The German Peace Settlement and the Berlin Crisis

by

Manuel Gottlieb

(University of Wisconsin—Milwaukee)

New York

PAINE-WHITMAN PUBLISHERS

1960

FIRST PRINTING

Printed in the United States of America
©

TABLE OF CONTENTS

PREFACE

THIS BOOK deals with the quest for East-West settlement in Germany and its outcome of crisis in Berlin. Quest and outcome are treated only in their germinative phase closing in June, 1949 with the emergence of two Germanies, eastern and western. These have since grown farther apart in institutions, ideas, and class alignments. No effort is made in this book to chronicle or to evaluate this divergent development. For this task, the author is neither prepared nor especially suited. Rather we deal with the movement of the forties out of which these two Germanies were born. Thus, in form our book is historical. But in purpose and in substance, it is highly contemporary. The diplomatic and international positions of the sixties were fixed both objectively and subjectively in the forties. The issues of difference evolved in the forties still agitate foreign policy. The diplomatic struggle about Berlin still revolves in the sixties about the issues fought out in the forties by means of airlift and blockade. Since 1949, the lines of divergence about Berlin and Germany have not hardened; they have merely become hallowed. German policies are not invented, induced, or inferred; they are memorized. We cannot break the spell of past encounters until we return again to their scene and acquire a deeper and truer understanding of them. That is the purpose of this book.

The deeper understanding sought traces much of the indecision and controversy in the German peace settlement to the ambivalent cast of German policy which in the East and West simultaneously pursued antithetical objectives. As ambivalence became worked out, an honorable East-West peace settlement became possible. A united and liberal, but neutralized, disarmed and probably semisocialized Germany could have

vii

played a buffer role separating and bonding together East and West. Our leaders rejected this line of settlement partly because they distrusted partnership with the Soviets, partly because they underestimated Germany's reparation potential, and partly because they sought to use Western Germany as a springboard for mobilizing Western Europe into closer forms of political association binding together the Atlantic community and safeguarding its economic institutions from those forms of creeping socialism made possible by the isolated national democratic state. The crucial role played by the reparations question is fully disclosed in our work.

The professional student of international or German politics will find evidence in almost all chapters of fresh source materials some of archival origin. The last chapter provides a decoded analysis, novel and I believe impartial, of the true course and character of the Berlin crisis. The careful index owes to the devoted labors of my wife, who also helped in the preparation of an earlier version of the manuscript.

Manuel Gottlieb

Milwaukee, Wisconsin
April 20, 1960

INTRODUCTION

WE MAY SAFELY SAY that the paramount problem of our age concerns possibilities for achievement of an honorable and livable peace settlement between East and West. This task of settlement resolves into a set of problems which are domiciled in many territories and turn around many themes. These problems grew out of local situations which are conditioned by special circumstances of setting and action and which have for that reason a certain scope for local resolution.

This scope is both limited and contingent. The development of events in the problem areas is influenced by the worldwide trend. Likewise, local policy will be designed to carry out a larger strategy. But overall trend and larger strategy in turn are outgrowths of developments arising in the major problem areas. The relationship between overall trend and problem area, global strategy and local policy is thus organic and dynamic. Influences arising at any point are transmitted through the whole but are transformed as they work their effects in an ever newly developing situation.

Thus it is that fruitful understanding of the possibilities for East-West settlement should have a worldwide focus and an organic point of view. It is as a contribution toward such understanding that this book has been written. It attempts to provide a study of the larger problem of East-West settlement so far as this had a German setting and involved East-West relationships within and over Germany. We presuppose only that light is shed on the course and outcome of the East-West settlement in Germany by enquiry which focuses primarily on the German scene and does not directly concern itself with the moving currents of the larger worldwide setting. We know that in this form the results of en-

quiry are incomplete and provisional. But we also feel that in this form
our results have a solid footing as far as they go. And there are special
grounds for believing that these results can contribute to the larger
understanding for which we all grope. No single localized problem area
was more central in position, more strategic in location, more pervasive
in its effects than Germany. In this theater of action we can watch the
play of settlement possibilities of unusually wide scope and promise.
Nowhere did the Eastern and Western worlds meet with greater comity
of aims and with fuller recognition of mutuality of interest than in
Germany. The antagonism to the late enemy—once so dreaded and
powerful—simmered, and it nourished the sense of alliance which had
grown up out of wartime partnership. To Germany were sent gifted
soldier-statesmen capable of handling the ordeal of settlement. Finally,
in Germany East and West provisionally were prepared to aim at halfway house, a neutralized buffer area between the two.

In the beginning the quest for East-West settlement in Germany
ran an outwardly hopeful course. The territory was divided without
bickering. The capitol city of the country, Berlin, was put under a
common garrison and joint occupation to permit the city to serve as a
common headquarters and seat of central government. A machinery of
Allied cooperation and consultation was contrived and certain working
institutions were constituted. The two great contentious issues of settlement—Soviet claims on German eastern border lands and upon German
industrial resources for equipment and products as reparations—were
roughly resolved in compromise. Attuned to this record of achievement,
the commanding Generals and their staffs entered with relative enthu-
siasm into the task of planning the peace settlement and of conducting
their zonal occupations in the spirit and within the framework of Allied
accord.

Yet this attempt at settlement, entered into so auspiciously, hardly
got under way before setbacks slowed its momentum. These setbacks
took on larger importance as more progress in settlement was achieved.
When conditions had become ripe to consolidate a new united and
neutralized Germany under a common East-West overlordship, the
ability to contrive settlement was paralyzed. In the situation of stalemate which resulted, by a curious paradox the intimacy of purpose and
solidity of achievement which had laid the basis for settlement became
a source of aggravation. Agreements that facilitated unification ham-

pered zonal management; joint institutions became irritating entanglements.

The end of this first quest for East-West peace settlement in Germany is well-known: collapse of joint institutions, termination of arrangements for consultation and collective action, near-war in Berlin,
imposition of sanctions along the zonal boundary line. From a partnership designed to cement alliance and to bring East and West together,
the German affair became a source of embroilments which accelerated
tendencies to polarization in Europe and which contributes potently to
the making of ultimate catastrophe, World War III.

This shift from white to black, from cooperation to tension, makes
up an important theme of contemporary international politics. What
went wrong with this first effort at East-West peace settlement in Germany? What contributed to the setbacks which finally paralyzed forward action? What were their deeper sources and conditioning causes?
Why were they not foreseen and adapted to or provided against more
successfully by wartime planning?

It is the answers to these questions and not the German development *per se* around which this work is organized. Hence we do not
provide a balanced and exact description of the outward course of
events which marked the German development. For this the reader can
turn to many other works framed to meet this need. We have, however,
carried narrative enquiry far when our questions are involved. Thus the
reader will find in this work most of the events, conferences, agreements, personalities which loom large in the narrative and monographic
accounts. Only here they are viewed from a different perspective.

To permit this perspective to stand out clearly, the statement of
facts in which it is developed has been cast in non-specific terms. The
text accordingly has been freed from the task of conveying detailed
information even where this would be of general interest or where the
results of fresh research were presented. This specific information is,
however, liberally provided in the footnotes where the specialist will
find much factual data as well as indication of the materials and reason-
ing available to support the unfamiliar or questionable generalizations
of the text. When familiar ground is covered we have used footnotes to
permit brevity in discussion. Since footnotes sometimes distract, only
their little warning signs will be found in the text; most of their body
has been removed to the rear of the work.

This extensive footnoting and the bulk of the appendixes involved may yield the impression of a more solid scholarly foundation than the work has. No such deception was intended. The bulkiest apparatus of scholarly reference cannot buttress the comparatively slender foundations of historical reference on which an interpretive essay on this theme at the present time can build. Only two manuscript collections out of the hundreds that ultimately will be available were used. Unfortunately, scholarly investigation on a monographic scale has only begun to supply the verified knowledge which a general survey relies upon. This network of monographic investigation was imperfectly replaced by working over source materials with moderate intensity and considerable unevenness. The sometimes scandalous gaps in this respect are recognized. But the point of diminishing returns can come rather quickly in battle with a virtually unending mass of undigested source materials approached for survey purposes. Systematic use of available secondary and published primary accounts helped but did not make up for the absence of monographic investigation.

Under these circumstances effort at interpretation was quite naturally grounded in knowledge gained and research carried on in my professional capacity with American military government in Germany. Although my role during the three years I was in Germany was secondary in every respect, my position was sufficiently central and my responsibilities were sufficiently varied to bring me at some point into contact with many of the policies, problems and issues which are treated in this work. This contact afforded access to "inside" opinions and the flow of office paper in which they are embodied. At some crucial junctures this contact brought knowledge of fundamental importance though not yet incorporated into current writing.

Moreover, the capacity in which I technically functioned in military government—as economist—brought me close to those fundamental problems of the peace settlement which turned around issues of an economic nature. With three of these issues, that of monetary reform, economic controls, and occupation costs, I was occupied in the course of my regular duties; a fourth issue, that of reparations, I was able to follow at near hand. All of these issues have complex economic bearings which cannot be brought under control without working through a good deal of technical information and analysis. With regard to certain crucial phases of these issues dealing with monetary reform and reparations, I have by publication in professional journals submitted before my professional colleagues a full statement of the technical analysis of which only a summary account is provided in this book.*

Since personal experience was so central in providing the basis for this enquiry, I do not apologize for using my own manuscript materials and studies out of all proportion to their intrinsic worth. But for the same reason, this enquiry becomes suspect in terms of the attitudes involved in its making. Insights and knowledge bought with personal experience are usually blinkered. These blinkers were most in evidence in the early phases of the writing which were soaked in contemporary judgment, were intended to work exposure or blame and were preoccupied with the shortcomings of American policy. As the research progressed and the writing took shape, the focus of writing shifted. It became apparent that the German development did not readily lend itself to personalized categories of blame or guilt and that the stream of causation ran in very complex currents. These currents could be traced and their manifestation in concrete situations understood only if the mind were permitted to roam freely and conscientiously over the materials to be elucidated. Coming to this project without any very deep predisposition assisted in refocussing the enquiry. Finally, occasion for this refocussing was provided by the circumstance that an early version of the enquiry had to serve as a doctoral dissertation at Harvard University and had to pass muster with two very keen-minded savants—J. K. Galbraith and C. J. Friedrich—who were not at all disposed to let my nonscientific attachments play too prominent a role.

But precisely because elucidation is involved, sloughing off bias in its cruder forms leaves the more room for its subtle forms. One possible source of such subtle bias is the disproportionate availability of source materials. We of the West think of Soviet policy as a monolithic block in which there are no options, no divisive currents, no controversial areas. There simply is the policy, its strategic justifications and doctrinal supports. Except for grotesquely distorted echoes, we generally know little of the debate out of which the policy emerged, of the deviant opinions

* See the following papers by the present author: "The German Economic Potential," *Social Research*, XVII (1950) 65–89; "The Reparations Problem Again," *Canadian Journal of Economics and Political Science*, XVI (1950) 22–41; "The Capital Levy and Deadweight Debt in England—1815–40," *The Journal of Finance*, XVIII (1953) 34–46; "The Capital Levy After World War I," *Public Finance*, VII (1952) 356–384; "The Failure of Quadripartite Monetary Reform," *Finanzarchiv*, XVII (1957) 398–417.

thrust by the wayside, of the play of "inside" judgments. Since so much more is known about Western policy determination in its divisive aspects, these tend to figure more prominently in this work.

This bias in turn is accentuated by the fact of nationality. I am an American, I feel as an American, I have pride in America. Other powers may err, but why should she? In the mythology of every country its existence is construed as a blessed act of that Providence which also brought other peoples into existence. Although the scientist in me naturally attempted to suppress this guileful presumption, the suppression undoubtedly was incomplete. It is likely that bias persisted in the form of a tendency to treat the policy of other nations as fixed but ours as variable. There is some justification for this. We were less committed by tradition or suffering to any fixed course toward the German peace settlement. The war for us involved only a small loss of men and it generated the blessing of enabling us to test our productive mettle and to achieve full employment levels. Hence it was easy to presuppose that of all the powers America should be most free from compulsive thinking and narrow interest outlook.

A work of elucidation is shaped as much by presupposition as by outright or subtle bias. These presuppositions and the social thought epitomized govern the way in which a problem is formulated, evidence weighed, emphasis distributed. Comment on these presuppositions is not intended to advertise private opinions but rather to bring to the surface influences which run underground in this work. These influences tend to resolve around three issues which will be briefly discussed: economic collectivism versus private enterprise, the liberal versus the closed state and social drift versus responsible action.

With regard to collectivism in economic life, the analysis of the text may suggest that economic policy should strive for collectivism in institutions and non-market controls in mechanism. This inference would be misleading. The author holds no general formula which he would administer as so much patent medicine to remedy the sicknesses of different societies. He would judge the fitness of the remedy by the needs of the case.

The needs of the case primarily focus in the author's view on the response to dislocation, impoverishment and development. By dislocation is meant serious injuries to the productive organism either at home or, with reference to sources of supply or markets, abroad. By impoverishment is meant shrinkage of national income per capita and reduced levels of consumption relative to those expected norms around which incentives are organized and income budgets are balanced. By development is meant economic flow on an expanding scale as contrasted with the mere reproduction of the social economy on an unchanged basis.

This study was written on the assumption that relative to the ability of any given society to handle large-scale overhead political organization and directive mechanisms, successful societal response to impoverishment, dislocation and developmental needs will generate collectivism and controls. Conversely stated, collectivism and controls are the dimension of positive response to marked needs growing out of impoverishment, dislocation or development. Just as the maintenance of life in a besieged city requires increased solidarity and sharing, as a herd under attack may band together for mutual protection, so social patterns under strain will tend to become more cohesive and solidaristic.

A similar kind of balance was felt to prevail on the front where the liberal polity is challenged by the closed state. The author's personal idiosyncrasy is that of the liberal polity. But as a social scientist he feels no sense of absolutism about a polity for which social and cultural prerequisites of a very high order are required, which can prevail as a stable and functioning regime only under highly specialized conditions, and which has emerged out of a long and complicated process of social development that cannot easily be short-circuited. Far from being the universally desirable mode and measure of political organization, the liberal polity can maintain itself only over a relatively small segment of geographic space and historic time.

Although the German community of 1945 certainly met some of the conditions which permit the establishment of a liberal polity, it is a major presupposition of this work that these conditions were insufficient for its success. Many of the tensions, institutions and attitudes out of which fascism had drawn inspiration and by reason of which the liberal strain in German society had been weakened were still present and potent. No stable and tested leadership or network of social organization had emerged by which the common man in his daily life could become politically effective. Finally, many of the basic needs of German society were inherently incapable of being satisfied by the slow working of self-governing processes in the liberal polity. These needs called for quick and drastic action essentially through use of dictatorial power. Hence little patience is exhibited in this work toward the ritualistic emphasis which latter-day American policy laid on conformity with the formal requirements of the liberal polity.

The third general topic of predisposition is the balance between drift and responsible action. By "responsibility" is meant the capacity to exercise the options involved in a course of events with a minimum consistency and a due regard for relevant potential developments and ultimate values. Conversely, drift will characterize any course of events which is not to a marked degree guided by responsible action. Events tend to drift of their own accord while responsibility cannot be wholly extruded. Drift and responsibility are thus not mutually exclusive categories but are dimensions of response fused over the range of social action in patterns of infinite diversity and shading.

It became increasingly clear in working out the major problems of this book that the foreign policy involved in the German peace settlement did not—in the Western world at least—emerge out of a responsible stream of decisions. The division of labor in making decisions and in action was too finely worked out. Even those few actors in high position with special intellectual qualities were unable, it appears, to develop much perspective on events in course and in the making. In any case, they were not free agents able to respond to random insights. They had to act through hierarchy and to wear its blinkers. Their minds were nourished on filtered information. In making their judgments they were subject to what Burke so aptly called "the domineering necessities which frequently recur in all great affairs." Thus there was a tendency to drift on a current not shaped by responsible action. The individual actors were in the position of the stones and beams which Hegel once said "obey the law of gravity—press downward—and so high walls are carried up."

A course of drift is not to any marked degree subject to responsible control. But the options taken in this course must draw upon some relatively consistent texture of thought. Since this thought accommodates contradictory interests and expresses rather than previses events, it is basically ambivalent. Ambivalence grows out of uncertainty and involves simultaneous pursuit of irreconcilable objectives and the holding of antithetical attitudes. The intellectual orientation which harbors uncoordinated elements of thought and desire and which sustains the illusions and distortions which a course of drift requires may be characterized as ambivalent.*

The roles of ambivalence and drift are most clearly seen in settlements between relatively independent powers. An act of true settlement must be made by persons willing to stake their imperfect foresight on a commitment which forecloses future options and trades off esteemed national rights. This action hurts a latent national pride. Its risks are enhanced by the reluctance of other powers to provide guarantees which would attest to their good faith. The calculations on which the commitment is based must be sufficiently clear-cut, certain and persuasive that the drag of inertia and the impulse to caution can be overcome; and the calculations also must demonstrate that further negotiation will not bring better terms or permit the development of a stronger bargaining position.

Yet these calculations can rest on nothing better than a series of informed guesses about the future supported by obscurely known tendencies of the immediate past. And these calculations must be made in a context of thought readily subject to the psychic mechanisms of distortion, transference and stereotyping. These mechanisms are felt in the self-governing processes by which a society directs itself as they are felt in the shaping of personality. But they probably have their widest ambit in foreign affairs. There the impulse to use the foreigner or stranger as scapegoat goes to work. This is partly because the moral bookkeeping within the nation in foreign policy—and particularly in conducting war and making peace—is extremely lopsided. Reward, sacrifice and policy-voice are highly discrepant. Resentments have to have some outlet. In both domestic and foreign affairs the channels of access and influence by which a given social stimulus ultimately evokes an adequate political response easily get clogged or feed back in reverse. In domestic affairs where a long period of time usually is available these channels can be cleared; in a peace settlement it is time that is at a premium.

* The concept of ambivalence is used throughout this work with the specialized meaning assigned in the text. The concept has been borrowed from Freudian psychoanalysis where it relates chiefly to an individual ego and its involvements. In employing the concept in a larger social context, necessarily its meaning somewhat shifts. There is sufficient carryover to make it worthwhile to retain the term itself rather than to invent a new term.

Finally, the calculations out of which the act of settlement emerges must in the Western world be made by leaders who as professional politicians would, in Keynes' poignant language, "have succumbed long ago in the bitter struggle for the survival of the unfit—which politics is—if they had ever formed the habit of allowing the merits of what was put before them to obscure their judgment." Political judgment tends to run in terms of access, influence, compromise. The Western political leader is, in Lippmann's words, "a perpetual office seeker," always "on trial for [his] political life [and] always required to court [his] restless constituents." As such the Western political leader is "lofty in his attitude toward the masses and fluctuates among lip-service toward their stereotypes (which he calls 'public opinion'), uneasy fears when they begin to want something hard ('pressure groups') and panic when they act to get it ('revolution')." His ammunition, Lerner concluded the indictment, is "abstractions"; his tenacity is "nil"; "a purpose to him is like a work of art meticulously carved in butter."* This delineates with some caricature the average type whose limitations can be transcended or obscured when outstanding personalities like Roosevelt, Truman and Churchill are involved. Yet even at this level the capacity for firm decision was near paralyzed by the fundamental American policy of delaying all basic European decisions on the peace settlement until a peace conference; and even at this level the tendency to abstraction and the inability to penetrate to essential issues of political-economic process blurred the vision and encouraged thinking in terms of simple

* Walter Lippmann, *Essays in the Public Philosophy* (Mentor Edn. 1954) p. 28 f; J. M. Keynes, "The United States and the Keynes Plan," *New Republic* (1940) p. 157 f; Max Lerner, *It Is Later Than You Think* (NY, 1943 edn), p. 4 f. We delineate above primarily the liberal politician which is the generic American type. The true conservative leader and the socialist politician are varieties of the type with distinctive characteristics. Roosevelt and Hull—and in a somewhat different way Truman and Byrnes—were typical American liberal leaders whose faults and virtues shine through the whole record of German policy-making. By contrast the Soviet leaders and particularly Stalin show up in the documentary records as trained realists. Decisive characteristics of wartime American German policy stemmed primarily from the basic American wartime strategy of postponing the settlement of frontier issues and reparations questions to some general future peace conference. That this strategy was designed to thwart Soviet expansionist aims or any Soviet expansion beyond their 1937 frontier is quite clear. But this strategy in turn was quite suited to the mentality of the liberal politician who functions at his best in this atmosphere of ultimate moral purpose, of maneuver, of indirection.

stereotypes. Moreover, the peak personalities are bound by the common opinion for which they speak and which they represent. Yet these were the chosen instruments through which the work of settlement was to proceed. Is it so remarkable that they were inadequate for the task?

The tendency to fumbling leadership and to drift will be strongest when settlement is attempted between Power areas cleft by a cultural gap. Of such nature were the relationships of the Graeco-Roman empire with its surrounding peoples, of the medieval Christian and the fluid Mongol and Moslem worlds, of the decaying Turkish realm and the advancing Western world. As the cultural gap narrows and bonds of solidarity thicken, relationships between states become civilizational in character and become to a greater or lesser degree infused with responsibility. Yet so powerful are the forces making for drift that even within as solidary an association of societies as the Western Christian world, with its relatively high level of integration and respect for law, the main *modus operandi* for inter-state adjustments has been predominantly that of drift around relationships of power.

The predominance of drift is much less marked in the intimate relations of a solidary society which has taken on the political form of a confederated union. Yet it has become almost a canon of political science that the member states of such a union only rarely can be expected to take decisive action in concerted form by means of negotiated agreement. The tendency to drift and scope for drift are effectively reduced only when a society has worked out for itself the means by which social pressures quickly can be brought to the political surface; by which the necessary degree of equalization of wealth and power can be achieved; by which interest groups can be transmuted and reduced to a common denominator; by which divisive forces are reduced through social conventions, the habits of compromise or ceremonial observance; and by which the verdict of some authority within the society is commonly recognized as binding. Under these conditions the tendency to drift can be partially obviated and responsible actors can work out those deliberate acts of settlement by which a society attains a relatively clear-cut structure without losing the capacity for effecting peaceful change.

If these factors which condition the respective working of drift and of responsible action in complex societies and civilizations are borne in mind, there will be less tendency to complain at the outcome of the

German postwar peace settlement and there will be more understanding of the forces which ran through it. It will then appear miraculous not that the East-West peace settlement in Germany was muffed but rather that it came so close.

If this is true then the persistent conclusion which emerges from our enquiry—that not blame or deserts but tragedy was involved—has much significance. Is this a foreboding of a "time of troubles" which may be beyond the capacity of our familiar secular life institutionalized in Great Power politics to rectify? Are we now all so caught in the postures of antagonism and weighed down with the traditions of our past and the compulsive drives of our ideologies that we cannot be expected to work out the complex questions of a major intercivilizational settlement by responsible means? And if we cannot muster responsibility and consistency of purpose sufficient to this end, can we drift into livable settlements? We are not concerned in this book with answering these questions. But we may note here that in the past such drift was relatively easy due to the "immutable condition," as Burke put it, that in "large bodies the circulation of power must be less vigorous at the extremities" and that accordingly "authority" must be "weakened" by "distance." This condition governed the relationships between co-existing civilizations separated by rough terrain or long water passages at a time when travel was difficult, when production depended largely on muscle power and traditional handicraft skills and when warfare was conducted chiefly by soldiers on foot or on horse using simple weapons of low destructive power.

But the orbit of civilization has now greatly widened, power within them has become centralized and the space between them has shrunk in consequence of a revolution in social technology. By this revolution man's ability to produce has multiplied, population density has increased greatly, the span of central control over human organization has widened, powerful devices for large-scale indoctrination of mind have been created and warfare has been given new dimensions through which to attack and destroy. It is much more difficult than it once was to drift into intercivilizational settlements, and it is much more destructive than it once was to attempt to fight them out. Can a new equilibrium be reached, or has our secular world now become Frankenstein's Monster? This well may be the central question of our age, but we cannot pursue it further here.

CHAPTER I

THE POLICY OF AMBIVALENCE

I. A Shared Occupation

THE GERMAN POSTWAR PEACE SETTLEMENT was only a phase of the effort to form a new world equilibrium between East and West after the defeat of the Axis powers. The working bases for this effort were the present and prospective positions of the respective military forces as victory approached. Soviet armies, after pushing the Germans out of the Soviet Union, pursued them around the Black Sea, into the Balkans, up the Danube Valley and down the Baltic coast across the Polish plains. Once the West decided to capitalize on its great maritime resources, the strategy was to direct the Western thrust into the more exposed coastal and peninsular areas of Axis-held territory. By 1943 the Soviets had retaken most of European Russia while the Western powers had swept the Germans from North Africa, had converted the Mediterranean into an Allied lake, and had established a foothold in Italy, which was knocked out of the war as an independent political force. By the late fall of 1944 the German armies were pushed back near their frontiers and virtually all the "satellite" as well as Axis-conquered territories were, or were in process of being, "liberated."

The distinctive characteristic of "liberation" was that, country by country, it was achieved separately by East or West but never by both. The army which moved into a territory in pursuit of German forces or to overthrow a satellite regime constituted itself the supreme authority there. This was true for the West in North Africa, Italy, France, Belgium, Norway and Greece. It was true for the Soviets in Poland, Hungary, Roumania, Bulgaria and Czechoslovakia. In all these countries, the authority of the occupation was exercised with rigor in varied forms and to different ends by both East and West.

1

The legitimacy of these regimes of unilateral power was conceded grudgingly and provisionally. Legitimization was expressed negatively by failure to take explicit and public exception even where, as in Poland, the Soviets instituted a regime which cut across a "government in exile" friendly to the West. Elsewhere this implicit approval was supplemented by joint signature of armistice terms and membership on a council of "Allied authorities." In other cases there was participation in ambassadorial advisory councils. "Influence" was even allocated by a numerical coefficient.[1] Over the whole was thrown the carefully wrought drapery of agreed Allied purpose in reconstituting a "democratic" and "anti-fascist" Europe. This was a special diplomatic way of indicating to wary partners the need for caution and of expressing the compounded note of solidarity and contingency involved in the legitimization of unilateral occupation regimes. As such, it indicated the grounds on which rights of access and special pleading would later be claimed.

Unilateral occupation conceivably could have extended to the main source of Axis power, not just to its satellite and peripheral domains. If the military forces of either East or West had broken through German lines on one front and had overrun Germany while the other front held, Germany would have been unilaterally occupied as Japan later was. A military break-through against German resistance was not precluded. Support within Germany for the Nazi policy of last-ditch resistance was weakening.[2] But the dictatorship of the Nazi party was well-entrenched. And Hitler was a demoniac leader who still wielded magic. His hold was greatly strengthened by Roosevelt's unconditional surrender policy which weakened the impulse to revolt and discouraged those Germans who were seeking Western contacts and getting rebuffed.[3] Under these circumstances German resistance remained tough, as was strikingly brought home to the West by the disabling effect of the German 1944/5 winter offensive. The possibility of a negotiated armistice became negligible. The likely outcome was that the armies of East and West would fight their way into the country and hence would meet one another *within* and not *outside* the territories inhabited by peoples ethnically and politically German. This meant that in some significant sense the occupation of this central Axis power—and hence the balance of power within Europe—would be shared.

Once the groundwork of Allied wartime policy and military strategy was so laid that a shared occupation would be its probable outcome, it became desirable to demarcate in advance the boundaries of the shared areas. Otherwise these boundaries would become objects of contention to be fixed by the last round of fighting or by German decision. On the basis of a British proposal advanced as early as February 1944, an agreement on occupation zones was reached in the spring of that year and ratified by the respective governments in the fall. The agreement was predicated upon the simple premise of allocating to each of the three major partners of the alliance a roughly equal share of German population of convenient access with internal frontiers falling on the nearest provincial boundary line.[4]

More was required, however, than the bare act of territorial allocation. Both East and West had pledged themselves to fight German armies but also to overthrow the political regime which had sustained these armies. Only extended occupation would enable either East or West to do this. The Soviets would not easily give up a zonal control won from an enemy which had devastated a broad belt of Soviet territory. The Western powers wished to curb the aggressive inclination of a people whose armies had three times in a century invaded Western territory. Economically, extended occupation would signify a nourishing flow of reparations Eastward to repair war damage. For the West, such an occupation would bring secure control over the Ruhr coal mines which were vital for the Western European economy.

The probabilities were strong, then, that occupation of Germany after her unconditional surrender would run deep and be long. The insistence on unconditional surrender signified just this. The occupation regimes thus prolonged would need some form of mutual legitimization. This would strengthen the position of the occupying forces vis-a-vis the asundered German community. It would make possible an indispensable minimum of solidarity initially required between the zonal regimes; and it would provide an ideological cloak under which the occupation forces could entrench themselves in their respective domains.

The mutual legitimization which was worked out consisted of a series of overlapping pronouncements framed in broad terms. At bottom was the simple assertion of the "supreme authority" to be exercised in Germany by the military commanders of the occupation forces "each in his own zone of occupation."[5] This grant of power was spelled out by agreements which accorded to the occupation authorities collectively and separately a range of specific functions and rights stated in language so sweeping as to exclude few actions from their gambit.[6]

II. Impulse to Bifurcation and Overlap

The occupation at its outset, then, was a *legitimized* occupation shared by East and West over a militarily partitioned Germany. Such a shared occupation would exhibit tendencies both toward bifurcation and overlap, intricately interwoven with each other. The immediate objective of occupation, to uproot the Nazi regime, was common to both East and West. This regime did not hang on a few leaders holding high political office. This regime was rather constituted by the activist core of a generation which had taken over leadership of and become rooted in the entire social structure: farm organizations, labor organizations, factories, business and welfare associations, schools and universities, radio stations, newspapers, the army, government offices, and police bureaus. Hence "removal" of the Nazis and "uprooting" their regime was a special way of characterizing the positive action of re-placing the Nazified elite with a new managerial elite which would take custody of the vacated power positions.

This new elite strata naturally would be composed of accessible persons in whom the occupying powers could have "confidence." Con-fidence rested on the expectation that orders would be executed reli-ably. Confidence also required that the interests and outlooks of the ap-pointees would be congruent generally with those of the occupation, that secret sabotage or desertion would be unlikely, and that the authority vested in the position would be used to carry out the ob-jectives of the occupation. The candidates for office who would merit the confidence of the occupation tended to link themselves with two focal centers of anti-Nazi resistance. One of these was the right resistance with a core of the old ruling classes of the Bismarck empire: the rural gentry, the ex-nobility, rightist politicians, conservative churchmen, bankers, businessmen and investors. These in the main were nationalist fellow-travellers of fascism mobilized by Hitler for service of the vaunted Third Reich. As defeat loomed nearer, this group moved increasingly into op-position, drawing with it—from the Right—sympathizers from Nazi ranks, from the German high command and even from the Nazi inner circle. At the same time, on its leftward side, this group drew closer to the liberal, Christian and social democratic opposition on whom would fall the main work of mobilizing mass support for a new regime. This motley gathering was held together by common antagonism to the Nazis, by dislike of Nazi "excesses," but chiefly by desire to end the lost war with greatest advantage by sparing the country conquest by combat and stopping the crucifying Allied air war against the German urban population. Though there were fringe factions who flirted with the idea of dealing with the Soviets, the predominant leaning was to the West out of a basic community of culture, class interest and fear of Russian retribution. The tactical goal was a palace revolt to be achieved by assassination of Hitler. This almost succeeded in the coup of July 1944. Though the most active leaders of this resistance were killed in the bloodbath that followed failure of the attempted coup, some leaders and the body of followers survived.[7]

The other center of anti-Nazi resistance was of leftist inspiration. It had a core of communists of chiefly worker background, flanked by left-wing socialists, fellow travellers and an appreciable number of turncoat army officers whom the Soviets had captured. The communist movement had first taken the form of a deviant fraction within German social democracy. Inspired by mass revolt, by Russian example and by their own revolutionary leaders, the communists unsuccessfully bid for power in 1918/9. Defeated during the transition from the collapsing Bismarck Reich to the Weimar republic, they bade their time, became a section of the communist international and proceeded to educate and develop a strong following in important industrial areas of Germany. Much of this following was lost through fascist repression. But in most industrial localities various forms of left-wing organization or activity continued to crop up among a core of faithful and well-indoctrinated workers and party supporters.*

The left resistance to the Nazi regime sought no coup but rather to form radical cadres who could organize mass action.[8] These cadres

---

* See the scholarly and illuminating survey by W. H. Kraus and G. A. Almond, "Resistance and Repression under the Nazis," *Struggle for Democracy in Germany* (G. A. Almond, ed., Chapel Hill, 1949), 33–63. During the year 1944 alone there were 6500 arrests on grounds of "communism-Marxism" (p. 61). "Strong anti-Nazi attitudes were prevalent apparently among workers in all large German cities, particularly in the north throughout the war. . . . Among 58 interrogations of industrial representatives in five heavily bombed large cities, exactly half referred to more or less widespread worker antagonism to the regime and only three denied this." United States Strategic Bombing Survey, *The Effects of Strategic Bombing on German Morale* (Washington, 1947), 52.

gained in energy and support as popular resentment welled up against the Nazi policy which converted the country into the final battle theater of a war already lost. In some areas they were able to facilitate the surrender of towns and cities, to prevent demolition or to aid the entrance of Allied troops.[9] Generally, however, the thread of discipline sustaining Nazi rule snapped only with the appearance of Allied troops, and that event in most cases preceded open anti-fascist activity. In most of the principal German cities the anti-fascists of the left, working in the form of loosely organized local movements, stepped forward to carry on some of the emergency functions of government, to ferret out Nazis and to offer assistance to military government.[10]

These two resistance movements had comparatively few active members. But their respective attitudes diffused rapidly once the Nazi regime broke down. These movements represented, with varying degrees of distinctiveness and with considerable overlapping, the viewpoints of most of those who offered to participate under the occupation in rebuilding a new political life. In making appointments from this spectrum much would be left in all zones—particularly in the early phases of the occupation—to accidents of accessibility and of personality. But in the main the response of the thousands of commanders and officers exercising the authority of military government would be that of a filtered cross section of their home community. The culture of this community would mould the standards of "efficiency and reliability" codified in manuals, training courses and directives. In the process of giving effect to its own culturally prescribed and codified directives, each occupation would thus tend to give confidence to the resistance movement more responsive to its aims and outlook.

The types of political regimes which had to emerge from the Eastern and Western occupations might be differentiated only slightly at the outset. The tendency to differentiation would be reinforced by the divergent responses given by the east and west to the German need for basic institutional reorganization. This reorganization was called for on various grounds. Wartime ideology in East and West alike singled out as a prime security menace the landed and titled gentry who constituted the backbone of national German power ever since the rise of Prussia and who still wielded authority over semi-feudalized peasant villages or estates located chiefly in eastern Germany.[11] Similarly destined for liquidation was the German version of Big Business, i.e. the network of interwoven quasi-public corporations in the fields of industry and finance which played a dominant role in the German economy. Corporate leaders had in many instances collaborated closely with the Nazi regime or had been involved in its rise to power. These leaders exercised large responsibilities which would need to be handled in the interests of the occupation. Corporate net incomes would be needed for public use. Finally, the industrial facilities involved comprised the heart of heavy industry whose products would necessarily be closely regulated in the interests of reconstruction and recovery, of foreign trade management and of military security. For these reasons it would be advisable everywhere to sever the thin threads which linked corporate management hierarchies with the key ownership interests, the stock market and the control groups, and to cast the corporate system in new forms.[12]

The urge to social renovation and property reorganization in agriculture and industry was heightened by other pressures. With the close of hostilities, the disappearance of the Nazi regime, and the abrupt stop of armament production, the wartime economy would disintegrate. But the old peacetime economy could not simply be dropped in its place. The business world would find that its old supply and demand relationships were twisted out of shape by the impoverishment and dislocation resulting from war, the cessation of imported supplies, the disappearance of old markets, and acute shortages of power and materials. The process of reconversion would thus involve recasting the entire economy—its productive operations, supply flows and product designs—to correspond with new conditions of economic life. This process of reconversion, unless guided by central planning, would move slowly and hesitantly into an uncertain future. On its own steam, reconversion would be marred by upsets, diseconomies and waste of resources. Alignments of supply and of market values would be unstable since firms depended on each other in complex patterns which would continually shift as improvisation proceeded and as underlying objective conditions and subjective dispositions would alter. The need for centralized planning would be the greater, the more heavy the priority placed upon satisfaction of Allied economic demands, upon repair of war damage and upon rebuilding of bombed cities and transport facilities.[13]

Centralized economic planning can be achieved in many ways and through many institutional forms. But under conditions of pressure and acute scarcities, planning leans heavily upon controls, allocations and rationing which serve as so many means by which use of money income is restricted and by which basic economic decision-making is centralized and coordinated on a large scale. The requisite central and field staffing and a vast body of usable controls and regulations had been evolved. The continued use of these controls for planning purposes was anticipated and favored at all levels of German society. It was only necessary systematically to elaborate and overhaul these controls, to give them more permanence of form, to infuse a new spirit into them and to alter their purpose from planning for war to planning for recovery, reparations and rebuilding.

To this program of action called for in agriculture, industry and economic method there was joined the need for a revolution in finance. The Nazi war had been financed by deficit spending which had built up a five-fold expansion in purchasing power and as well a swollen public debt which could not be serviced out of prevailing or anticipated tax yields.[14] The bulk of the public debt was carried by financial institutions where it served as backing for the larger stocks of currency and deposit claims which the public preferred to hold as liquid assets. During the war this swollen stock of liquid assets lay dormant because it was insulated from markets by official controls and expectation of victory. But these assets would become activated with military defeat and would then undermine wage and price controls, hamper effective planning, demoralize business life, divert resources from essential uses and foster black markets.[15] These excess monetary assets would need to be liquidated by outright monetary reform which would scale down monetary holdings and thus bring the supply of liquid assets into nearer accord with real assets and goods availabilities. Such action would be in accord with the instinctive German belief that the Nazi currency and war debt were doomed with the regime that sponsored them.[16]

Monetary reform would itself lead to measures touching a deeper need, namely that of property equalization (*Lastenausgleich*) to spread more equitably the burdens of the lost war. The main burdens were of course shouldered by the concentration camp and bombing victims, by the front-line fighters, by their widows and orphans and by those soldiers destined for prolonged captivity or disabled in mind or body. Then there were the millions of Germans who left all their possessions in eastern border lands and fled before Soviet armies and the many millions who were bombed out by the Allied air war against the German urban population. The forthcoming occupation would bring many confiscations of home and business property, arising in part from territorial seizure. Finally, monetary reform would impact unevenly within the German community since it strikes directly at all those individuals—chiefly of the working and lower middle classes—whose prewar property and wartime savings were held in the form of liquid claims in contrast to farmers and business men whose wartime assets and property generally were concentrated in equities and tangibles. Thus while possibly one German family out of ten would come out of the occupation without serious damage to person or goods, at least two out of ten would be beggared or seriously incapacitated while seven would be damaged to varying degrees in goods and in person.

The pressure in the German community for readjustment of these disparities, which bore little relationship to deserts or equity, was strong.* No new regime could become settled without attempting such readjustment. But such readjustment would not be easy to contrive. The physical possessions of the lucky, the well-off and the well-placed

* This at any rate was the universal German cry, whether faintly or loudly, ingenuously or with sophistication, for the record only or with serious intent. An authoritative survey of the literature reported that "it is suggested therefore by all authors that not only financial assets but also real assets should be subject to a burden." OMGUS, *A Plan for the Liquidation of War Finance and the Financial Rehabilitation of Germany* (a report by G. Colm, R. Goldsmith, J. Dodge, dated 20 May 1946, with a separate volume of appendices, Berlin—hereafter cited as *C-D-G Report*), Appendix Z, 5. A characteristic statement of the Minister-Presidents of the American zone in 1945 stated that the rebuilding of German democracy was possible only if monetary reform was carried through with strict regard to the principles of justice; the burdens of the lost war should be shouldered by the German people in accord with economic capacity and relative needs; the goal was an equity-oriented equalization (gerechten Lastenausgleich). (See mss. undated statement submitted through the Laenderrat in late 1945 or early 1946.) As late as 1 March 1948, a party committee of the conservatively-oriented CDU in a document not designed for publication developed proposals for one-time property taxation and Lastenausgleich. CDU-CSU Deutschlands, subcommittee report, "Vorschlaege über Fragen der Währungsreform und des Lastenausgleiches" (Frankfurt AM, 1 March 1948—typewritten). In circles of Ruhr industrialists late in 1945 willingness was expressed to shoulder a 30 percent capital levy if it were coupled with drastic monetary reform. Binder, "Die Sanierung," 31. On the other hand a secret bizonal committee of finance ministers advised the occupying powers in late 1947 in favor of a capital levy but with a rate structure between 5 and 10 percent graduated in two or three brackets. This example indicates the danger of judging real attitudes by the modes of their expression. Only one conservative economist, Adolph Weber, is on record in contemporary publication as having opposed the notion of burden-equalization as unrealizable. See his *Wohin Steuert die Wirtschaft* (Munich, 1946) 52 ff.

could not simply be piled in a heap and divided. Command over these possessions would need to be mobilized so that income and work opportunities resulting from them could be applied to promote the general welfare of those most in need of rehabilitation. This mobilization could not be achieved by raising taxes to be paid out of current income. The pressure on national income of taxation needed to defray current public expenditures and forseeable occupation charges approached tolerance limits.[17] This mobilization could be achieved on a considerable scale and in a short time-period only by imposing an extraordinary levy on property. This levy could be collected most easily by transferring to the government property rights over claims to future income without entailing active managerial responsibilities. These property rights stem largely from modern corporate and financial organization which by separating control and ownership of capital have made it possible to regroup property rights and income claims in a short time-period without crippling business incentives or disorganizing business management. But by the same token this mode of mobilizing resources for *Lastenausgleich* carries with it a considerable potential for socialization of the properties affected.[18] This potential for socialization would obviously be more effective in conjunction with the drive toward centralized decision-making and property-reorganization which was elsewise called for.

This underlying drive toward socialization, collective control and institutional and class reform would naturally be greeted sympathetically and given ready response by the Soviets. The Soviet leaders came to power by giving land to peasants. The Soviet economic system pivoted about mobilization economics carried to a high point of tension by means of price controls, rationing and allocations which were customary methods of Soviet economic management. Soviet officials were experienced in the art of collecting foodstuffs in a hungry land. Soviet response would not be hampered by the need to ensure equities in individual cases or by concern for established property rights.

There was in all these respects some overlap of the Western with the Soviet position. The West in its turn had experimented with the techniques of planning and through taxation it had learned to carry a long way the technique of partial confiscation. The Western tradition in America venerated the family farm and was repugnant to landlords and titled aristocrats. In a war setting the West had come to feel at

home with mobilization economics which had also won a certain emergency standing in coping with the needs of devastation and mass dislocation. The West had long ago lost the 19th century sense of absolutism in property rights. The West was prepared to use the methods
of social liquidation to cut out the Nazi abscess in German society. But
though the overlap with the Soviets went far particularly as concerns
first steps and intentions, the differences with the Soviets were also
systematic and profound. The West would move less quickly in taking
the requisite measures. There would be many gaps between program
and realized action. Action when taken would be encased in safeguards
designed to protect individual equities. Programs put into effect would
not need to be carried so far or buttressed so securely or enforced so
vigorously. Finally, a strong current in Western ideology pulled in a
contrary direction.*

The impulse to social bifurcation thus arising was magnified in
the German case by two potent tendencies. The first was the differing
conception, East and West, of the ultimate nature of the enemy manifested in Nazism. For the West this enemy primarily was fascism itself,
the broadside use of state coercion to regiment a community. In these
terms the main task was to decentralize and disperse public power and
to revive a love for and tradition of liberty. Mingled with this primary
stress was a secondary note which with varying degrees of emphasis
looked to change in social structure. The Eastern interpretation reversed this primacy. Fascism was seen as a manifestation of the will to
power of a dominant class—the still feudal rural gentry, the capitalists,
the corporation magnates—who could or would no longer rule with
safety through a democratic republic. In these terms a democratized
Germany would be achieved by socialization or by redistribution of the
real power positions controlled by the former ruling classes. Only
against this primary stress on social renovation did the Marxist interpretation permit an infrequently sounded emphasis on the need for
humanist values and the desire to overcome traditional German ser-
vility.

This real policy divergence was enhanced by the wide difference,

* That the Eastern and Western worlds are permeated by similarities as well as
marked by differences has been noted by many, though possibly only James Burnham
in his *Managerial Revolution* (NY, 1941) probed fully on a broad level of generaliza-
tion into the basis for similarity in terms of converging "managerial" societies.

East and West, in historic background and national interest out of which German policy would grow. For the East the background was of tension through long centuries in territory which had few natural barriers to separate Slav and German populations. The continuous pressure on this frontier was indicated by its changing contour and irregular shape as well as by the long periods of settled collaboration punctuated by invasion and attempted conquest. The German-Slav struggle which began in 1941 was thus tinctured with memories of old conflicts, devastations and foreign rule. The image of the German problem cast up by the historic experience of the Anglo-Saxon West ran in quite different terms. Only for a generation or so before World War I had the Germans been regarded with fear. A cultural community subsisted between the Anglo-Saxon and German worlds manifested by kinship in language, common experience of the Reformation, and association in the medieval European community. With a land base far from Europe and with access to and dominion over empire, the Anglo-Saxon powers had never been interested directly in German territories. The warfare which had ravaged Slavic lands hardly touched the homes or the youth of the Anglo-Saxon West. This varied experience and background would leave an impress on German policy and thus tend to reinforce the impulse to bifurcation which already was so powerful.

III. Partition or Unification

It was the strength of this impulse to bifurcation mingled with an overlap of interest and action which constituted the crux of the German problem. How could wartime policy planning adapt to it? The simplest line of policy to adopt and the easiest direction in which to move was probably that of partition inherent in the profound tendency to bifurcation. This perspective could be accepted as bedrock and deliberately facilitated in inter-Allied agreements. The task of policy then would be not to obstruct the impulse to bifurcation: to ease the way for a clean-cut break between the partitioned zonal areas; to settle frontier lines that would be least disruptive, easiest to sustain and administer; to unscramble to the greatest extent possible the mixed and floating population; to separate the webs of joint administration and of communication and transport, and to reorder their strands on zonal lines; and to foster any separatist tendencies which would culminate logically in satellite regimes bound to the respective cultural and economic worlds of the East and West.

Viewed in this context, the policy of partition had its merits. It would accept as immutable the political and cultural gap between East and West. It would discount the possibility that a partnership could be sustained even between an East in its most democratic and a West in its most liberal transmutation. East-West relationships would be spared the aggravations arising out of condominium over a country undergoing social reconstruction. Finally, a clearcut partition which corresponded to inner German social division would do much to break up that monolithic Germanic state which had been forged by the Junkers and Hohenzollerns and consolidated in a century of capitalist development. "Balkanization" will reduce power potential. In the wartime mood this was widely held to be desirable. As Churchill put it, the Allies "all feared the might of a united Germany."[19]

But to these merits of partition there corresponded marked drawbacks. In the course of the development of the 20th century German economy the relatively self-subsistent communities of the Middle Ages were stripped of their localized character and transformed into specialized organs of a modern industrial society. In the process of transformation many of these communities had grown into cities which had drawn citizens and capital from all over Germany. Specialization was facilitated by the emergence of centralized bureaucracy and by the easy flow of transport and communication on a well-conceived and complex network of carriers. Regional division of labor in agriculture as well as in industry had gone a long way. Even many of the less important fabricated products were made from component parts or materials processed in scattered parts of the country. The ties which bound the economy together were reinforced by those measures by which it was converted to a war economy. The strains of reconversion and the adaptation to the impoverished conditions of postwar life could best be handled with the use of all Germany's postwar resources tied into an integrated economy.

Partition had other drawbacks. The whole course of modern history warned against an attempt to divide an ethnically single people with a historically evolved and rooted community of culture. No effective German leadership would rise to collaborate with an occupation based expressly on partition. The families and kinship units of which the German people were composed had transplanted themselves on a large scale during the preceding century of capitalist development. Movement increased throughout the war and was accelerated tremendously by forced migration at the war's end. These migrations increased the separations among family units and their kinship groups. Partition thus would cut through kinship ties and property entanglements on a large scale.

Contemplation of these drawbacks to partition would lead to consideration of the alternative goal of policy, that of achieving occupation objectives in a unified Germany. The Eastern and Western conceptions of the German problem overlapped enough and values enough were common to both to permit a certain but limited range of congruous program and joint action. Although the overlap had been magnified in the ideology of wartime alliance, its full extent and depth was probably greater than the retrospective view can readily envisage. In this perspective, the elements of congruity in Eastern and Western policy and action would need to be consolidated and extended so that Allied purposes could be effected primarily through central German agencies. If the administrative apparatus of centralized control over national life broke down in the last stages of the war, priority would be given to its reconstitution. This apparatus with its myriad agencies for control over banking, taxation, transport, foreign trade, rationing and food collection and distribution would be reactivated under some kind of caretaker management until a new provisional political leadership could be given contingent custody. Although zonal in form, an Allied occupation under such conditions would be unified and national in content. The larger weight of Allied authority would be exerted not in the provinces but at the center. The specific power of zonal authorities gradually would be limited to police and garrison duties and such special projects as demilitarization, handling displaced persons, cultural propaganda, denazification and dealing with war criminals. The principal aim of occupation policy would be to withdraw its local controls as soon as effective central government had been restored.

This policy might be difficult to carry out if habits of local control became rooted because drawn out Nazi resistance made nationwide institution of the occupation a gradual rather than a sudden action. But once the machinery of national life began to turn, such a course would develop momentum. The operations of a central regime could be hampered. But without creating a furor its existence could not be dissolved by any one of the occupying powers. By playing the role inherent in the situation of broker between the occupying powers, the newly established German leadership could win confidence and enlarge the sphere of its real if not its formal authority. All this, however, presupposes a considerable measure of agreement between the Allies over a wide range of problems, including the order of Allied objectives, the distribution of German revenues available for use within or outside of Germany, and the disposition of like German resources.

Thus both partition and unification had merits; neither policy was free from hazard; and both involved immense difficulties in design and execution. Success in neither direction could be guaranteed. But the German situation was unusually plastic, while the German people had a deep instinct for order and for obedience to legitimate authority. Hence it seems not too controversial to conclude that if Allied agreement and resources had been thrown behind either policy, with astute management and good luck either could have succeeded. It would be necessary only to decide one way or another and then to employ the concentrated resources of policy to back up the decision.

But the process of choice would not be easy since it would involve foregoing an alternative line of action. The strain of making a choice could for a time be avoided by attempting to carry out both policies concurrently. Any sustained and organized effort to do so might even show certain initial successes. It would be possible to reestablish the central machinery of German political and economic life but to allocate to the center the vaguer functions of "coordination" and "planning" while assigning to the zonal level operative authority. Or conversely, it would be possible to establish behind a front of unification a group of purely zonalized regimes held together chiefly by the incessant talk of unity and by preservation of external frames of action and organization. There were many different ways to move concurrently and irresolutely in the directions of both partition and unification. But none of these ways could lead to constructive outcome and movement along all of them would be accompanied by controversy and frustration. The precious initial fund of Allied good will and German plasticity would be depleted. In the end, the area of overlap in policy and action between East and West would recede. Divergences in various spheres would obtrude more or less speedily and explosively and in aggravated form. The peace settlement would be plagued with the drawbacks of both policy courses without being facilitated by the merits of either.

Yet precisely this—most undesirable—solution to the dilemma of policy-making on Germany was adopted by the Allies during the war and was applied in the occupation. This basic fact—so simple and controlling—was at the bottom of the subsequent tortuous course of the German development. It is therefore needful to enquire as carefully as the available material will permit into the way this policy was designed; the nature of those interests and drives, rationalizations and ideas which motivated it; and the means by which it was put into effect.

IV. The Policy of Ambivalence

A policy which attempts to move in opposite directions at the same time might fitly be termed a policy of "contradictions." But "policy" is the work of the human mind with its quest for light and penchant for rationalization. Hence it is more appropriate to think of the policy in question as one of ambivalence, which tends to arise as a product of strain occasioned by uncertainty, and which psychologically involves simultaneous attraction toward and repulsion from its object. The wartime setting out of which a postwar policy had to emerge was permeated by both strain and uncertainty. The military outcome until the closing phases of the war was itself liable to sudden shifts. This objective uncertainty was magnified by the difficulty in communicating the full import of evolving complex military and diplomatic patterns to the large number of persons who would contribute in small or large ways to the shape of German policy. The fog of official ideology blurred vision. Nor was it easy to take the bearings of the worldwide situation or to foresee the kind of policy which the various Allied countries in their postwar moods could be expected to support. Neither was it certain what policies they would in fact carry out.

Hence it was, as President Roosevelt wrote at a crucial stage of American planning, convenient to suppose that "in their occupied territory they [the Soviets] will do more or less as they wish." Uncertainty about Germany's real condition also was prevalent and it was not unnatural to "dislike making detailed plans for a country which we do not yet occupy."[20] Churchill protested "lawyer's agreements made in all good faith months before and persisted in without regard to the ever-changing fortunes of war."[21] Accent therefore would be laid on caution in commitment, on deviousness in expression, on extending the period of forward options, and the while on steadily building national power. This was the policy of ambivalence writ large. To devise the requisite formulas was not difficult. The language of diplomacy was readily adaptable to such purposes. The tendency to slide into ambivalence was also facilitated by the perhaps unconscious but understandable impulse to think of partition in terms of freedom of action for our side while thinking of unification in terms of the restraints it would impose on the other side. By stressing these aspects separately, diverse interests could readily be accommodated.

These interests were mobilized around a constellation of ideological drives which unwittingly sanctified the central pivot on which the policy could best hinge: namely, the destruction of the centralized machinery of German national life. This goal, restated as a "grass roots" approach to rebuilding a "healthy" political structure with responsible "local" government, picked up that distrust of coercion and of central authority latent in the Western liberal and radical tradition. At the same time, the policy of ambivalence in its openly partitionist aspects could mobilize the support of groups of varying political complexion for whom destruction of the German machinery of central government appeared as a deserved form of punishment or as essential—even as tantamount—to uprooting the Nazi regime.

Finally, the policy of ambivalence suited a situation in which public opinion and important policy-making circles were too divided to reach any clearcut decision. There was strong support East and West for the policy of clearcut partition. The main proponents were the German-haters, the army chiefs and the American and British chiefs of state. But the opposition to partition was very strong particularly in America where it included the state department, key members of the cabinet and a powerful bloc in Congress. Neither group was in a position to obtain a clearcut decision. A "compromise" was needed which would not foreclose options and which would satisfy most of the adherents of both camps. The formula of ambivalence suited this situation. It perhaps embodied the only kind of solution that could have been negotiated not only *between* but *within* the governments concerned.[22]

The policy of ambivalence first was presented, in a suggestive way only, by Hull in October 1943. It was not then embodied in formal international agreement although Hull reported that it seemed to win general approval.* At any rate it came to be the accepted mode of think-ing about the resolution of the German problem. This approach con-ditioned the negotiations and structured the agreements reached during 1944/5 in the European Advisory Commission and at Yalta. Through these agreements the policy of ambivalence bore its first fruit—the Control Council, an agency which was to accomplish "coordinated administration and control" of the mutually sanctified, but militarily partitioned, zonal regimes.[23] The Control Council was a special standing diplomatic conference whose members, the four Zone Commanders, were explicitly deprived of plenipotentiary authority.** The pretentious language used to characterize the scope of the Council and its sub-ordinate working committees—"matters affecting Germany as a whole" —grew in part out of the real presupposition that a working ma-chinery of German central government would survive the war and would be reactivated under Central Allied control. This presupposition, explicitly written into the 1944 agreements on the Control Council machinery, grew out of negotiations in which the U.S. Department of State was relatively free to work out a statement of German policy along "unifying" lines.***

But while the U.S. Department of State was able to reach the EAC agreements in 1944 on zonal allocation and a Control Council, the De-partment was unable to fashion in like manner the policy directives

* See the plan for German settlement summarized in Hull, Memoirs, II, 1284–1287. In this form the policy of ambivalence is indicated only generally, with strong emphasis on "decentralization" by "assigning to the state units control over a wide range of administrative functions and by encouraging any movement that might emerge within Germany in favor of the diminution of Prussian domination over the Reich." At the same time the German economy was to be drained to the maximum to "pay reparations for the physical damage inflicted upon the USSR and other Allied and occupied countries." Stalin was described as being "enthusiastic" about the proposal, and the Soviets and British gave it general concurrence. Ibid., 1602.

** The characterization of the Control Council as a "standing diplomatic con-ference" is not vitiated by the instruction in its charter that the "Control Council whose decisions shall be unanimous will ensure appropriate uniformity of action by the Commanders-in-Chief in their respective zones of occupation and will reach agreed decisions on the chief questions affecting Germany as a whole." The lack of plenipotentiary authority was specifically noted in the foundation statement that "supreme authority in Germany" was to be exercised by the Zone Commanders in their own zones and in the Control Council "on instructions from their Governments."

*** See U.S. Dept. of State, Foreign Relations of the United States, The Con-ferences at Malta and Yalta 1945 (GPO, 1955) p. 125, 126. This basic collection of documents will hereafter be referred to as Yalta Papers.

which were being issued to the American occupying forces and which would condition overall policy undertakings in Germany. The policy position of the State Department was undermined by the strong attack of the U.S. Treasury aided and abetted by the Army. Both organizations were more inclined to a "zonal" or "partitionist" solution or at any rate to a "tougher" policy which won the favor of President Roosevelt. Roosevelt had no compunctions about abruptly shifting the policy course. He in any case wanted to work out the basic agreements in personal diplomacy; he was insistent about preserving freedom of maneuver; and he urged thinking in terms which would permit shifting positions at a later date. This was the policy of ambivalence writ large. It was elucidated in an American directive which became in effect a statement of the joint U.S.-British position and which seemed to express effectively the common ground which had been reached between the three powers on the operative phases of postwar German policy.[24]

In this directive, JCS 1067, the policy of zonalization was worked out with a thoroughness which left the nature of the process and its outcome in no doubt. Thus care was taken at the outset to emphasize that the American commander was clothed with "supreme legislative, executive and judicial authority in the areas occupied by forces under your command." This authority was to be "broadly construed" and to include "all measures deemed by you necessary, appropriate or desirable in relation to military exigencies and the objectives of a firm military government." Civilian movement in or out of the zone was to be only "by your authority." Courts were to be reopened "to exercise jurisdiction within the boundaries of your zone" under such "regulations, supervision and control as you may consider appropriate." An "interim program" for "reopening" and conducting educational institutions was to be put into effect "within your zone." The social insurance system and the German pension system was to be modified zonally. A zonal program for agricultural resettlement was to be instituted. An estimate of zonal requirements for supplies "necessary to prevent starvation or widespread disease" was to be forwarded, while the zone commander was to "take all practicable economic and police measures to assure that German resources are fully utilized."* "Appropriate controls" over

---

* The fact that this zonal economic autonomy might lead to disparate ration levels was recognized by the instruction to "urge upon" the Control Council the establishment of "uniform ration scales" to be applied throughout Germany.

foreign trade and foreign exchange were to be established within the zone. Revenues and facilities were to be requisitioned directly from the German provincial financial authorities. Banks, security exchanges and financial regulations were to be put into effect on a zonal basis. German government expenditures in the zone were to be put under "general supervision." Properties and facilities of the former national government were to be impounded or blocked and subsequently handled only under zonal military authorization.[25]

The tendency operative in the directive to entrench zonal power was furthered by the omission of reference to a central German government or to its pervasive central administrative and law-making machinery. Though it was not expressly required that these be dismantled if they survived the war, this was everywhere implied. German "authorities" and "agencies" were referred to as a species of local fauna. The guiding principle was "decentralization of the political and administrative structure of Germany and the development of local responsibility." To this end "autonomy in regional, local and municipal agencies of German administration"—all subject to zonal control—was to be "encouraged." It was desirable "to decentralize the structure and administration of the German economy to the maximum possible extent." This was to be effected by action to "restore essential public utilities and industrial and agricultural activities . . . as far as possible on a local and regional basis"—that is, under zonal control and on a zonal basis.

But if the imperatives of the directive—and of the structure of international wartime agreement it epitomized—fostered the entrenchment of zonal power, this tendency, true to the policy of ambivalence, was held within elastic restraints. Development of zonal power under the rubric of decentralization itself implies limits to zonalization. The idea of decentralization connotes the continued existence of a unifying framework holding together that which is dispersed. This unifying framework was further propped by the ban on constructive or rehabilitory programs. This ban hindered positive action in the zone which would break through the external uniformity of German institutions and laws carried over into the occupation. The responsibility for the resulting paralysis was rather cynically shifted to the powerless local German authorities.

These elastic restraints on zonalization were supplemented by an attitude of permissiveness with respect to establishment of certain types of central agencies or the undertaking of quadripartite unifying action.

Over a narrow range of functions, chiefly negative and repressive in character, action expressly was to be based on inter-Allied agreements reached through the Control Council.[26] In cautious language the directive permitted the establishment of "centralized administration" or "central control" over "essential national public services" which ran to the heart of modern government. Yet this impulse to retie the threads of unified national life was undermined by the discrimination between "administration" and "government," by the express intent to permit central controls merely to the "minimum extent . . . clearly essential" to carrying out the repressive and negative purposes which dominated the directive, and by the emphasis on the role of the Control Council as a source only of "policy."[27] Characteristically, "proclamation" of the dissolution of the German army, of the Nazi party and its formations was assigned to the Control Council, while the "effectuation" of these policies was left to the zones.[28]

Indeed the relative balance between zonalization and unification was so lopsided as to jeopardize the ability of the Control Council to emerge as a stabilizing force in the occupation. Fortunately for the policy of ambivalence, ballast in offset to zonalization could be found in two other areas, Berlin and currency. The agreement to partition Germany into zones meant that Berlin—which had to fall within one of the zones—would become assimilated into a zonal regime unless special arrangements for it were worked out. In order to be on hand, military currency had to be printed before invasion. Minimum financial precaution would suggest an effort to arrange either mutual acceptance of separate currencies at an agreed rate of exchange or shared use of a single currency. The Allies could not avoid some form of advance action on Berlin and military currency; and the outcome of this advance action would vitally affect the course of the German peace settlement.

V. Berlin and Currency

In its beginnings Berlin was chiefly a provincial trading and administrative center. It grew great with the rise of the German economy which became more highly differentiated as it industrialized. To varying degrees the whole of Germany became a zoned hinterland interlaced in a variety of ways with the capital city. Closest bound to Berlin were its suburban offshoots. The extent of interweaving declined as distance from Berlin increased and as the orbits of other metropolitan areas and trading centers approached. Between Berlin and the province of Brandenburg a particularly close connection existed reflecting the old Berlin which had been the political and administrative capital of the province. Dense interrelationships also characterized other territories now in the Soviet zone. Of prewar commodity shipments to and from Berlin between 43 and 59 percent arose within or terminated in the present Soviet zone. Much of this trade flowed on an intricate network of inland waterways which linked together the upper Silesian area fed by the Oder with the lower Elbe running through central Germany and into the North Sea port of Hamburg.[29] Because of these connections with the North Sea and Rhine ports, a sizeable percentage of Berlin's commodity shipments—15 to 23 percent—either originated or were terminated within the area of what later became the British zone. The relative share of Berlin trade falling within the American zone shrank to a much lower level, 3 to 6 percent, while the lower Rhineland territories under French control interacted directly with Berlin by commodity shipments only to the extent of 1 to 2 percent.[30]

If for purposes of direct commodity shipments Berlin was most closely integrated with and dependent upon its surrounding territories, for certain key industrial products and services integration was at a uniform level throughout Germany. Berlin was the center of development and production for electro-mechanical products. The clothing industry was concentrated in Berlin for reasons comparable to those which have made New York, London, and Paris clothing manufacturing centers. In the realm of services the integration of Berlin with the total national life was most outstanding.[31] This was particularly true in the field of government. Of the city's prewar productively employed population some 16 percent were in direct government service while another 8 to 10 percent were in quasi-governmental services such as education, cultural activities, health and welfare.[32]

The economic dependence of Berlin upon the integrated functioning of the entire economy was matched by an equally close political and cultural interdependence. The inhabitants of the city had been drawn from all Germany. The city contained many of Germany's outstanding cultural institutions. Leaders of a wide array of organizations —in politics, business and art—made their home in Berlin. Residents of the city owned property located for the most part all over Germany while property within the city was controlled by institutions drawing

THE POLICY OF AMBIVALENCE

financial support from outside the city. City and hinterland were thus phases of an organic life which had historically developed.

The fate of Berlin early became involved in the fate of the inter-Allied negotiations which resulted in the agreement on zone lines. The distribution of German territory on the basis of rough thirds left Berlin well within the zone which would by reason of contiguity be allocated to the Soviets. In the British proposal which served as the basis for later zonal arrangements it was indicated that Berlin, as the capital city, should be governed directly as an enclave under inter-Allied occupation. This was accepted by the Soviets and later by the Americans. The plan specified that the city be carved into sectors, and that each sector should be occupied by one of the Allies. The respective local commanders were to sit together as the Kommandatura and govern Berlin "jointly" in matters of common concern.[33]

Soviet relinquishment of physical control over the city is itself a testimonial to their faith in the wartime alliance. Provision for a limited Western garrison and inter-Allied control of certain facilities such as those of the central German government and of Allied headquarters and living quarters, would have satisfied the desire for a more intimate form of condominium in Berlin than was in prospect for occupied Germany as a whole. The relinquishment of the city to inter-Allied control was possibly designed to facilitate the work of the central German government and its machinery of administration.[34] Too, the Soviets may have wished to manifest by their agreement on Berlin their appreciation of the need for joint controls over the centralized facilities of German life.[35]

But it is also likely that, under the conditions of taking over in Germany in 1945, the Soviets were reluctant to carry through the agreement on Berlin. The Nazi policy of last ditch resistance had severed many of the threads which bound the nation to its capital. The machinery of central government had been destroyed and the tendency toward autonomous zonalization was in full swing.[36] At any rate, the Berlin agreement was implemented only by dint of pressure. In the final stage of the war German military resistance melted at the thrust of Western armored divisions. In a wild pursuit during two weeks in April the American forces overran a sizeable portion of the territory allotted to the Soviet zone. Churchill pleaded for a continuous advance but Eisenhower wanted to avoid an obvious rush for position and checked the advance of the Western armies.[37] Later, Churchill urged that the overrun territories previously allotted to Soviet control be retained under Western control. This went farther than American policymakers deemed proper considering the clear commitment on zonal lines and the still unfinished war in the Far East. Hence, withdrawal of American troops was coupled with admission of Western troops to their assigned sectors of Berlin and the provision of suitable channels of access for their support.[38] When this arrangement was consummated, sizeable Western military contingents moved into the wrecked city. With this touch of constraint the occupation attained a common capital and a joint headquarters—at once a hostage to Allied success, a stimulus to cooperation and a potential trouble spot.

A joint occupation of Berlin went far to link the militarily partitioned zones. A second practical arrangement, less devised by plan than extorted by circumstances, was the provision of a common military currency in addition to the use of the old Reichsmark currency. Each combat army as it approached Germany had to carry a stock of German currency usable for military procurement, for troop payment and for the support of military government operations. To this end early in 1944 an Anglo-American project was launched to print Allied military marks in Washington according to a design and on a scale determined by Anglo-American agreement. The Soviets were interested in use of a common military currency but plainly intimated that some of the printing should be handled in Moscow "in order," it was laconically stated, "that a constant supply of currency may be guaranteed to the Red Army."* While the statement had a distrustful ring, American officers could feel sympathetic with the thinking behind it. "It disturbed the mental equilibrium of the Allied Commander and of his commanders down the line," stated a ranking American staff officer, "to run out of anything, particularly anything as important as money"; and the best way to prevent a shortage was to control the sources of supply.[39] After extended negotiations the Soviets threatened that if plates were not made available a separate Soviet currency printing program would be

* U.S. Congress, Senate, *Occupation Currency Transactions*. Hearings before the Committees on Appropriations, Armed Services, Banking, and Currency, 80th Congress, 1st session, (Washington, 1947). Appended to these hearings is a collection of documents—including cables, minutes of conferences and meetings, texts of decisions, instructions, and reports on negotiations—bearing upon the handling and issuance of German military currency and subsequent transactions. The collection is extremely valuable both for the light it sheds on this episode and for information on certain other problems which will be dealt with later.

undertaken. A decision was reached on April 14 to send the plates and requisite printing supplies to the Soviet Union. The actual range of agreement or understanding that accompanied this action was meager.[40] It appears that the transaction was opened and closed with the shipment of currency plates and printing supplies and the payment duly made by the Soviet government upon presentation of invoiced cost by the American Treasury Department.[41]

But, thin though the agreement was, and thinly though it hung upon a single transaction, enough occurred to help to link together with an interchangeable military currency the payment communities that would emerge in eastern and in western Germany. The assimilation of one Allied military Mark to one standard Reichsmark in German currency meant that both East and West, through the military Mark, had bound themselves to the same currency system. The mode of monetary action helped to deprive the system of enduring economic value. Each side possessed large quantities of a currency already weakened by inflation. Nevertheless, the zones were bound together in the unifying constraint of a common monetary system. This currency and the shared capital in Berlin together gave the policy of ambivalence vitality enough for the Control Council regime to have a chance to become born. Whether the regime could survive its birth would depend upon the ability of its parental custodians to agree on the disposition of German assets, resources and frontiers. The problems of disposition were various but came to center around the Oder-Neisse frontier and the taking of German reparations. The challenge of these problems and the response they evoked presents a story so complicated that it deserves for its exposition the clean canvas of a fresh chapter.

CHAPTER II

THE CORE OF CONTROVERSY AT POTSDAM

I. The Oder-Neisse and Reparations

A COMMON MILITARY CURRENCY and a joint occupation of Berlin gave the Control Council regime a chance to come to life. But that life would be puny and shortlived unless the territorial confines of the Control Council regime and its liabilities for reparations were definitely fixed. A territorial issue arose chiefly from the Soviet demand for those eastern German border lands, stripped of their indigenous population, which lay east of the Oder-Neisse river. A reparations issue grew out of the Soviet demand for ten billion dollars (1938 worth) in reparations.* At bottom the two questions turned about what the Soviets and the Slav world for whom they spoke would get out of Germany by the way of land, goods and services in return for misery endured and the blood shed in withstanding German aggression.

The rationale of controversy over the Oder-Neisse issue is easy enough to trace. The Poles were pressing ardently a policy of westward expansion partly to offset their loss of territory to the Soviets.[1] Though this expansion would benefit Poland, the Soviet indirect advantage was considerable. The territorial cession would bind the Poles and the Soviets to the peace settlement. It would help adjust the Polish people, traditionally anti-Russian, to the shift of Polish eastern territories to the Soviets. The Oder-Neisse frontier would give a new Poland economic elbow room and new coal resources on which to base extensive indus-trialization. Finally, the new frontier would be marked by a river channel which has some military significance.[2]

---

* For detailed analysis of German reparations, see my two papers: "The German Economic Potential," *Social Research*, XVII (1950) 65–89; "The Reparations Problem Again," *Canadian Journal of Economics and Politics*, XVI (1950) 22–41.

Western opposition to the Soviet territorial objective had no deep basis in principle. The normative proscription—at least for advanced Western peoples—of coercive change of settled frontiers without the consent of the indigenous population remained in effect. But its application to the case at hand was waived. This act of waiver grew out of wartime hatred of the Germans and desire to exact retribution from them. Then too, the West felt there was a case for revision in the frontiers concerned. On the Soviet-Polish side the case for revision was well-founded since it concerned a Ukranian people living in a border area which the British in the early twenties would have turned over to Soviet custody. Revision of the Polish-German frontier was legitimized by the fact that World War II had started over its enclaves and corridor. The Soviets with British support persistently urged Westward revision of these two frontiers.[3] Although Hull formally bound the Americans not to support changes in frontiers during the war, a shielded American support seems to have obtained both at Teheran and at Yalta.[4]

What was disputed was not the principle of major frontier revision but chiefly its extent. The Soviets wanted this frontier placed at the western Neisse river. The British with American support urged that the frontier line be placed eastward following the eastern Neisse. The territory between these two rivers supported a population of some three million persons and amounted to about a third of the total eastern territorial gain. On this issue of the Western versus the Eastern Neisse line, the West released the moral indignation hitherto held in suspense. They also argued on grounds of economic feasibility. Loss of the Oder-Neisse area would bring Germany's total resource loss to 25% of her arable soil, 20% of her timber stand and 14% of her coal mines and other energy sources. With absorption of expelled populations added on, this resource loss would tend to translate itself economically into coal scarcity, lower levels of feeding, maldistribution of population and unemployed surplus labor. This resource loss would translate itself socially into a pauperized mass at the base of the German social structure.

The bulk of the territorial gain would inure directly to Polish benefit. Soviet gain out of settlement was primarily to take the form of reparations to help repair damage and loss arising out of the war. Soviet civilian and military casualties ran up to fifteen million persons. The belt of Soviet territory that was occupied, fought over and devastated included her most productive farmlands and many of her important industrial areas and urban districts.[5] These social and industrial losses rolled back advances which had been achieved since 1921 by dint of sustained privation and austerity. It was hence understandable that on reparations Stalin "spoke with great emotion" and that extraction of a sustaining flow of reparations in goods and services was a fundamental Soviet objective in a German peace settlement.*

The proportions and composition of a sustaining flow of reparations are interrelated. Reparations could be drawn from three possible sources: services of German labor performed in the victor countries; withdrawals from the current flow of industrial production; and one-time seizures from the German stock of wealth primarily consisting of dismantled plant equipment but also including such items as stocks of gold and precious metals, merchant shipping and rolling stock, titles to wealth and investments owned by Germans in foreign countries. Reparations from these varied sources could be drawn in varied combinations, with different aggregated yields, and over varied time-periods.

The question of time-periods is relatively simple. All the countries concerned had an urgent preference for immediate as contrasted with deferred command over resources; and there was a recognition that reparations arrangements should not require many decades for their consummation. Regarding magnitude and assortment by sources, the relationships are more complex. With a relatively low order of magnitude, reparations could be collected indifferently from any of the three

* Stettinius noted that during the Yalta discussions Stalin "spoke with great emotion which was in sharp contrast to his usual calm, even manner." On several occasions, the account runs, "he arose, stepped behind his chair and spoke from that position gesturing to emphasize his point. The terrible German destruction in Russia obviously had moved him deeply." Stettinius, *Roosevelt and the Russians, the Yalta Conference* (W. Johnson, ed., New York, 1946), 264. Byrnes also reported that "during all the consideration of the German question [at Yalta] reparations were the chief interest of the Soviet delegation." James Byrnes, *Speaking Frankly* (New York, 1947), 26. Byrnes continued to believe that reparations was a crucial Soviet objective in Germany. See *Ibid.*, 194. Reparations was uppermost in Soviet war aims literally from the start of their discussion. See a report on Eden-Stalin discussions of December 1941 in Cordell Hull, *The Memoirs of Cordell Hull* (2v., New York, 1948), II, 1167; R. E. Sherwood, *Roosevelt and Hopkins, an Intimate History* (New York, 1948), 388, 713. Reparations ranked along with the Polish western frontier as the dominating theme in the Big Three discussions on Germany at Teheran, Yalta, and Potsdam. See the illuminating treatment in A. B. Carr, *Truman, Stalin and Peace* (New York, 1950), 40, 41–44; 65. The U.S. State Department advised Roosevelt of the basic Soviet interest in a sustained reparations flow. *Yalta Papers,* 166–171.

sources in any pattern found desirable. However, as the magnitude rises beyond certain critical points, the composition of reparations by source becomes increasingly affected. In this reciprocal connection between overall magnitude and composition lies the nub of the problem.

The critical point touching composition would be most quickly reached in utilization of labor service performed abroad. At the outset of the occupation a significant amount of labor service would be performed by large numbers of Soviet and French-held German prisoners-of-war who could not be repatriated over-night. Some delay of repatriation would ease manpower shortages. However, delay of repatriation long after the armistice would become progressively less profitable and more difficult. Exploitation of an army of aliens living without a normal community environment and without family life was morally too repugnant to be carried very far in times of peace without arousing intense opposition within Western countries. Nor presumably would the Soviets desire to take even the larger part of their reparations in services unwillingly performed under expensive supervision at a small net return. Their own supply of unskilled labor, granted military demobilization, was relatively large and their needs were greatest for skilled labor, industrial equipment and fabricated products.

Soviet needs would hence be met more adequately by taking reparations in the form of *goods* and *things* rather than *personal service*. However, there were only limited stocks that could be taken from the German economy without unduly squeezing the German standard of living or hampering the ability of the German economy to repair war damages and to become self-sustaining. Practically none of the foreign assets, including merchant shipping, gold stocks and foreign investments, could be taken without enhancing import requirements or injuring export capacity and thereby weakening at vital points the ability of the German economy to become self-supporting. Moreover, by common usage these foreign assets if seized would be distributed as reparations not according to the incidence of needs or deserts but according to the accident of location. Finally, German-owned foreign investments could not simply be seized and dismantled. These investments could in the main only be administered; most of these investments were not at the time very profitable; and the larger part of the income accruing was not immediately transferable across frontiers.

With regard to wealth located within Germany, the outlook for most categories was not much better. Allied strategic bombing had greatly depleted stocks of household effects and furniture, household appliances, libraries, office machines and store equipment, railway rolling stock, dock and harbor equipment, inland watercraft and power stations. The categories of removable wealth which were relatively free from wartime injury and which were available in relative abundance within Germany comprised her stocks of industrial equipment. Desirable items included woodworking machines, scales, cranes, stationary engines, boilers and heating equipment, printing presses, research laboratories, vending and washing machines, weaving looms, electrical equipment, and machine tools. This industrial equipment was generally housed in sturdy buildings located outside the heavily bombed urban centers. Repair and replacement of industrial equipment more than kept pace with bomb damage, leading to increases during the war in equipment inventories. The margin for removal thus occasioned was further enlarged by the buildup of prewar inventories during the armament effort and by the fact that German industry was geared to single-shift operation and to a liberal margin for industrial expansion.[6]

But though available for use as reparations, total stocks of removable equipment would not enable reparations claims to be pushed very far. Gauging by stocks of machine tools, the total 1938 value of industrial equipment allowing for a fifty percent depreciation for aging would run to some 13 to 15 billion 1938 Reichsmarks or between 3 to 4 billion 1938 dollars.[7] Most of this equipment would of course be required to meet the peacetime needs of a self-sustaining German economy equipped to maintain a tolerable standard of living for its population and to permit reconstruction of her destroyed urban centers and damaged industrial facilities. Much of the equipment was too old to warrant dismantling or was structurally imbedded and could be removed only with prohibitive dismantling and packaging costs. In other instances dismantling would leave valuable building facilities inoperable. A sizeable margin for dismantling would remain and this margin could be widened somewhat by lowering German living standards, chiefly by depriving Germans of imported amenities and by enforcing chiefly a cereal diet. With a given standard of living, the scope for plant removal could be enlarged by forcing concentration of production, by inducing multi-shift plant operation and by fostering regimented patterns in society and politics. However, application of all available pressures could hardly permit removal of half of Germany's available equipment inventories and most probably the margin for removal consistent with leaving a viable Germany would not exceed a third. This means that in dollar values the removable margin of industrial equipment would not exceed a few billion 1938 dollars. This much could be removed only by dint of costly dismantling charges and by leaving a trail of disruption in the bottleneck areas of the German economy.

While a program of equipment dismantling would thus quickly yield little, retention in Germany of this same equipment and utilization of it to produce reparations products would promise much. It is a distinctive characteristic of modern industry that it turns out an annual product many times the value of its own equipment. The value of this annual product is resolved into services of the innumerable varieties of labor, capital facilities and enterprise drawn from the whole of industry, from primary product production and from transportation and communication. Use of industrial equipment permits this conglomerate of resources to be mobilized for reparations purposes and converted into fabricated products that may readily be removed. This mobilization and removal occur under relatively amiable conditions, cause little disruption, are assimilated in form to everyday life, and tend to diffuse rather than concentrate resentments. The fertilizing flow of products thus tapped could continue for many years, could be turned in different directions and could be adjusted to the needs of recipients.

From this analysis it is obvious that a total reparations drainage on a scale of a few billion dollars could probably be handled by one-time removals from Germany's installed equipment and from her choice foreign and liquid trading assests. By adding to this some utilization of enforced labor service possibly the total yield of reparations could be built up to something near four billion 1938 dollars. But if reparations demands were pitched any higher than this or if Soviet claims were to rank high, they could only be satisfied by cutting down the scale of dismantling and tapping an enlarged stream of German industrial production.

It was essentially this tapping of current production which underlay the Soviet reparations position consistently maintained in all the wartime discussions. All three sources of reparations were to be tapped on a scale designed to yield over a fixed time period running up to at least a decade some 20 billion dollars in 1938 values of which one half would go to the Soviet Union. This was tantamount to a request for a Soviet share of 10 billion dollars in 1938 values with an equivalent share, if desired, for the other Allies. The implications of this reparations goal and time-period on the composition of reparations by sources, on German living standards, societal patterns and economic viability could not be spelled out in advance. The Soviets made only a weak effort to do so. But reparations on or near the scale indicated would involve reliance primarily upon withdrawals from current production over an extended time-period. To facilitate extraction of these withdrawals, utilization of labor in enforced service in the devastated areas and one-time seizure of industrial equipment through dismantling would need to be confined to a minimum if only to sustain adequate motivation at working German levels. For this same reason a reparations program on the scale indicated could be carried out only if the overall yield and time-period were definitely stipulated in advance as a primary target of the Allied occupation in Germany. This would stabilize expectations, facilitate flexibility in programming, increase German incentives to fulfill the requirements imposed upon them and confine Allied controversy chiefly to the ways and means needed to reach a given goal but not to the goal itself.

II. The Western Reparations Position in Evolution

The most general basis for Western opposition to the Soviet reparations position was the difficulty of ascertaining before the end of hostilities the extent to which German reparation potential would survive wartime destruction. This uncertainty virtually precluded those clear-cut guarantees—in terms of amount, arrangements and duration—which could have persuaded the Soviets to pool their zonal resources with those of the Western zones. Mere promise of a liberal reparations policy would for the Soviets be inadequate. The West, in turn, was reluctant to name a figure, however guarded, in the context of a settlement which involved taking extensive territories from Germany and resettling in a smaller country some seven to ten million persons formerly living outside its boundaries.

Opposition to the Soviet reparations position arising out of uncertainty over the extent of reparations potential shaded into opposition grounded on adherence to a fundamentally different version of a reparations settlement, spearheaded on the American side by the Secretary of the Treasury, Henry Morgenthau. In this version reparation was regarded as a by-product of the elimination of German war potential.

This was to be achieved by removing German wealth-producing capacity to the maximum extent. Equipment or facilities which could not be removed as reparations would be destroyed. Removals primarily would consist of equipment from heavy industry and would be carried to the point of imperiling Germany's ability to achieve self-support at a low standard of living. To cut off removals at this point would help to render unnecessary permanent subsidization from American sources of a pauperized Germany. Further to assure minimum invocation of American assistance, no guarantee would be placed on the amount of reparation to be realized. While removal and destruction were in process, no reparations would be taken from current industrial production or commodity stocks. These rather would be mortgaged as means to finance essential imports. After the desired amount of wealth was removed or destroyed, no basis for taking additional reparations would exist and the reparations problem would disappear.

This positive version of a reparations settlement was reinforced by disparaging any attempt to collect current reparations. The reparations experience in the Twenties was represented as a process of gouging America to build German industry. The desirability was stressed of permanent destruction of Germany's industrial potential.[8] This would ease the pressure on British industry and in anticipation promote the possibilities for a quick British recovery. Weakening Germany to help Britain strongly appealed to Roosevelt and, in conjunction with the promise of a large loan, won Churchill over to the Morgenthau position in September 1944.[9] At the Yalta conference Roosevelt under pressure of negotiation wavered in his loyalty to the Morgenthauist position and established—or appeared to establish—an accord with the Soviets. This accord was based upon personal loyalty to an informal understanding expressed in vague and equivocal terms.* The key personalities in-

* This wavering of Roosevelt to the Morgenthauist position was evidenced not in the introductory plenary discussions, which were extensively reported upon in the various memoirs (Leahy, Byrnes, Stettinius), but rather in the discussions by the foreign secretaries. The basis for these discussions was provided by reparations plans submitted by each delegation (see Stettinius, *Roosevelt and the Russians*, 165–229 for the texts and debate). The American and Soviet plan had parallel provisions on types of reparations (capital removals and current products), time limits (two years for capital removals and ten years for current product) and bases for distribution of reparations among recipient countries (priority for countries "which have borne the main burden of the war and have organized victory over the enemy"). Indication of restraints on reparations arising out of foreign trade deficits was conspicu-

volved were soon removed from active responsibilities by illness or death. In any case, the accord was undermined by the main drift of American policymaking which, after the conference, crystallized along Morgenthauist lines.[10]

This American position on reparations had significant implications for the balance between zonalization and unification which could be

---

ously absent from the American, though not from the British, plan. (*Ibid.*, 39, 254.) The only important U.S.-Soviet difference was American unwillingness to stipulate a fixed sum and term of years without closer consideration than it was then possible to give of the economic potential in Germany which would be used for reparations purposes. This difference was whittled down by a subtle shift in wording. The Soviets asked for "clarification" of the American provision which stated that a reparations commission would take "into consideration" the Soviet proposal for 20 billion dollars of reparations. The "clarification" was to take the form of adding the phrase "as a basis for its studies." This was to mean that the final figures "arrived at by the commission might be a little more or a little less than this [20 billion dollar] figure." (*Ibid.*, 230 ff.). That the U.S.-Soviet accord thus resulting rested on more than a placatory verbal gesture is variously indicated. Stettinius is reported to have explicitly endorsed the Soviet $20 billion figure as "reasonable" though he asserted he could not commit American policy. *Yalta Papers*, p. 809. Thus the British steadfastly refused to accept the U.S.-Soviet formula (of taking the Soviet proposal "into consideration" as a "basis for its studies"). Then two curiously worded notes passed by Hopkins to Roosevelt attest to the meaningful nature of the formula (cf. *Ibid.*, 264–5; Sherwood, *Roosevelt and the Russians*, 861–862). Furthermore, in the final plenary session of the conference frequent reference was made to the split between the "American-Soviet proposal" and the British view. Thus Stalin referred to the "American-Soviet proposal that there should be twenty billion dollars of reparations with 50% to the Soviet Union." He indicated the nature of the tentativeness of the figures by noting that since they were to be used "as a basis for discussion," they "could be reduced or increased by the Commission at Moscow." See Stettinius, *op. cit.*, 264, 266, 272. The texts of the Hopkins notes are as follows:

"Gromyko just told me that the Marshal thinks you did not back up Ed [Stettinius] relative to reparations—and that you sided with the British—and he is disturbed about it." (This note was passed during a plenary session which followed the foreign ministers' discussions. The other note was passed at the final plenary session when Stalin backed away from an earlier impulse to give in and insisted stubbornly on his reparations position.)

"The Russians have given in so much at this conference that I don't think we should let them down. Let the British disagree if they want to continue their disagreement at Moscow. Simply say it is all referred to the reparations commission with the minutes to show that the British disagree about any mention of the ten billion [the Soviet share, under the 50% arrangement]." The detailed compilation of materials on Yalta fully confirm the account given in the Stettinius volume and in the sources as noted above. See *Yalta Papers*, 702 f., 808 ff., 875 f., 902 f. Feis (*op. cit.* 536 f.) also thinks an ambiguous—or treacherous—accord was established.

worked out in the projected Control Council regime. The American position would eliminate that category of reparations removals—drainage over a decade or more from German current industrial production—upon which reparation to the extent contemplated at Yalta would have had to depend for fulfillment. Large scale reparation of this category could have been raised only by unified management of the German economy and by collection of reparations in a single pool subject to allocation by percentage shares.[11] Unified management of the German economy would presuppose or call into existence a nucleus of central German government and an Allied counterpart mechanism of custodianship. A program of extensive current product reparations would thus strengthen the tendency to unification.

The elimination—entire or in the main—of this category of reparations correspondingly would weaken the centralizing impulses of the Control Council regime. The other two categories of reparations which American policy permitted—labor services and one-time capital removals—did not require or set in motion a German central government. Reparations in the form of services would consist chiefly in the utilization by Allied powers of German prisoners of war. In whatever manner future provisions for labor services might be worked out, they would not presuppose centralized mechanisms in Germany. Capital removals were to be carried through in a relatively short time period, two years. Planning for and inspecting removals could be handled by inter-Allied personnel, whereas executing the program could fall with logic to the zone commanders who were responsible for maintenance and custody of the zone and for movements within or across its frontiers. Interest in maintaining the economic viability of the zone would tend to hold in check excessive zeal for wholesale reparations removals. Under these conditions the zone of origin would be a more appropriate basis for reparations distribution than a national pool. Some kind of pool would be required to handle the reparations claims of the non-occupying powers but this pool did not need to include all of the zones. American policy accordingly shifted away from the principle of a single national reparations pool with its presupposition of a single economy and a unified frontier control.*

* In *Speaking Frankly* Byrnes has told how he felt that "if reparations were to be drawn from all Germany we would have to demand an accounting from the Soviets," (83), that control would have to be established over objects removed from Germany as military loot or as "restituted" objects, that "we were sure they could not even

III. The Potsdam Effort at Resolution

The fully crystallized American policy on reparations and the continued Western dislike of acceding to the full measure of the Oder-Neisse frontier collided with the Soviet position at the Potsdam conference. The discussion was acid, frustrating and unsuccessful almost to the end. Under pressure of what virtually amounted to a U.S. ultimatum, a halfway compromise and halfway truce was patched up, loaded with hedges and retreats designed in the now characteristic spirit of ambivalence.* These in the main accepted the predominant

---

approximate an accurate valuation of what had been taken," and hence "we realized that the effort to establish and maintain such an accounting would be a source of constant friction, accusations and ill-will." Therefore, "Mr. Clayton, Mr. Pauley and I concluded that the only way out of the situation was to persuade each country to satisfy its reparation claims out of its own zone." This would seem to indicate that the U.S. had renounced a policy of joint economic fusion of a character which would "demand" a very close "accounting" of income and outgo. In a later context Byrnes argued that "even then it was provided that production available for export should be used to pay for necessary imports first and then for reparations; a provision which clearly called for over-all economic planning and administration" (167). A reparations pool seems to have been discarded to avoid problems of "over-all accounting," but check-up on the disposal of proceeds of all exports was "clearly called for" in the name of "over-all economic planning and administration." It appears that Mr. Byrnes' fears were based partly on misinformation and partly on distorted or unclear thinking. The British and American armies as well as the Soviets had a very elastic concept of military booty. Under this cover the British through 1947 were shipping out large quantities of German metal scrap. The problems involved in the definition of "booty" and "restitution" were not simple and could not be hastily resolved amidst recrimination. But under General Clay's guidance an acceptable if not too stringent definition of "restitution" was later reached. Aside from "booty and restitution," exclusive zonal control of frontiers and of shipping under military license and control would permit much laxity in the use of German resources. In the final analysis this laxity could only be reduced if a German government were to come into existence and if the flow of reparations and the fulfillment of other claims were to create the leverage for going ahead with the peace settlement. To shy away from the policy of a reparations pool because of the difficulties of "accounting" was in fact to shy away from starting on the path of a united Germany and to reinforce the tendency which was strongly pressing for partition.

* Byrnes has described in detail how the two major unresolved issues of the Oder-Neisse and reparations, joined with the mode of admission of Italy and the Balkan states to the United Nations, were grouped into a single American proposal to be discussed later that day. "I told him [Molotov] we would agree to all three or

balance of *fait accompli*. The Soviets controlled Poland and eastern Germany and had tentatively established the Oder-Neisse frontier by consigning territory east of that frontier to Polish administration. This action could be rationalized as military necessity and it clearly was not going to be reversed.* The West therefore acceded to the formal exclusion from Control Council jurisdiction of the German territories east of the Oder-Neisse river. These territories were assigned to Polish and Soviet custody. The deportation of their indigenous German population into what remained of Germany was approved; and thus by implication and without stipulation to the contrary the emptied territories were laid open for resettlement. Having thus effectively fixed the German-Polish frontier the agreement specifically characterized the territorial cession as "provisional" and left the final determination of the frontier to some future peace conference.

If the territorial question lay within the Soviet orbit of power, the reparations question lay primarily within the Western orbit. The West controlled the greater bulk of productive resources and assets liable for seizure or exploitation as reparations. German stocks of gold and precious metals had been evacuated from Berlin and captured by Western forces. German shipping was in Western hands. Most German foreign investments were located in areas beyond Soviet control: in Western Europe, in the European neutral countries, in the Mediterranean and overseas. Finally, the heart of German industrial power in the Ruhr and some 70 percent of Germany's industrial output was located in the Western zones. The West therefore laid down the terms of a reparations settlement. Only captured German shipping was to be pooled and distributed by thirds. All other goods and services were to be handled on a zonal basis and were to be distributed on the simple premise that he who had would control and keep.

For this purpose, within and outside Germany, the line was adopted which marked off the Eastern and Western orbits. The Soviets

---

none and that the President and I would leave for the United States the next day." Byrnes, *Speaking Frankly*, 85. For description of the session, see Leahy, *I Was There*, 422–424; P. E. Mosely, "The Treaty with Austria," *International Organization*, IV (1950), 229; Truman, *Memoirs*, I, 400 f.

* "We had recognized from the outset, however, that we would have to accept for the time being the Polish administration of this part of the Soviet Zone. It was an accomplished fact and we could not force the Russians to resume the responsibilities they had voluntarily resigned." Byrnes, *Speaking Frankly*, 81. Truman felt that this proposal "represented a very large concession" on our part. *Memoirs*, I, 400.

renounced all claims to Western-held German gold stocks; to German-owned investments located overseas or in Western Europe and in the major neutral countries; and, with certain stipulated exceptions, to business properties and shipping lying within the western zones of Germany. Soviet reparations claims were to be satisfied by "withdrawals" from the Soviet zone of Germany and by assumption of German foreign assets located within the Soviet orbit: Finland, Bulgaria, Roumania, Hungary, and eastern Austria. Reparations from these sources would be shared by the Soviets with Poland in accord with a bilateral agreement to be reached privately between these two countries.

The Western powers in their turn specifically renounced all claims to industrial properties in the Soviet zone or to German foreign assets in areas under Soviet occupation. Western reparations claims were to be satisfied exclusively from German gold stocks in Western possession, from German foreign assets not under Soviet control, and from the resources and wealth of the western zones of Germany. Whatever would be drawn by way of reparations from these sources would be shared by the Western powers on terms privately negotiated by them with the many smaller Allied powers, other than Poland, who would not directly participate in the occupation.

These reparations arrangements were recognized by astute observers as strong reinforcement of the partition potential inherent in a zonalized occupation.* But true to the policy of ambivalence this re-

* A selection of pertinent comments follows. "Whatever the basic causes, the most striking indication to date of the flow of events toward partition is the Potsdam decision on reparations. Instead of treating Germany as a unit for reparations exactions, Russia is invited to collect her share from the eastern zone and the Western Powers from the western zones. . . ." E. S. Mason, "Economic Relationships among European Countries," *Proceedings of the Academy of Political Science,* XXI (1946), 3. "The system that we have adopted [for reparations purposes] takes into account the same solid realities that were recognized in dividing Germany into Zones of armed occupation. . . ." E. S. Pauley, cited in World Peace Foundation, *Documents on American Foreign Relations,* 1945 (L. M. Goodrich and M. J. Carroll, eds., VIII, Boston, 1948), 223. "I concluded that the only way out of the situation was to persuade each country to satisfy its reparations claims out of its own Zone," Byrnes, *Speaking Frankly,* 83. "Auf der Grundlage der in Potsdam beschlossenen getrennten Behandlung der Besatzungszonen in der Reparations-frage erwiesen sich alle anderen Vereinbarungen, Deutschland wirtschaftlich und politisch als eine Einheit gu behandeln als illusorisch." W. Cornides and H. Volle, *Um den Frieden mit Deutschland,* Vol. VI of "Dokumente und Berichte des Europa-Archive," ed. and compiled by W. Cornides and H. Volle (Oberursel, 1948), 38. A journalist commented that the extent to which the handling of reparations had produced the effects of an eco-

inforced course of zonalization was given only veiled expression and at least in surface effect was overbalanced by renewed emphasis on unification. Provisions to this effect—frequently borrowed verbatim from JCS 1067—were adopted with little debate. They dominated the text of the conference agreement and gave it a characteristic stamp.*

These provisions all tended to establish elastic restraints on the trend to zonalization without, however, entailing a positive decision to unify. Thus "certain essential administrative departments" were to be "established." But these departments, which were to function under the "direction of the Control Council," were to conform in their behavior to the principles which entailed "decentralization of the political structure," which asserted the need for "local responsibility," and which proclaimed that "for the time being no central government shall exist." The proceeds of exports, which need not be inclusive of reparations deliveries, were reserved for financing essential imports. But the imports were to be those "approved" by each of the four zone commanders in connection with working out "the economic balance of Germany."[12] Then again, Germany was to be "treated as a single economic unit." But this economic unity was to be "established" not through central administration under law but through "common policies" to be "applied" with "account appropriately taken" [by the zone commanders] of "varying local" [i.e. zonal] conditions. These policies were to shape up a "balanced economy." But what was to be balanced was the distribution of

nomic iron curtain splitting Europe in two is not generally appreciated," S. Lubell, "The Shape of Peace," *Providence Journal Bulletin*, 14 September 1946. Ginsburg felt that "use of zonal boundaries to define reparations areas was surely an unqualified evil . . . [and] the core of the problem." Ginsburg, *The Future of German Reparations*, 25.

* Even the timetable of work done at Potsdam is significant. "Previous discussions in the European Advisory Commission on the political and economic principles for the treatment of Germany had already brought the various views close together. Only a few hours of additional discussion in the first three days of Potsdam were needed to complete the agreement on principles." P. E. Mosely, *Face to Face with Russia*, Headline series, 9. That the agreement embodies an American designed and drafted settlement is readily apparent from the marked coincidence between the text of JCS 1067 and the "Political and Economic Principles to Govern the Treatment of Germany in the Initial Control Period," embodied as section III of the Potsdam Protocol. According to Leahy's authoritative account, this section III of the Protocol was presented as a "recommendation of the Foreign Ministers" which "followed very closely the American paper that had been prepared on the subject," adopted at a plenary session on July 19 after "little discussion" (Leahy, *I Was There*, 401).

commodities "between the several zones." And this distribution was to be achieved not through market exchange or even through a central economic control administration but "in the manner determined by the Control Council," i.e. through *ad hoc* agreements negotiated between the zone commanders. These agreements were to keynote on "equity" which signified that no rights were settled and that issues would be resolved by bargaining limited by precedent.*

This same interweaving of zonal power and unity runs through all the major policy provisions of the agreement. It was the essential content of the stipulation for "uniformity of treatment of the German population throughout Germany . . ." This uniformity was to be achieved only "as far as is practicable" since the zone commanders acting as the Control Council would not be able to restrain the impulse to divergence which would grow out of zonalization. The improbability of such restraint was indicated elsewhere by description of the principles governing Allied policy in Germany as "coordinated." Zonal divergence which in the one case was expressed as practicable uniformity in the other case was allowed by prescribing coordinated policies.[13] In all these varied ways the zone commanders were confirmed in their zonal power but were admonished to exercise it prudently for the purpose of preventing the zonal economies from growing too far apart, of according some license to other zonal economies and of preserving a semblance of outward uniformity. Each of these provisions also had in it a contingent claim on the resources and policies of other zones and a potential charter for lodging complaints and for pressing measures of rectification.

Only one feature of the settlement could induce a counter draft to zonalization. This was an agreement to transfer eastward as a Soviet share one tenth of the capital equipment dismantled within the western zones. Another fifteen percent was to be transferred eastward in exchange for reciprocal deliveries of raw materials. Taken by itself this was a straight East-West deal on zonal lines. But it created leverage for achieving a basis for economic unification. The capital equipment to be dismantled from the western zones had to be judged by the West "unnecessary for the German peace economy." The nature and extent of

---

* This provision was written as follows: "Allied controls shall be imposed . . . to insure in the manner determined by the Control Council the equitable distribution of essential commodities between the several zones so as to produce a balanced economy throughout Germany and reduce the need for imports."

this economy was not specified. If this economy were treated as bifurcated into East and West, the Western zone commanders would insist on retaining in their zones relatively large plant capacity. An integrated Germany using to the best advantage its combined resources—wherever they were located—could be self-sustaining with a substantial reduction of industrial plant capacity. If the Soviets were to realize any considerable gain from the provision—zonalized, on its face—for transfer eastward of a share of plant equipment dismantled in the Western zones, they would have to persuade the Western zone commanders that they were committing their zone to the hazardous goal of economic unification.

However, the Soviet incentive for this commitment was not of a high order. The direct inducement was only a small net share—ten percent—and the supplemental share of fifteen percent was contingent upon furnishing reciprocal deliveries of equivalent value. To get these shares a complicated series of intermediary agreements had to be contrived involving a census of the larger part of German industry, conduct of property appraisal on a large scale and design of a plan which encompassed the whole of economic life. While these agreements were being reached and their results tied down, it would be hard for the East to commit their zone to unification or to refrain from utilizing rights to make reparations withdrawals from their zone. But it would be difficult for the West to carry these agreements all the way to completion and upon their basis to commence the dismantling of German industry without receipt of guarantees which would reaffirm the promise of unification. Much would obviously depend upon goodwill in negotiation, upon mutual faith in good intentions, and upon the time that would be involved in reaching and executing agreement. Any lapse of good faith or good will would enable either side to bring negotiations to a standstill and thus to retreat to the solid reality of zonal power.*

* That both sides could at will so retreat was at the bottom of the Potsdam cross-zone reparations arrangement. Both East and West had to agree to the adequacy of a list of reparations deliveries moving eastward. Neither side was bound to so agree. There was binding only on the general principles that were to guide the calculations whose ultimate outcome would be a delivery list, on a time-limit of six months, and on the percentage share of dismantling to be allotted to the Soviets. Strictly speaking both sides bought no rights but only a basis on which to work out an agreement without pledge of result. It is amazing how under pressure of negotiation and interest, the plain words of the agreement could have been interpreted so frequently as conveying "rights" or "interests" which had been "violated" by the "other side."

But though easy to take, the decision to retreat would not be lightly made. Successful carrying through of the unity option could shift the balance between zonalization and unity in the projected Control Council regime. Unity already had on its side a single currency, a shared capital city, a common antagonism to the late enemy, and a desire to carry dismantling a long way in order to assure destruction of German war potential. The Soviets had an urgent interest in a settlement which permitted them to dump a few million Germans from east of the Oder-Neisse and Sudetenland across Western zonal lines, to involve the West as accomplice in the removal of the Germans from their eastern territories and thus to add sanctity to the new German-Slav frontier. Both sides needed time to consider, to test the German potential, to examine the bearings of the world-wide drift. Their armies were tired of fighting and their civilian populations would have been disconcerted by a break in an alliance which had been touted as the key to peace. Finally, the world of illusion in which many of the actors in the German situation lived—a world faithfully reproduced in the policy of ambivalence—laid great stress on the challenge of cementing East-West unity in Germany.

CHAPTER III

THE EASTERN ZONE

I. Antifa Front and Communist Program

LOCAL COMMITTEES formed by anti-fascists of the left were the starting point of political development in eastern Germany.* Broadly speaking, these ANTIFAS, as they were called, were greeted by the local Russian commandants; their development was, however, discouraged by German Communist leaders. Some members of the right resistance and of the older liberal opposition to Hitler were drawn, hesitantly at first, into administrative positions. The reluctance of conservatives to collaborate under a Soviet occupation was diminished greatly by Soviet recognition of a number of their Berlin leaders who had at least a semblance of national prominence. These men were acknowledged as the provisional leaders of their respective political movements which were to operate in Berlin and in the zone. Along with two bourgeois liberal centers for political activity, two leftist centers were recognized under the respective leadership of the social democratic underground in Berlin and the German communist party.[1]

Recognition was reciprocal. For the Germans, it meant access to Soviet-controlled facilities for influencing public opinion as well as the right to organize a political following and to hold political office. It also signified German acceptance of the legitimacy of the Soviet occupation and willingness to function under its general direction. For the Soviets, it signified tolerance of activities and viewpoints which at times assaulted cherished Soviet beliefs. It also signified withholding direct coercion and pettifogging restrictions, although the activities of the political parties were subject to important indirect limitations including occupation approval of party functionaries, registration of membership

* See earlier, pp. 4–6.

lists and access to closed party meetings.[2] Facilities for speech and paper were allocated so as to favor the left parties but channels for public expression existed for all.[3] As in the western zones, editors of papers were licensed and subject to a disciplinary code which limited the range of public expression. The proscripted topics were attempted defense of the Nazi regime or of the war or open opposition to the occupying power or to the Potsdam agreement. Next to this were reparations, dismantling and the German-Polish frontier—the "most dangerous subjects for discussion."[4] On issues of domestic, political, economic and social reconstruction, a margin of tolerance appears to have existed.

This margin of tolerance was widest at the outset of the regime.[*] It was manifested in a variety of ways, including the relatively open election of 1946 which yielded a balance of power between left and right that probably closely reflected actual voter preferences at the time.[**] There was genuine collaboration in the writing and adoption

[*] That the political regime, with the proscriptions and within the limits indicated, was unexpectedly open at the outset of the occupation is admitted almost universally. ". . . The effects of Russian pressure were just beginning to be felt and had not yet blurred the political picture as they were subsequently to do." V. F. Eliasberg, "Political Party Developments," *The Struggle for Democracy in Germany* (A. A. Almond, ed., Chapel Hill 1949) 231. Even Kurt Schumacher referred to "einer relativ recht grossen Freiheit beim Aufbau der politischen Organisation" in the earlier phase of Soviet zone development. Schumacher, *Nach dem Zusammenbruch* (Hamburg, 1948), 84. H. R. Külz in his authoritative article noted three "distinct phases of development" in the Soviet zone, of which the first phase ran from 1945 through to the end of 1946 and was "not unlike developments in western Germany." H. R. Külz, "The Soviet Zone of Germany," *International Affairs*, XXVI (1951) 157.

[**] The ballot was fairly secret and the counting of the votes was correct and public. According to Külz, the second period in the Soviet zone, which opened in 1947, was one of "struggle between the democratic and the total communist forces in the zone and ends in March 1948 with the victory of the latter." The third period was one of "thorough totalitarianism" which apparently has not yet "reached its culmination." Of the five Land Minister-Presidents, three were of SPD vintage, one of LDP and one liberal; the governments functioned subject to parliamentary responsibility, and thus "even in the Soviet zone the first period of administration and political reconstruction terminated with a somewhat favorable outlook for the future." At the time of the Marshall Plan, or through the summer of 1947, the "real struggle between communists and non-communists for power in the zone had . . . only begun and the CDU and LDP were then by no means mere satellites of the SED." *Ibid.*, 157, 158, 164. Even Löwenthal reports that the ANTIFA consultation was under "constant pressure." Löwenthal, *News from Soviet Germany*, 19 f. The official OMGUS report notes a number of occasions within the sphere of local govern-

of state constitutions.[5] Procedural safeguards and ameliorations were obtained as the price of liberal support for measures of social reform. This support was not yielded automatically under pressure but had to be earned through negotiation.[6] Some of this give and take was due to the ease with which prominent figures in the regime could go over to the West through Berlin or across zonal lines.[7] While the Soviets were able to apply pressure to the bourgeois and liberal leaders, these leaders could apply some counter-pressure to the occupation since numerous flights or withdrawals by noncommunist leaders in the eastern zone would embarrass the Soviets. Similar tensions were felt within the merged socialist-communist party. Some of the older SPD leaders worked uneasily in harness and their defection would put in jeopardy the new left party.[8]

The loose ties of interest between occupier and occupied was paralleled by closer bonds which linked together the German political leaders. Partly this was due to common subjection to the authority of military government which was stringently applied in the earliest phase of the regime. The role of a political opposition was undesirable in any case since it would deny the opposition parties their share in distribution of office and influence on policy. Also, no one party could claim a popular mandate. The leadership cadres of the left were badly depleted by Nazi repression and combined forces were needed to cope with emergency conditions. Many of the German leaders had had com-

ment as well as in Land assemblies when relatively important questions were concerned where the political struggle was lively and the two bourgeois parties played no satellite role. OMGUS. *Government and Administration, Soviet Zone*, paragraphs 43, 51, 55, 74. Within the ANTIFA assemblies the OMGUS report goes on to state, the early SPD leaders "put up no resistance," not out of "timidity" but because they had no political line of their own and "attempts to inspire them with ideas were unsuccessful." The source of the "attempts" is not noted. "Of the other parties, three men tried to exert opposition on the problems of state reform, on expropriations and on KPD domination in the administration," but they were victimized. However, the report infers that "the whole style of discussions within these committees . . . [became] more moderate in accordance with the new policy towards the CDU and LDP." *Ibid.*, paragraphs 202–203. Equally illuminating was the *Economist's* comment apropos the expulsion of Jacob Kaizer from the zone. "The Soviet political administration has hitherto shown forbearance; it has attempted to gain rather than to extort support." *Economist*, 3 January 1948, 3. "Bis zu den Entscheidungen um den Volkskongress war bei allem Druck der auf der Bevölkerung vor allem auf der verantwortlichen der nichtkommunistchen Parteien lastete noch eine gewisse Möglichkeit politische Eigenleben zur Geltung zu bringen." Jacob Kaiser, "Ein Ordnendes Wort," *Der Tagespiegel*, 18 February 1948.

mon experience in the anti-Nazi underground or in concentration camps and this led to a solidarity of outlook which facilitated joint action.[9]

Accordingly, political life in the eastern zone developed on the basis of a partnership of the political parties who in concert ran the newly formed governments, central administrative agencies and public organizations. As is frequently the case, this partnership did not signify full parity. The two left movements were predominant in social movements and organizations growing out of the labor movement, such as trade unions and cooperatives. Governmental cabinets and high level political appointments were shared on an explicit coalition basis while throughout public life there was at least a show of general representation.*

To maintain partnership on a continuing basis agreed principles of action and a machinery for collaboration were required. These principles were provided by a basic agreement negotiated between the leaders of the four political movements. A machinery of consultation was set up in the form of arrangements for a secretariat and regular meet-

* In detail it appears that the bourgeois-liberal groups dominated the highest executive positions of the newly founded central agencies; that Land Minister-Presidencies were distributed among the four movements; that departments of interior, education and economics were usually SPD or KPD, while departments of finance, agriculture and justice were usually allocated to the bourgeois parties; that trustworthy communist or left SPDers were installed in the police bureaus; and that the general policy was "collegial" management, with the top executive staff of important government agencies distributed among parties. Even as late as 1947 the members of the two left parties did not predominate in the civil service. The estimates that county directors (Landräte) and mayors (Oberbügermeistern) were KPD in two-thirds of the cases seem dubious because of the relatively small numbers of KPDers. Nettl goes so far as to say that "the period May 1945 to October 1946 was really the period of ascendancy for the Social Democrats in the eastern zone" due to SPD predominance in the higher executive positions. Nettl, *Eastern Zone*, 81 ff, 93, 97 ff. Staff in universities and schools was renovated to make room for Marxists who were far from being given a monopoly of teaching positions. "In the Soviet zone the replacement of university teachers has so far been far less radical than one would expect." W. Friedmann, *The Allied Military Government of Germany* (London Institute of World Affairs, London, 1947), 182 f. For an illuminating set of materials on communist policy toward education, see *Um Die Erneurung der deutschen Kultur* (protocol of conference, Berlin, 1946), particularly 62 ff, 65 ff, 76 ff, 101 ff. On sharing in political office and governmental control, see the scrupulously accurate and well-informed report, OMGUS *Government and Administration*, Soviet Zone, paragraphs 50, 51, 206–9, 211–2; Peter Nettle, "Inside the Russian Zone," *Political Quarterly*, XIX (1948) 201–233.

ings of ANTIFA committees to be held at all governmental levels.*
These committees were to attempt to work out action projects and to
resolve issues of difference on the basis of a balanced tri-partite program. This program emphasized the need to win Allied confidence, to
respect the authority of the occupation and to accept the obligation to
pay reparations. Then, leaning to the right, it promised to respect freedom of spirit and conscience and to institute a liberal polity (Rechtstaat). On the left, it stressed the need to purge the community of
Nazism, to rebuild an anti-fascist republic and to reconstruct the economy to provide work, goods and housing.[10]

One of the planks in this united front program involved loyal fulfillment of Soviet occupation requirements. These laid major stress on
taking into the German community by express arrangement a large
influx of refugees chiefly from Poland. While their reception and the
resultant program of absorption was a one-time operation it was also
massive. Far-reaching measures were required to prevent the refugees
from constituting a dissatisfied and disaffected group.[11] Paramount
emphasis on a more continuing basis was given to mobilization within
the economy of a transferable margin of resources to be made available
to the Soviets for their use in Germany or abroad.** At first the Soviets
were most interested in satisfying reparations requirements by dismantling. Dismantling teams made up of operating industrial specialists
were hatched in droves out of Soviet ministries and industrial organizations and trailed the Soviet armies as they stepped into their occupation

* These consultations, held under the title of ANTIFA committees became, in
the words of the OMGUS report, "the real instruments of control in the eastern
zone." See OMGUS, *Government and Administration*, Soviet Zone, paragraphs 198–
199; Gordon Schaffer, *Russian Zone of Germany* (SRT Publications, U.S.A. 1947)
71 ff. For the basic documents involved, cf. *Einheitsfront* 5–14, 34–7. Nettl stated
the ANTIFA "represented a sort of supra-party unity on questions of fundamental
importance such as denazification . . . [and] through its cohesive influence political differences were kept out of reconstruction as a general rule." This unsound
characterization is supplemented by clumsy observation which has a kernel of truth;
namely, that "during 1947 it gradually developed into a means of compromising the
bourgeois parties by associating them with almost all major public actions of the
SED . . ." Nettl, *Eastern Zone*, 102.

** "The first aim of the Soviet policy was no doubt a purely economic one," B. R.
Kuelz, the LDP leader of the eastern zone wrote after his flight to the West, "to get
as much reparations as possible out of the Zone." Kuelz, "The Soviet Zone of Germany," *loc. cit.*, 163. In the same terms, see Russell Hill, *Struggle for Germany* (New
York, 1947), 173 and Nettl, *Eastern Zone*, 199–231, 304–14.

posts. These teams were not subordinated to local Military Government and worked directly for some Soviet home organization. They were energetically searching the Zone for suitable equipment and frantically organizing its earliest possible dismantling and shipment to the Soviet Union. The dismantling fever was at its height in late 1945 and as a philosophy of reparations was supported by influential groups in the Soviet Politburo.* Even when dismantling was at its height, however, the Soviets through local military government were undertaking to re-activate industrial production partly to provide for the needs in goods and services of the Soviet combat armies which were in Germany await-ing demobilization.[12] Hence the later shift of the main focus of Soviet reparations policy from extracting dismantled equipment to withdraw-ing current product only accentuated a mode of utilization of German resources which already had been developed on a large scale, although the range of usable products was widened when the locus of consump-tion was shifted from within to outside Germany.

The onus of Soviet requirements on the German economy—on transportation and foodstuffs for provisioning troops, on taxes for fi-nancing, on commodities and services for occupation maintenance and on reparation via dismantling or current product—was sufficiently heavy and given sufficient priority during the early phases of the occupa-tion to turn the Soviets into the major claimant for allocations and the chief beneficiary of economic revival.[13] The loyal fulfillment of Soviet occupation directives was a common task accepted by the German leadership both Right and Left and constituted a major premise of German political action.

The other planks of the united front program laid stress on purging Nazism from the German community, achieving economic recovery and rebuilding a liberal polity (Rechtstaat). This framework of action was broad and flexible; it could accommodate Soviet and communist objectives. For the Soviets it would permit a program of radical anti-fascist action designed to uproot enemies of the Soviet occupation and

* Through publication by former Soviet personnel engaged in reparations work, this phase of Soviet action in Germany has been treated in many interesting details. See G. Klimov, *The Terror Machine, The Inside Story of the Soviet Administration in Germany* (trans. from the German, NY, 1953) 197 ff; R. Slusser (editor), *Soviet Economic Policy in Postwar Germany, A Collection of Papers by Former Soviet Of-ficials* (NY, 1953), particularly V. Alexandrov, "The Dismantling of German In-dustry," 14–18, and 18–60.

to favor interests friendly to the Soviets.* It was, however, consistent with Soviet interests that social reorganization stay within the area of overlap in East-West agreement on Germany in order to avoid sharp offense of the Western powers, to attract the middle groups in German political life and to escape isolating from the German community the communist and socialist movements upon which the Soviets primarily relied. Social action within these limits in fact would entrench these groups in leadership of the German community.

This policy could be pursued successfully by the German communist party only if this party turned aside from its traditional goal of seeking to establish an outright proletarian dictatorship and a structure of government on the Russian model. This traditional goal, on the basis of which the communists had fought the social democratic policy of establishing a democratic republic in 1918, had been in the process of slow modification since 1933. It was finally disenthroned by the catastrophe of war and German defeat together with partial occupation of Germany by the Soviet Union. Under these circumstances communist objectives could best be achieved by building a radical democratic republic in company with social democrats and bourgeois liberals.**

* This combination in Soviet policy of desire for reparations with stress on political control or social reform was noted by many observers and critics who failed to point out that the two policies were not contradictory but, within limits, would support each other by turns. For example, an official American statement asserted that Soviet policy in Germany revolved around the desire to "reconcile the pressing need for maximum reparations from Germany with a desire to rebuild a German state that will be friendly to communist ideology and to broader Soviet aims in Europe." U.S. Department of State, *Occupation of Germany: Policy and Progress, 1945–1946,* Department of State Publication no. 2783, European series 23 (Washington, 1947), 59. General Clay likewise stated two Soviet objectives in Germany: "to exact the maximum of reparations" and to "establish the type and kind of government which could be controlled or at least exploited to the full by a police state." *New York Herald Tribune,* 18 May 1949. See also Nettle, "Inside the Russian Zone," *loc. cit.,* 231–232; W. Friedmann, *Allied Military Government,* 24 ff., 138 ff., 183 ff., 240 ff.; J. Warburg, *Germany: Bridge or Battleground?* (New York, 1947), 51 ff.; Neumann, "Soviet Policy in Germany," *loc. cit.,* 166 ff.

** That the strategy outlined above was in fact that of the German communists and that this did involve a significant programmatic shift in communist ideology could only be demonstrated by a study of the complex evolution of communist thought and program since 1917 in Germany, in the Soviet Union and on an international basis. Early in the history of the communist movement any strategic objective short of proletarian dictatorship and any political form other than the Soviet was laid aside as "treachery" and "opportunism." During the Twenties some shift away from this

The new republic would be nurtured by a military government pledged to uproot the Nazi regime and its sources in the social system. The process of this uprooting would equip the new republic with the facilities and habits of coercive control and would generate a convenient and flexible ideological basis for its exercise.*

doctrine of purity, whose latterday expression had essentially aimed at copying Russian experience, was made by the efforts to work out a theory of a "united front." A further shift was made during the Thirties with the development of "popular front" regimes in which the communists participated. The present status of this gradual shift is the post-World War II doctrine of "new democracy," which has found widespread expression in communist writing and which in varied forms has been applied in China, in the Balkans and central Europe and in eastern Germany. On this new form of communist strategy, see R. Schlesinger, *Marx, His Time and Ours*, (London, 1950), 234–242; S. L. Sharp, "New Democracy: A Soviet Interpretation," *American Perspective* II (1947). In his worthwhile study on *New Constitutions in Occupied Germany* (Foundation for Foreign Affairs, Pamphlet no. 6, Washington, 1948), Harold Lewis characterized the German adaptation as an "ideology rationalizing the realities of the existing political and social organization of the eastern zone," and, as such, as an "ideological facade." *Ibid.*, 33–34. That more than a facade was involved would seem to be indicated by the convincing nature of the reasons mobilized behind the program from the point of view of realizing orthodox communist objectives. On this, see Tibor Mende, *Europe's Suicide in Germany* (London 1946) 88 f, 198 f. Communist leaders also explicitly argued that they had made a real turn in policy and outlook. See Otto Grotewohl, *Im Kampf um Deutschland, Reden und Aufsätze* (2v., Berlin, 1948), I, 45, 111 ff, 279; *Bericht vom 15 Parteitag der Kommunistischen Partei Deutschlands* (Berlin 1946), 99–119; A. Ackerman, "Wohin soll der Weg gehen," *Einheitsfront*, 34–37; Walter Ulbricht, "Erste Funktionärkonferenz der KPD Gross-Berlin," *Ibid.*, 15–33; Ulbricht, "Strategie und Taktik der SED," *Einheit*, I (1946), 257–271. The turn in communist strategy, although explicitly made with avowal of previous "error," was predicated upon real conditions which hardly permitted another course and was guarded by escape clauses which would permit a later reversal. Nonetheless, the program which the communist party agreed to in its fusion with the socialist party under Grotewohl would have been unacceptable a decade before and would have been denounced as gross opportunism two decades before.

* "A democracy can only subsist if it destroys the enemies of democracy," wrote Grotewohl frankly. These enemies, he asserted, stand "outside the constitution and the laws." They will be "suppressed by the coercive power of the state." There are "no basic rights for those who would use the basic rights to undermine (untergraben) the political, social or constitutional basis of the state." There was later the same determination in the western zones to "outlaw . . . outrightly and directly . . . associations whose purpose or activities 'are directed against the constitutional order or the concept of international understanding.'" Arnold Brecht, "The New German Constitution," *Social Research*, XVI (1949), 451 f.; Grotewohl, *Deutsche Verfassungspläne* (Berlin, 1947), 68. In the eastern zone repressive measures were consti-

Repression would logically be accompanied by expropriation. This was a time-honored means by which to consolidate a new regime and it would constitute an efficient method of denazification. It would remove from politically dangerous persons the means for sabotage or subversion.* The estates of the Junkers and landlords were obvious targets which had been noted not only in eastern but in western war aims. The breakup of cartels and trusts and the removal of the industrial leadership integrated with the Nazi war economy had been marked out in Allied ideology. These actions had an independent rationale. They would work needed social reforms; they would loosen the German social structure and promote vertical social mobility; they would place resources needed for reconstruction under collective control; and they would facilitate squeezing available surpluses out of the German income structure.

If denazification, decartelization and demilitarization provided captions for energetic pursuit of communist objectives, the effort to achieve without external aid the final plank of the anti-fascist program, economic recovery, would culminate in a planned economy. Finally, even building a democratic republic would provide raw material for the pursuit of communist objectives. By giving emphasis to local self-administration, new levels of popular initiative could be tapped; persons formerly inert politically could be drawn into activity.[13a] Proportional representation and party solidarity—two time honored German political devices—would assure party control of legislative assemblies. In election campaigns policies would be explained and propaganda disseminated. These advantages were to be obtained by cooperation in building a democratic republic. Building such a republic entailed few risks since unsettled conditions and the continued presence of the occupying power assured a prominent political role.

To these challenging opportunities in the limited program of the anti-fascist front was added also the inviting prospect of fusion with left-wing social democrats. The social democrats, along with the communists, had been targets of persecution under the Nazis. They too felt

---

tutionally aimed at "Faschismus und Militarismus, Monopole und Grossgrundbesitz" but of course they permitted repressive action against any movement deemed subversive. *Idem.*

* ". . . If any one should wish to establish a republic in a country where there are many gentlemen, he will not succeed until he has destroyed them all. . . ." N. Machiavelli, *The Prince and the Discourses* (Modern Library ed., New York), 256.

the need for radical action to uproot their enemies in the German community.[14] If the communists met the social democrats in support for democratic political institutions and renounced the aim of soviet revolution, the programmatic basis would be constituted for fusion of the two parties which alike sprang from the labor movement and had kindred creeds.[15] The desire for fusion was widespread among radical workers and many SPD leaders.[16] Though it was achieved by dint of Soviet pressure and some direct coercion, fusion was too persisting and operated too smoothly to be attributable primarily to maneuver or pressure.*

Soviet control favored radical action which was fostered by practical economic needs and denazification measures. But radical action on a scale which would put the eastern zone too far out of line with the western zones would hamper the achievement of German unity. This unity was warmly regarded by the German left. In the absence of unification their loyalty to the occupation would tend to deprive them of political independence.** Through unification and settlement the focus of

---

* That sustained Soviet pressure also was required to bring about the fusion is indicated. And yet the fusion, although fathered with an element of force, was too free from later feud and division to have been in the first instance due to Soviet pressure or communist maneuver. In these terms, see the accounts of Eliasberg and Tibor Mende as cited above. For the SED view of the events, the best source is Grotewohl, *Im Kampf um Deutschland*, I, 107–112. For the SPD version, the classical source is K. Schumacher, *Nach dem Zusammenbruch*, 84–108, 113 ff.

** That this was desirable to the Soviets did not necessarily mean that it was wholly attractive to the German left. Grotewohl once frankly—almost belligerently —asserted that it would be impossible to work against the occupying power, that "good relations" with it were indispensable and that "es ist doch ein lächerliches Wortspiel davon zu reden oder nicht anzuerkennen dass nicht alle politischen Parteien in Deutschland mehr oder weniger mit Abstufungen selbstverständlich unter dem Einfluss der Mächte stehen, die in den betreffenden Zonen die reale Macht ausüben. Sie sind von ihnen zugelassen, sozusagen geboren, werden beobachtet und ihre tätigkeit wird von den Besatzungsmächten reguliert." Grotewohl, *Im Kampf um Deutschland*, I, 225–226, 238. So also it was in the West. Ehard once designated a course of action as "der Zuverlässigste Ausdruck unserer Loyalität gegenüber den Besatzungsmächten zu sein." See *Die Deutsche Ministerpräsidenten-Konferenz in München* (conference of 6–8 June 1947, Munich, 1947), 29. The *Economist* once noted that "from Germans east of the Elbe claims to unity are heartfelt and sincere; they are a plea for rescue." *Ibid.*, 1 November 1947, 707. This probably was felt not a little by the communist-socialist SED leadership. It is one thing to rationalize one's domestic aspirations in terms of eulogizing foreign achievements; it is another kind of experience to govern one's country under foreign domination. The continual

political interest within Germany would shift from issues of the war and occupation to issues of domestic policy. While unification would jeopardize the entrenched communist position in the eastern zone, it would open prospects for socialist combination in a united Germany. Finally, the unequivocal tradition of revolutionary Marxist struggle for a united and indivisible republic and against separatist and particularist currents was a potent factor.[17] In response to all these motivations, the communist and left socialist leadership of the eastern zone shaped its domestic as well as its interzonal policies on the hope of unification of Germany and neutralization under East-West guardianship.[18]

The multiparty regime which emerged in the eastern zone was thus the product of a delicate balance of inducements, pressures and restraints. The Soviets wanted bourgeois-liberal collaboration in order to strengthen their occupation tenure and to establish relationships which would be needed in a unified Germany. But though they offered bourgeois-liberal groups a role in zonal life, they could not allow them freely to oppose reparations or the Oder-Neisse, to challenge Soviet authority, to identify themselves aggressively with the West or to obstruct a reform program. Yet restraints needed to be administered gently so as not to erase those expectations upon which the will to collaborate depended.

The German communists with their left-socialist allies functioned as the connecting link between the occupying power and the bourgeois-liberal groups. They were ideologically bound to the occupation to whom they were indebted for position and favor. Like the occupying power, they looked forward to unification and wanted bourgeois-liberal collaboration. But to them it was essential that collaboration should not cripple their radical reform program and that the federalized political structure—which was one sector of this program and a common link with the bourgeois-liberal world—should not unduly hamper the planned economy necessary for organizing economic recovery. To carry through a radical reform program and a planned economy in coalition with bourgeois-liberals and within a political framework of a federalized state would strain communist skill in negotiation and self-restraint in handling power.

---

preaching of the SED leaders that partition meant colonialism was uttered with too much warmth to be wholly without implicit reference to the regime to which partition would tend in their zone.

In accepting the authority of the Soviet occupation the bourgeois-liberal groups echoed the legitimization of this authority expressed in the Control Council regime with its explicit aim of German unification. Partly they merely expressed recognition of military defeat. Under unification these groups could look forward to fusion with their colleagues from the West and to corresponding liberation from unilateral Soviet control. The bourgeois-liberal groups therefore were willing under Soviet direction to risk collaboration with the communists in a radical program of social reform. But the strain of this collaboration could be endured only if the reform program did not outrun certain boundaries and if political power was maintained primarily upon the local state-oriented basis which was crystallized early in the occupation.

To steer an independent course was not easy for the activists among the bourgeois-liberal groups. They were personally insecure and were jeered at as Soviet puppets. Their chief resource in the coalition hinged upon the prospects for quadripartite settlement and the embarrassment which they could cause the Soviets by withdrawal of support or flight. A rare order of personal courage and political understanding was required to lead these movements. Much was owed to Jacob Kaiser, the able leader of the Eastern zone CDU. He was the leading exponent of the idea of Germany as bridge between East and West. He managed to preserve his independence in Soviet zone politics and to develop a philosophy of progressive social action.*

II. Social Reorganization and Economic Revival

The program of social change worked out by communist-socialist strategy and applied through the give and take of the ANTIFA united front ran through most phases of economic and social life. But perhaps its pivotal actions revolved around land reform which worked a social transformation in the villages. Land reform was achieved by expropriat-

---

* "It seems to me that above all the great task given to Germany, among the circle of European powers, is to find the synthesis between the eastern and western ideas. We have to be the bridge between east and west, at the same time, however, searching for our own way to new social formations." J. Kaiser, *Der Soziale Staat* (Berlin 1946), 8. Eliasberg also pays tribute to Kaiser, who "not only succeeded in preserving his independence . . . but acquired in all four zones a reputation as the leader of the progressive forces in the CDU." Eliasberg, "Political Party Developments," *loc. cit.*, 265. See also Joesten, *Germany: What Now?*, 91 f.

ing the property rights of the former Junkers and landlords over some seven thousand estates which had dominated rural life and the production of marketable foodstuffs in eastern Germany. To these properties were added certain public lands and a small number of medium sized farms seized under denazification proceedings. About two-thirds of the land fund which was gradually deposited in this way was broken up into small holdings and distributed chiefly to poor peasants, estate hands and refugees resident in the area.

The remaining land fund was composed chiefly of large forest properties and special-purpose estates, such as seed farms and breeding stations, which had to be operated intact. These properties were placed under cooperative or local governmental or state control while rights of ownership generally passed to the state. Livestock, outlying buildings and minor equipment were generally distributed among land recipients. But the larger machinery and buildings together with processing equipment and mills were vested under the joint control of a newly formed state agency which leaned heavily on cooperative village action and the participants in the land distribution program.*

These changes were carried out during the fall and winter of 1945/6 by revolutionary mass action. This mass action though incited by communists and socialist agitation arose from "an authentic initial stirring" of public opinion.[19] The action was authorized by state decree which directed local villagers in popular meetings to form land distribution committees. These were instructed to compile a list of lands open for distribution and to distribute the same among eligible persons according to specified rules and procedures and subject to corrective

* On the land reform, see the exhaustive and scholarly survey and analysis by Dr. Philip M. Raup, *Land Reform in Postwar Germany: The Soviet Zone Experiment* (doctoral dissertation, University of Wisconsin, Madison, Wisconsin, 1949) chap. V, chap. VI, sec. 4. Dr. Raup was closely concerned with formulating and executing American land reform policy in the American zone of Germany; he disclosed himself in his dissertation a profound student of German agrarian history; and he was fortunate in being able to combine field visitation and personal interview with documentary research and statistical analysis. For other accounts of lesser value, see the pamphlet by the chief of the eastern zone agricultural department, Edwin Hoernle, *Die Bodenreform* (Berlin 1946); *CFM Report*, Section IV, Part 4, Agriculture; Foundation for Foreign Affairs, "Agrarian Reform: A Test of Allied Occupation Policy," *American Perspective*, I (1947) 181–202. A much less adequate and sharply-toned survey is that of Frieda Wunderlich, "Agriculture and Farm Labor in the Soviet Zone of Germany," *Social Research*, XIX (1952), 198–208.

action and confirmation by the higher governmental authorities.[20] With the whole countryside mobilized into action, the land reform was carried out in a burst of energy which was attended by little or no violence and surprisingly little disorganization.[21] Since many of the newly formed farms were without adequate buildings, equipment or livestock, the land reform was buttressed by campaigns carried on to remedy these crucial shortages.[22] Though the changes in land tenure and management were sweeping, harvest yields in eastern Germany were not reduced beneath levels reached in western Germany in the crop year following the reform. However, agricultural output in the year after may have been adversely affected.*

Any adverse effects of land reform on food production were more than offset by the heightened efficiency of food collections. The process of land reform brought forward a new rural leadership which assisted in establishing a new system for food collection.[23] Delivery quotas now were fixed and publicized in advance at a level which took a steep fraction of crop yields and of meat and other farm produce at controlled prices. Compliance with these delivery quotas was maximized by vigor-

* So far as acreages and harvest yields go, official Soviet reports to the Control Council indicate somewhat higher returns for the 1945 and 1946 crop yields than were achieved in the western zones. Thus in 1946 for the whole of Germany sown areas of grain, oil crops, potatoes and vegetables were 89.4 percent of 1938 while Soviet zone achievement was 94.8 percent. Soviet zone acreage yields for major crops were reported for 1945 and 1946 at about the all-zone average. See CFM Report, Section IV, Part 4, Agriculture, 2d section, factual report, 2–4. In terms of food collections, the data brought together in the same report, Part 3, Food and Rationing, indicates that eastern zone food collections were about on a par with the western zones. Thus while some 49% of eastern zone grain output was made available through collections to non-self-suppliers, the corresponding ratio for all of Germany was 45%. But the positions were reversed with potato collections. Soviet zone meat collections held up better. This performance on collections is of course a by-product of the entire agricultural regime and is no measure of the specific effects of land reform. Furthermore, western data on food collections became increasingly unreliable. See later, 80–81. For the crop year 1947 and later years, eastern zone crop yields have been less than in Western Germany. See Raup, op. cit., 320–336. After bringing under survey the various responsible causes, Raup concludes: "The ravages of fighting, the seizing of livestock for reparations, the requisitioning of farms for the subsistence of the Red Army, the shortages of commercial fertilizer, tractors, equipment and supplies and land reform, all combined to reduce post-war agricultural production in the Soviet zone to below 50% of prewar levels or some 15% lower than in the US/UK zones. In very general terms it seems unlikely that land reform alone can be held responsible for more than 10% of this 50% decline," 337.

ous enforcement proceedings.* But at the same time cultivators were given the right to sell any post-delivery margin of produce in special markets at higher prices.[24] Some effort was made to gear distribution of farm supplies and needed manufactured goods into the food collection program by relying upon the newly formed cooperative centers to aid in trade which was put under single agency control at all governmental levels.

The net outcome of the reform was of course a rural universe of small to medium sized peasant holdings. But land farmed this way will absorb surplus population and will lead to a democratic rural community.[25] Land reform helped to assimilate through resettling some of the trained farmers expelled from East of the Oder-Neisse frontier. Peasant holdings were rendered more feasible by a vigorous program of cooperation which had won a strong position in the German pre-war rural community.**

* See Löwenthal, *News from Soviet Germany*, 130 ff. There are many indications that, as Schaffer put it, the administration of the new quota system "during the first year" involved "plenty of mistakes. . . . Assessments of the proportion of the harvest each peasant was called upon to deliver were frequently arrived at by rule of thumb without proper regard to the difficulties or to the nature of the soil." It appears that "local authorities and in a number of cases, local Red Army Commands acted ruthlessly and foolishly and peasants were promptly gaoled." As Hans Liebe noted in his authoritative "Die Organisation der Landwirtschaft," *loc. cit.*, 194, "das Instrument . . . als solches besagt jedoch wenig, ausschlaggebend ist die Art und Weise in der es gespielt wird." Liebe noted that collection would be particularly handicapped in the eastern zone due to damage and dislocation. "Unter diesen Bedingungen konnte nur unter scharfen Zwang erreicht werden, dass die Bestellung durchgeführt und die Ernährung der Bevölkerung gesichert wurde. . . . Da vollkommen neue Wege gegangen wurden, waren zahllose Schwierigkeiten zu überwinden." Under-collection was not always punished. Thus adjustments in quotas were made for the poor 1946/7 crop yield. But Liebe reports that milk and meat deliveries were enforced "in the strictest manner" and that accordingly, in contrast to the western zones, there was very little peasant accumulation of inventory in the form of increased livestock. *Ibid.*, 198–199.

** See on these topics, the suggestive and judicious analysis of Raup, *op cit.*, 390–409, and particularly 406, 318 ff, 417 ff. Cooperative patterns of activity and purchasing were widely developed in the German villages; but apparently they were directly invoked by land reform which, as it were, deposited a network of cooperative organizations as the residual owners of the undistributed estate facilities and buildings. It appears that the active nucleuses of these organizations, which were called Gegenseitige Bauernhilfe, were formed by the some fifty thousand land reform committees. See Hoernle, *Bodenreform*, 22–24; Hans Liebe, "Die Organisation der Land-

This comprehensive program of land reform and of change in agricultural economic policy—this social revolution in east-German villages—was paralleled by an equally vigorous program of monetary reform.* During the active combat period commercial banks were generally closed. By decree they remained closed. All financial claims and liabilities of financial institutions were thus voided along with the Nazi public debt which served as their main backing. In consequence an economy which had operated on the basis of high liquidity suddenly was drained of nearly four-fifths of its monetary assets. Acute commodity scarcities and relative monetary reflation by means of Soviet currency issuance diminished but did not cut away the market tension which the initial monetary reform had created. This market tension made it possible to continue old price and wage levels without encountering excessive strain and it strengthened the desire to acquire money in the regular course of trade.[27] As in the western zones a black market existed and individual producers improvised in newly developing markets and with new products to adapt themselves to the continually changing conditions.[28] However, the gap between market and controlled price levels was narrowed and the enforcement work of the price control authorities was reinforced by regulative efforts of trade unions and work councils.[29]

Qualitative credit control was facilitated by gradually reopening a compact network of banks operating at the direction of the state economic authorities. The reopened banks were composed of former branches of the central banking system and of the cooperative rural and savings bank systems. The old Reichsbank system had conducted a commercial banking business both in its head offices and in its branches. Hence the process of rebuilding the financial structure led, without outright socialization or assumption of new state functions, to a socialized financial structure.[30]

Industrial reorganization was achieved by a threefold process. In the first place, direct nationalization was applied to the coal industry and its offshoots—to coal mines, coal processing and distributing facilities and power plants. All of these were placed under a central zonal administration. Nationalization here arose in the first instance—as in

---

wirtschaft in der sowjetischen Besatzungszone," *Wirtschaftsproblems*, 188 f., 201 f. See J. H. Clapham, *The Economic Development of France and Germany* (3rd ed., Cambridge, 1928), 221–228 on rural cooperative traditions in Germany.

   * On the need for reform, cf. earlier chap. I, pp. 8–9.

laborite England—out of need to ensure maximum mobilization of resources by planned production and distribution of a basic industrial
resource, coal.[31] Moreover, most of these properties were segments of
large-scale corporate organizations and were accommodated to management within a bureaucratic framework.

Another and somewhat overlapping action, since it embraced one-
third of the coal mining and briquetting resources in the zone, vested
126 properties under direct Soviet management. These properties had
been scheduled for dismantling under the Allied reparation program
and they were concentrated in heavy industry, covering the product
groups of coal processing, chemicals, electro-technical, machinery and
vehicle output. In the main they also comprised the zonal establishments of the large multi-plant corporate combines and trusts which
were scheduled for corporate reorganization in any case or—in the
case of a proprietary establishment such as Flick—for expropriation as
a measure of denazification. That is why, although a quarter of the
industrial output of the zone and 18 percent of its industrial employment was concentrated in these properties, so few business organizations were involved.[32] Soviet managers were installed and apparently
they were able, with the help of the trade unions, to take over the properties and operate them without sizeable disruption or sabotage and
without significant use of direct coercion. Acceptance of the sequestration doubtless was aided by belief that these choice enterprises were
saved from dismantling and kept in operation. Also, the Soviets were
shrewd enough to announce originally the sequestration of 200 properties
and then to return 76 properties for German disposition. This sustained
the hope that other properties in time also would be returned.[33] In supplement to this formal acquisition of German property certain informal
acquisitions developed through direct realty purchase or through the
formation of commercial and banking concerns given privileged status
within the German economy partly to support the operations of the
Soviet sequestered enterprises (SAG) but partly also to carry out foreign trading functions of a kind which had not yet developed in the
German administration.*

* For detail, see Nettl, *Eastern Zone*, 225–31. The scope and authority of these
supporting operations, which were handled by a battery of impressively entitled
"organizations" can be overestimated. Thus the establishment of a series of Intourist
restaurants, described by Nettl as "the expropriation of German hotels and restaurants by Intourist" was only a repetition on a lesser scale of the Western practise of

A third mode of industrial reorganization grew out of the disposal of properties taken into interim custody or property control under general directives prepared in similar form by all the occupying powers. These properties embraced all former Reich establishments, properties of the Nazi party and its affiliates and properties belonging to leading Nazi members and active associates generally subject under early military government rules to "mandatory arrest." In the western zones, these properties remained nominally "blocked" and except in the cases of public property or where sequestration was ordered by court action they eventually were returned to their former owners.* In the eastern zone, these properties were turned over early in 1946 to the Land governments for disposition.** With the sanction of a popular referendum

requisition of the best hotel facilities for occupation use. A commercial company, Derutra, is alleged to have "controlled the Baltic harbours of Wismar, Rostock" and others. Compare with this the well-informed article, "Seehafen und Flusschiffahrt im Ausbau," *Die Wirtschaft,* II (1947), 217 ff. It is as easy to misunderstand the extent of such "commercial penetration" as it has been for eastern observers to read "imperialist penetration" into strange sounding organizations with commercial functions or New York branch banking facilities chiefly for occupation personnel established in the western German economy.

* These properties were seized in the American zone under Military Government Law no. 52. Under its broad provisions, at the high point of holdings and aside from foreign-owned properties taken under protective custody, 64,367 individual properties were under property control in the American zone alone, with an average value of 109,000 RM and an aggregate value of 7 billion RM. See OMGUS, *Report of the Military Governor,* Finance, July 1946–June 1947, cumulative review, no. 24, 62 ff. By June 1946 these properties included a classification of some 5,040 industrial units or items of equipment. The value of controlled properties belonging to the Nazi party and its members at that time amounted to 3 billion RM. *Ibid.,* no. 12, 22. A similar program of property control under the same law was carried on in the French and British zones. Sanderson notes that "as a result of the blocking of properties of Nazi organizations and leading Nazis and of certain other assets the occupying authorities found themselves custodians of a huge amount of wealth. . . . In the British zone all coal mines, steel plants and the I. G. Farben and Krupp combines as well as many other properties were sequestered." Sanderson, "Germany's Economic Situation and Prospects," *loc. cit.,* 150.

** The Soviet Order no. 124, issued 30 October 1945, was modelled after the provisions of the U.S. Law no. 52. See *Befehle des Obersten Chefs der Sowjetischen Militärverwaltung in Deutschland* (Berlin, 1946), Heft I, 20–22. Pressure for disposition of the properties also was felt in the western zones. "As the number of properties under control increased, it became imperative to come to some decision regarding their disposition." OMGUS, *Monthly Report of the Military Governor,* Finance and Property Control, June 1946, no. 12, 23. Disposition, however, was lame and halting

in Saxony, quasi-judicial tribunals in which all the political parties
participated were formed to pass judgment on the affected persons and
properties.* About 3,000 industrial properties, involving one-third of
industrial employment and between 25 and 30 percent of industrial output, were sequestered and converted into formal state-owned business
—*Landeseigene Betriebe.*

More than any other single program in the Soviet zone, this one
tended to strain the limits of overlap in the Control Council regime and
bourgeois-liberal participation in the political coalition in the zone.**

---

and in the case of Nazi-tainted properties was effected only by action of denazification
tribunals. Soviet zone action was aimed at a swift solution which would end provisional status for so significant a segment of the business life of the zone.

* Though the referendum was somewhat demagogically formulated, it was a
real one and doubtless expressed the popular judgment that, as Ulbricht put it in a
contemporary comment, "diesmal sollen die Grossen gehängt werden und nicht die
Kleinen." See his comments on the expropriation of property of Nazi activists and
leaders in *Demokratischer Wirtschaftsaufbau*, 14. On the referendum, see Schaffer,
Russian Zone, 47 ff.; M. Fechner, "Wirtschaftliche und politische Bedeutung des
Volksentscheides im Lande Sachsen," *Die Wirtschaft*, I (1946), 65–67; Risch,
"In den Händen des Volkes: Landeseigene Betriebe in Sachsen," *Ibid.*, 163–165.
The referendum was a brief broadly stated proposal on confiscation and disposition
of Nazi property. One of its key clauses ambiguously included properties of war
criminals, leaders and active followers of the Nazi party and Nazi state and also "die
Betriebe und Unternehmen die aktiv dem Kriegverbrechen gedient haben." Article
I of the proposed law, reprinted in *Tägliche Rundschau*, 28 May 1946. The accompanying state government communique explains, however, that the proposal
was aimed more narrowly at the Nazi party, its organs and formations and "influential and active Nazis or supporters." The action was endorsed by the anti-fascist
bloc. In an interview a few days later with the leader of the LDP in Saxony, it was
emphasized that the frame of reference of the entire action would be "exclusively"
that of "Kriegsverschuldung." *Ibid.*, 19 June 1946.

** The party struggle on the sequestration issue came out in the open in connection with a decision reached by the zonal sequestration commission regarding
500 hangover cases whose disposal had been delayed. This decision "mit eindeutigen
Belastungsunterlagen präsentierte, wurde deren Behandlung von Vertretern der
LDP und auch der CDU unter Drohungen abgelehnt; man inszenierte Kabinettk-
risen, mobilisierte unter Berufung auf angelichen 'Verfassungsbruch' die Ältestenaus-
schüsse der Landtage, bemühte das Thüringer Oberverwaltungsgericht, forderte
parlamentarische 'Pärteausgleichsausschüsse' zur Entschuldigung der enteigneten
Verbrecher usw." A constant struggle appears to have been underway in the various
state governments, with the LDP allegedly leading a drive for reimbursement, and
for revision of the sequestration listings. "Bis in die jüngste Zeit hinein kam insbeson-
dere die LDP unter Ignorierung des geschilderten Tatbestandes mit immer neuen
Revisionswünschen." The LDP appears to have sponsored a list of 160 firms which

Stripped of its guises and regarded in its naked results, it effected a significant measure of property socialization. Yet the action appears in the main to have been inspired and executed in the spirit of denazification. It began with disposition of blocked properties under property control. Inclusion within it of the extensive properties of Nazi organizations or former Reich government enterprises, of branch properties of the corporate combines which had been dissolved by Soviet or by Control Council action and of abandoned properties could well add up to the total which was sequestered with little departure from denazification.* At any rate, considerable and varied evidence points to this conclusion, such as bourgeois-liberal representation on the tribunals, the relatively large number of properties returned to former owners or remanded to local governments and cooperatives, the scattered pattern of sequestered holdings and the fact that so many of them were of a small size which ordinarily would not be tackled in the opening phases of socialization.** This sequestration of property of Nazi activists or sup-

---

they wished to be returned and which were not small but large and medium in size. See W. Kling, "Der Kampf um des Volkseigentum," *Die Wirtschaft,* III (1948), 513–515. See also for the same picture, Löwenthal, *News from Soviet Germany,* 112–114.

* Even the denazification tribunals in the American zone, with their predominantly white-washing outcome, fined 524,000 persons and confiscated in part or in whole the property of 21,690 persons. OMGUS, *Monthly Report of the Military Governor,* June 1948, no. 36, 10. Most of these confiscations were not however, registered in military government property control statistics which showed only 2,466 units of property valued at 49 million RM confiscated under the denazification law in contrast to 57,530 units of property valued at 2,717 million RM released to owners. OMGUS, *Report of the Military Governor,* Statistical Annex, May 1949 no. 27, 260. As of 31 March 1949 a considerable number of valuable properties remained "blocked" pending appeal and other action. *Ibid.,* March 1949, 25. For totals of Nazi-tainted properties in the eastern zone, see note below.

** Thus in Land Saxony, out of some 4,000 properties examined by the commission about one-half, consisting of small properties belonging to "die kleinen Pg's," were returned to their owners. Of the remaining 1860 properties or property shares, about 40 percent—chiefly consisting of trading and service enterprises—were remanded to local governments or to cooperatives or were given up for sale, 379 properties being in the latter category. In Brandenburg, of the 2079 properties examined by tribunals, 700 were returned to the "nominellen Pg's;" and of the 1300 enterprises retained, about half were remanded to local governments or cooperatives, while 500 properties were retained in Länder hands. The pattern was similar for other states. The percentage of socialization that resulted in individual industries was highly irregular, varying from 100 percent in mining and gas and power generation (most of which was municipalized or quasi-socialized) to 13 percent in the woodworking in-

porters was of course categorical and was modified only by exemption of small proprietors, traders and craftsmen. In effect, a property levy in kind was applied to larger property owners who were members of the Nazi party or of any of its militant organizations or who were conspicuous supporters or beneficiaries of the Nazi regime.*

Economic revival apparently was fostered on the balance by the quick nationalization actions which brought management of a crucial section of heavy industry and of widespread productive facilities into close relation with the main centers of official economic decision. Particularly in the case of the coal industry, way was made for revival and controlled utilization of coal output. Revival was promoted by the concomitant general upgrading into management of militant workers who carried a spirit of initiative to their work, who were identified with the new regime and who wished it to have mass support and to mobilize the

---

dustry. The small size of many of the properties is indicated by the low average employment per enterprise and the fact that many enterprises with employment under ten and under fifty were state-owned. On all this, see M. Fechner, "Wirtschaftliche und politische Bedeutung," loc. cit., 66 f.; "Planmässig und Rentabel Arbeiten, Aufgaben für die Betriebe des Volkes in Brandenburg," Ibid., II (1947), 100 f.; "Vom Konzernsystem zur neuen Industrieordnung," Ibid., 4 f.; F. Seume, "Organisationsformen," loc. cit., 233–245; "Die Wirtschaftliche Entwicklung sowjetischen Zone," loc. cit., 1033–1037; "Der Wirtschaftsplan 1949/1950," Die Wirtschaft, III (1948), sonderheft, July 1948, 3 ff.; Schaffer, Russian Zone, 48 ff. Neither Külz nor Kaiser after flight to the West placed this expropriatory action in another light than primarily denazification. This indicates that some doubt is to be placed in the characterization by Löwenthal of the confiscation tribunals as a "caricature" of socialization. Löwenthal, News from Soviet Germany, 112–114.

* See Nettl, Eastern Zone, 76 ff., for lucubrations on the "exploitation" by the communists of "the prevalent anti-Nazi feeling" and of carrying out "every kind of activity under the cloak of denazification." The leaders of the left put the case differently. They could not forget that half the German electorate of their free will in 1933 voted for Hitler, that the mere "external defeat" (äusseren Niederwerfung) of the enemy would "yield little." They noted that in 1918 also the monarchists, the militarists and reactionaries hid in the corners and Ludendorff fled to Sweden. But, they said, "soon he came back . . ." and so it is also certain "dass noch allzu viele ihre Faust in der Tasche ballen und nur darauf warten, dass sie sie uns wider an die Gurgel pressen können." Max Fechner, "Erfahrungen aus der Aktionseinheit," Einheit, I (1946), 4. The eastern zeal for effective denazification was not a "cloak" or "disguise." Confiscation of properties of state enemies by categorical action was a device of policy used widely during the American Civil War, was favored in various forms within western Germany and was given partial expression in the Austrian denazification law which laid special income surtaxes on all certified Nazi party members.

industrial resources of the zone.* Compliance with allocation and price control was bolstered by this transformation in management. The quality of local economic planning and administration was improved by the solidarity of viewpoint and interweaving of position among the new officials.

Soviet supervision and drive was an important ingredient in sparking recovery. Soviet officials were experienced in the art of collecting foodstuffs in a hungry land. Trained Soviet economists and managers helped to reorder the bureaucratic establishment which the Nazi war economy had left behind. They introduced a stern note of insistence upon fulfillment and execution.[34] They directly introduced the quota controls and two-price system for farm procurement.[35] They propagated a creed of labor, fostered the upgrading of manual workers into management and stimulated programs for arousing worker response in carrying out production objectives. Yet they unceremoniously sponsored speed-up and incentive devices—including use of food supplements—to get more work done at less cost.[36] They were on the lookout for inept management and stressed the need to assure profitable and not merely socialized enterprise.[37] Finally, the Soviets, inspired both by missionary zeal to transmit a faith and by the more prosaic motive of establishing themselves as the main customer of German industry, provided integrated economic control on the zonal level.

With Soviet driving force behind it and with the positive support

* Citing data on "social origin" of managerial staffs, Stolper, without quite knowing whether to be horrified or pleased, states that "thus almost one-half of the socialized industry is actually run by workers." Stolper, *German Realities*, 117. This upgrading from the workbench into managerial and directive elites embodied a healthy adjustment in the German social organism which was characterized in general by an excessive sense of class distinction and segregation with very little of the American or Soviet pattern of upward social mobility. The method of upgrading apparently occurred to some extent spontaneously, as with the case of abandoned properties cited by Schaffer, *Russian Zone*, 29, 173, but to a greater extent by central direction as a means of obtaining "controllers" when property was placed under control. The new custodians had been recruited, said a Saxon state government functionary in December, 1945, from the enterprises themselves. "Das hat den Vorteil, dass der Treuhänder einmal mit der Belegschaft verbunden ist, zweitens den Betrieb genau kennt und weiss, was überhaupt da ist. Auf diese Weise sind die Betriebe verhältnismassig schnell angelaufen." *Neuaufbau der Deutschen Wirtschaft*, 63. As Fritz Voight pointed out in his valuable study the former militant workers now upgraded into management presented themselves in a different light to their former associates. See "Die volkseigenen Betriebe," *Schriften des Vereins für Sozialpolitik*, Neue Folge, Bd 2 (1950) 367 ff.

of the new leftist elite and the labor movement, industrial recovery proceeded at a remarkable pace in spite of the fact that the main fruits of recovery and as much as 50 percent of industrial output were at least initially at Soviet disposal for occupation maintenance or reparations shipment. Economic recovery was held back by lack of raw materials, by inability to obtain hard coal and coking products and steel from the Ruhr and by the almost complete absence of foreign trade except for programmed importation of certain materials, chiefly textile fibres, from the Soviet Union. The recovery process was hampered, however, not only by these material shortages but also by the absence of a well coordinated economic administration. The central zonal administrative departments were well organized and staffed. But they functioned in the main as advisory organs of the zonal headquarters staff of Soviet military government and performed chiefly legislative, research, and inspection duties.[38] State governments and local agencies and movements organized under their wing had taken over most operating responsibilities in the economy and in politics. This was the outcome of early needs and circumstances. The breakdown of communications and the vestment of broad authority in regional and local military government generated counterpart patterns in German politics. The reviving political and industrial life of the zone drew upon local energies and initiative.[39] The new central banking system was organized on a state basis. Denazification and the resulting property seizures were under the wing of state governments. Building up the authority of local government fitted into the plan of preparing the eastern zone for organic fusion with western Germany. It also enabled the Soviets to retain the main lever of control, the prerogative of zonal coordination.* The Soviets could deal with untoward local tendencies by amplifying the authority of central agencies and then playing off the one against the other. On the German side an emphasis on local control stimulated local initiative and made for flexible and responsive government. Furthermore, both the Germans and the Soviets seem to have anticipated that, while zonal agencies probably would pass into or even serve as

* Nettle, "Inside the Russian Zone," loc. cit., 215–225. Nettle stressed the fact that domination of zonal integration gave the Soviets a freer hand in zonal exploitation and in carrying out their reparations policy. "In fact it was essential that no non-Russians and only a few Russians should have an overall picture of the activities of these Soviet [SAG and trading] companies." See also Nettl, Eastern Zone, 304 ff.

partial basis for a future central German government, the newly established state governments would enter such a regime relatively untouched.

However well motivated, politically sound or unavoidable, placing the main focus of economic planning and administration in the hands of local governments wreaked havoc on the functioning of a planned economy.[40] It led to a duplication of planning staff which was spread thin on the state, the zonal and the local level and thus worked ineffectively everywhere.* It dispersed responsibility and generated conflict between zonal agencies and Land governments.** It freed the zonal agencies from any part of parliamentary control and made of them a caricature of bureaucracy while it freed the local operating agencies from the responsibilities of assuring optimum zonal results. Chiefly from this emerged the main weaknesses of Soviet zone planning: profusion of planning on a local level, over elaboration of directives and questionnaires and inadequate coordination of resources on a zonal basis.[41] In the earliest stages of the drive to reactivate the economy, little positive strain resulted from this overlapping planned economy. But the revival of production rather quickly ran afoul of shortages which required for their resolution a centralization of resources, a concentration of output and of investment planning which under existing conditions could only be crudely approximated.[42]

* Thus the first zonal plans for 1946 were made up by three planning agencies: the Land governments, the central administration for industry and the Soviet economics department. See the comparison of all three in Kromrey, "Entwicklung der Planungsarbeit," loc. cit., 5, and Nettl, Eastern Zone, 166. See also the description of the enormous planning and staff apparatus for a Land government in Gregor, "Die Wirtschaftsplanung eines Landes," Methoden der Wirtschaftsplanung, 6–11.

** While Nettle probably exaggerated the case, he thought that the central thread in the political development of the eastern zone lay in the "struggle between the central administrations and the provinces." See Nettle, "The Eastern Zone," loc. cit., 210 ff. and for more detail see the larger work, Nettl, The Eastern Zone, 130–3. Through 1946 and early 1947 the central administrations were empowered to intervene in state management when quotas were unfulfilled. "Such central interference became frequent during and after the hard winter of 1946/7" and brought "the latent conflict out into the open." Allegedly, the defence of the state viewpoint was led by the Saxon government which was well organized and well backed. "By the summer of 1947 the position had become acute. Reports indicated that the meetings between the provincial ministers and the presidents and vice-presidents of the Administrations were increasingly stormy . . ." Ibid., 131. A kernel of truth probably underlay this somewhat overdramatized portrait.

CHAPTER IV

THE WESTERN ZONES

I. Overlap and Variety

LIFE IN THE WESTERN ZONES of Germany ran in grooves similar to those of the eastern zone. In both areas the occupying powers with their headquarters in Berlin and their sources of authority at home wielded power over an inchoate German community struggling to assemble some authority unto itself in an atmosphere permeated by poverty, disorganization and the shock of war and defeat. The relationships between rulers and the ruled were basically the same. The occupying armies uniformly entered Germany with a marked anti-German feeling tempered by the need to mobilize some support for the occupation. The emergent political forces in the German community bore a common non-Nazi stamp; and reaction and extreme nationalism were in hiding in both areas. The parties which came to life in the West when political activity was allowed leeway were similar in origin and complexion to those recognized early in the occupation of eastern Germany.[1] The policy of coalition government was adopted with varying degrees of emphasis throughout Germany.* Likewise, political and institutional reorganization everywhere came to center around state governments.[2]

Stress was laid on social reform and institutional change in the Western, as in the Eastern, occupation. The West believed it desirable to democratize German life by eliminating absentee ownership of land,

* "In wide and dominant circles of all the essential political party organizations in western Germany, even after the elections in the states, the coalition system was held to be desirable, praiseworthy and coveted." Sternberger, "Parties and Party Systems," loc. cit., 28. See also Eliasberg, "Political Party Developments," loc. cit., 253 ff.

67

by fostering trade unions and cooperatives, by divesting the old owners of heavy industry and of the corporate combines of their strategic positions and by uprooting the forces of militarism and reaction from German society. Denazification laid its stamp on social life, East and West, with its massive programs of removing Nazis from office and high position and interning Nazi leaders and prominent Nazi personalities.

The uniformity of grooves for economic life was yet more apparent. The occupation forces of the West took nothing from German current production formally entitled as reparations. But they exerted a corresponding pressure on economic life by drawing on German resources and production for a wide variety of occupation purposes. Most akin to naked reparations were the gains yielded by underpriced exports of coal and timber.* Displaced persons with privileged status within the German economy required subsidies, camp facilities and supplies on a sizeable scale.[3] The largest source of drainage was maintenance on a comparatively indulgent basis of large occupation forces. This cost between 4 to 4.5 billion RM annually during 1946/8 in use of German

* Coal was billed for exports at the comparatively low price of 10 dollars per ton average through to the middle of 1947 and was underpriced so far as market values were concerned. On French gains through overpricing of imports and underpricing of exports, see F. Sanderson, "Germany's Economic Situation and Prospects," *Struggle for Democracy in Europe,* 157. Timber exports were clearly underpriced. British-French interest in German timber was very strong and constituted besides coal the second most important resource exploited for occupation benefit. Both Britain and France organized special timber cutting organizations. Clay frankly stated that "this question of timber exports to the United Kingdom was one of reparations not one of exports." Bipartite Board, *Minutes,* Bib/M(47) 6, 154. For an extremely severe criticism by an American timber specialist on British zone practice, see Bipartite Control Office, *Report by Forestry Timber Department,* U.S., Bico/P(48)95, 31 March 1948; and for the British reply see Bico/P(48)102, 13 April 1948. For a reliable general treatment, see Walter Grottian, *Die Krise der Deutschen und Europäischen Holzversorgung,* Deutches Institut für Wirtschaftsforschung, Sonderheft no. 1 (Berlin, 1948) 20–30, 46–49. See also J. Speer, "Die Krise des deutschen Waldes," *Die Gegenwart,* IV (no. 90, 1949), 25–28; *Die Deutsche Ministerpräsidenten-Konferenz in München* (Munich, 1947), 65–68, 111 ff. The American position was that the timber cut should not exceed twice the annual growth. This was accepted by the British and was incorporated into the Paris Marshall Plan report as a basis for European economic planning. See Committee of European Economic Cooperation, *Technical Reports,* Vol. II, issued as U.S. Department of State Publication no. 2952, European Series 29 (Washington, 1947), 367–369.

manpower, facilities and current industrial output.* Although Anglo-American occupation personnel were not provisioned—as were the Soviets and the French—from German foodstuffs, the total Anglo-American drainage for occupation costs on a per capita basis was as high as in the eastern zone and the French drainage rate was higher.**

* See the carefully worked out estimate and analysis in Eduard Wolf's authoritative study, "Aufwendungen für die Besatzungsmächte, Öffentliche Haushalte und Sozialprodukte in den einzelnen Zonen," Deutches Institut für Wirtschaftsforschung, *Wirtschaftsprobleme der Besatzungszonen* (Berlin, 1948) 120, 126. See also the somewhat looser but more inclusive study, timewise, of the Institut für Besatzungsfragen, *Occupation Costs: Are They a Defence Contribution?* (Tübingen 1951), 7–9, 18 ff, 22 ff. For a detailed picture for one zone alone see the OMGUS report cited n. 3, above, pp. 20–6. Of bizonal occupation costs, approximately a billion RM of (annual) purchases from current industrial production was registered in the bizonal area during the winter and spring of 1947/8. In terms of critical supplies directly consumed (coal, electric power, foodstuffs), the rate of occupation drain was about 5 percent while in terms of overall industrial output the rate of drain probably ran to 10 percent. The labor services of 700,000 Germans, employed in various capacities, accounted during 1946 and 1947 for 1.5 billion reichsmarks. The rest of the outlay went into new construction, transportation and communication services, building maintenance and rentals and troop payroll outlays. These data are drawn from my study, *Stingy Finance and Laisser-Faire, an Essay on U.S. Financial and Economic Policy for a Post-Financial Reform Western Germany* (OMGUS, Office of the Economic Advisor, Berlin, August 1948–mimeographed), paragraphs 51–55; Bipartite Board, *Inclusion of Occupation Costs in the Bizonal Budget*, Bib/P(48)37, 11 March 1948.

** The French zone was two-thirds above the bizonal area in its occupation costs outlays on a per capita basis, and it took about 67 percent of tax revenues, the highest in Germany. E. Wolf, "Aufwendungen," *loc. cit.*, 120 ff., 126 ff., 128 ff., 135. The drainage on social product by occupation and reparation costs was higher in the French zone than in the Soviet zone (28 percent over 26 percent); for the various types of occupation costs discussed by an informed source, see "Die Finanzielle Last des Südwestens," *Wirtschaftszeitung*, 2 May 1947. What this rate of occupation costs meant was pointed out in a memo by the author, "Drainage of Resources in the French Zone by Occupying Forces" (OMGUS, Office of Economics Advisor, 26 March 1948–typewritten). Of the food crop, 3½ percent of the potatoes were taken, 33 percent of eggs, 12 percent of fruit, 15 percent of the wine, 32 percent of the cheese, etc. Of total industrial sales during the first six months of 1947, 15 percent was sold to the occupying forces and 22 percent of net industrial product. On the general sense of colonialism which pervaded life in the French zone by way of housing, requisitions, political supervision, in order to provide a proper mode of life for these 180,000 Frenchmen (an official figure which includes civilian dependents and affiliated service personnel), see Freda Utley, *The High Cost of*

Finally, the western Berlin enclave became a special source of drainage. The eastern sector of Berlin was assimilated quickly into the adjacent Soviet zone economy. But the isolated western Berlin enclave with its two million inhabitants took from the western zones valuable foodstuffs, coal and other essential supplies without returning noteworthy compensating values.*

The economic penetration embodied in the Soviet trading companies and AG trusts found real counterpart in the Western zones, although penetration was not carried to assertion of prerogatives of ownership. Outstanding instances of Western penetration into operating levels of the German economy were the British coal and steel control organizations which through outright sequestration took over operational responsibility for the coal, iron and steel industries. As in the eastern zone, the properties of I. G. Farben were placed under direct occupation custodianship; and in the American and French zones this custodianship was extended to the zonal branches of the former large banking chains.[4] Moreover, as in the east, penetration was extensive in the realm of cultural services including newspapers, radio stations and commercial air lines.[5] As in the eastern zone, the properties of the Nazi party, its main affiliates, members and active supporters were provisionally blocked and placed under custodians appointed by and made responsible to military government.[6]

Similarity extended to the non-institutional plane. Acute shortages

---

Vengeance (Hinsdale, Illinois, 1950), 232–269; "Colony on the Rhine," *Economist*, 12 June 1947, 68 ff.; Edgar Morin, *Allemagne Notre Souci* (Paris, 1947), 17–25 (a picture of Baden-Baden and French headquarters), 147–152 (economic controls).

* During 1946 and 1947, when the economic life of Berlin was not yet disrupted by blockade or rendered uncertain by threat of war, this drainage ran to between 400 and 500 million RM calculated on a legal cost basis and with importation being held down to a minimum. The dollar value of this deficit, computed for the value of imported materials at the port and of export coal values alone ran to about 140 million dollars. See a tripartite paper, Bipartite Board, *Trade Deficit, Western Sectors, Berlin* (report to the Economics Advisors, 30 July 1948–mimeographed). Of course as Berlin ration, fuel, power and other requirements have been scaled up both the RM and dollar costs have mounted, as was pointed out by a 1949 study. Bipartite Control Office, *Bizone Investment of Counterpart Funds*, BISEC/Memo 9 (49) 25, Annex K. See also U.S. Congress, Senate, *Extension of European Recovery*. Hearings before the Committee on Foreign Affairs, 81st Congress, 1st session (Washington, 1950), 203 ff. For a mistaken estimate of 75 million dollars, see U.S. Congress, House of Representatives, Select Committee on Foreign Aid, *Final Report on Foreign Aid*, 80th Congress, 2nd session, 116.

existed, east and west. Food was rationed at levels which hardly sufficed to feed families on a diet loaded with cereals and potatoes sparsely supplemented by fats, sweets and meat. Medical supplies were short everywhere. Even after two years of occupation, pre-war levels of economic activity were less than 50 percent achieved. Because of scarcities and the pressure of surplus purchasing power the apparatus of the war economy—with its paraphernalia of rations, allocations and economic planning—was as familiar in western as in eastern Germany.*

In these and cognate respects the same elements were present in the occupying regimes in eastern and western Germany; but they were combined in differing patterns. The anti-Germanism common to both was tinged in the eastern zone with anti-fascism while the Western attitude was more commonly tinctured with anti-Hitlerism and anti-radicalism. Hence the Western armies which came into Germany with instructions to ban German political activity rejected or suppressed ANTIFA movements in their areas or reduced them to accessory agencies in intelligence operations.** The early Western ban on political

* When a liberal Westerner, the SPD mayor of Bremen, W. Kaisen, visited the Soviet zone and reported on his trip, he noted that the eastern as the western zone economy bore the stamp of "private enterprise," but it was "more closely subjected to state controls and administration." W. Kaisen, "Blick in der Ostzone," *Weser-Kurier,* 7 August 1946.

** In Bremen the organizations were tolerated but "under control." In Leipzig they were "disbanded" and the leadership was required to inform on violations. In the Ruhr area the ANTIFAS "in every case investigated met with hostility from MG although this hostility has not everywhere resulted in an outright ban" except in Essen. According to a trustworthy summary account, "most of these organizations were reduced to the role of informers on the location of prominent Nazis and automatic arrest cases." Office of Strategic Services, Mission for Germany, USFET, *Field Intelligence Studies,* no. 7, "The Political Situation in the Ruhr," 3 ff.; H. O. Lewis, *New Constitutions in Occupied Germany* (Foundation for Foreign Affairs, Pamphlet no. 6, Washington, 1948), 2; Kraus and Almond, "Social Composition of the German Resistance," *Struggle for Democracy in Germany,* 67 ff. An important contrast between eastern and western Germany was that to be found in the role of the "Kzer"— the men and women from concentration camps. In the eastern zone these were given special assistance and pushed into positions of leadership. In the western zones they were accorded no prerogatives and found little favor in the eyes of the occupation authorities or the German leadership. A. D. Kahn, *Betrayal, Our Occupation of Germany* (Warsaw, 1950), 43–58; Eugen Kogon, *Der SS-Staat* (2d ed., Berlin, 1947), 366 ff.; G. Schaffer, *Russian Zone of Germany* (SRT Publications, U.S.A., 1947), 17 ff., 67 ff.

activities and all meetings and associations tended to nourish particularism in the German community and to hinder the drive of anti-fascist forces. The tendency toward conservatism which resulted was reinforced by the pattern of appointments to political office. These fell within the same range as in the East—from communists to repentant Nazis—but the proportions differed. Communists and militant socialist spokesmen seldom held leading positions in the West while the conservatively hued civil servant, the clerical leader or rightist fellow traveller—frequently installed on clerical advice—fared well.[7] This was as true of French appointments as of those of the British and the Americans.[8]

A similar contrast in emphasis appears in denazification. All zones were denazified, but in different ways and to differing degrees. On any criteria, denazification perhaps lagged most in the British zone.* Even

* The sharp-tongued Schumacher once commented on this British leaning toward mild denazification that the bizonal agreement had delivered from the American side the capitalists and from the British side the Nazis. (Speech cited in Otto Winzer, *Sozialistische Politik, eine kritische Stellungnahme zu Reden und Aufsätzen von Dr. Kurt Schumacher* [Berlin, 1947], 78.) The measurement of the pace and character of denazification in its many dimensions and through its many complexities cannot be attempted here. We might merely note that analysis of the mass of information and data presented in a summary Control Council report speaks tellingly of a prominent British tendency to lag behind in most phases of the problem. Thus as of 1 January 1947 only 520 persons had been individually tried on war crimes and 3038 were held in custody, while comparable figures for the American zone were 610 and 12,425 and for the Soviet zone were 14,240 and 14,820. ACA *Report to the Council of Foreign Ministers from the Allied Control Authority in Germany,* CONL/P (47) 7–15, Denazification section, Part 2, p. 1. It is also odd that though 26,351 former SS officers were interned in the Soviet zone and 25,382 in the American zone, only 11,279 were interned in the British zone. *Ibid.,* Part 3, p. 1. Moreover, of the members of criminal organizations (under decisions of the International Military Tribunal), 27 percent were quashed or acquitted and the great bulk of those sentenced were given monetary fines or imprisonment terms of a year or less and hence already served in internment. Out of 14,629 cases disposed of, only 95 persons were sentenced to more than two years and only 4 persons to more than five years. Control Commission for Germany, British Element, "Trial of Members of Criminal Organizations," *Reports,* III (February, 1948), 9–12. The British staffed their major central zonal agencies with conservatively oriented personnel to a large extent tainted by collaboration with the Nazi regime. This was so notorious that General Clay in a basic strategy conference with the U.S. zone Minister-Presidents took official note of what he stated as the "statement frequently made that [Bizonal] amalgamation requires Germans of the American Zone to work with members of the Nazi party of the British Zone." This statement was enlarged by the Minister-

where it was executed with the greatest energy in the West, as in the American zone, its outcome was unsatisfactory. The Americans started possibly more radically than the Soviets with mass internment of Nazi activists and prominent supporters, trials programmed for industrialists and bankers, across-the-board removals of party members from responsible positions and mass property blocking. Unfortunately, the program was dragnet in scope covering the entire adult population and mechanical in form. It depended almost exclusively upon Allied initiative and lacked adequate provision for local enforcement. It was ripe for scuttling when its pursuance was turned over to a conservatively oriented German community and occupation surveillance was later withdrawn.[9] The economic base of the nazified elites—in business property, in corporations, in farms or in banking—was relatively untouched. Only a handful of outstanding Nazi figures or particularly incriminated personalities were specially penalized or deprived of privileges other than rights to vote or to hold public office. The main role of denazification was temporarily to remove Nazified elites from leadership positions throughout Western Germany and thus to permit the pre-nazi elites or the nationalist camp-followers of Naziism to take over. This significantly accelerated retirements and in-rank promotions and thus facilitated the emergence of new leadership cadres throughout the Western German community. The whole process has been aptly called the method of "artificial revolution."[9a]

A gap between high purpose and depressing levels of achievement was characteristic of the social reform program generally. It probably showed up least in the American endeavor to build a politically balanced anti-fascist press. But trade unions which were encouraged were not given concrete functions in economic life and in the American zone they were incompletely re-equipped with the facilities which had been taken from them in 1933. Educational and school reform was adopted as a pet occupation hobby but little school reform resulted. Land reform was advocated but too tepidly to obtain results from a German leadership opposed to radical action. The lesser emphasis on dynamic social reform together with the early ban on meetings and political activity, the suppression of spontaneous local anti-

President of Bavaria who charged that "it is possible in the British Zone for a man to become a ministerial director whom we couldn't even hire as a mail carrier." OMGUS, "Conference of Lt. Gen. L. D. Clay and Minister-Presidents of the American Zone" (protocol of conference, 23 February 1947–mimeographed), 8–9.

fascist activity, the appointment of a predominantly conservative leadership and the mechanical or muted denazification led to a regime of political stagnation. In effect, Allied power was used to tide over a crisis an "intact social structure" headed by an old bureaucracy. This "immobilized and atomized society" then was allowed to institutionalize slowly by direction from above.[10]

II. Stagnation and Deficit

Political stagnation was complemented by economic stagnation. This took its point of departure from the literal disintegration of the war economy which occurred during the closing phase of the war and the opening phase of the occupation.* A new postwar economy adapted to the new conditions of life was not to be the product of centralized planning agencies. The former branch offices or provincial ministries who, with the collaboration of the local chambers of commerce, were entrusted with custody over economic affairs, were inept at this larger task. Only the French, with the motive of obtaining a large share of the product, attempted in their zone to provide a zonal planning apparatus to direct the process of reconversion.** American zonal control and planning was nondescript in character.*** The British occupation ad-

---

* Cf. earlier, p. 7.

** The zone was ruthlessly controlled, and its industrial production was directed by control of transport, coal and raw material allocations. All foreign trade was directed, marketed and priced by a French military government agency and between 85 and 90 percent of exports were shipped to France. By underpricing exports and by overpricing imports the formal approximate balance of payments which French statistics showed, indicate, according to American reports, a concealed profit running to an outside limit of 50 million dollars in 1947. See also "Ungelöste Probleme der französischen Zone," *Die Wirtschaft*, II (1947), 430–431; Fred H. Sanderson, "Germany's Economic Situation and Prospects," *loc. cit.*, 157; G. Stolper, *German Realities* (New York, 1948), 70 ff.; H. Wegner, "Die Zonen und der Aussenhandel," Deutches Institut, *Wirtschaftsprobleme*, 108–111.

*** It is hard to do justice in this context to the gnarled story of economic policy and administration in the American zone in its zonal aspects, particularly since the necessary monographic investigation chiefly of the Länderrat and its functioning has not been made or published. For discussion of limitations, see Hans Möller, "Die Wirtschaftsplanung in der U.S.-Zone, Zentral Instanz ohne Zentralismus," *Wirtschaftszeitung*, I (15 September 1946); "Vorstadien der Wirtschaftlichen Einheit, Das Beispiel der U.S.-Zone," *Ibid.*, I (16 August 1946). Clay emphasized that the Länderrat was not established primarily for action purposes but to achieve "co-

ministration had a readier faith in zonal control and economic planning but the network of zonal agencies which they carried over intact from the Nazi regime did not appear very effective.[11] In both zones was retained an outer shell of regimented economy in the form of price and wage controls and formal allocation authority. Official energies concentrated on maintaining a flow of foodstuffs and coal through the rationing system, on keeping public utilities in operation, on taking care of emergency needs and on mobilizing the labor force for employment. The "fusion" of the economic control authorities in the Anglo-American zones introduced a certain element of order and forward planning into the few items under central disposition or influence such as coal movements, imported foodstuffs and import and export trade. But the bizonal administration lacked executive authority and could not issue binding legal mandates. Lines of authority between it and the occupying powers and the Land economics ministries remained unclear and overlapping to the end. Consequently, little direction of reconversion was yielded by bizonal fusion.*

---

ordination" and to lead the German officials "to a better understanding of the federal type of government." Clay, *Decision*, 86, 95–103. Zink notes that "perhaps the very complexity of the coordinating machinery has contributed somewhat to defeat its primary purpose." Zink, *American Military Government*, 75. On the extent of the authority of the Land governments over economic affairs, cf. OMGUS, *Land and Local Government in the U.S. Zone of Germany* (prepared by Comstock Glaser, Civil Administration Division, Berlin, 1947), 55–65, 72 ff.

* In these terms, see "The Battle of Minden," *Economist*, 26 April 1947, 6–9–11; O. Emminger, "Wirtschaftsplanung in der Bizone," Deutsches Institut, *Wirtschaftsprobleme*, 147–175. The principal bizonal planning instrument was the organization of a unified coal and later iron and steel distribution plan of which Emminger gives a detailed account. Absence of control over administration led to marked deviation between the control plan and the realized pattern of coal consumption as well as to marked incongruities in this pattern. The waste of coal "through misuse, diversion and inefficiency was prodigious." Cf. D. D. Humphrey, German mss. Chapter XI, "The Black Gold of the Ruhr," p. 14. This judgement was based upon a detailed statistical review of coal consumption by major consuming groups during 1947/8 and their respective or indicated productive output. The electric, power, chemical, railroad and coal mining industries were receiving about twice as much coal per unit of output as before the war. Much of this coal was presumably diverted to other uses. In a well-known speech V. Agartz, the then chief of the bizonal economic "department" at Minden scathingly indicted the futility of his own organization. "Die Wirtschaftspolitik ist heute durch die Länderstellung völlig aufgespaltet." V. Agartz, "Die westdeutsche Wirtschaftskrise," *Die Wirtschaft*, II (1947), 176. Note the comment of the former chief of the central administration for commerce and trade

In the main, reconversion was directed by the improvisations of the managers of the some 47,000 industrial enterprises licensed to resume production in the western zones who operated within the limits of their coal and energy allotments as widened or narrowed by supplementary trading. Their dealings chiefly involved efforts to form new supply and demand relationships which would be in accord with the new conditions. Such relationships ordinarily would have been formed with money. Sellers accepted money freely only in the black market. The maintenance of legal price ceilings combined with the policy which reopened banks and released for circulation the mass of purchasing power accumulated under the Nazi war economy made other sellers unwilling to accept money in trade. A varying fraction of the output of many, perhaps most, firms was sold on the black market to gain access to funds to be used for replenishing losses from sales at legal prices or for procuring on the black market items which were not otherwise obtainable. In general, however, legal price norms if not precise levels were respected. Offer in barter or trade of part of plant output or inventory was used in procurement to supplement or replace money payments. This mode of procurement by direct trade was informally sanctioned by helpless control officials. They resorted to the same device when they endeavored to get supplies moving out of other jurisdictions. Compensation trading became the dominant form of marketing for commodities or services not in the embrace of public control or subject to special allocation or rationing programs.[12]

The *Sachwertbesitzern*—the possessors of real goods—functioned at the center of this trading universe while the grey mass of wage-earners, clerks and stipendiaries stood on its fringes. This contrast of position harbored a wide potential for exploitation. Wage and salary earners were mobilized in employment by labor offices which issued ration cards. Labor services were extracted in exchange for an allotment of paper currency scaled at legal wage levels, supplemented by small gifts, bonuses in kind or a quasi-legal noonday meal. With his allotment of currency the wage earner could procure through the rationing

in the Soviet zone after his flight to the West. "It is understandable that the American and British military authorities were not in a position to take a hand in clearing up disorder to the same extent as the Russian administration. They do not know this poverty, this muddling through in the midst of general insufficiency while the Russian officials have learned how to deal with such conditions at the decisive moment of the history of their country." Hugo Buschmann, "Plan for the Organization of the Economic Administration in Germany," 14.

system without marked difficulties—though not without disparities of treatment and aggravating delays—the essentials for bare survival. In this way wage-earners could command access only to a somewhat reduced share of current social product.*

The most onerous effects of the western stagnant economy were felt, however, not in maldistribution of social product *per se* but in warping the process of reconversion to a peacetime economy. This process was hampered by the clumsiness of compensation trade as a device for indirect exchange, the energy wasted in the effort to make it work and the absence of a uniform measure of value. Misdirection of resources and energy was evidenced in small things: the zeal for garden cultivation, the search for direct farm connections, the overburdened rail services, the introduction of wage payments in kind, the concentration of production on items least amenable to official control and the hoarded inventories.[13]

Waste and misdirection of resources were possibly more harmful in those industries amenable to official control whose products were distributed through allocations. This was the situation of the coal, iron and steel industries which had been sequestered, placed under special Allied scrutiny and made the object of much of the work of the economic control administration. The coal mines were so efficiently controlled that they could not even procure enough of the near valueless reichsmarks

* The most perceptive analysis of this aspect of the stagnant economy came from the trenchant pen of that remarkable political leader Dr. Kurt Schumacher. See particularly his addresses before Social Democratic Conferences: *Sozialismus, eine Gegenwartsaufgabe* (Hanover, 1946), 12–14. "Das Resultat ist dass die deutsche Arbeiterschaft noch niemals einen so geringen Realwert gehabt hat wie heute." *Deutschland und Europa* (Hanover, 1947), 6; *Die Sozialdemokratie im Kampf für Freiheit und Sozialismus* (Hanover, 1948), 3–7. Among American commentators, the analysis of Horst Mendershausen just cited is the most penetrating. Labor's share of current product was probably not much greater in the eastern zone. There the lion's share of current industrial product went to the Soviets rather than to the *Sachwertbesitzern* who played a much smaller role in the east due to the socialization of much of their property, the curtailment of purchasing power by closing the banks and the subjection of reconversion to more planned direction. Eastern zone workers however probably could command through their wages a greater access to a wide range of incidental services and small products which the compression of liquidity in the eastern zone would put within their range of purchase. It may also be noticed that compensation trade was generated in the east by scarcities and by organization of a planned economy chiefly on a state basis. Hence it was not the incidence but the degree of pervasiveness of compensation trade which characterized the western zone economy.

from their sales to satisfy the financial obligations incurred in carrying on their operations. The mines had to be subsidized by transfers which ran up to nearly a billion RM through 1947. Compensation trade was of course barred. The effects of such thorough control over the industry's business operations were tragic. The resources of the industry were continually drained away without bringing a return flow of materials and foodstuffs or providing the leverage by which these could be procured.* This weakness in the economic base of the industry was reinforced by the British sequestration which tended to isolate mine management from the zonal and Land economic administrations which were most able to bring resources to bear on manpower recruitment, mine management and procurement.

In addition the industry was hampered up and down the line by unimaginative leadership and by weakened incentives. Partly this flowed from retention practically unchanged of the old management and cartel and syndicate business organization.** This management was

* The most fundamental fact in the economy of the British zone was that the British gave it over to unrequited exploitation by her two Western allies by delivering to their zones for rudimentary return about one-third of the Ruhr coal output, together with a share of its electricity and gas. This cost the British zone somewhere near 250 million dollars in 1946 computing drainage to the French and American zones and to Berlin of about 15 to 20 million tons of coal valued at $15 per ton. One bizonal paper in referring to shipments of coal, power and steel to the French zone notes that "at present trade in these items goes on in the habitual manner on a German to German basis—bills presented in RM and payments made in the normal way." Bipartite Board, Economic Panel, *Billing the French*, BIECO/P (47), 28 February 1947, 2. Indeed the French were requested specifically just prior to the Moscow conference to settle for the balance of trade in allocated items by payments in dollars—a demand which helped bring the French into Bizonia where things proceeded in the "normal way."

** Cf. A. M. Hillhouse, "Report on Organizations and Practises in the Ruhr Coal Industry as Observed January 13–18, 1948" (OMGUS, Finance Division, 31 January 1948–typewritten); "Die Deutsche Kohlenverwaltung," *Der Wirtschaftspiegel*, III (1948), 22–30. The British comment in reply to strong Soviet and French criticism that denazification was carried out "to a considerable degree" and by 1 July 1946 would be completed after an investigation then under way had wound its course indicates that the British tread lightly in this area. Cf. ACA, *Preliminary Report of the Committee of Coal Experts on the Measures to increase Coal Production and the Principles of Allocation of German Coal* Corc/P(46)289, 6 September 1946, Appendix A(1), and A(5), to CEC/M(46)22. More to the point was the French complaint that "the supervision of the work is entrusted to the old German managements" who do not act "energetically" and are "incapable or do

not dynamized by socialization or by the acquisitive energy of private enterprise or even by the force of determined foreign control.[14] The British seemed as a matter of policy to bear lightly wherever sensitive issues of German initiative or worker resistance were concerned.* Worker incentives to produce were blunted by a wage system which did not tie earnings very closely to output.[15] The British control authorities had no positive program of action. Finally, early in the occupation German incentives were depressed when the Allies loudly proclaimed their intent to export a large fraction of German coal output regardless of German needs.**

The net result of all this may well be considered the "most costly failure of the United States in Europe" or "one of the major scandals of the occupation period."[16] Though the facilities, the manpower and the equipment for comparatively speedy recovery were either on hand or capable of being mobilized, the production of Ruhr coal which the German economy needed so badly and which all Europe wanted lagged unmistakably and unforgivably. In terms of pre-war levels only 25 percent was achieved in 1945, only 40 percent in 1946, only 50 percent in 1947 and only 60 percent in 1948. Since coal was so fundamental to the western zonal economy—as a prime cash export, as the main source of electricity and gas, as industrial fuel, as a prime source for steel, as a base for synthetics, as a means of space heating—the low level of coal output in combination with the hampering effects of the stagnant economy was in the main responsible for the slow pace of economic recovery

---

not concern themselves sufficiently with the implementation of the directives which they receive." *Ibid.*, 7. See also Fred Sanderson, "Report on Trip to the Ruhr, July 6–9, 1948" (OMGUS, Office of the Economic Advisor, 16 July 1948–typewritten).

* In reply to French criticism of "management and supervision," the British noted the importance of not inciting "passive resistance such as arose in the Ruhr during 1923. A similar attitude on the part of the mine workers now would have a most disastrous effect upon production." ACA, *Preliminary Report of Coal Experts,* Appendix A(5), 3.

** See U.S. Department of State, *United States Economic Policy toward Germany,* Department of State Publication 2630 (Washington 1946), 76–7 for the text of the July 1945 directive which specified that 25 million tons of German coal should be exported by April 1946 regardless of the "delay" in "the resumption of industrial activity in Germany." Actually the directive was annulled in practise but its frightening language (export was to proceed even though it might cause "unemployment, unrest and dissatisfaction among Germans of a magnitude which may necessitate firm and rigorous action") left traces on German attitudes.

in the western zones and for their conspicuous lag behind recovery in eastern Germany through 1946 to 1947.*

The lag behind the eastern zone was embarrassing since it bore an inverse relationship to the more promising productive potential of the western zones and the larger area open for integration there. Moreover, the eastern recovery had proceeded with the handicap of Soviet reparations withdrawals while western lag occurred in spite of Western subsidy. This subsidy was largely incurred in importing foodstuffs to make up for the over-all inability of western Germany to feed itself and its eastern refugees at tolerable ration levels with low prevailing crop yields. But food was also imported to make up for the weakness of the western German food collection and distribution system. This was based on locally controlled and state directed food collecting and marketing agencies functioning under programs constituted of delivery quotas on the one hand and corresponding schedules of food movements from surplus producing to concentrated urban areas on the other. These programs were arrived at through a complex process of negotiation. Initially only military government at the state level and German state governments were involved but later zonal and bizonal agencies on both the German and Allied sides were brought in.[17] The food collecting agencies had little control over the distribution of farm supplies. They were unable to apply effective sanctions for noncompliance. They could offer the grower little beyond payment in irritatingly low money prices at a time when most other wholesale buyers were offering "compensation trade." Notwithstanding, with their programs in hand

* In terms of comparative economic revival, and comparing 1946 with 1936, Soviet zone coal output was 98 percent and the Anglo-American zones were 53 percent; industrial output by sales value was 45 percent for all Germany and 51 percent for the Soviet zone; social product (value) per capita had fallen 18 percent in the Soviet zone against 25 percent for all of Germany. See statistical data for 1948 and previous years in Deutches Institut, *Die Deutsche Wirtschaft Zwei Jahre Nach dem Zusammenbruch* (Berlin, 1947), 270 ff. Industrial output indexes prepared under eastern auspices showed the eastern zone finishing 1946 with an industrial output index of around 50 against 33 to 34 for the Bizonal area. *Die Wirtschaft*, II (1947), 344. For similar results, see O. R. Donner, "Das Volkseinkommen Deutschlands 1946" (an unpublished study by one of Germany's leading national income statisticians prepared under OMGUS auspices, Berlin, 12 March 1947—mimeographed); OMGUS, Special Report of the Military Governor, *Economic Data on Potsdam, Germany* (Berlin, 1947), 80; Sanderson, "Germany's Economic Situation and Prospects," *loc. cit.*, 128 ff., 160.

these agencies were supposed to collect all marketable farm produce
and to thin out local feeding levels by large-scale movements of food to
urban areas in other jurisdictions.*

* This complex problem is badly in need of investigation. One of the interesting
projects for a monograph would be disclosure of the broad margin of error and systematic bias in west German food and agricultural statistics. On this, see Bipartite
Control Office, *Report on Bizonal Administration,* Bico/Sec(47)17, 4 September
1947 (prepared by Hugo Buschmann). The official reports vacillated between stress
on unbelievably high collection quotas with apologies for lax performance and excellent explanations for breakdown in food collection and distribution. For the
former, Clay describes the quotas as between 83 and 86 percent and notes that "collecting food in Germany during these years was difficult." Clay, *Decision,* 271. For
the latter, see "Bauern Ohne Vertrauen," *Die Wirtschaftzeitung,* I (20 September
1946); "Sieben Fragen zur Ernährungslage," *Frankfurt Neue Presse,* 14 October
1946. See also the interesting article, "Harvest Survey Reveals More Grain," OMGUS,
Information Bulletin, III (15 September 1946), 3. In Wuertemberg-Baden one military government investigator disclosed "unreported productive land equal in total
to an entire county (Kreis)." OMGUS, *Economic Policies, Programs and Requirements in Occupied Germany* (Berlin, September 1947), 170. "Any Land which really
succeeds in squeezing more of its produce into legal channels fears that the net result will be simply that its share of imports will be decreased." *Idem.* The increasing
disappearance of German food supplies so far as actual fulfillment of ration needs
were concerned troubled Clay. While in Congressional hearings the German food
collection system was praised, although shrewd Congressmen remained skeptical
to the end, in the privacy of Bipartite Board and staff meetings the sheer arithmetic
of the problem aroused indignation. In the middle of 1947 Clay thought that the
use of constabulary would "have good effect on the farmers and would definitely
impress upon them the determination of MG to pursue the collections." A little later
he was puzzled to note that "we had imported more than twice as much food as in
the previous years without bettering the ration." But in February, 1948 he really got
indignant, for the data showed "that the amount of food collected by the German
authorities was negligible," for "imported foodstuffs were practically equal to the
ration fulfillment." It was then that the General came to the point of demanding that
police be employed in connection with the food census law. Was Robertson joking
when he drily noted that "it was possible to use troops to collect cattle but that such
use was difficult in the case of potatoes and grain?" Clay was aware that the German
administration would never really work hard if they believed that "we will always
cover the deficits" or if food help was on an open-ended basis; he was also aware
of the need for a broad program of subsidies, priorities and incentives designed to
make organized collection more attractive. In Frankfurt they struggled with the
manipulation of import quotas. But after the ludicrous experience of the food census
law enacted by the direct order of military government, the German mal-administra-
tion of foodstuffs was substantially taken for granted. See Bipartite Board, *Minutes,*
Bib/M(47) 5, 13, 14 and (48), 1, 3, 4, 6, paragraphs 136, 239, 256, 264, 292, 295,

But even this generously scaled importation of foodstuffs need not have occasioned a deficit of the scale actually experienced. The food imports were simply put through the rationing system and given in exchange for reichsmark balances of very little value. Although the German community would have cooperated readily, no compensatory arrangements were made except in coal and timber to use the authority of military government to requisition German industrial production to pay for food imports. Nor was effort applied to dispose of food imports within Germany on terms designed to yield a flowback of serviceable industrial products. Instead the Anglo-American occupying powers indulged the hope that imports would be paid for by the proceeds of foreign exchange which German traders would make available by sale of their output in foreign countries.

This hope was futile because none of the preconditions for its fulfillment on any appreciable scale were present. Through 1946 and the spring of 1947 responsibility for foreign trade in the Bizone was scattered over a host of Allied and German agencies interwoven to a greater or lesser degree with provincial government organs.* The physical and

301, 348 and the papers therein cited. For certain futile gestures in the direction of "incentives," see BICO, *Interim Report on Incentives*, Bico/P(48)42/3, 7 April 1948. For comments and analysis of the so-called "pantry law" episode, see almost any German newspaper or periodical during the months January-March 1948, such as *Stuttgarter Zeitung*, 13 March 1948. On reliance on the device of manipulation of import quotas and differential ration levels as "punishment" and "incentive" with regard to collections, see BICO, *Indigenous Supply Programs for Grain and Flour in 1947/8 Year*, Bico/Memo(47)19, 29 September 1949. See the illuminating discussion of the attempt to use differential rationing in the third session of the bizonal Laenderrat, Frankfurt, BICO, *Summary Record of the Third Open Meeting*, Bico/P (48)138, 14 May 1948, item 4.

* Responsibility during most of 1946 and 1947 for foreign trade on the German side was concentrated in special agencies organized on a Land basis and integrated with the Land government but also functionally related to a bizone German foreign trade bureau integrated into the Bizone Economic Department. On the Allied side there was even more overlapping. Under the first Bizone fusion agreement, roughly through the end of 1947, the main functional Allied foreign trade offices remained Land agencies formally designated as local JEIA offices which, though functionally tied to local military government, were "integrated" with a Bizone JEIA office which had more direct authority over imports than exports. But JEIA in turn had an authority which overlapped both with its monetary counterpart, JFEA, and functional finance and economic officials in Berlin. Only after the January 1948 bizonal reorganization was Allied responsibility for foreign trade adequately centralized in JEIA which in turn was given full authority over the branch offices.

organizational, not to speak of the incentive, preconditions for a revival of private trade were achieved only in rudimentary form through most of 1946 and 1947.[18] Official Allied and German controls constituted an interlocking series of obstacles which greatly hampered importation not handled directly on a high government level and which penalized rather than rewarded most exporters.*

A narrowly conceived foreign trade policy reinforced and supplemented the network of obstacles to private trade. This policy presupposed a pauperized "disease and unrest" economy which could only trade on the basis of individual transactions for dollars and not for goods.** This led to a curious "wheat-coal" disease-and-unrest economy in its foreign trade relations.[19] Wheat was imported from America; coal was the principal German export. Potential import offers of Dutch vegetables, Norwegian fish or Italian fruits were translated into their wheat equivalent calorie-wise to establish an offering price which a disease-and-unrest economy could afford to pay. Customers who wanted German goods were required to pay gold or dollars since the most urgent export need was to earn dollars to pay for wheat imports. Mutual trade in less essential goods would have been advantageous, but programmed mutual trade on a negotiated basis ran afoul a celebrated American principle of antagonism to barter-type trade agreements. In

* On importation this was notoriously true partly due to the inefficiencies of the newly organized JEIA and JFEA but basically attributable to the reluctance of the Military Governors to authorize import expenditures except through processes which permitted their personal review of essential developments through a variety of reporting and "budget" devices. See on this Bipartite Board, *Minutes*, discussion of category B budget programs, Bib/M(47), paragraphs 87, 123, 133, 146, 180, 240. Many of the key purchasing decisions were made directly by the Military Governors, as for example penicillin, commercial messages, medical supplies, milk and herring purchases and tobacco purchases. The export penalization came about partly due to the repeated series of approvals which an export contract had to undergo, stringent provisions for advance payment guarantees, and a double-checked program to ensure that RM payments to exporters would be on a verified legal price basis without any relation to foreign currency gains. The 5 percent incentive device was only slightly helpful and it became effective only in 1948.

** "When in 1945 I asked General Draper to give prime attention to building up exports, I told him that all sales would have to be in dollars and that purchases must be restricted to essential raw materials which after manufacture into finished products in Germany would bring many times their cost when exported." Clay, *Decision*, 196.

a trading community nearly starved of dollars or gold and with highly unsettled economic conditions, "the United States thrust the policy which would destroy Germany as both exporter and importer and imposed the dollar requirement in the most critical trading area in Europe."[20]

CHAPTER V

THE CONTROL COUNCIL REGIME

I. The Control Council and Berlin

THE ZONAL REGIMES of eastern and western Germany were built up in accord with the policies laid down by the military government concerned. But military government was not only applied separately in the zones but also collectively as the Control Council. To rule effectively in this capacity the zonal delegations which made up the Control Council invested their meetings and concerted decisions with the ritual and some of the paraphernalia of independent power. Laws were enacted and proclamations made known under the name of the Control Council and published in an official gazette issued under its imprint.[1] Important species of property were vested in its name; and the property of the former Reich government and of the Nazi party nominally was subject to its disposition.[2] Pervading much early Control Council negotiation was the vague assumption that established Reich legislation could be amended or revised only by its action.[3] Certain sovereign prerogatives in the field of foreign affairs were exercised through it.*

Along with ceremonial stature, an imposing physical machinery for collaboration developed in the Control Council regime. At its center was the Allied Control Authority located in Berlin and headed by the

---

* Missions of other Allied governments were accredited to it. It communicated through its secretariat with foreign governments. It regulated the extent and character of German communications and transport arrangements with other countries. It assumed responsibility for the return of Germans in neutral countries, German prisoners of war not held by the occupying powers and consular services for Germans abroad. Foreign trade nominally was conducted and export proceeds nominally were held in its name. OMGUS, *ACA Enactments*, I, 49, 62–63, 126, 176, 204, 206; II, 82, 122, 125, 169; III, 169, 171.

four zone commanders sitting together as the Control Council. Under the Council was an elaborate hierarchy of working organs composed of the upper levels of the four staffs of military government. In a somewhat different category were nine quadripartite agencies such as the Berlin Kommandatura and the Nüremberg Tribunal with specialized functions and varying origins.* Many hundred Allied personnel, aside from a small army of clerical administrative workers, probably were engaged in this monumental effort at condominium.[4]

Condominium had to be exercised at every stage by *ad hoc* quadripartite negotiation. On its own account this was a source of strain. Negotiation tended to lapse into the conventional methods of diplomacy and to convert small concerns of German life or procedural questions into negotiational hurdles. The Nüremberg Tribunal was dismantled partly because of this element of strain.[5] Yet important offsets to this tended to facilitate negotiations, most effectively where a stream of quadripartitely determined executive decisions was not required. For one thing, a certain fraternal air surrounded the commanding generals who alike were commanders of military forces and chiefs of military government.[6] On lower levels, negotiators frequently could respond primarily to professional arguments, to *esprit de corps*, or even to the sheer spirit of conviviality.[7] Such collaboration of course was restricted whenever German interests to any important degree were mobilized behind the negotiations or when Allied interests in the home country or within the home governments were active. These pressures sometimes

* The most important of these had been directly constituted by governmental agreement: the Berlin Kommandatura which functioned under the Control Council for the administration and coordination of occupation policy in Berlin; the Nüremberg Tribunal established under charter to try the ranking Nazi leaders and lay down fundamental policy on treatment of war crimes and war criminals; a naval commission for the purpose of carrying out the Potsdam decision on disposal of the German shipping fleet; a rudimentary intelligence agency. Other agencies soon were established by the ACA to carry out various specialized purposes: a commission to control I. G. Farben, another to handle and investigate German foreign assets, a third to organize and give practical direction to vast interzonal movements of persons, a fourth to trace missing Allied persons, a fifth to provide housekeeping facilities and administrative arrangements. See *Ibid.*, I, 15; U.S. Department of State, *Germany, 1947–1949, The Story in Documents*, Department of State Publication 3556, European and Commonwealth Series 9 (Washington, 1950), 52; U.S. Department of State, *Trial of War Criminals*, Department of State Publication 2420 (Washington, 1945), 15 ff.; OMGUS, *ACA Enactments*, I, 35, 37, 41, 184, 198, 225, 315; IV, 96.

were pushed back as far as they could be out of an instinctive staff tendency to resist intruding forces, to widen their areas of personal responsibility and in result to further the tendency of the Control Council regime to become a source of self-generated activity.

At the center of this machinery of collaboration and serving partly as its ballast was the copartnership over Germany's capital city, Berlin, which was converted into a Europeanized and inland Shanghai.[8] The copartnership rested on a solid basis of occupation rule exerted separately by each occupying power over its assigned sector of the city. Each military government assumed responsibility for provision of food, power and other supplies and services needed to maintain the population and facilities of its sector.[9] To this end the West obtained after much negotiation rights of moving supplies and traffic through the Soviet Zone by rail, air, highway and waterway.* Within the sectors in turn each occupying power exerted the full authority of military government over the ward (Bezirke) administrations which had customarily transacted the larger part of the city's business.** Though financially the city remained

* In a very important agreement, Western air channels were recognized as open for flight without previous notice and rules to promote air safety over Berlin were laid down. With regard to train service, the Soviets insisted on Soviet control over locomotive and train operations within the Soviet zone. However, complex administrative arrangements were worked out to ensure Soviet service to sixteen trains per day and the net of rail lines was later extended. Besides provision for Western telephonic and cable lines running through the Soviet zone, certain facilities along the Autobahn were arranged. OMGUS, ACA Enactments, I, 50–53, 149–162, 227; Clay, Decision, 26, 361.

** In such matters as political affairs generally, press and information control, school and church affairs, restitution, courts, welfare and police the autonomy of the district administrations relative to the Magistrat was recognized on both the German and the Allied side. If the traditional administrative structure did not offer a foothold for sectoral control, special arrangements could be made as in the resolution of conflict over police organization. OMGUS, ACA Enactments, IV, 70–72; OMGUS, A Four Year Report, 63. All administrative operations, noted the former mayor of the city, that did not by their nature require centralized control—such as statistics or financial administration—were decentralized to the districts which had a very broad field of operations. In 1939 the all-city administration employed 12,000 persons, the district administrations some 60,000 persons. G. Böss, Berlin von Heute, Stadtverwaltung und Wirtschaft (Berlin, 1929), 17 ff.; Berlin im Neuaufbau, 25. This tendency to sectoralization was so strong that even in the heyday of the condominium regime it found juridical expression in the October 1946 city charter. The final sentence in Article 36 of the Provisional Constitution for Berlin read: "the Bezirke Administrations are subordinate in their activities to the Military Government

assimilated to the Soviet zone, since the banks in both areas remained closed, the payment restrictions on monetary transfers to the West did not hamper economic dealings.[10]

On the basis of this sectoral power, a complex pattern of condominium was developed. On the German side this was embodied chiefly in the city Magistrat, the all-city administration which had been set up by the Soviets upon capture of the city and which was continued after the Western powers moved in. The Magistrat's range of authority was considerable. Though all goods and services were separately provided by each occupying power, supplies of foodstuffs, coal and power were pooled and operated on a citywide basis subject to uniform standards. A limited extent of coordination was achieved over other industrial products and services, particularly building and manpower control.[11] Courts, schools, banking, price control, social insurance, labor offices, cultural facilities, and public utilities were all operated on a citywide basis. The police department was in form a single one though executive control was achieved on a sector basis.

The extent of this all-city German administration entailed corresponding responsibilities upon inter-Allied cooperation. Every action of the Magistrat—including removals, appointments, rulings, decrees, budgets—required the approval of the sector commanders sitting together as the Kommandatura. The Kommandatura had to give permission to the Municipal Bank to discontinue payment of one percent interest on current account deposits, to confirm appointments and ration norms, to assent to election dates, to organize the in-movements of coal and foodstuffs and the major principles which would guide their distribution within the city.[12] To facilitate action the lower organs of the Kommandatura were permitted to communicate to German officials their directives without formally clearing these through higher channels. The very intimacy of this partnership which involved a continuous stream of joint executive decisions gave it a certain solid footing. But some precarious inter-allied differences were not infrequently compounded by divergences having their origin chiefly in personal predilection. Hence this city administration could only be nursed along through resolution of a succession of crises at the Control Council level where there was

in the respective sectors." OMGUS, *ACA Enactments*, IV, 47. Employment patterns also reflected sector predominance, for the district administrations employed 57,000 as against 9,000 in the all-city offices. *Berlin in Neuaufbau*, 26.

greater latitude for compromise and a lesser degree of emotional involvement.[13]

II. The Achievements of the Control Council

An impressive façade of ceremonial observance, organization and condominium was built up by the zone commanders acting in concert as the Control Council. Concurrently an extended effort was made to give generalized expression to the ideological overlap which permeated zonal life and to mark out its bounds, point up its directions and indicate its standards. This work necessarily went slowly; it touched on sensitive issues; it was not motivated by compelling practical needs. Yet within the first eighteen months of the Control Council's existence an ambitious series of policy declarations, sometimes in the form of detailed enactments, were worked out under quadripartite auspices covering a miscellaneous ensemble of fields which ranged from manpower controls to church affairs, educational reform, marriage, prison custody.[14] Agreements on other important issues—including trust-busting (called decartelization), social insurance and principles governing trade unions and political parties—had surmounted the major hurdles.[15] In this work both East and West exhibited a spirit of moderation and aimed at creating a sort of halfway house. The East accepted the fundamental principles of a liberal state; the West leaned in the direction of social reform and property reorganization.

This attempt at ideological codification shaded into a parallel effort to maintain a uniform outer frame of economic life throughout the various zones. To this end, Reichsmark currency was made legal tender in satisfaction of debts arising from interzonal trade. Tariff schedules for communication and transport were raised by quadripartite enactment. The German tax system was revolutionized through a series of laws which raised to a new height its revenue potential and revised many of its fundamental features. Patterns and levels of price and wage control inherited from the Nazi regime were frozen and by specific inter-Allied decree upward adjustments on any important scale were made subject to specific quadripartite agreement.[16] By virtue of these actions the Zone Commanders undertook collective responsibility as the Control Council for the management of the financial frame of a fully controlled economy. This management involved making adjustments in the scale of money payments permitted major types of transactions in private and public affairs.* In consequence the financial frame of the various zonal economies was maintained on a quadripartite basis even though the actual course of reconversion going on within those economies and the disposition of output produced was wholly under zonal management.

These functions of normal civil government assumed by the Control Council were carried out hand in hand with repressive and punitive undertakings. One such involved the trial of Nazi and wartime leaders by the quadripartite International Military Tribunal at Nüremberg.

* This work of adjustment varied in different fields and was most successful in the earlier period of the occupation before negotiational rancor was aroused by basic conflict. This rancor probably was felt least in the important area of taxation which had been reorganized by issuance during 1946 of ten fundamental tax laws which revolutionized the German tax system. These laws left many inequities and asperities to be adjusted. Though no basic revision was undertaken, no less than five separate amendments received Control Council imprint during the year following the issuance of the basic legislation and some of these touched issues of consequence. For brief discussion, see OMGUS, *Report of the Military Governor,* Finance, no. 24, cumulative review, 5–7; Mabel Newcomer, "War and Postwar Developments in the German Tax System," *National Tax Journal,* I (1948), 5–11. The most important of these amendments reduced by more than half the effective rate of taxation enacted the year before on tobacco and cigars—an action which was brought on by German resistance to these taxes. But the experience through 1947 indicated increasing strain in negotiations. The effort to mitigate the severity of the Control Council income tax law received Control Council imprint in January 1948 with an emasculated content. See Walter Heller, "Tax and Monetary Reform in Occupied Germany," *Ibid.,* II (1949), 219, n. 9. The experience with price control, which was explicitly frozen on an ACA basis for "basic commodities" which were thereafter by agreement listed in detail, showed about the same degree of flexibility. Not too much trouble was encountered in negotiating minor adjustments of which three were put through in 1946, while five individual adjustments were agreed to quadripartitely through November, 1947 (sugar beets, calcium carbide, coke oven gas, sulfuric acid, calcium superphosphates). On these changes, see OMGUS, *Report of the Military Governor,* Trade and Commerce, no. 17, cumulative review, 34–36; no. 29, cumulative review, 20. Real trouble was occasioned in negotiating a coal and steel price increase for which the British had pressed persistently since October 1945. Since Soviet opposition here was mixed with a partial U.S. and French inclination to "hold the line," negotiational problems of inter-Allied control cannot be held responsible for failure to take the requisite action. For brief review, see *idem.* An ability to carry through more drastic and varied adjustments in a frozen pattern was indicated in the field of wage control. Some eight industries, employing 30 percent of the manual workers in the American zone, were given margin for wage changes of an appreciable size. For brief survey of these actions, each of which had to be separately negotiated through the Control Council machinery, see *Ibid.,* Manpower, Trade Unions and Working Conditions, no. 32, cumulative review, 20 ff.

The decisions and judgments of the Tribunal constituted a broad basis from which to develop standards, priorities and principles for denazification.* These were spelled out in quadripartite agreements which provided for removal of Nazis from leading positions, establishment of war crimes tribunals and adoption of general measures designed to discourage resumption of Nazi activity or expression of Nazi doctrine.[17]

The demilitarization agreements of the Control Council also were extensive. Under these agreements armed formations were to be disbanded, military institutions dissolved, military fortifications and underground facilities destroyed, armament plant dismantled, scientific research drastically curtailed and revival of militarism discouraged.[18] Some approach to a time-table for operations in at least two of these areas was obtained; frequent and detailed reporting threw light on zonal progress in other areas; and in connection with dismantling armament plant a specific program for quadripartite interzonal inspection was instituted.[19]

Although achievement in these repressive areas of Control Council activity was noteworthy, East-West collaboration reached its height in carrying out the two great punitive undertakings of the Potsdam agreement. The first of these involved loyal Western fulfillment of the Potsdam agreement directing the expulsion of the German population from the Sudetenland and the eastern territories "provisionally" ceded to Poland and to the USSR. Though this agreement did not obligate the West to open its zonal borders to the expelled population, these borders were opened wide enough to take in some 60 percent of the programmed exodus. Nor did the West dally over making the practical arrangements with the local, frontier and transportation authorities to handle a migration of some three million persons to be completed within fifteen months.

* Though the International Military Tribunal was organized apart from the Control Council and the Potsdam agreement, it functioned virtually as a part of it. Its decisions were incorporated by reference into basic Allied law to govern war criminal and denazification proceedings. The agreed documents of the prosecution, including the indictments and more particularly the long Tribunal judgments, took on great importance. Over the larger area of decisions the Tribunal was agreed, although the Soviet dissent on the acquittals of Schacht, Papen and Fritzsche and on the failure to declare the Reich cabinet and General Staff war criminal organizations had important implications. See OMGUS, *ACA Enactments*, I, 306–310; *Final Report . . . on Nüremberg War Crimes Trials*, 139–154. For the text of the Tribunal judgment and the Soviet dissent, see *Trial of the Major War Criminals before the International Military Tribunal* (Nüremberg, 1947–1949), I, 216–350.

Finally, the Western military government put the necessary pressure on the local German authorities to ensure their cooperation in receiving and providing for the expelled populations.[20]

The Potsdam reparations agreement had provided in one of its sections that the capital equipment found unnecessary in the Western zones for a German peacetime economy should be dismantled, used for reparations and in part distributed to the Soviets. A list of eastward reparations deliveries was to be agreed upon within six months. How could that list be contrived? It would have been simplest for the West to have made the requisite surveys and calculations and at the end of six months to have offered a list of reparations plants scheduled for dismantling and from which the Soviets could choose for their quarter share. But even if the West had undertaken to make the requisite decisions on their own determination, still they would have needed to become appraised of plant capacity that was to be retained for the use of the civilian German economy in the Soviet zone. The Soviets could only make the determination of needed plant capacity in their zone in coordination with the Western determinations. A common plan for a mutually agreeable level of industry would need to underlie both Western and Eastern determinations on needed and surplus plant capacity. The Soviets, moreover, would want to be sure that the West was dismantling to the largest possible extent since the larger the extent of Western Zone dismantling the larger the reparations flow to the Soviets. The West in turn would want to make sure that the requisite capacity was actually being retained in the eastern zones. The plants would need to be jointly appraised for purposes of determining a property value since the appraised value was needed in order to allocate a Soviet share. The Soviet quarter of dismantled plants could not be measured by considering every plant of equal value. Since the mutual interest was a strong one it was decided to negotiate jointly all the decisions needed to result in a final list of Western reparations deliveries. In these joint negotiations it was assumed that the industrial resources of the four zones were effectively pooled. To the western powers this assumption meant that through a reparations settlement effective quadripartite control would be extended in some form to the eastern zone. The assumption for the Soviets signified that through a reparations agreement they would obtain access to a liberal share of the industrial equipment of the western zones for use or transfer eastward as reparations.

Decisions required to derive necessary plant capacity for a peacetime German economy mutually governed each other with a varying discretionary range. Thus the over-all standard of living left to the Germans would govern rates of consumption and capital requirements for consumer goods. But a given living standard could be approximated in different ways and aggregate product requirements would depend upon the size of the population. The determination of population and living standards would involve specification of calorie needs. These could be met by different patterns of food consumption and these in turn could be satisfied by different combinations of German food output and food imports. These imports in their turn would require that some industrial capacity be allocated to support export trade though the make-up of this trade was subject to variation. Over-all levels of metal production, both ferrous and nonferrous, would control the projective output of metal-using goods and equipment; but here too a wide range of output could be obtained from a given materials base by variation in the pattern of commodity usage.

The fact that ranges of variation bounded discretion in coming to the basic decisions involved in the level of industry plan provided the handle by which so complex a project was driven within a short time-period through the Control Council by processes of *ad hoc* quadri-partite negotiation. Taking this handle, the Allies considered each decision separately, laid down their demands, talked fast and hard and in the end accommodated to one another by compromising on some middle range of values. The French and Soviets tended to pull requirements down while the British tended to pull them up. The Americans under Clay's and Draper's driving leadership clung to a middle position which on the balance won out sometimes through outright horse trading.*

The outcome was a level of industry plan which wiped out three fourths of Germany's metallurgical, chemical and heavy equipment and machinery industries and totally prohibited products with direct mili-

* "In fact, Dave Ginsburg and I told [Draper] . . . that when the Agreement was published, his picture would be on the frontispiece and underneath, in true Time style, the captious caption, 'Divide-by-Four'." So reported D. D. Humphrey in his account of the negotiations by which the level of industry plan was determined in the Economics Directorate. See his German mss, Chapter VII, "The Control Council's Greatest Achievement," 7. Horse-trading and "divide-by-four" characterized the agreements on estimate of German population, the needed amount of exports, the size of needed steel capacity and other basic pivots of the agreement. See B. U. Ratchford and W. D. Ross, *Berlin Reparations Assignment* (Chapel Hill, 1947), 91, 119–130, 150–165.

tary significance. The plan projected an over-all level of industrial output and a corresponding level of plant capacity officially estimated at half the prewar (1936) average or about the equivalent of the level of output reached in the bottom of the great depression. In operation the decline in output would have been greater than this because of a number of specific imbalances and shortages projected in the plan which resulted from the piecemeal nature of its negotiation. Outstanding examples of imbalance were in electric power, cement, petroleum refining, heavy chemicals and an extraordinarily tight balance of imports and exports.[21]

The level of industry plan, reached in March 1946, was only a frame which needed elaboration and implementation. It later was extended into areas where detail had been avoided or totally new plans were drawn up for areas such as fishing and shipping capacity which had not been covered.[22] Side by side with extension went the work of taking a census of industrial capacity actually in existence and of reaching agreement upon standards to be used for measurement of capacity. This census once taken was subject to verification by a program of inspection which at its height involved 20 inter-Allied inspection commissions travelling through the four zones to verify statements of retained capacity in all zones and of surplus capacity in the western zones. The next step was to distribute, industry by industry, required plant capacity between the eastern and western zones since upon this distribution hinged the extent of plant dismantling forthcoming from the western zones. In addition, agreement was obtained on an eight-point list of principles for the selection of particular plants.[23]

This cleared the way for compiling lists of plants within all four zones to be retained as essential and of plants to be removed from the western zones. By the end of 1946 retention lists were compiled for virtually all restricted industries and most of them were agreed. Dismantling lists for the western zones were less extensive. Of an estimated 2,000 eligible surplus plants only 740 plants were agreed by the end of 1946. For over half this number the agreement was tentative and for purposes of valuation only. A mere 290 plants were approved for valuation and notification of availability as reparations. Actual allocation or assignment for reparations to a given recipient country numbered again only half this total. Physical dismantling and deliveries had miniscule proportions.[24] Forward progress was hampered by innumerable detailed controversies on particular industries concerning eligibility for and extent of reparations, the appraisal of present capacity, the selection of particular plants or plant valuation.[25] But the major decisions involved in carrying out the Potsdam dismantling plan had been made, vested interests in its success had been created, a working procedure had been devised and an apparatus to this end had been mobilized on the Allied and on the German side.

III. Pathways of Unification

The work of the Control Council proceeded on the premise of German unification. This premise had some embodiment in quadripartitely directed actions which reestablished circuits of economic interchange between the eastern and western zones. Temporary movement of persons across zonal lines was facilitated and certain agricultural and power and gas grid exchanges were arranged.* Virtually unrestricted postal and communications exchange was reopened, easy circuits for rail and water transport were provided and an agency was established in Berlin under quadripartite direction to clear and settle reichsmark payments in trade between Berlin, the eastern and the western zones. While these actions permitted resumption of interzonal east-west trade this revived only slowly to the extent of 100 million marks of programmed trade during 1946 which was less than one-tenth of prewar trade between these areas.[26]

East-west interzonal trade could have been stepped up somewhat if more effective clearing agreements had been reached and if more coal and steel products had been available from the Ruhr. But the principal block is traceable to the framework within which trade was conducted. This framework essentially did not involve money for settling transactions. Incentive for engaging in trade was lacking unless individual transactions could be organized by the initiating parties on a reciprocal

---

* The exchange of power and gas on the old grid was partially restored on a balanced basis. Permanent migration of persons between zones was still forbidden except for returning prisoner of war and voluntary interzonal exchanges; but temporary movement of persons across the east-west line for commercial or official purposes was facilitated. Arrangements were made for pest and disease control and for a limited exchange of seeds and fertilizer supplies. *CFM Report*, Section IV, "Economic Problems," Part 3, Food and Rationing, 2; Part 4, Agriculture, 2–5, Appendix A, paragraphs 3A1(a), (b), (c), B, 4, 7, 8; Part 7, Internal Trade, 1–3; Part 9, Transportation, 205; Section VII, "Population Transfers," Part 4, German Refugees, 9–10. OMGUS, *ACA Enactments*, I, 56, 119, 227, 280, 295, 303, 321; II, 89, 155; IV, 55, 96; V, 71, 84, 86.

basis. There was none of the network of ties which currents of trade weave for themselves with the aid of sound money.

If economic connections were limited, the fissure between eastern and western Germany was complete in social and political realms. Neither any nationwide administrative centers nor any trace of central government functioned. Every nationwide body of importance in public or private form—clubs, professional societies, political parties, trade unions, corporations—had been dissolved and reconstituted on a basis which did not cross the east-west line. Even the laws enacted by the Control Council on social and political matters were enforced, implemented and adjudicated in the respective zones according to the unfettered discretion of the zone commanders.

The zonal areas, east and west, thus were effectively sundered despite the pressure for unification exerted by the Control Council regime. This pressure came to focus first on the creation of the central administrative agencies promised in the vague terms of the Potsdam communique. Agreed upon plans for six key central administrative agencies were worked out in the Control Council machinery in a short enough time.[27] True to the Potsdam formula the planned agencies were not endowed with independent power by way of control of facilities, funds or zonal operations; and technically no provision was made for interlinking them since they were subordinated directly to the corresponding functional organs of the Control Council.[28]

The second major center of centralizing pressure revolved around nationwide merger of political parties and trade unions.[29] For the Soviets these measures would anchor the foundations of the Control Council regime and would correspondingly narrow the Western range of choice. For the West, these measures would open up so many avenues by which Western influence could be transmitted and applied wherever the merged organizations, with their predominantly non-communist leadership, would be active in the Eastern zones. German leaders and public opinion supported these measures and pushed ahead wherever possible in their execution. Though the western Social Democracy remained passive or hostile, both the trade union and the liberal-bourgeois political leaders of East and West developed various forms and organs for interim meeting and action pending a definite decision on merger by the Control Council.[30]

However, actual formation of the central administrative departments and fusion of the trade unions and liberal-bourgeois political parties was stopped by the French veto in the Control Council. The Soviets believed that "France was receiving too much financial assistance from the United States to maintain such strong opposition unless it met with our acquiescence."[31] The Soviet suspicion was essentially correct. France was unquestionably dependent upon American assistance, dollar loans and coal allocations.* Moreover, her zone was so small that it could have been neglected in unifying action without incurring danger that the French would continue to stand out.[32]

Acquiescence in the French veto, however, did not have the conspiratorial character which the Soviets inferred. There was genuine irritation with the French in Berlin and in Washington.[33] But the French had made it plain that their opposition was implicit with national honor. And within a policy of ambivalence the achievement of any one of the vetoed actions promised only modest fruits. Certainly neither the formation of central agencies nor the unification of parties or unions by themselves would have altered the complexion of the Control Council regime. Central agencies set apart from the active currents of national life would have been stillborn. National parties and trade unions as isolated national entities could hardly have become vital institutions. These measures in combination would have created something of a groundwork for unification. But this groundwork would have seemed anomalous in a political and economic setting of zonalization. This feeling of anomaly and of the thinness of the proposed unifying measures probably was at the bottom of Anglo-American toleration of the French veto. The Anglo-American powers were unwilling to humiliate the French by coercive means over concrete decisions of limited weight and uncertain quality. They were not so wrong in this. The means for vitalizing the Control Council regime lay in another quarter, monetary reform.

Monetary reform already had been partially carried through by the Soviets in their zone by closing the banks and voiding the Reich public debt. After some degree of reflation by Soviet currency issuance, the relative liquid asset supply of the eastern zone was about a third of that of the western zones where the banks had been reopened.[34] The resulting

* It is sufficient to note that a two billion dollar loan was granted to France in May 1946, that French troops landed in Indo-China on British sufferance, that French economic life hinged upon receipt of Ruhr and American coal. For a case of brutal use of U.S. power against the French, see W. D. Leahy, *I Was There, The Personal Story of the Chief of Staff to Presidents Roosevelt and Truman* . . . (New York, 1950), 372 ff.

disparity in market conditions made a fundamental gulf between the eastern and western economies. It was provisionally dammed off by application of restrictions on east-west monetary transfers but its elimination was the critical prerequisite to restoration of preconditions for a smooth flow of economic interchange between eastern and western Germany.* This hiatus between the zones could be eliminated only by carrying through a monetary reform which would even up monetary conditions in the two areas, repudiate the old Reich debt and drastically liquidate the monetary overhang. Reform was expected by Germans and urged by all shades among German political groups.** Reform was

---

* The payment restrictions prohibited monetary transfers east-west except in conjunction with current commodity transactions. Their existence was sanctioned by the Western powers. See *CFM Report*, Section IV, Part 10, (e) Banking, paragraphs 15, 20, 23, 27. The need for restrictions has been variously indicated and was felt most acutely in the earliest phase of the Occupation. Wolf, "Geld," *loc. cit.*, 221 f; G. Schaffer, *Russian Zone* (SRT Publications, U.S.A., 1947), 46 ff.; J. Kuczinski, "Geld und Geldwert," *Die Wirtschaft*, 1 (1946) 114 f; *Tägliche Rundschau*, 23 January 1947; Bruno Gleitze, "Zur Finanzpolitischen Lage Ende 1945," (typewritten statement by a prominent SPD economist serving in the Soviet central administration for finance), 2–4. The peril for unification involved in the east-west monetary hiatus was most clearly outlined in Eduard Wolf, "Der Geldüberschuss" (Deutsches Institut für Wirtschaftsforschung, Berlin, April 1946—typewritten study prepared for the Institut) 113–5; "Um die Zukunft der Kreditwirtschaft," *Wirtschaftszeitung*, I (17 June 1946).

** Reform was widely anticipated and made up a prominent theme in German rumour reports. See OMGUS, *Report of the Military Governor*, Finance and Property Control, no. 5 (November, 1945), 13; *Ibid.*, no. 6 (December, 1945), 8–9, 15; no. 24 (June, 1947), 37 ff.; *CDG* Report, Appendix P, "German Public Opinion on Monetary and Financial Reform." See also unpublished reports of local military government units and of intelligence and information control agencies. Extracts are given from these that the flavor may be judged: "Another sore point . . . is the increasing wave of rumours concerning the future status of the German Reichsmark." "The expected devaluation of currency is having a considerable effect on civilian economic life." Reference is made to "the many censorship submissions referring to large stockpiles of goods from various sources." "Uppermost in the German economic mind are apprehensions concerning devaluation of the Mark which is widely held to be impending." The desire for immediate drastic reform was possibly most widespread in the eastern zone where it was popularized in the catching phrase of "Strichtag"—drawing the line with the past. But the immediacy of reform on a somewhat less drastic basis was also believed desirable in the West. Binder reported that at the December 1945 Frankfurt conference: "Gegen gewisse Wiederstand wurde in der Konferenz zunächst eine Übereinstimmung nach der Richtung erzielt dass die Währungsreform nicht mehr aufschiebar sei." Binder, "Die Sanierung von Deutschlands Währung und Finanzen" (Tübingen, 1949—mimeographed), 2. Only later

needed to enlarge the role of markets and of decentralized decision-making and as well to regularize Soviet and French exploitation of the German economy.[35] It also was needed to undermine the black market and to cut off possible currency reserves secreted by the Nazi underground or flowing illegally across frontiers.[36]

Those who believed that reform would be premature overlooked its renovating effects on production and its far-reaching dynamic influence in the society as well as in the economy.* Reform could not have been confined to mere readjustment of financial claims. It required either centralization of control over and access to old currency plates and reserves coupled with possible calling in for redemption of currency notes of high denominations or printing a new currency for com-

---

during 1946 and 1947 did Western German opinion favor delay. On this shift of opinion, cf. E. Wolf, "Probleme der Finanziellen Kriegsliquideriung" (Vortag am 13th Diskussionsabend des Deutsches Instituts für Wirtschaftsforschung, Berlin 4 December 1946—mimeographed), 10.

* See Wolf, "Probleme der Finanziellen Kriegsliquidierung," 10 ff. for a statement of objections to immediate reform; and for a later version, see H. Mendershausen, "Prices, Money and the Distribution of Goods in Postwar Germany," *American Economic Review*, XXXIX (1949), 647. For an effective rebuttal, see OMGUS, *A Plan for the Liquidation of War Finance and the Financial Rehabilitation of Germany* (a report submitted by the Colm-Dodge-Goldsmith mission to Germany which includes the text of the report with a preface dated 20 May 1945 and a collection of supporting studies as appendices, paged non-continuously and dated 10 June 1946) [hereafter cited C-D-G Report], 3–4; Wolf, "Probleme der Finanziellen Kriegsliquidierung," 12–15; H. Sauermann, "The Consequences of the Currency Reform in Western Germany," *Review of Politics*, XII (1950), 179 ff. It was well said in rebuttal that "waiting until general economic conditions improve involves the risk that the confidence in the currency and thereby the incentive to work and to sell may deteriorate further" and that "the economic chaos that is likely to result from an undetermined postponement of financial reform would probably destroy for a long time to come the chance of creating any . . . central government in a democratic state." *C-D-G Report*, 3–5. In none of the surrounding countries which put through monetary reforms of a more or less drastic character was the complex dialectic of delay given validity. As Leon H. Dupriez brings out in his classic monograph, *Monetary Reconstruction in Belgium* (New York, 1947), it was desirable to act not in the full tide of a course of economic recovery which planning and executing reform would only unsettle but "before any reorganization of economic activity" and preferably while the public still was in commotion. *Ibid.*, 13, 81. For a general survey of European monetary reforms, see F. H. Klopstock, "Monetary Reform in Liberated Europe," *American Economic Review*, XXXVI (1946), 578 ff. The date of publication of this article is suggestive of the way in which timing was viewed in financial reform thinking in countries other than Germany.

mon use in the entire country. The unifying effects of a sound currency would have been reinforced by the necessary reinstitution of a central banking system to replace the old Reichsbank network and to serve as a means for carrying out the reform, as a custodial agency for the new money and as a source of credit control and inter-regional credit and payment clearing.* Finally, monetary reform would have been felt to be incomplete without an effective program of *Lastenausgleich*.**

A monetary reform which created a central bank, which reorganized the universe of debts and financial claims payable in money, which centralized control over the old or was coupled with issuance of a new currency, which imposed a levy on tangible property on a scale and in a form designed to equalize war burdens and losses—such a reform would create the social basis for a new Germany. It would set this Germany in a single mould and would by its dynamizing effect go a long way toward generating new trends toward unification. Central departments would have been vitalized in operation against the background of a central bank, merged unions and merged parties. The heads of the agencies and of the bank would have been forced by the pressure of intertwining activities to meet jointly and to work out comprehensive programs. Once this corner was turned other central agencies would have been created since incipient projects to this effect made headway under relatively discouraging conditions.[37] If the agencies formally would have been powerless, the prestige which their recommendations would possess and the clear tendency of the occupying powers to widen German latitude to facilitate inter-Allied agreement would soon have vested in these departments much of the substance if not the outward form of a provisional German government. This would particularly have tended to become true if the departmental chiefs and their advisory councils had been selected from among the different political parties or, in other words, if the central German leadership had been composed on a united front basis.[38]

---

* "A financial reform for Germany as a whole requires common measures in the four zones, as well as an essential minimum of central institutions such as an agency for the issue of currency and the determination of a consistent credit policy." *C-D-G Report*, 4.

** On the need and call for *Lastenausgleich*, see earlier, pp. 8–10.

CHAPTER VI

QUADRIPARTITE MONETARY REFORM[1]

I. The French-Soviet Position

MONETARY REFORM was objectively and administratively feasible. It was called for by fundamental German and Allied interests. Expectations of monetary reform had already paralyzed the limited steering function which a weak and worthless currency could have. Neighboring countries had either opened the gates for price inflation or carried through monetary reforms of one or another kind. Reform was required to curtail the black market and minimize profiteering. Action also was desirable to avoid a race for occupation expenditure of unlimited currency reserves. Monetary reform was partially carried through in one zone and was needed urgently on an all-Reich basis. Every long run consideration of ostensible occupation policy called for reform. If all this is true, why and how could monetary reform have been delayed for three dreadful years? How could the action have been missed in the early period of the Control Council regime? What forces, what instructions, what viewpoints blocked successful negotiations? These questions are not easily answered and answers do not fall into any clear-cut mould.

Perhaps the first requirement was a policy favoring drastic monetary reform and the formation of a unified regime throughout occupied Germany. In the early period of the occupation policy formation was complex. In the home countries authority over German affairs was likely to be divided among two or more main governmental departments with a corresponding dispersion of responsibility. Since knowledge in governmental capitals about precise conditions in Germany was uncertain and fragmentary, policy instructions had to be left general, vague, or contingent. Broad latitude was necessarily given to the responsible Theater

101

Command in posing problems and developing the direction of negotiations. But neither the Commanding General nor his principal staff officers were singly or collectively likely to have well developed opinions on problems of monetary policy. Much would be left to the principal monetary advisor. Over-all occupation policy would be involved both by way of encouragement and specific prohibitions. At one stage or another home government assent would be involved.[2] Thus the factors in policy formation were complex and interrelated.

Once a clear-cut mandate was adopted, it would be applied successfully only if the principal negotiating representative with his close staff associates agreed with and strove to carry out that mandate; if these representatives had the confidence and support of the person charged with over-all responsibility for military government; if the execution of this mandate was not hindered by hostile or incongruent over-all occupation policy; and if the representatives of at least one influential occupying power were able to take the lead, give support to weaker colleagues, and develop and push through a program by utilization of all available resources of position and policy. These are basic requirements, and if they fail in any of their interlocking parts—governmental mandate, willing and able staff negotiators, support of the theater topside, and congruent over-all occupation policy—no further progress along the pathway of monetary reform can be made.

Some central German banking organization was a necessary component of a master agreement on financial reform. Oddly enough, this issue was dormant until the late winter months of 1945/6. The British delegation were interested in centralized financial action but their efforts in this direction took the form of proposals for a central administration, expenditure control, and tax adjustment. Neither the French nor the Soviets sponsored action. The American delegation was caught in the throes of Morgenthauism and had neither the capacity nor the personnel to take large views, but fortunately the Morgenthau influence lifted sufficiently to permit a plan for a central banking structure. This envisaged a highly federalistic system of state central banks banding together in a central banking "commission" subject to the control of an Allied banking agency and endowed with sweeping authority over both federal and state banking and credit questions. Although this solution was prejudicial to the long run institutional requirements for centralized finance in Germany, it suited a transition period in which the occupying powers would unwillingly give up direct control over their zonal banking systems or permit the immediate re-creation of a centralized banking system.

The solution drew support from all concerned parties. It provided for dismantling the large banking combines and their network of affiliated branches. This appealed to the Soviets and to the French. The French were also satisfied with the general decentralization bias of the proposal so far as German institutional structure was concerned. The British were induced reluctantly to approve the proposal on account of the elements of centralization which it did provide. Thus sustained, the proposal won general approval at the committee level in the early spring of 1946. It was never carried out, since by the time it reached higher Control Council levels the prospects for financial reform and effective unification had begun to falter. However, a precondition to monetary reform was accessible if a master agreement on monetary reform itself came within reach.[3]

Since available information on the origin of French policy is slight and since French policy played either a secondary or negative role during the period, a survey of the ability to reach a master agreement may well commence with review of the French position. There is nothing to indicate that the French control authorities and their directing staff in Paris had worked out any particular policy for monetary reform. No sign of such a policy was indicated by formal or informal publication or in negotiation. A French government had only recently been installed and the directive layers of the German occupation were hastily recruited, chiefly from the retreating Vichyites and from the contingent from North Africa which participated in Allied invasion of occupied France in 1944.[4] Further, the decisive voice in French policy through 1945 and part of 1946 was that of De Gaulle and his political associates. Taken together, these circumstances ensured that a program which would tie together and dynamize the Allied occupation and give a progressive solution to German problems would not emanate from Baden-Baden.

There were indications that the French would not block financial reform, although they would not initiate it. Over-all French occupation policy was oriented to maximum exploitation of German resources, and with a weak currency there were limits to the efficiency with which this could be done. In the Control Council negotiations of 1945 the French representative was rather colorless and participated only slightly in debates on monetary reform, although he evinced understanding of the need for curative action on the debt front. Specifically, he clearly rejected the anti-reform outlook of the British delegation and supported a partial repudiation of the Reich debt. Beginning with 1946, the principal French spokesman in Berlin on financial matters was experienced in economic affairs, personally able to cope with large questions of financial reconstruction, and apparently sympathetic to action on the currency question.[5]

There were perhaps two decisive features which would have led to imposition of a French veto. The first would have been stringency in the allocation of currency to finance occupation spending which could not be handled through Länder budgets. The French were ambitious spenders. Considering the smaller size of their zone and its more meager equipment and resources, they exploited their zone as successfully as did the Soviets. The French zone supported a relatively dense layering of occupation personnel who were billeted and provisioned from German resources; in addition, French economic policy in Germany was oriented to requisitioning, from German industrial production and forestry, resources for maximum export at official prices.[6] This policy, particularly in its earlier phases, depended on possession of liberal currency supplies. Hence French assent to monetary reform would have been contingent upon comparatively generous allocation of currency available directly or indirectly for the issuing authority. Since the Soviets would have made a similar claim, this aspect can be handled in discussing the Soviet program. Limitations found palatable by the Soviets would have been deemed acceptable by the French.

A second possible objection is more weighty and was rated by British opinion as decisive. It concerned French hesitations growing out of the centralizing aspects of monetary reform.[7] Issuance and control of new currency is centralized by its nature. But the French were not opposed *per se* to active measures of economic unification of Germany; their opposition to unification was contingent upon the association therewith of elements of a central German government. They were opposed to the formation of important German governmental agencies before French territorial and political demands on Germany had been settled. Agencies shaped along federalistic lines and subordinate to Allied executive bodies were viewed more indulgently. In the spring of 1946 the French concurred in plans for a reconstructed banking system which would have culminated in a German counterpart of a Federal Reserve Board functioning under an Allied banking commission. Execution of monetary reform inevitably would have fostered pressures for over-all political centralization, but at its inception and during its earliest phases the approved plans would have sufficed. Thus, sustained French opposition to monetary reform appears unlikely, granted a federalized banking system and liberal distribution of funds for occupation spending. The French would never have initiated monetary reform; they might have dragged in the later phases of planning; they almost certainly would not have blocked it altogether.

The Soviet position differed from the French in many respects. It was dynamic, positive, and sweeping. Though we have no inner documentary evidence on the Soviet position, the grounds for inference provided by public action and Soviet participation in Control Council discussion are persuasive. This evidence indicates readiness in the fall and winter of 1945/6 to agree with a policy of immediate and drastic monetary reform. By their actions within their zone and during Control Council negotiations they indicated from the earliest period their repugnance to any legitimation of the Nazi war debt. They plainly desired to eliminate inflationary pressure and to organize a new banking system. To the extent permitted by continuation of the old currency, they did this unilaterally in their zone. The Soviet representatives definitely desired to extend this policy to other zones and to complete it with new currency. In supplement to monetary reform proper the Soviets proposed a capital levy in January 1946.[8] They also approved the formation of a provisional central banking system. Thus with respect to the essential components of monetary reform—a central bank, monetary liquidation, and equalization (*Lastenausgleich*)—the Soviets were positively oriented.

The principal Soviet representatives were competent in monetary matters and evinced keen understanding of the broad aspects of the question. Although they were close negotiators, they appreciated the need for compromise. However, in place of a detailed program they seemed to have a very general position marked out by a series of antipathies and attractions. The absence of program is suggested by the nature of their statements in Control Council debate and their failure to advance positive proposals except for the capital levy. The principal Soviet representatives were relatively preoccupied with zonal concerns. They probably lacked the ability to develop a program utilizing to the maximum the available common grounds and couched in terms which would not offend Western sensibilities. It is also possible that topside

Soviet strategy makers in Germany did not grasp the unique strategic character of monetary reform.[9]

A possible source of Soviet objection to immediate monetary reform, the desire to retain authority over the unlimited currency issue of military marks, diminished in importance. Certainly during the year 1945 the rate of Soviet military spending financed by military mark issuance was extremely high. Soviet combat armies were only gradually repatriated during 1945 and the following year and their maintenance costs were correspondingly large. The armies were provisioned chiefly from German sources; tax receipts were slow in starting to flow; and a backlog of troop pay roll was paid in nonconvertible German currency. The extent of currency issuance by Soviet sources is not known, although estimates by well-informed sources do not run to more than 6 to 8 billion Reichsmarks or a rate of somewhat less than a billion RM a month during the 1945 occupation period.[10]

During the last quarter of 1945 taxation began to provide revenue for a considerable part of this load. Over 500 million RM is known to have been obtained for occupation spending from tax resources. The newly formed German governments had taken hold and the wheels of economic life and payments flows were beginning to turn. Demobilization continuously cut away the size of the occupation forces. Stern pressure was placed upon German governments to deliver a maximum of their tax revenue for occupation purposes. Whole categories of German civil expenditures were postponed or prohibited, quarterly budgets were enacted and their execution was rigorously watched to ensure delivery of budget surpluses at all government levels, from Gemeinde to the zonal administration. An important factor in budget revenues was the alcohol excise which was boosted in October 1945 by 3,000 percent as well as other Control Council tax increases enacted over the winter of 1945–6. Since Soviet zone alcohol production was sizeable, the alcohol revenues—which during 1946 alone reached 3 billion RM and accounted for 40 percent of total tax revenues—helped turn the financial tide in the Soviet zone. As a result of swelling revenues and severe German expenditure controls some 7 billion RM were raised from German budgets during 1946 out of a total 10 billion RM revenue. Since it is highly dubious that expenditure outlets for this revenue were available, the Soviet report officially made in July 1946 and privately explained to eastern German finance ministries during the winter of 1945–6 that military mark issuance had ceased is highly credible.[11]

Out of all this grows the inference that in the first stages of the occupation the Soviets would have resisted issuance of a new currency because of their immense spending requirements preceding troop demobilization and the resumption of full scale tax payments. Issuance of a new currency during the latter months of 1945 and possibly the early months of 1946 would only have been possible if sizeable currency allocations had been made to the Soviets and if future grants of currency to the occupation had been based on liberal principles. This was the pattern encountered in Austria and the circumstances in Germany were similar. The Soviet army finance administration seems to have been organizationally separate from the financial staff of military government, but both groups apparently were aware of the desirability of restoring financial discipline and were willing to move in this direction.[12] Without the prompting of inter-Allied settlements, Soviet requisition on their zonal budgets for occupation spending fell from 7 billion RM in 1946 to 4.2 billion RM in 1948.[13] That leverage existed for a resolution of potential conflicts in the general area of currency allocations was indicated during the hastily conducted "last minute" currency reform negotiations of February and March 1948. Agreement quickly was reached on terms acceptable to the Western powers on allocation of currency for purposes of occupation spending.[14] The principal Soviet negotiating representatives wanted a reform, reform was congruent with their basic occupation policy, and their currency spending requirements after 1945 would have permitted participation in reform. But the Soviets do not seem to have had a governmental mandate to take the initiative and apply the sustained pressure needed for successful negotiation of the requisite broad program of action. It is also dubious that on the Theater level the Soviets could mobilize the negotiatory ability, tact, and diplomacy required to carry such a program through.

II. British-U.S. Opposition to Monetary Reform

The leadership potential which the Soviets lacked on the issue of monetary reform the British probably had. But this potential was utilized in opposing, not sponsoring, reform. British policy consisted of a stubborn fight to orient Control Council policy along lines of misapplied monetary orthodoxy. The principal British staff member responsible for the development and negotiation of financial policy was S. P. Chambers, a Treasury representative with a ready wit and charming manner which gilded outdated conceptions of monetary policy and public finance. Although able in negotiation, he was unresponsive to the need for drastic monetary action inherent in the German situation.[15] During U.S.-British discussions on financial policy early in 1945, Chambers argued passionately that the fate of the occupation hinged on realizing balanced budgets during the initial period of the occupation.[16] In a detailed British program for financial policy, the themes attended to were the need for additional RM printing facilities, resumption of tax collections, expenditure control, administration of tax offices, and similar matters.[17]

This program was translated into a series of working proposals which were presented for Control Council negotiation. To a substantial degree these proposals determined the course of quadripartite policy during the first six to nine months of the Control Council regime. The principal papers involved were comprehensive proposals for tax increases, expenditure and loan controls, handling of the Reich debt, a central finance ministry, and a relaxation of price control.[18] The proposals stemmed from a policy of avoiding monetary reform.

Recognition and resumption of payments on the service of the Reich public debt was specifically suggested. In the Berlin negotiations, the British stated frankly that they favored "complete recognition" of the Reich debt even though "this would mean over a period of years rising prices and wages so that the burden of the debt on the income of Germans was reduced to manageable proportions." The relative excess in liquid assets was to be handled by a policy of "steady increase both of prices and wages over a period of two or three years" in the order of "a 200 to 300 percent rise." A first step in this direction was the proposal to raise coal prices by 66 percent and to establish limits for the quick increase of food prices up to 10 percent and other prices up to 50 percent.[19] The expanding national income fed by this controlled inflation would enable a reorganized tax system equipped with higher rate levels to bring in the revenues required to balance budgets and to help "drain off as much as possible of the dangerously large excess of free purchasing power which is now present in the German economy."[20]

British expenditure proposals required local and state governments to balance their budgets and, aside from short term cash advances, to resort to indebtedness only to finance capital improvements. Deficit financing for major expenditure areas was to be placed under centralized control. Great importance was attributed in the British view to exchange of full information regarding emergency and occupation expenditures imposed upon German budgets by the Allied Powers to permit gauging of the public finance burdens. The "most important and the most urgent action" was "probably to balance revenue and expenditure."[21]

If the policy of drift and adjustment to the institutional *status quo* was defended, the policy of financial reform and capital levy was attacked on all fronts. Monetary reform was in Chambers' view discredited by its full or partial invalidation of the Reich debt. This would render the banks "insolvent" and would mean in turn that "all the savings banks and other credit institutions which have large deposits with the bigger banks would also be insolvent and the whole existing financial structure would collapse like a pack of cards." There was something disturbing to the British about the outright Soviet policy of closing the old banks and "smashing the big German banks." The policy of reform would "shake the confidence of the Germans in the Mark" whereas Chambers' policy of inflation would presumably strengthen that confidence. He argued that in place of an oversupply of currency was a dangerously short supply and that "drastic overnight cutting down of the value of the mark would result in an acute shortage of actual currency in places where it is needed." When these arguments did not avail, the policy of reform was shunted off by prediction of its failure unless budgets were brought into balance beforehand. "We should consider the question of the oversupply of the currency when we are satisfied that there will be no further oversupply. It would be premature to take drastic measures with respect to the currency if we left expenditures by governmental authorities exceeding the revenues."[22]

The British opposition to monetary reform was strong. Even an aggressively oriented American policy might have been stalemated by British objection after French and Soviet support had been won. To argue thus, however, is to overestimate the deep-rootedness of the British position. The Labour Party victory in 1945 would have permitted an appeal to a friendly and progressively oriented British Government to change a Theater policy developed on a philosophy which played havoc with defeated Germany and which was strangely out of tune with a Labour government. The Americans and British were intimately associated in an array of enterprises; and the fate of the British economy was contingent upon the protracted negotiations for a British loan then in course. With this source of pressure available and the political complexion of Britain to reinforce it, a London veto of a conservative Theater policy probably could have been obtained. To have achieved this result, a resolute monetary reform policy and skillful and able leadership would have been needed on the American side. These did not then exist and later only slowly and partially came into existence.

The story of the development of American policy on monetary reform is complex with its many strands sometimes tied in curious knots. The first draft directive for the determination of monetary policy in areas controlled by Western armies under General Eisenhower actually was comparable to the Soviet policy of immediate monetary reform. This directive, which was dispatched to Eisenhower in May, 1944, ordered military government to close the banks and financial institutions, ban service on the Reich debt, declare a general moratorium, reopen banks when deemed practicable but keep accounts and deposits blocked except for "limited withdrawals for necessary living expenses to avoid personal hardship and to permit essential business enterprises to carry on authorized operations." High denominations of outstanding currency were to be called in for blocked deposit if necessary as a "measure of inflation control."[23] A few months later this policy was reversed on application of the U.S. Treasury Department. The need was alleged for a drastic revision of the May, 1944 directive deriving from a study of recent military government experience in Italy and reconsideration of the issues involved. There should be a "minimum of financial controls or regulations until it is possible to introduce a comprehensive anti-inflationary and control program following an opportunity to observe" post-occupation conditions in Germany as they actually developed. Pending this more detailed study it was inadvisable to attempt the May, 1944 program before "adequate preparations" were made to ensure its "administrative feasibility," bearing in mind that "a comprehensive program cannot be practically placed into effect in the first few weeks or more of occupation."

In line with this argument the directive was revised by making the closing of banks and institution of a moratorium discretionary rather than mandatory; the directive on blocking of accounts was deleted as was the discretionary instruction to call in large denomination currency notes; and the prohibition against service of the public debt was replaced by a provision requiring the resumption of debt service. The revised directive was issued in August, 1944 and determined SHAEF policy.[24]

By the time the final directive was issued in April, 1945 as part of the basic occupation directive known as JCS-1067, the specific Morgenthau imprint was more clearly identifiable. There was a specific injunction against measures designed to "maintain, strengthen or operate the German financial structure" except for the negative purposes specified in the directive. Opening banks was mandatory, though stock exchanges, insurance companies and other non-banking financial institutions could be closed for as long a period as was deemed appropriate. No directive was issued to maintain uniform monetary conditions throughout Germany. Financial policies were to be promoted in the Control Council only as might be necessary to carry out the negative purposes specified in the directive. A general excuse or mandate for inaction was provided by the instruction to shift responsibility for public finance measures on to the German "authorities."[25]

Lewis Douglas, originally recruited to serve as the Military Governor's financial advisor, understandably resigned when his efforts to modify the directive to permit the exercise of economic and monetary controls were fruitless.[26] Appropriately, General Clay appointed the Morgenthau representative then at General Eisenhower's headquarters as his principal financial advisor. Under this leadership for the first six months of the Occupation the Finance Division in Military Government industriously worked to carry out this directive.[27]

The outright Morgenthau representative in finance was soon replaced, but the constraining force of the Morgenthau-oriented JCS-1067 directive held over. It was sufficiently modified to free the American representative from the task of stating that American policy favored resumption of service on the Nazi debt. On a "personal" basis it was even possible for the principal American representative participating in the November-December 1945 monetary reform discussions to advocate a policy of drastic monetary reform.[28] However, there was no governmental mandate to back up action.

The lack of an appropriate governmental mandate was not made up until a mission of specialists, headed by two well known economists, was dispatched to Germany to devise an anti-inflation and financial rehabilitation program. Working intensively for ten weeks, the mission produced the Colm-Dodge-Goldsmith Report with its complex and thorough going plan for the reconstruction of the German financial system. In this process the Theater Commander, his headquarters staff, and the principal finance negotiator were persuaded of the need for monetary reform and given a working program for its consummation.

There were long delays before Washington assent was obtained. The mission plan was complex and Washington objections were not ill-taken. After direct petition by General Clay to Secretary of State Byrnes, the plan finally was approved in late August 1946.[29]

On 2 September 1946 the American plan was introduced into the Coordinating Committee of the Control Council and on 7 September it appeared on the agenda of the Finance Directorate. The discussions of monetary reform broken off some nine months before thus were resumed after sixteen months of occupation had elapsed. The Soviets and the French gave immediate assent. The Theater opposition of the British had been undermined by appeal to London and by considered reflection in Berlin. Within three days, on 12 September, agreement on the broad principle of drastic monetary reform accompanied by some kind of capital levy was obtained.

III. C-D-G Plan Negotiated

Quadripartite agreement on the principle of immediate and drastic monetary reform was reached in September 1946, but the agreement was to bare principle only. There were many combinations of methods to use and as many difficult decisions to make. The same combination of methods could be given different quantitative expression. No one was certain of the order of magnitude of German social product, or of the production potential and goods availability which might appear in the period immediately following monetary reform. Judgment was involved in the endowment of the German economy with sufficient liquidity to meet its liquidity requirements without overindulging spending proclivities. Special arrangements would be required for the conversion of funds by business enterprise, persons contaminated with Nazi background, governmental agencies, and foreign persons. Virtually all these questions had political aspects which one or another of the occupying powers felt not to be congruous with its interests. Above all, how could this agreement be negotiated before the hourglass of quadripartite unity had run out? By September 1946 the slow tempo of diplomatic negotiations needed to be accelerated or no agreement could result.

This need for quick action and for a clear-cut solution was both fostered and hindered by the Colm-Dodge-Goldsmith report which constituted the main starting point of the post-September 1946 monetary discussions. The report did valiant service to the cause of reform in a number of respects. It gave monetary reform prominence as a measure of occupation policy crucial for the fate of the peace settlement and German economic recovery. It threw the weight of its cogently argued position in favor of a comprehensive solution which liquidated and did not merely block the monetary overhang and the Reich government debt. Furthermore, it concentrated attention on the need to accompany monetary reform with complementary measures which were either to precede or to follow the reform itself: adjustments in price and wage control, institution of expenditure controls and realignment in basic areas of German expenditure policy, settlement and limitation of occupation costs, and reconsideration of the tax structure. Finally, the report furthered the cause of the association of monetary reform with fundamental measures of property taxation and burden equalization, and it worked out proposals to this end which cut deeply into the established property and income system and still did not assume the political form or give promise of assuming characteristics of formal socialization. To the extent that the American and the British Governments were persuaded of the need for measures of a complexion which included a capital levy collectible in kind—and this was a *sine qua non* of agreement with the Soviets on monetary reform—much of the credit may be laid to the Colm-Dodge-Goldsmith mission report.[30]

The most distinctive feature of the C-D-G plan was the combination of monetary reform proper with an extensive program for equalization of property holdings to spread more widely and equitably within the German community the losses arising out of the war. We have already pointed out how deeply felt and insistent was the call in the German community for an effective program of equalization-of-burdens or, in the German, *Lastenausgleich*.[31] The German community was less aware that any effective and speedy *Lastenausgleich* could only be carried through by virtual state appropriation of wealth holdings and claims through measures which bore considerable potential for socialization of the properties affected.[32] (See chapter I, pp. 8–9). This handing over of property to the government was projected on a large scale in the C-D-G Report. Two measures of extraordinary property taxation were devised to this end. The first measure would have stripped from the banks and financial institutions virtually all of their 40 billion RM holdings of corporate and municipal bonds and building and land mortgages—which comprised their most valuable category of assets—and placed these obligations in a changed form in the hands of a government financial agency. This was to be achieved by first *liquidating non-Reich indebtedness* at the same ratio as monetary assets (90 percent) and then *replacing the liquidated private debt with a debt owed to the public*. In addition to displacement of private debt, a fraction of the clear equity of all tangible income-bearing property was to be placed under debt obligation bearing a low rate of interest. For unincorporated property this obligation was to take the form of a conventional type mortgage instrument or participation share. For incorporated property the obligations were to be manifested provisionally in a special issue of corporate stock entitling its holders to a share of disbursed earnings. At the 50 percent rate suggested in the C-D-G Report these obligations, together with those replacing private debt, according to preliminary estimates would have brought in some 96 billion RM. Since the rate of interest as well as the annual rate of repayment was left flexible, the proposed mortgage on property would constitute a powerful tool for government policymaking.

This levy laid on tangible property and given scope by the conversion which it effected of private debt into a kind of public mortmain could not take account of the property owner's circumstances or resources. It accordingly left need for a supplementary levy which could be graduated in its incidence to take cognizance of the innumerable disparities of wealth, income and personal position cast up by the war and its aftermath. Therefore the C-D-G plan provided for *a progressive capital levy* to be imposed on the relatively well-to-do, in respect of their net equity positions, and to be collectible in cash or securities. The proceeds of the capital levy, pooled with the returns of the mortgage-type obligation imposed on tangible property and augmented by properties confiscated from Nazi party organizations or activists, would give to the government an ample resource base with which to effect equalization of wartime losses and to give assistance in rehabilitation.

If the C-D-G Report made extensive inroads on the property structure and moved far in the direction of collective controls and the equalization of wealth, care was taken to cast these property inroads in a form designed to minimize their socialization potential. Partly this was to be achieved by taking a large portion of the newly centralized claims on wealth in the form of a simple debt instrument given ample security by the imposition of a property mortgage and the ground for this was cleared by liquidation of private debt. This liquidation was not called for to any important degree to eliminate inflationary pressure; it had not been featured in German plans.[33] It was an action chiefly defensible in terms of minimization of the socialization potential inherent in large-scale measures for wealth-equalization.

This potential was further narrowed by the report's recommendation that management of the seized property and income claims be segregated in a *distinct government agency* not dependent on central government leadership or direction. The functions of this agency were to be confined chiefly to managing the assets entrusted to its custody, certifying claims of loss or damage arising out of the war or the occupation and passing received funds to certified claimants on a basis varying chiefly with the extent of loss or damage to property. Thus the socialization potential of the entire process was confined chiefly to creating a pool of income and wealth claims of property owners and retransferring the resulting income flow in a manner primarily designed to reflect the world of property and income relationships which existed before the war. Agency discretion was to be relatively broad over fiscal and financial policy but relatively narrow over industrial management and fund expenditures with moderate allowance for social priorities. These aspects of the C-D-G program would appeal to Western predilections just as the massive inroads on property would appeal to Soviet predilections.[34]

Probably only this balanced appeal enabled the proposals to make such rapid headway in the quadripartite negotiations which opened in September 1946. Within a few months—as diplomatic time-tables run—an amazing body of agreement was registered, utilizing the main elements of the C-D-G plan and modifying it chiefly with respect to the mode and rate of liquidating the monetary overhang. The over-all design of the C-D-G plan was followed toward treatment of private indebtedness, imposition of a mortgage plan on tangible property, and enactment of a progressive capital levy. The main areas in which agreement had not jelled were currency allocations to the occupying powers, detailed provisions of the capital levy and the degree of primacy that property damage and loss was to receive in retransferring income in the "Lastenausgleich." Later events showed that there was little ground for conflict on the first question.[35] On both latter questions the tenor of American thinking seemed sufficiently accommodating—both with respect to the need for severe rate structures and collection in kind in the capital levy and for modification of the stringent property criteria of the C-D-G Report—to make unlikely the floundering of the entire agreement in controversy over them.[36]

In any case, negotiation did not reach these points because it stalemated over the report's recommendation that monetary reform be coupled with the issuance of new currency. This had been strongly urged in the report apparently without much reckoning with the complications involved in the 12 to 15 months delay involved in printing a completely new currency in Germany. This preference for new currency is explicable partly by its obvious psychological advantages, partly by the illusion that it would facilitate solution of quadripartite access and control over currency plates and reserves, and partly by the drift of prevalent opinion in western Germany which favored new currency issuance. In any case, the currency recommendations of the report were accepted implicitly by the British and the Americans and apparently were favored by the French and the Soviets. It was assumed readily that currency printing facilities in Washington or London or Paris could be drawn upon if needed, subject to willingness to shoulder for a time the expense involved.[37]

However, when the Soviets proposed that *currency printing facilities in Leipzig be used jointly with those in Berlin*—to spare recourse to non-German facilities, to save foreign exchange and to shorten the delay inherent in printing—a snag was struck. The French and British accepted the proposal which stipulated that currency notes in Berlin and Leipzig be printed "under identical quadripartite control in both towns." The Americans objected and insisted that currency printing should be conducted only in Berlin "since quadripartite control should be exercised in a town under quadripartite administration." The issue was carried to the Moscow conference in March 1947 and left unresolved. Since the other three parties did not propose alternative arrangements capable of winning American support and the Americans did not budge from their "Berlin only" stand on printing, the financial reform negotiations were dropped.[38]

Motives on the American side for this outbreak of controversy are easy enough to establish. We had had enough, wrote General Clay in his authoritative account, "of Soviet promises in the printing of Allied military currency."

We had paid dearly for the set of plates we made available to the Soviet Government in this case. We did not intend to be placed in such a position again and our government was firm in this view.[39]

This statement was backed by a charge that Soviet issued marks had been converted into dollars on a scale which on the highest estimate reached 300 million dollars. This undoubtedly was the main point of reference which sustained what in effect was an American veto to an otherwise agreed plan for Berlin-Leipzig currency printing.

IV. The Army Overdraft

At first glance the facts on military marks seem alarming. The American government had printed a currency to be carried with Western armies into Germany and used there to finance troop pay and needed military government operations. The United States turned the engraving plates over to Russia with paper and ink. No agreement laid down conditions limiting the printing of military marks or controlling their issue; there was no information on the amount of printing or issue aside from a Soviet statement, which our responsible authorities would not confirm, that their military currency issuance had ceased in July 1946.*

The Soviet marks could not readily be distinguished from marks printed in America. Indisputable evidence demonstrated that the Soviet issue of military currency was on a scale considerably greater than that of the three Western powers. Moreover, the Soviet practice of paying troops in marks and not converting marks into rubles practically enforced the injection into circulation of the entire Russian issue while the larger part of the American and British issue could return through purchases in army canteens or conversion by Army finance offices into foreign currency. A considerable part of the Russian military currency issue gradually percolated from the Soviet zone and Berlin into Western occupied areas of Germany or became otherwise accessible to enterprising Americans. Thus the American and the British armies in Germany took in more military marks in receipt through sales and currency exchange and conversion than they issued.

An excessive rate of conversion of local currency into dollars was not, however, exceptional to the German case. A similar over-conversion appeared in every major military theater outside the American continent. With the military establishment at war strength and spread over the world, the foreign exchange business of the armed services became, as one observer and participant noted, "tremendous," involving

* See earlier discussion in chapter II, pp. 26–28.

dealings in 34 different currencies and the handling of over 11 billion dollars in transactions.[40]

American military and financial wartime policy favored the right of troops located out of the American Theater to draw part of their pay in local currrency and to reconvert on demand. The alternative of providing American military personnel with an "unconvertible" ration of local currency was rejected on the grounds that this would be a limitation of the "rights" of American military personnel.[41] Attached to this was also a desire to minimize the exploitation of indigenous resources by Allied military forces and to give some support to the local currency. American currency was used for troop pay and local spending in the North African and to a limited extent in the Italian operation but its use was found unsatisfactory.[42]

Payment in and utilization of local currencies was the key to American financial policy for American forces in enemy or liberated areas. The soldier was free to determine for himself the portion of his earnings which he wished to allot, save, or spend.

Whenever he desired the soldier could at any Army installation convert such portion of his pay drawn in a foreign currency which proved excess to his needs back into dollars at the same rate at which the pay was drawn.[43]

This policy in its essentials was recognized by Congress in a public law enacted late in 1944 which authorized foreign exchange transactions by the armed forces.[44] To the limited extent that any danger was anticipated of black marketeering and conversion of money holdings "improperly acquired" it was expected that utilization of the disciplinary sanctions of the army would confine "excess conversion" to some tolerable minimum. These sanctions were effective while major fighting was still in progress. When American military forces had spread themselves throughout their zones of Italy, Austria, Germany, Japan, and Korea and a static position was achieved, the process of excess conversion gathered apace. There was a manifest unwillingness among staff officers to take measures which would effectively eliminate military privileges with respect to currency conversion and use of army transport facilities for the transfer of illicitly acquired articles and merchandise.[45]

Moreover, since the difficulties of control and the propensity to violation were underestimated, the process of developing effective controls was slow.[46] The first formal control of a quantitative nature was the imposition of currency control books which registered in a personal book every currency conversion under a rule which limited conversions into dollars substantially to official payroll income. This was introduced in November 1945 after much damage had been done. The books were easily counterfeited, the audit system was weak, fraud by troop and officer personnel was not uncommon, control over duplicate issue and forgery was nondescript, and sizeable expenditures were routed through facilities not capable of being tied up with the control book system.[47]

Although these leaks were quickly apparent in the German theater, a more stringent currency control book system was not installed until 20 June 1946.[48] And not until the use of convertible currencies for troop pay was stopped in September 1946 and a military certificate system was inaugurated did the Army get out of the foreign exchange business. Only then did the drainage on its dollar resources stop. But it was sixteen months after the end of the war in Europe before Army staff members reluctantly concluded that their basic policy on conversion did not work.[49]

There is no particular indication that the leakage of dollar resources by excess army conversion was appreciably greater in Germany than in other areas due to Soviet access to American currency plates. Though Theater fiscal officers alleged Soviet currency printing and easier conditions of issue as a contributing cause to excess conversion, no similar imputation is apparent from War Department studies and reports. Concern with the problem was manifested before close contact had been made with Soviet forces in Berlin.[50] There, where US and Soviet army contact was most continuous, the total amount of excess dollar conversion brought considerable gain to Americans stationed in the city but contributed only slightly to the Theater total.[51] Consideration of the total conversion deficits experienced in the various currencies, contrasted with the size of the armed forces located within the areas concerned, would roughly indicate that the German deficit was not unusually large.

At the time currency conversion was banned in September 1946, the accrued German deficit is reported at 250 million dollars in comparison with a total of 130 million dollars outstanding for other areas, chiefly Japan. The deficit in Italian lira is reported at 155 million dollars and as growing out "of the same type of situation," while a French franc deficit with a more mixed origin of 29 million dollars was indicated. A much earlier compilation of excess currency conversions showed a pattern in which the German mark was less prominently displayed, with 34, 20, 13, 11, and 3 millions being the respective holdings of marks, guilder, schillings, yen and crowns. A US Treasury spokesman asserted that the excess holdings of non-German currencies were in his judgement "equal in proportion to the German problem . . . in relation to the troops."[52]

General Hilldring, who played an active role in developing US policy in this area, flatly stated that in his judgment the Russian printing of military marks and our excess troop conversion are "very indirectly if at all connected." The contact between American and Soviet troops was "confined to relatively small areas where our troops are located . . . in Berlin . . . and along a short frontier between our zone and the Russian zone." Along our zone line there was very little contact "but the conversion of marks to dollars occurred all over the American zone." In Hilldring's opinion "there is plenty of currency legitimately introduced into the economy of western Germany by us and the British and the French to make possible this and even a larger conversion."[53]

This testimony is the more impressive since there is no little ambiguity in the Army presentation of its case and in Army statistics. The basic reports of the Army Fiscal Director were not released for publication and it is significant that the records on which these reports were based were explicitly withheld from independent Treasury audit and inspection. It is curious that a War Department Staff Study in April 1946 would list the excess German mark holding at 34 million dollars; that two months later an analogous study should list the holding at 111 million dollars; and that the holding three months later should be cited by General Clay as 300 million dollars, by the War Department at 250 million dollars, and by General Clay's financial advisor at over 200 million dollars.[54]

At least an appreciable portion of the "excess mark holdings" may have originated from military marks issued to friendly Allied governments and missions, dispensed to UNRRA, or used to make up for German currency shortages in the early phase of the occupation.[55] It has been charged that military mark supplies in the Western zones of Germany were loosely handled without adequate controls for issuance, that shipment was made by weight and case and that basic accounting sheets have not properly been audited. It has been admitted that the British and French joined the Soviets in issuing 1000 mark notes which were widespread in the American zone and which were generally believed to

be issued only by the Soviets. Though early directives apparently stipulated that a permanent record of currency conversions on a cumulative
individual basis was to be maintained, no such records were in fact made
available. These discrepancies and ambiguities suggest that the problem of the so-called "Army mark overdraft" is related far more to internal
US procedures and fiscal delinquencies than to Soviet monetary policy,
although this policy was an important contributing factor.[56]

However dubious and ill-founded may have been the case that
shared currency plates with the Soviets and laxness on printing arrangements with them cost America dear, the winged word had gone out.
Newspaper stories publicized the way in which the "Soviets Pried
Money Plates out of US." Congressional interest was concentrated on
ferreting out the culprits "who acquiesced on behalf of this government
to give the Russian government these plates." Responsible senators felt
that the experience demonstrated the need for the closest security controls on currency dealings with the Soviets.[57] This agitation in Washington greatly narrowed the American range of discretion on dealings with
the Soviets about access to printing plates for a new German currency.

Although rigid persistence in a course which continued to hold
French and British support was understandable on the Soviet side, the
Soviets were not committed to maintaining a position which frustrated
reaching a desired goal. Opportunities for intermediation were provided
both by the Moscow conference to which the issue of currency printing
was referred, and by the rare fact that America's two Allies were supporting the Soviets. These opportunities were neglected not because the
issue was unamenable to adjustment but rather because of undermined
interest in quadripartite monetary reform as a dynamic act of fusion
accomplishable within the framework of the Control Council regime.[58]

At the start of the year—in February and March 1946 when the
C-D-G mission was at work—the Control Council regime was ready for
growth. By the spring of 1946 the preconditions for quadripartite agreement on monetary reform probably had matured so far as the U.S., the
British and the Soviets were concerned. Delays—even though those
delays were short according to customary intra-governmental and
diplomatic timetables—held up the final preparation of an American
program until May 1946 and its issuance as a governmental mandate
until late August 1946. Quadripartite technical negotiations were commenced only in September 1946 and could be brought to completion
only through the winter of 1946–7. By this time the tenability of the

Control Council regime itself had come under such insistent question as to paralyze the possibility of its further development.[59] Under these circumstances the currency printing controversy seems to have served as a catalytic agent. Through it the negotiations could stalemate on an issue which would facilitate scapegoating and yet avoid premature commitment of policies to be executed at a later stage.

CHAPTER VII

THE BREAKDOWN OF AMBIVALENCE

I. Dismantling and Concurrency

THE RAPID DECLINE during 1946 in the tenability of the Control Council regime was in part the outgrowth of inability to carry through the level of industry plan agreement for reparations from the western zones. While the plan was being negotiated, it was anticipated that its execution would give rise to strain. These forebodings looked more serious when they were translated into detailed showings, industry by industry, of the plant capacity to be retained under the plan in contrast to what was needed to support the German economy at a minimum level of subsistence. Yet the discrepancy between planned capacity and needed capacity involved too large a segment of reparations potential to be adjusted by piecemeal negotiation without further horsetrading. This made the West determined in the view that if the plan had to be carried out with all its stringencies, the integrated economic life of the zones which it presupposed had to be "concurrently" brought into existence. By constant reiteration, this doctrine of concurrency came to be a fundamental American theme.*

* Clay has well stated the position: "I felt strongly that we were being placed in the position not only of financing reparations to the Soviet Union but also of agreeing to strip our own zone (which had insufficient industrial capacity for self-support) without getting the benefits which would come from the amalgamation of all zones." L. D. Clay. *Decision in Germany* (New York, 1950), 121. Marshall gave a clear statement of the case at Moscow: "the United States holds that the provisions of the Potsdam protocol for the delivery of plants for reparations and for the economic unification of Germany to include a common export-import plan must be carried out concurrently." U.S. Department of State, *Germany, 1947–1949, The Story in Documents*, Department of State Publication no. 3556, European and Commonwealth Series 9 (Washington, 1950), 411.

123

The West asked for uniform food ration levels and fusion of the leaking food reservoirs of western Germany with the better guarded food-stocks of eastern Germany.[1] They also demanded that the more quickly revived coal industry of eastern Germany send westward a part of its output under a program of joint allocations on the basis of common needs.* Finally, they insisted that some form of import-export agreement be reached which would tend to pool export proceeds and spread the burden of carrying western import deficits and as well would prohibit explicitly the withdrawal of current product reparations from any zone while any other zone was meeting an uncovered trade deficit.**

* See the brief summary of issues in the *CFM Report*, Section IV, Part 8, 4. The main facts of a very complicated matter are apparently as follows. Interzonal coal allocations up through the second quarter of 1946 revolved around settlement for Berlin needs, a peculiar formula for exchange between east and west on an equivalent basis, and a Ruhr export quota. In the spring months of 1946 the Ruhr coal output sank almost one-fourth, while Soviet zone coal output surged ahead to nearly the prewar levels. Soviet zone coal retentions were out of proportion to those of other zones and the Americans introduced the proposal for an interzonal coal pool with allocations based on some objective (capacity) index of need. Cf. ACA, *Coal Allocation for July 1946*, DECO/P(46)258, 12 June 1946. At this time it was discovered that Soviet coal allocation figures had not included a significant amount of coal directly converted into other energy at the mines. "The method of allocating coal between zones," notes the American memo in closing, "has remained practically unchanged since that time. Under these methods the Soviet zone is receiving 37 percent more and the Western zones a correspondingly lesser amount than objective need would support." CFUL/P(46)102, incorporated in *Ibid*. The question was not resolved, but the French and British delegations were converted to the American view of the desirability of a raid on Soviet zone coal availabilities. This tripartite position was set forth. ACA, *Preliminary Report of the Committee of Coal Experts on the Measures to increase Coal Production and the Principles of Allocation of German Coal*, CORC/P(46)289, 6 September 1946; OMGUS, *Enactments and Approved Papers of the Control Council and Coordinating Committee* (7v., Legal Division, Berlin, 1946–1948), IV, 110–119; and ACA, *Minutes of the Coordinating Committee*, CORC/M(46)47, 10 September 1946. General Clay bluntly posed the issue as to whether "coal would be made available from the Soviet zone for the common coal pool." The Western delegations insisted on a common coal pool starting as of the moment. The Soviets asserted willingness to join a common coal pool whenever responsibility for the "planning of coal production" would also be fused. The three Western representatives, noted the Soviet delegate, "while considering Germany as one economic whole in respect of the allocation of coal, do not recognise her as one economic whole in respect of planning of coal production." The latter, the Soviets insisted, was basic to the former.

** Cf. *CFM Report*, "History of Discussions with a view to the Establishment of An Export-Import Plan for the Whole of Germany," App. E. to Part 8 of Section IV

The West pushed these measures in negotiation. When the Soviets did not yield, sanctions were applied in May, 1946. General plant dismantling in the American zone was stopped, giving the Control Council regime its first real jolt.*

The core of the difficulty in the Western doctrine of concurrency was that it was incompatible with itself. It attempted to join two processes of fundamentally different character: dismantling, which was piecemeal in its nature, and economic unity, which was organic. Once agreement was reached on plants to be dismantled, delivery could proceed piecemeal. This was not true of economic unity. Resources of food or coal could scarcely be pooled in common allocation programs without concurrent pooling of responsibility for management and policy; and neither allocation nor management nor policy could be pooled by degrees. Economic unity is indivisible and inseparable from establishment of a nuclear center for provisional German government, i.e. from political unity. Furthermore, each step toward unity would be a step away from

---

as well as appendices F, G, H.: cf. also *Ibid.*, Part 6, "Export and Import." The essential features of the proposals for an export-import bureau were (a) banning reparations withdrawals within any zone until foreign trade balance for all zones was achieved on the basis of agreed import-export plans; (b) pooling export proceeds from all zones; (c) some form of sharing in the over-all deficits (British plan) or some form of lien on export surpluses (U.S. plan). Using the veiled language of such negotiations, the Soviets replied that they would be quite ready to enter a foreign trade pool after the list of reparations deliveries had been determined and after over-all production planning was shared. The import-export issue was the trigger issue in controversy. See Clay, *Decision*, 120–123.

* This was "our first break with Soviet policy in Germany," notes General Clay, and it involved facing a "major decision which was certain to have lasting effect on our relationship with Russia." The Soviets undoubtedly were angered by American resort to a physical sanction. While the British did not follow suit, they carried out dismantling at so slow a rate as virtually to involve the same end although to the last they "denied the allegations of bad faith . . ." However, the British asserted that Soviet representatives inspecting property potentially due them "have always displayed exacting meticulousness in every matter and this has largely contributed to the delays." Further, "uncertainty" about the program had a "natural reaction" on the Germans involved in dismantling. Finally, "as a result of the failure to achieve economic unity in Germany the amount of reparations to be taken from any zone cannot finally be determined." These arguments, plus the fact that reparations shipments from the British and the American zones were substantially the same, seem persuasive on the issue of "faith." See *Ibid.*, 120; J. Joesten, *Germany: What Now?* (Chicago, 1948), 219–220; *CFM Report*, Section V. Reparations, Part 8, "Valuations and Physical Removals," 4–6.

zonal autonomy. All this the Soviets sensed. Thus they developed their own doctrine of concurrency: that limited measures of asset pooling ought to be accompanied by concurrent responsibility over production and economic administration.*

Because limited fusion made sense to the Soviets only in this more extended form, they also insisted that it could not be commenced unless the total amount of reparations due from dismantling were fixed firmly. The Soviet share had been stated only percentage-wise at Potsdam; and the level of industry plan had set out the general procedure for translating percentages into amounts. But the plan was tied to assumptions which provided options for revision. Before concrete plant allotments could be made to the Soviets the four powers had to traverse a tangled web of intermediary investigations and actions in order to assemble for the Western zones an agreed list of reparations deliveries complete down to inventories and evaluations. In the absence of guarantees from the West that these deliveries would reach a stipulated figure, what the Soviets would get depended on what the West would agree to give. Hence the Soviets plainly told the West that their zone would not be committed to fusion before they had in their hands a specific and irrevocable list of reparations deliveries.**

* This was variously emphasized by the Soviets. Thus they urged that the level of industry plan needed to be supplemented by "an overall economic plan for the restoration and development of a peaceful economy . . . which would establish . . . specific minimum obligations . . . for each of the four zones." The Soviet delegation "cannot accept the viewpoint by which the problem of allocation of production is placed independent of the coordinated efforts in the field of production because without production allocation is impossible." *CFM Report*, Section IV, Part 8, Soviet unilateral statements. In the Soviet version, pooling of resources would mean that "each commander must be responsible for putting into operation all the industrial facilities of the zone." Clay, *Decision*, 122.

** This was stated with exceptional clarity at the crucial May 4, 1946 meeting of the Coordinating Committee of the Control Council at which the import-export issue came to a head and General Clay announced that "all reparation dismantling had been discontinued in his zone . . ." The Soviet representative stated that "implementation of an Export-Import program depended on the plan for reparations and the level of post-war German economy. In order to prepare such a program it was essential that the following questions should be settled. (I) The determination of the plants to be delivered on account of reparations; (II) the determination of the plants to be left in Germany and the nature of their products; (III) the determination of those plants which must be destroyed as constituting a war potential. Until these three points were settled he considered that it was difficult to discuss a common Import-Export program." The British chairman then restated the Soviet

The effort to develop the Potsdam reparations unity option thus led to irreconcilable positions, East and West. Neither side was willing to give the blank check which was needed for the option to be carried through to completion. Perhaps it was unavoidable that this conflict was exacerbated by being publicly aired. The West justified its push for current effectuation of limited fusion and dismantling for reparations purposes by characterizing extraction of reparations from the Soviet zone as illicit and the counterpart—on some readings, the cause—of the Western deficit.* In this way the West could rationalize the policies which had led to lagging recovery and deficits in the Western zones. On the other hand, in the light of the Soviet doctrine of concurrency, the measures of limited fusion urged by the West could be seen only in their invidious and discriminatory aspects. They appeared to be unprincipled calls upon eastern German resources to subsidize western German defi-

position as involving "agreement with the economic principle of the treatment of Germany but considered that they could not be put into effect at the present time." The Soviet spokesman in reply stated that "Soviet policy was in accord with paragraph 14 of the Potsdam Protocol, Section III dealing with treatment of Germany as an economic unit but that the Soviet delegation interpreted this paragraph to mean that a common Import-Export program was dependent upon the realization of the three concrete prerequisites that he had already specified. He continued that it had been stated in the course of the meeting that the implementation of the reparations plan had been discontinued. He reminded his colleagues that the plan had already been delayed, for which delay the Soviet delegation could not accept responsibility." ACA, *Minutes of the Coordinating Committee,* CORC/M(46)23, paragraph 243. Compare Clay's account, *Decision,* 120–3.

* The following statements are typical: "We and the Americans," complained Bevin, "have had to buy food and other goods to send into Western Germany while the Russians are taking similar goods from Eastern Germany into Russia." The American delegation in the Control Council charged that "the facts that some Occupying Powers are themselves paying for the substantial deficit on necessary food imports at the same time that other zones have an exportable surplus is evidence of the failure to treat Germany as an economic unit." This course of events, charged Clay, "represented indirect payment for deliveries to the Soviet Union by the United States and the United Kingdom." Through relief, charged Herbert Hoover in his influential report on German industry of 1947, the U.S. and Britain are "paying Russian and French reparations." These charges of course embodied chiefly scapegoating over the lagging and deficit-haunted recovery of western Germany. See U.S. Department of State, *Occupation of Germany: Policy and Progress, 1945–1946,* Publication no. 2783, European series 23 (Washington, 1947), 225: *CFM Report,* Section IV, Part 8, U.S.-British statement, 4; Clay, *Decision,* 121; G. Stolper, *German Realities* (New York, 1948), 310.

cits. As such they were objectionable on all counts. They would attempt to take from the poor and to give to the wealthy nations and thus to redistribute wealth perversely. They were not justified by German structural resource imbalance.* There was no food surplus in eastern Germany available to help in western German feeding.[2] The eastern zone was afflicted by refugee inflow to an even greater degree than the western zones.** And the Western powers had taken the initiative in establishing the principle of exchange of equivalents as the basis for East-West interzonal allocation of essential items.[3]

II. The Search for Settlement

The stalemate of concurrencies on the Potsdam unity option became involved with the other developments going on in the Control Council regime. The zonal regimes which had grown up under the policy of ambivalence diverged sufficiently to strain at the limits of overlap on which Control Council collaboration was based. This collaboration, moreover, had been given an unstable, lopsided form through inability to realize in good time those centralizing and unifying measures—monetary reform, establishment of central agencies and nationwide fusion of political parties and trade unions—which would have

---

* In terms of industrial output, urban population, crop land, timber stand and other wealth indexes the U.S.-British bizonal area was in a much stronger position than either the French or Soviet zones. While war damage was universal, the eastern zone came out with the shorter end of livestock, railway rolling stock and inland waterway vessels. See OMGUS, Special Report of the Military Governor, *Economic Data on Potsdam Germany* (Berlin, 1947), 12–14; *CFM Report*, Section IV, Part 4, Agriculture (showing data on draft power and livestock per zone relative to prewar), 6–8; *Ibid.*, Part IX, Transportation, App. 2; Deutsches Institut für Wirtschaftsforschung, *Die Deutsche Wirtschaft Zwei Jahre Nach dem Zusammenbruch* (Berlin, 1947), 269, 275.

** Though the population increase for Potsdam Germany in 1946 over 1939 for the same territory was 10.6% and for the three Western zones some 13.4%, the increase in population of the Soviet zone was 14.4%, only the American zone having a higher net rate of increase. For this, see any tabulation of the results of the October 1946 all-German census conducted under Control Council auspices. So far as movements of German expellees are concerned, the official CFM report as of 1 January 1947 credited the Soviet zone with receipt of 5.02 million expellees as against 4.16 million for all the Western zones. The two sets of data showing over-all population change and expellee movements are reconciled by an adjusting movement of refugees between zones. *Ibid.*, Section VII, Population Transfers, App. L.

buttressed and dynamized it. Inability to achieve these measures made it difficult to glide into that program of limited fusion which might have satisfied American concurrency doctrine. In turn, limited fusion was unworkable without these measures. Yet the stalemate of concurrencies sufficiently aggravated the atmosphere to hamper taking the vital monetary reform action.

It was thus found impossible to move forward constructively by piecemeal negotiation and partial agreement. The policy of ambivalence was played out. Constructive forward action could only be taken upon conclusion of an overall settlement which would bring together congruent forms of action and avoid the hazards of piecemeal negotiation. In reaction to the strain of the search for settlement the occupying powers would tend to prepare some form of retreat. On the eastern side this required no basic reconstruction since only one zone was involved and the basic measures establishing the eastern regime were taken early in its course. This was not true of the West. Three zonal areas were involved in western Germany and on the whole the course of policy had favored deliberate delay of basic decisions. Preliminary moves would be needed to smooth the way for a suitable provisional arrangement for the Western zones in case quadripartite stalemate should endure.

These moves would be welcomed by the Americans since they could assure the supply sources of Ruhr coal, steel and power without exchanging equivalent values.* Special relationships between the British and American zones were bound to exist in any case because of the Bremen enclave, managed by the Americans, which tore an awkward hole in Britain's zonal territory.[4] Furthermore, the principle of pooled resources which had developed under the single command of the wartime period had never been dissolved completely and it appears that the export proceeds of the two zones were committed to some form of joint disposition.[5] British interest in joining with the Americans was stimulated by an intense need for financial support for imported foodstuffs and other supplies to reactivate zonal economic life and Ruhr coal output.[6]

Sustained by these practical impulses, the quest for some way out of the Potsdam stalemate led in July-September 1946 to the first move toward Bizonia, the "fused" British and American zones.[7] Bizonal fusion arrangements were made effective in December 1946 by an intergovernmental agreement which sketched in the enduring design of Anglo-

* See earlier, p. 78.

American partnership, provided for financial responsibility, constituted operating agencies, made fundamental commitments on German resources and pledged Anglo-American action toward fulfilling German needs.[8] This agreement indicated that the Western powers were preparing an easy exit if a quadripartite solution was not obtained.

Reconnaissance along the path of partition was not the only reaction to the Potsdam stalemate. The common ground which had developed in Germany under the Control Council regime could be used as a basis for settlement. For one thing, the Council's negotiating apparatus had evolved a tradition and momentum which would facilitate inter-Allied control over a future central German government. The capital of a post-settlement Germany could be the Berlin enclave which had been built up under Control Council administration for a unifying role. In demilitarization and denazification, as in many sectors of social life, codification of Control Council agreements and decisions would have disclosed an already prepared and solid base for settlement. The financial frame for a post-settlement economy even had been carried forward and partially revised to suit it to the new post-war conditions.[9]

Broad bases for agreement also characterized areas of zonal life which were not expressly shaped by Control Council enactments. This was outstandingly true of the political regimes which had crystallized under the occupation. Everywhere some play was permitted German opinion and political life was given some range for self-determined expression; but everywhere this political life developed under occupation pressure. Partly because of and partly in spite of this, the political movements which had sprung up within the several zones were relatively homogenous. Their chief theaters of activity were the some sixteen independent state governments carved by the occupying powers out of the former Reich and converted into the focal centers for German political life. A wide though variable range of authority in all zones was exercised through the state governments. After pruning, these state governments and political regimes could be fitted into some form of federal union.

By and large, East and West agreed on the major principles of a federal union and the key steps required to bring it into existence. State governments were to retain extensive areas of authority and to wield independent power; they were to be represented through the upper house of a bicameral federal legislature; the central government would exercise constitutionally delimited functions; civil liberties and the principles of a liberal state would be constitutionally secured; a provisional German central government could be established by drawing primarily upon heads of the state governments; and an elected parliament would be convened at an early date.*

This outer frame of agreement was accompanied by divergences in detail and in emphasis. Central contentious issues were the amount of authority which a German central government should have to direct economic controls or to develop a planned economy, questions of civil liberties, use of the method of proportional representation in electoral procedure and the mode of contracting the authority of the occupation within the separate zones. Disagreement on these matters was real. Yet no occupying power had to sacrifice any vital national interest to resolve them. The Soviets had a potential interest in weakening German central government in order to protect the zonal regime which they had fostered. While the British under Bevin spoke with an American accent at Moscow, they were potentially closer than they seemed to the Soviet plan in socialization and economic controls as well as in their constitutional tradition of parliamentary supremacy, a weak upper chamber and absence of a judicial veto.

Divergences between the occupying powers undoubtedly could not have narrowed to the point of devising through quadripartite negotiations the text of a German constitution or a detailed scheme for German political structure. This would have strained the capacity of a more solidary alliance. But the frame of agreement was large enough and the issues of divergence were few enough to permit concensus to be reached on a procedure for establishing a provisional central German govern-

* The Soviet version of a plan for a future German political structure and for a provisional central government can best be studied directly from the main Soviet texts presented in V. N. Molotov, *Speeches and Statements at the Moscow Session of the Council of Foreign Ministers, 1947* (published by Soviet News, London, 1947). *A Summary of Agreements and Disagreements on Germany* (1st ed. Civil Affairs Administration, February, 1948), 152–173. For a competent general survey, see W. Friedmann, *The Allied Military Government of Germany* (London Institute of World Affairs, London, 1947). Friedmann noted that "the constitutional schemes of the four powers proved less divergent than the deeper underlying differences on social and political principles;" and despite "Molotov's protest against federalization," the Soviet proposals "envisaged a Bundestatt, with both central and federal Parliaments, and an interim administration on the lines of the Potsdam agreement." *Ibid.*, 98.

ment, on ordering all-German elections and on minimum stipulations to which a constitution drawn by the Germans should conform.*

Political developments which had taken root in zonal life could have culminated in a political structure for a unified Germany. But polarization was well advanced in institutional structure and class elite relationships.[10] This polarization, however, would have been reduced or displaced by the formation of new centers of economic power and institutions which would have followed from peripheral accompaniments of settlement. One of these was the *Lastenausgleich* program of the C-D-G Report which had been quadripartitely approved as a phase of monetary reform. By reorganizing German property relationships and by establishing powerful new economic institutions, the measures involved in carrying a *Lastenausgleich* forward would have gone far to bring eastern and western Germany together.

This foundation for a united Germany would have been strengthened by settling the disposition of the corporate enclaves established by the occupying powers. These enclaves could not be continued unchanged under settlement. The U.S. insisted on dismantlement of the Soviet AG controls in the eastern zone. The Soviets insisted on sharing

---

* E. S. Mason, a member of the U.S. delegation at the Moscow conference, reached a somewhat similar conclusion. After review of the issues involved, he concluded that with regard to the establishment of a "liberal political regime" a "qualified yes" could be given to the question of whether or not East-West differences could have been "reconciled" without essential injury. "If the author is correct in his estimate of the situation, agreement could probably be reached with the Soviet Union on questions concerning the political structure of Germany, subject to the limitations mentioned above, if Soviet demands for reparations were satisfied," Mason, "Reflections on the Moscow Conference," *International Organization,* II (1947), 483 ff. C. J. Friedrich, who was a close observer with access to official information, emphasized the inadvisability of including in any German peace settlement "German constitutional arrangements . . . in any detail." Later, Friedrich expressed doubt that "agreement could have been reached on the German constitution at Moscow." Friedrich, "The Peace Settlement with Germany: Political and Military," *Annals of the American Academy of Political and Social Science,* 257 (1948), 125 f.; Friedrich, "Rebuilding the German Constitution," *American Political Science Review,* XLIII (1949), 467. On some of the disputed questions the Anglo-American position bordered on the doctrinaire. Thus, state governors in Germany rarely were outstanding political leaders and it would have been a mockery to confine a consultative political council of a provisional government to them. For an indication of how close the occupying powers were to agreement, see the American statement of 2 April 1947, cited in U.S. Department of State, *Germany, 1947–1949,* 190–192.

any special Ruhr controls.[11] But management through loosely framed quadripartite control was not feasible for enterprises dependent upon a continuous stream of operating decisions. The British had formally declared that the enclaves—at least under the Labor Party government— would not be remanded to private owners or the old management.* Return to the old corporate regime would have concentrated economic power in hands potentially too irresponsible to suit either a safely functioning German republic or the trustbusting qualms of American policy.

Under these circumstances the only possible mode of disposing of these enclaves in settlement was to remand them to the provisional control and interim custody of a central German government. Without this custody the German government would have been handicapped in organizing the resources and energy of the nation to carry out the obligations of settlement. Such action was urged by the Soviets, was supportable by the British with their penchant for socialization and was consonant with the earlier American desire to see industrial enclave arrangements removed.** Essential objectives in this move and objections

* In condemning them before the House of Commons, Bevin said that "these industries were previously in the hands of magnates who were closely allied to the German military machine, who financed Hitler and who in two wars were part and parcel of Germany's aggressive policy." See U.S. Department of State, *Occupation of Germany*, 226 ff.

** At Moscow the U.S. position found "some special provision for the overseeing of Ruhr resources . . . advisable," but felt that this "should not interfere with German responsibility for the management and operation of Germany's resources." It is "only if the Germans take action contrary to the just interests of other countries that the attention of an international agency may have to be called to the question." U.S. Department of State, *Germany, 1947–1949*, 329; Clay, *Decision*, 321 ff. The Soviets expressly favored remanding large-scale corporate trustified properties to the German state. OMGUS, *A Summary*, 120. In Soviet zone political life the assumption commonly was made that the SAG empire was not intended to be permanent and had a certain trusteeship status. Ulbricht in a programmatic speech in 1947 noted that some of the SAG enterprises already had been returned to German disposition and "wir hofien dass später auch die anderen SAG-Betriebe volkseigene Betriebe werden. Daraus ergibt sich dass wir uns zu den sowjetischen Aktiengesellschaften ebenso verhalten wie zu den volkseigenene Betriebe." W. Ulbricht, *Brennende Fragen des Neuaufbaus Deutschlands* (Berlin, 1947), 35. For the same viewpoint, see Otto Grotewohl, *Im Kampf um Deutschland, Reden und Aufsätze* (Berlin, 1948), II, 333. In Soviet zone statistics the Soviet AG's were apparently assimilated with the "volkseigene Betriebe." See for example, *Die Wirtschaft*, sonderheft "Der Wirtschaftsplan 1949/1950," July, 1948, 3 ff. For a time the SAG's were consolidated on a commercial footing as, it seems, a more or less permanent part of Soviet occu-

to it probably could have been reconciled by basing the action on general inter-Allied agreements that would protect Allied property interests, fix clear-cut coal export policies, permit inspection at will and stipulate that settled forms for handling the enclaves could be determined only by a fully responsible German government.[12]

Once remanded to a provisional German government these properties undoubtedly would have been socialized in some far-reaching sense. The left parties, the trade unions and many bourgeois-liberal political leaders would have opted for this.* It would have gone well with German tradition which in the past had assimilated large elements of socialization into a pattern of capitalist enterprise. Throwing off interim governmental custodianship would have encountered practical difficulties.** The enclaves were suitable for socialization since they had been carved out of those sectors of business organization in which the motor drives of private property and profit seeking in the main had been displaced and in which patterns of competitive business organization were inherently difficult to achieve.[13] Socialization would have simplified the economic steering incumbent upon modern governments and facilitated carrying out regulatory controls. Socialization would have disposed of the elite industrialists and put their wealth to collective use. By forming new power relationships within the society, it would have tended to narrow the gap between the eastern and western regimes and to decrease the strain involved in their consolidation within a single polity.

---

pation. *Die sowjetische Reparationspolitik seit 1945* (Sopade Denkschrift no. 29, Hanover, 1950), 22–26. But within half a decade the corporations were relinquished and reparations was ended. See documents collected in B. Ruhm von Oppen, *Documents On Germany Under Occupation 1945–1954* (Oxford, 1955) pp. 594–597.

* See the report of the decision of the conference of state Minister-Presidents of the Bizone, "Recommendations to Increase Ruhr Production," *Frankfurter Rundschau*, 8 June 1948, which recommended socialization. The CDU leadership in the early phases of the occupation was partial to "social" solutions. See "Rechts von der SPD, zur politischen Genealogie der CDU," *Die Gegenwart*, IV (1949), 9–12; H. Meyerhoff, "Parties and Classes in Postwar Germany," *South Atlantic Quarterly*, LXVI (1947), no. 3.

** It would have been difficult to sell any considerable number of enterprises by issuance of new securities. Break-up of the corporate combines and remanding them to new owners by conventional methods of corporate reorganization could have been carried out only on a limited scale and during the process incentives would be unsettled, access to new capital would be difficult and the general outcome would be problematic.

A similar foothold for settlement had developed in the other major concern of economic policy: namely, the extent to which industrial disarmament to achieve security and reparations should be carried at the cost of German economic livelihood. Experience in managing their zones and in attempting to negotiate and carry out a dismantling plan had indicated that dismantling was not the cure-all it was thought to be at Potsdam. Collection of reparations by dismantling industrial equipment avoided problems of money payments but led to haggling over each potential item of equipment and its fair value, which by omission or commission could enter into settlement. German sensibilities were irritated by dismantling out of all proportion to the extent of their loss or of Allied gain. The labor of dismantling absorbed economic energy better put to other use. Finally, to push dismantling to the point of crippling the German economy no longer seemed necessary in view of fuller perspective on the postwar world and the real proportions of the German menace in it.[14] Hence America, Britain and the Soviet Union separately concluded that need existed roughly to double the levels of industrial production for Germany which had been set out in the level of industry plan of March 1946.

With this foundation in industrial strength, a renovated and united postwar Germany could have mobilized its resources for quick recovery and reconstruction. But this happy development would take place at Soviet expense just as settlement on the March 1946 basis was designed to be reached at German expense. For Soviet relinquishment of their zone and rights to extract reparations withdrawal from it, they would receive in return a curtailed dismantling quota. The Soviets were too poor to be so generous. Hence they coupled acceptance of settlement with participation in the enlarged production and greater national income which settlement and curtailed dismantling would make possible. The issues faced at Yalta thus emerged again and the Soviets responded with the pattern of demands which had been presented at Yalta and dropped at Potsdam. They asked that current product reparation withdrawals be scheduled on a scale which would yield the Soviets from all sources, allowing for what they had already received, a total reparations benefit of 10 billion dollars. In meeting this challenge, Western spokesmen replied in kind by indicating that the Oder-Neisse frontier settlement also was still in doubt.

The breakdown of ambivalence and the emergent need for settlement thus turned the circle. The issues of the Oder-Neisse and of Soviet reparations claims on current product central to Yalta and Potsdam were pushed to the forefront again. This main theater of controversy shaded into a minor theater in which French opposition was expressed to the patterns of settlement toward which the achievements of the Control Council regime could lead. The French persisted in their original demand for a graded French annexation of the Rhineland and Saar and implantation of Western control over the Ruhr which was to be sundered from Germany. They also opposed any settlement which would raise dismantling levels and establish effective central German government with control over key economic resources and 68 million Germans. The French preferred maintenance of zonalization and military rule gilded by the Control Council mechanism at about the *status quo*. This zonalized Germany would be permitted a weak form of confederation. Its industry would be dismantled, its labor permitted to emigrate, its coal supplies reduced by forced exportation of coal and territorial dismemberment in the West.[15]

Thus an Anglo-American conflict with the Soviets over the reparations benefits of carrying forward the Control Council regime into a full-scale settlement went on hand in hand with a conflict of the Potsdam trio with the French over the Control Council regime and the settlement issuing from it. Though the scope for divergence and the depth of the conflict was of comparable order in both cases, the balance of forces differed markedly. The French zone was a mongrel little territory inhabited by some 5 million Germans without effective lines of interior transportation. After loss of the Saar, the zone was not supportable in isolation from Western Germany.[16] The French economy was in chronic crisis and dependent upon America for aid in money, coal and foodstuffs.[17] Hence France could have protested but she could not have blocked a German settlement nor could she have withheld her zone of Germany from inclusion within it. Her irritation could have been assuaged in any case by the fruits accruing to her out of any reparations settlement which would obtain Soviet assent, by continued voice in Allied councils in Germany and by a coal export agreement to relieve pressing domestic anxieties.[18]

It was otherwise with the Soviets. Their zone already was prepared for partition. It embraced a considerable territory over which close Soviet control was exercised. The zone was supportable in estrangement from western Germany through integration with the contiguous Eastern world. Unlike the French, the Soviets were independent of Western largesse. A settlement could not be pressed upon them but only reached with them through the give and take of negotiation.

In some ways the prospects for settlement were improved by the new setting for negotiations. One of the main disputed questions, that of the Polish frontier, had in fact been irretrievably determined by inter-Allied action in removing German inhabitants from the Oder-Neisse territories and thereby opening them up to Polish resettlement. This resettlement had gone ahead without Western objection. The Poles could hardly then, short of war, be induced to undo the resettlement. Nor could the Soviets be expected to upset their carefully wrought Polish alliance. Finally, many expelled German families would be reluctant to return to their former homes out of fear of living in an eastern borderland or because they had become rooted in the new Germany. Thus though the new frontier had yet to win diplomatic approval, it was anchored solidly enough.*

Inability to maneuver on the frontier issue increased the pressure on reparations. Yet prospects for settlement in this area were improved. The nature of the problem was now manifest. Various possibilities for its solution had been probed, and a clear picture had been obtained as to the extent of German reparations potential.

* It is doubtful, e.g., "that even the present leadership of Polish Communism would meekly accept a reversal of Soviet policy on the issue of the Oder-Neisse line." A. B. Ulam, "The Crisis in the Polish Communist Party," *Review of Politics*, XII (1950), 96. For an indication of the permanence of the frontier change, see Clay, *Decision*, 76; Friedrich, "The Peace Settlement," *loc. cit.*, 122; Stolper, *German Realities*, 226; U.S. Department of State, *Occupation of Germany*, 25.

CHAPTER VIII

REPARATIONS AND FOREIGN DEFICIT

I. Reparations Potential and Foreign Deficit

THE SOVIET REPARATIONS CLAIM was for 10 billion dollars in goods and services valued at 1938 prices. But this was an all-inclusive claim and in part it was already fulfilled. The extent of fulfillment at the time the settlement issue came to climax in 1946 and in 1947 cannot be precisely determined. This extent was itself increasing as time went on. But available research indicates that known extractions by the end of 1947 ran to near 35% and that with close bargaining perhaps 50% of the gross total could have been written off as fulfilled.[1] The known values include an allowance of 770 million for dismantled equipment and 1.5 billion dollars for reparations withdrawals from current product.[2] The Soviet share of the German merchant marine was booked only at near 25 million dollars.[3] The Soviet share of seized foreign German assets runs to around 775 millions for assets in Finland, Austria, and in Hungary; total realizable foreign assets probably amounted to near one billion from all eastern countries.[4] The 10% share of equipment dismantled as reparations from the Western zones ran only to around 25 million dollars and probably could not have exceeded 50 million.[5] Thus we can add up around 3.3 billion of reparations fulfilled in minimal values. These values are very conservatively appraised and no allowance is made for assets withdrawn for use in Germany or for labor services performed in the Soviet Union. Could a 50% writeoff for previous or scheduled fulfillment have been obtained? This seems a reasonable assumption. In 1950 and again in 1953 the Soviets waived fulfillment of almost half of their

138

original reparations claims of ten billion dollars. Western negotiators
were armed with plausible and well-informed estimates of fulfillment,
emanating partly from German sources, which ran well in excess of five
billion dollars.[6] However, it may be doubted that the Soviets in 1946 or
in 1947—i.e. at a time when the reconstruction needs in the Soviet
homeland were so urgent—would have permitted a settlement on less
onerous terms. Hence we deal with a five billion dollar figure as a minimal Soviet price for a German peace settlement framed in other respects
along acceptable lines.

To this five billion dollar figure there must be added a non-Soviet
share of near equal size. There were large reparations claims from other
Allied countries ravaged or damaged through German aggression: chiefly
Poland, France, Jugoslavia, Holland, Belgium, Denmark and Norway.
Then there were sizable public and private pre-war debts held by
Western foreign creditors with a face value up to 3.5 billion dollars.
Besides there were accruing liabilities at a rate of nearly one half billion
dollars annually (in 1938 values) for American and British support of
their occupied zones of Germany. Finally, the French would never
accede to a plan of settlement which would not have laid some mortgage
on German Ruhr coal output designed to assure a generous supply of
low-priced coal or its equivalent in moderate commercial supply plus a
reparations quota. These Western claims were all indicated in the
negotiations and they could not have been overlooked in settlement. In
their own peace settlement with Western Germany in the years immediately ahead satisfaction of these claims was assured. This settlement included on the one hand provisions assuring a generous supply of
low-priced Ruhr coal provided the French and other Western European
coal users. The settlement also involved a debt settlement which fixed
on the Western German republic a foreign debt of nearly 15 billion DM
to be serviced at a 3% rate of interest and retired gradually over twenty-
five years. Annual payments were to commence at 567 million DM and
after five years were to step up to 750 million DM. Recognition in 1952 of
this debt settlement was a firm requirement toward release of occupied
status.[7] We can thus freely and readily assume that Soviet reparations
claims would have been matched by corresponding Western claims; that
these could have been spelled out in terms of money-flows or commodity values; and that to this extent a quadripartite peace settlement

with Potsdam Germany would have involved a reparations obligation by Germany totalling some ten billion dollars in 1938 values.

Clearly, the effective impact on the German economy of current product withdrawals totalling 10 billion 1938 dollars would depend upon the terms of its translation into current (1949–50) German Mark values, upon the length of time over which withdrawals would be spread and upon provisions for interest. If we allow for a 90% inflation of Mark prices between 1936–8 and 1949–50 and otherwise use going exchange parities, we equate one 1938 dollar in value to 7.5, 1949–50 Deutschemark.[8] The reparations bill on these terms would translate into seventy-five billion Marks of goods purchased at 1949–50 prices. With regard to time-spread and interest, Soviet proposals were liberal. The ten-year period for payment specified by the Soviets at Yalta was stretched out to twenty years in the Moscow March–April 1947 negotiations. Reparations drainage spread over twenty years without interest would thus amount to 3.75 billion Marks annually. Roughly speaking this annual payment would be doubled with a 5% interest charge as specified in the 1919–20 Versailles settlement and scaled up 60% by a 3% interest charge as allowed in the Western debt settlement of 1952. The Soviets however, did not choose to expand their reparations claims by requiring that they accumulate with interest. These claims were blood obligations and they were not regarded in the spirit of commercial calculation. Alternatively, the Soviets could have scaled down their reparations claims in half and asked for commercialized treatment by issuance of serialized interest-bearing debt. Perhaps their waiver of interest should be regarded as a kind of built-in concession or scaling down of the true amount which would otherwise be felt by the German economy.

How readily could a German economy unified in settlement have discharged annual reparations obligations averaging 3.75 billion Marks in 1949–50 values? How much true capacity was there annually to pay this sum of values in transferrable industrial products, useful services or foreign exchange? In appraising German capacity to pay we must try to erase from our minds the vision of the economically resurrected Germany which was to trace a record of amazing industrial recovery in the decade of the Fifties. On this record there can be no doubt of capacity to pay reparations on a more generous scale than we have indicated. Thus if we take industrial production alone in the first six years of the decade the following record was achieved:

(1936 equals 100)

| | East Germany | | West Germany |
	Official Estimate	Western Estimate	
1936	100	100	100
1950	111	85	111
1951	136	100	131
1952	157	107	140
1953	177	118	154
1954	195	125	172
1955	210	134	198

(Source: W. F. Stolper, "The Labor Force and Industrial Development in Soviet Germany," *Quarterly Journal of Economics*, LXXI [1957] p. 538.)

If we put these measures of industrial production on a labor force basis, the relatively greater speed of industrial recovery in Western Germany is nearly eliminated since the 1955 Eastern labor force was slightly below prewar levels while the Western labor force was greater by a fourth.[9] Combining the two Germanies we see that by 1950 industrial production had recovered its 1936 level and that by 1955 overall German industrial production was 80% over 1936 levels. Annual industrial production in both Germanies continued to rise in the later years of the decade at nearly as fast a rate. Yet the industrial production at 1936 levels supported a population with 67.3 million persons, only some 3% less than Germany's 1950 population of 69.1 million persons, at an average standard of living which exceeded by a third the European average.[10] In addition 1936 levels of industrial production supported a heavy rearmament program to equip the mighty Wehrmacht in the making. Soviet economists estimated that military expenditures in the six years before the war averaged annually about four billion dollars or about 15 billion Reichmarks.[11] If we take the West German development alone and plot gross national product by half-years from 1950 for the first three years of the decade of the 50's we see the testimony of German reparations potential spread out before us.

West-Germany Per Capita Consumption and Total Gross National Product by Half-Years in 1936 Prices.

	GNP (in billion M)	Per Capita Consumption
1936	23.96	384M
1950I	25.26	321M
1950II	29.58	379M
1951I	30.35	385M
1951II	32.38	391M
1952I	32.17	373M
1952II	34.49	426M
1953I	33.71	401M
1953II	37.51	463M

(Source: *Statistisches Jahrbuch für die BD 1954, p. 523.*)

The Western German Republic alone in the years 1950 and 1951—when her industrial strength was only beginning to show—was capable without budgetary strain of raising nearly a billion Marks annually for the support of Western Berlin and an average of six billion Marks for the support of the NATO military forces stationed in Germany.[12] The industrial recovery of the Eastern German Republic also proceeded under the handicap of support of a good-sized military force and reparations drainage as well.

But if we are to examine the problem of German capacity to pay as this problem was faced in disposition of the Control Council regime, we must erase from our minds the ready display of economic potential evidenced by the historical record in after-years and confine our view to that of the ailing, deficit-ridden pre-settlement Germany as it took shape under the Control Council regime. In this economy industrial production by the end of 1946 reached only a third of 1936 levels and by the end of 1947 hardly 46%. Obviously, the ability of the German economy to pay reparations depended in good measure on liberating its economic energies and resources, paralyzed in the Control Council regime, in settlement. Energetic monetary reform to provide a sound money as incentive for acquisition and as a ready facility for trade would have provided stimulus and basis for a revival of the German economy. Elimination of the zonal frontier line would have afforded an equally potent basis for resource-liberation.*

* The analysis following in the text is a condensed and only slightly revised version of a text prepared in 1949 and published in 1950. See by the present author,

The East-West zonal frontier line cut back to a twelfth the lines of trade and specialization which had provided the basis for German economic strength; this zonal frontier fostered duplication of resources. The adverse effects of partition implicit in the Control Council regime were augmented by the ruin which this regime spelled for Germany's largest industrial and urban center, Berlin. This great city with its prewar population of over four millions had been an important industrial workshop. Prewar Berliners by their enterprise and work generated some 10.7% of Germany's prewar national income, some 8.4% of her net industrial output, and some 7% of her industrial exports. Bombing, combat and dismantling hurt the city badly and particularly its housing, commercial and cultural facilities.[13] But the real damage to the Berlin economy issued from the Control Council regime. Wrenched from its hinterland, internationalized, dismembered into sectors, the economic energies of the city were paralyzed while its leadership role in commerce, finance and industry was gravely weakened. Settlement would have released the economic energies of this once vital center and turned Berlin from a deficit into a source of economic recovery.

Beside territorial partition which cleft Germany as a whole and as well its capital city, Berlin, there was another line of partition between the segment of the German economy functioning under German responsibility and the segment of the German economy which was put under direct control of military government through seizure, "blocking" or "confiscation." The most important and lasting of these acquisitions were the Soviet AG trusts and the Ruhr coal and steel properties under British control. Elsewhere there were thousands of properties under property control—banks, buildings, industrial firms, offices—placed under the "sterilizing custodianship of what can fairly be described as an army of Allied and German bureaucrats."[14] These Allied strangleholds on the German economy disrupted integrated economic planning and hampered industrial recovery. Removal of these Allied enclaves in the German economy would have promoted economic revival.

Finally, the Control Council regime involved a reckless exploitation of German resources to support and maintain the armed forces allegedly carrying out the occupation. In 1946/7 occupation costs in the narrow sense of the term were estimated at 7.5 billion RM or roughly

"The German Economic Potential," *Social Research* XVII (1950) 65–89 and particularly, p. 67 ff. We refer to that paper for the documentary support for the facts set forth in the text and for an evaluation of source-estimates.

one-third of aggregate tax revenues. In the two following years the financial burden of occupation costs ran to 20.5% of total tax revenues. In terms of resources involved, these expenditures claimed choice urban residential sites, about 5% of products in critical shortage (coal, food, electric power), about 10% of industrial output generally and the services of 700,000 workers or 3% of the labor force. Regionally this drainage was distributed among the zones with benign impartiality. Berlin and the French Zone were burdened with somewhat higher per capita charges while these charges in the Soviet, the American and the British zones were approximately on par.[15] Besides this official economic drainage there was private drainage growing out of the black marketing and smuggling activities of a horde of alien soldiery, freebooting civilians and displaced persons seeking private compensation for German wrong-doing.[16]

Some scope for curtailment of occupation charges would be afforded by enforcement of more abstemious modes of consumption upon army commanders who were enjoying in Germany the rare experience of access to resources which could be requisitioned without clearing through governmental budgeting controls.[17] Economies also could be obtained by depriving displaced persons camps of German subsidies and special status within the German community. But undoubtedly the main focus for curtailment was drastic reduction of the size of the military forces which had been stationed in Germany partly out of latent rivalry and prestige and partly because Germany provided free billeting, camp grounds, miscellaneous services and some contribution to upkeep. Early American policy pronouncements had strongly emphasized the need to curtail occupation forces and occupation costs.[18] The more closely these costs were assimilated to and charged off against reparations awards, the more stable the resulting patterns of settlement and the more ample the reparations potential that would be made available.[19]

Some progress toward curtailment had been made by negotiations in the Control Council on occupation costs and at a higher level on limitations of occupation forces. Experience in Austria showed that drastic reductions in occupation costs could be anticipated given a reasonable pattern of settlement.* A trimmed occupation budget—in addition to

---

* In the Control Council an elaborate agreement on occupation costs was in process of clearance. This agreement would have laid the basis for specific fund curtailment. See Allied Central Authority, *Report to the Council of Foreign Ministers from the Allied Control Authority in Germany,* CONL/P(47)

a disarmed Germany spared military outlays, a rehabilitated Berlin, a reassimilated Ruhr and corporate system and a reduction of foreign garrison—would greatly step up German reparations potential.

Did the postwar German economy possess the "capacity to pay" even after modification of the onerous Potsdam regime? Capacity to pay depends on the ability to raise the requisite financial means and to provide the requisite goods. Let us consider first the financial problem.

Since reparations goods are transferred from the national economy without reimbursement, this cost must be borne by government budgets or by the generation of some revenue source in local currency. The problem of German capacity to pay was approached in these terms by the Dawes Committee in 1924. The outer limit of capacity to pay was determined by the funds that could be raised for reparations purposes in a conventionally unobjectionable manner consistent with the maintenance of balanced budgets and overall monetary stability.

Ostensibly for this purpose, the Dawes Committee surveyed German taxing power and expenditure needs to measure that elusive margin between "the maximum revenue and the minimum expenditure for Germany's needs."[20] They found this margin for the time being was

7–15, section IV, Part 10, (d), Occupation Costs. See also the copious OMGUS brief, "On Financing of Occupation Costs" (Prepared for the Deputy Military Governor, Finance Division, July 1947—typewritten). At the Moscow conference Molotov indicated support of Byrnes' initiative in developing limitations on the size of occupation forces. See V. N. Molotov, *Speeches and Statements at the Moscow Session of the Council of Foreign Ministers, 1947* (published by Soviet News, London, 1947), 113. Molotov accepted the American proposal in principle but reduced the Western military contingent from 300,000 (suggested by Byrnes) to 250,000 and assigned parity in military holdings between the Soviet and the U.S.-British zones. It was chiefly this question of parity which stalemated later Control Council negotiations on the question of limitation of the occupying forces. See L. D. Clay, *Decision in Germany* (New York, 1950), 155. The acidity of the later discussions indicates that the chief grounds for their failure was the absence of a framework of settlement. While the Austrian frame of settlement was only partial, it permitted a considerable reduction of occupation charges. F. H. Klopstock, "Monetary and Fiscal Policy in Postliberation Austria," *Political Science Quarterly*, LXIII (1948), 108 ff.; M. Gottlieb, "Highlight Report of Vienna Trip, November 25–27, 1946," (OMGUS, Finance Division, 28 December 1946—typewritten); OMGUS, *Financial Exploitation of German Resources by the USSR* (Finance Division, November, 1947) 6. E. S. Mason noted, perhaps optimistically, that "a solution to this question" —that of introducing "fairly stringent limitations" on occupation costs—"could be found without much difficulty" within the framework of settlement. E. S. Mason, "Reflections on the Moscow Conference," *International Organization*, II (1947), 485.

non-existent. The Germany which they surveyed (in 1923–4) was just emerging from a long series of unbalanced government budgets resulting from continuous inflation, mismanagement of expenditures, and careless handling of revenues. Prospects for fiscal stability were uncertain. Hence the Dawes Committee wisely forbore from any general drain on German government budgets for the first two years. In addition to earmarking the proceeds of a single tax source, they laid a partial capital levy on industry and the railroads in the forms of new indebtedness, the interest service of which was earmarked for reparations purposes.

The situation after World War II was quite different. The process of inflation was stopped in its tracks by stabilization of the system of "suppressed inflation." In this setting, taxing power was raised to a high degree of potency by Allied tax increases. Civilian German expenditures were by design, inadvertence, and default subjected to a relentless compression, which made way for the large occupation costs, reparations, and other expenditures requirements imposed by the occupation.[21] Budgets in Potsdam, Germany during 1946 were thus approximately balanced. By the spring of 1948 they were placed in a surplus position. Economic revival generated by settlement would have immensely increased tax revenues. The same settlement would have caused occupation charges to dip somewhat. Thus there are good grounds to have expected that a settlement for Germany would have been able to afford considerable tax relief and still meet her relief and welfare needs and finance reparations without budgetary strain.[22]

Provision of funds out of balanced budgets was necessary to permit procurement of current produced product to be claimed as reparations. But the most ample financial provision would not itself make available the industrial abundance from which alone reparations could be paid. Did the ravages of war and peace leave the German people with a surplus of productive power beyond that needed to repair war damage and sustain life at some minimal level? Since industrial production by the end of 1947 had only recovered between 40–50% of 1936 levels, for the Control Council Germany, the proof of this abundance was not clearly evident.

Certainly, the Germany of the Control Council regime did not show up with the external signs of abundance and prosperity. The toll of war was felt most fully in the loss by bombing, combat and territorial cession of nearly 36% of Germany's dwelling structures, a ready target to the Allied air war against the German civilan population. This would mean regimented and crowded housing for many a decade ahead. Loss through cession of 26% of previous German food acreage would for years to come manifest itself in a coarser level of feeding and a reduced inflow of relatively expensive high-protein or tropical foods and stimulants which had become worked into the German standard of life. But badly housed and more poorly fed, a nation can still produce to excess.[23] Had the production capacity been depleted by the ravages of war or peace? What had the Council regime disclosed under this heading?

Here in the main, the disclosures had been highly favorable. The main requisite of industrial production, namely a skilled and mobilized labor force, had carried over from the prewar period, on virtually an unaltered scale. By December 1947 the reports from the Labour Offices showed that the number of gainfully employed by December 1947 had exceeded 1936 and had practically reached the employment levels of 1939. Although the productive quality of the labor force was somewhat deteriorated, a ready supply of industrial labor could be tapped with proper inducements.[24]

Would industrial labor have available industrial facilities with which to produce the abundance out of which reparations could be paid? There was clear and unmistakable testimony that this abundance of industrial capacity existed. Directly this was disclosed by the innumerable surveys of German industrial capacity carried out in connection with the Level of Industry Plan. These surveys showed a total excess plant capacity to produce in Western Germany alone, operating on a one-shift basis, of somewhat over 2000 industrial plants accounting for a high percentage of German industrial output. But the best evidence for this production potential was not the survey of the Control Council but the United States Strategic Bombing Survey. This Survey was carried on shortly after the war by a large staff of some 1200 persons which trailed the armies into Germany, closely examined and inspected several hundred German plants, cities and areas, interviewed and interrogated thousands of Germans, scoured Germany for its war records and published mostly during 1945 some 200 individual reports. The Bombing Survey teams included many competent economists and analysts attempted in their many summary reports to measure the effects of strategic bombing on the German war economy.[25] The startling fact which their reports underscored was that even under strain of war and the air-raid attack against the German cities and her industrial centers,

German gross national product rose during the war and was maintained during 1944 at an average level, not counting foreign contributions, some 25% over 1936 levels.[26] The physical volume of industrial production—covering mining, manufacturing and construction—continued to increase for each year of the war up through 1944.

Physical Volume of Industrial Production and
Construction Prewar Germany 1939–1944
(Indices, 1939 equals 100)

	1939	1940	1941	1942	1943	1944
Mining, Mfg. and Const.	100	106.5	116.6	118.1	131.8	132.6
Manufacturing	100	107.4	119.2	121.2	136.7	138.6
Bituminous coal (million tons)	187.5*	204.8*	247.9*	248.3*	264.5*	268.9*

(Source: USBS, *The Effects of Strategic Bombing on the German War Economy*, 1945, p. 27, p. 92).
    * Year ending March.

German industry was generously equipped with machine tools. The German inventory of machine tools rose by 1943 nearly 50% over 1938 levels.[27] German industry was equipped with machine tools at the end of the war on a virtual par with the United States.[28] Production during the war of new equipment was on a scale which considerably exceeded that needed to replace destroyed or damaged equipment. The mere slowdown of foreign deliveries which in peacetime years took a sixth of German machinery output more than offset the need to replace war damage.[29] The annual output of the machine tool industry when working at full capacity equalled nearly a tenth of the total stock of machine tools. Since the highest rate of equipment damage per year was about 6.5% of total machinery inventory, the mere channelling of current output more than offset war damage. Operation of industrial plant on a single shift basis through all the war years is another indication of generous equipment potential.[30] Moreover, production of coal and steel were well-maintained and even expanded through near the end of the war. Though the Ruhr coal and steel-working areas were heavily attacked by air raids, damage to facilities was largely superficial and production was maintained until the destruction in late 1944 of transportation facilities, whether by area or target attacks, led to the rapid collapse of coal and steel production. In the entire year 1943 air raid losses of crude steel production totaled 2.3 million tons as compared with actual output of 30.3 million tons.[31] In 1944 the more concentrated attack on steel and iron facilities extensively damaged "subsidiary plant facilities and the transport system in the producing area." But there was "comparatively little damage" done to "major production facilities." This is because "the machinery and equipment used in steel manufacture is massive and built to withstand great strains." The structural design of a modern blast furnace "resembles that of an air raid shelter built specifically to deflect bombs."[32] And the remarkable feature is that industrial production was maintained at high levels with a labor force composed nearly 30% of ill-treated foreign slave workers living in cities under heavy air-raid attack.

The conclusion to be drawn from the some 200 studies of the United States Strategic Bombing Survey was that German industrial capacity to produce was retained in Germany on a scale vastly exceeding the output requirements of 1936 or any comparable peacetime year. German industrial production was low in 1946 and in 1947 because of lax incentives to produce, demoralized organization, depleted supplies and lack of suitable overall inducements and facilities including money, trade and planning. The principal bottleneck area of the German industrial economy was in transportation. German railways and bridges were severely damaged by concentrated bombing attack, by combat and seizure of rolling stock, trackage. The German inland waterway and coastal fleets were either destroyed or confiscated. Ports and harbor installations were badly damaged. Industrial production could only revive as fast as transport facilities could be repaired and, we could add, no faster than coal and steel production would be revived. It can only be said that basic industrial capacity existed to support repair programs where needed and to thus carry output levels sustaining reparations deliveries and self-support of a demilitarized Germany.[33]

Internal reparations potential—sheer ability to mobilize funds by taxation and to produce industrially beyond self-support levels—was ample enough. But the losses arising out of the war and its aftermath more severely affected German ability to balance her foreign trading account and to achieve recovery without external assistance. The seeds of tension in this sector had been sown earlier by the peculiar way in which the German economy fitted into the 20th century world economy.

Industrialization and extensive population increase made Germany dependent on raw materials and foodstuffs imported on a deficit basis chiefly from oversea wheat belts and tropical areas. The free foreign exchange required to meet the deficit was earned through surpluses in intra-European trade and through special revenue sources such as German foreign investments, a thriving merchant marine and German pioneering in certain newly developed technological fields.[34]

Germany's dependence on outside trading incomes had become a source of concern to German students and publicists by the turn of the century.[35] Their forebodings were given substance by the changes growing out of the first World War which cost Germany most of her foreign investments and merchant marine, her position of industrial leadership which had been buttressed by patent protection in chemical and electro-technical products, and border territories which contained important industrial resources.[36] The persistent foreign balance deficits of the late Twenties at least partially reflected a condition of structural strain.[37] These deficits were eliminated during the Thirties but only by grace of favorable raw material price relationships and use of trading controls.[38] Hence return of raw material prices to more normal levels and stripping from the German economy the ability to exploit its trading position would tend to put the German balance of payments under strain.

This tendency to strain inherited from the past was intensified by changes growing out of World War II which undermined the two main supports in the trading relationships by which the German economy paid its way. First, possibilities for earning gold or dollars through surpluses on the intra-European trading account were cut away or narrowed due to deterioration in the economic position of the Western European economy as a whole in its economic relations with the outside world.[*]

[*] For a portrayal of the shifts in the underlying asset and income positions which account for the deterioration in Western Europe's relative trading position, see E. Ward, *The West at Bay* (New York, 1948), 22–100. On a more serious analytical level, see T. Balogh, *The Dollar Crisis, Causes and Cure* (London, 1949), 1–17, 136 ff., 226 ff. On the other hand, we are not supposing here that the balance of payments strain arising out of the unquestionable deterioration in Europe's real trading position may not be overcome by exchange rate movements of sufficient magnitude, given time enough for all the effects of price changes to work their way out in related and sticky markets. See H. Mendershausen, "Fitting Germany into a Network of World Trade," *American Economic Review Supplement*, XL (1950), 560 ff.

Moreover, while Germany's ability to earn gold or dollars through intra-European trade was weakened greatly, her underlying need for gold or dollars to meet her non-European trading deficit was increased due to weakened ability to obtain supplies from eastern Europe, Asia and Africa, increased dependence on western hemisphere grains and other edibles because of the loss of eastern food lands, and loss of shipping. When to these losses are added lost patents, confiscated German foreign assets and sundered banking and trade connections, it would seem unlikely that German commercial interests could be built up to their former level in the non-European Western world for a considerable future.[39]

The German foreign trade deficit which loomed ahead would be smaller the more favorable the terms of settlement to the German economy, the more rapidly economic recovery could be galvanized by appropriate measures of economic policy, the more prudent the management of German foreign trade and the more far-reaching the efforts made to curtail unessential imports and to foster by flexible protectionism local substitutes for products previously imported.[40] Nonetheless, even under the best foreseeable conditions some deficit for a transition period was unavoidable on the over-all trading account. Financial support to cover a current deficit would enable the managers of German foreign trade to refill pipelines, to withstand the pressures of seasonal unbalance and to permit trade in markets where rigid bilateral balancing could not at least at the outset be achieved. German gold and foreign currency reserves were confiscated and the process of trade recovery and economic expansion would be hampered if Germany were expected to accumulate a working cash balance out of current trade surpluses. The smaller the size of this working fund the more delayed would be the process of trade and economic recovery, the more effectively German commercial policy would be forced into the mould of bilateral and governmentally regimented trade and the greater would be the German need to utilize coal exports to Western Europe in bargaining to earn the required exchange.

The size of the deficit and of the needed loan would depend upon the terms of the settlement and attendant circumstances. But the scale of assistance needed was considerably less for a post-settlement united Germany than for a sundered Western Germany going it alone with an enclave in Western Berlin. Such a Western Germany faced intensified drainage of occupation costs; fructifying German trade with the east was obstructed or barred; unsettled prospects hindered long-run planning and investment; and the resource span of the working economy was narrowed and burdened as well with unproductive enclaves and artificial transport expenses. This indicates that the billion dollar deficit realized by Western Germany during 1948–9 was no measure of the need for assistance of a post-settlement Germany. Perhaps the Dawes Plan loan of 200 million dollars is more akin to the nature of the economic support required to enable a German republic to maintain itself in its first post-settlement year. At any rate, an amount between these two magnitudes and nearer the lower would appear the more reasonable projection for Germany's order of need for financial assistance under a quadripartite settlement.

The provision of external financial assistance to cover transitional deficits would generate the need for additional restraints on any feasible reparations program of withdrawals from current production.[41] Such withdrawals would need to be so scaled and organized as not to increase the need for aid or prejudice the possibilities for its repayment. This would mean that reparations installments should be tapered in their application according to the rate of recovery and that the full weight of reparations programming should not be applied until recovery was well under way. It would also mean that a charge should be levied on reparations withdrawals for the imported materials contained in them or used in their production.*

A more difficult problem was presented by protection of Germany's exportation from being "used up" in reparations. German ability to maintain exportation of choice items could be at least partially assured by a flexible system of commodity exclusions and limitations, by deliberate diversification of the assortment of goods permitted for reparations and by the greatest possible reliance on purchase in open markets rather than rigid requisition. At low levels of production little opportunity would exist for elastic arrangements, but the main premise of any reparations settlement was German industrial recovery to somewhere near prewar output levels. Given adequate internal production, the requisite diversification and flexibility in reparations programming would not appear unmanageable.[42]

Maintenance of German ability to offer export goods would be un-

* The Soviets appeared to resist this claim and asserted the right to take commodities in reparations without reimbursement for the imported materials in them or used in their production. But it may be surmised that Soviet assent to a settlement would not have been withheld on this account. OMGUS, *A Summary,* 113.

availing if the effect of receipt of reparations was that of diminishing the demand for those goods. This could occur since "Germany's reparations claimants are also her customers."* In the rapidly industrializing and collectivized economies under Soviet influence or control this impairment of demand for German goods by receipt of reparations was an unlikely prospect since their ability to absorb manufactured goods and equipment was almost unlimited. Under these circumstances the demand for German exports was governed primarily by the availability of export proceeds which receipt of reparations might even enlarge by improvement of export potential or of ability to produce and transport desirable export items.

The degree to which reparations would impair the demand for German exports in the western world is more uncertain. Choice export items could be withheld from the range of goods eligible for reparations purchase. Reparations could, moreover, be concentrated to a degree on special programs or consumption areas with a minimum direct effect on commercial relationships. But it would be very difficult to draw a commodity line between "commercial exports" and "reparations goods" without making the latter category a dumping ground for what in continental trade parlance is called "second-class" goods. German export relationships with individual countries had not settled into any well coagulated pattern and the commodity make-up was shifting and diversified. Moreover, even if reparations were permitted a recipient nation in a form designed not to impair demand for German exportation, the demand for products of other countries would to some extent be impaired.

These adverse effects could be confined to narrow dimensions only if

---

* Cf. D. Ginsburg, *Future of German Reparations* (National Planning Association Pamphlets Nos. 57–58, Washington, 1947), 38. "Will Germany be able to *give* these nations reparations . . . and at the same time *sell* them enough to maintain a tolerable standard of life within Germany's own borders?" Ginsburg admitted that reparations from the so-called restricted industries (chiefly metal and equipment) would not impair German export markets. But his argument that export markets for light consumer goods would be weakened by reparations within that category is self-defeating since he admits that Western European nations "have never looked to Germany for textiles or clothing" and Russia "now or in the long run cannot be expected to offer a commercial market" for products of this category. *Ibid.*, 39. What then makes the conclusion "unmistakeable" that "recurring reparations from the light peaceful industries would be, in all probability, at the expense of Germany's commercial exports from these industries?"

express arrangements were made by the principal recipients of Western reparations, Britain and France, who were scheduled to receive two-thirds of the Western share.[43] Given full employment and buoyant markets in these two countries, arrangements for maintaining reparations along with a balance of trade could have been worked out. In any case a German loss which was a British and French gain would constitute no net loss to the Western world. Admittedly, the insulation of reparations from commercial trading patterns would involve a considerable amount of bilateral trading relationships. This entire range of problems could be resolved if the Western countries were willing to receive their German reparations in the form of products selected and used in a manner and under conditions designed expressly to sterilize their adverse effect on the German commercial balance of trade or in the form of such free foreign exchange surpluses as might be realized by the German trading balance.

II. Illusion and Drift at Work

Ample reparations potential thus existed in Germany. But it existed only as the resultant of a complex and projective course of settlement. Reparations potential could not be read out of the surface situation or seen as the outcome of current drift. It could only be perceived by an intellectual effort, based on a vision of the rehabilitory leverage of settlement. It was necessary to push aside contemporary reality with its lagging recovery, deficits and scarcities. Such intellectual reconstruction was not to be had. Those who worked in Germany generally had their insight warped by preoccupation with familiar or pressing problems. Those working at a distance sometimes had more balanced perspective but less insight into forces operating below the surface.

Underestimation of reparations potential thus arising met little resistance from spokesmen of countries which suffered little or no direct damage from the war, which had little or no desire for German goods and which remembered the depressing experience of the Twenties when foolish American loans financed reparations payments. The inhibiting effects of the Potsdam regime were recognized but were rarely traced to their governing conditions. Potsdam Germany was readily rationalized in terms of Soviet and French obstruction, extraction of reparations at ¹o-American expense or, more often, destitution and disorganization ·l by the war and visible in wrecked cities, beggary and underfeeding. For such reasons reparations generally appeared in Anglo-American thought not as a catalyst of settlement which would liberate resources but as a drag on recovery, as an affliction on a suffering and destitute people and as an aggravation of the tendency to deficit.*

Concern with this deficit, overestimated through minimization of German economic potential and the rehabilatory leverage of settlement, took on something of the role in Anglo-American official thought which wartime losses had in Soviet thought. The deficit with its alleged burdens on Anglo-American taxpayers became an obsession. That the already accrued deficit grew out of the weakness of occupation policy more than out of a lagging German balance of trade was ignored. Insistence on sharing the deficit was propelled into the negotiations as a key issue.**

* The tenor of official American thinking on the question may be illustrated by the evaluation of reparations potential Marshall presented during an important East-West encounter in the Council of Foreign Ministers: "We will not agree to the program of reparations from current production which under existing conditions could only be met in one of two ways. The first would be that the United States would pay for such reparations. This the United States will not do. The only other method of obtaining reparations from current production from Germany at the present time and foreseeable future would be to depress the German standard of living to such a point that Germany would become not only a center of unrest in the heart of Europe but this would indefinitely if not permanently retard the rehabilitation of German peacetime economy and hence the recovery of Europe." For this statement, made on 10 December 1947, see U.S. Department of State, *Germany, 1947–1949*, 411. Ginsburg wrote that a reparations program "means an abandonment of the undertaking to permit them to raise their living standards to the level of those prevailing in the rest of Europe . . . , means the indefinite prolongation of stringent government controls . . . , means the indefinite continuance of the miseries of the last few years . . . , means for the ordinary German, hopelessness. One weeps not for Germans or Germany . . . but for Europe and the peace." Ginsburg, *Future of German Reparations*, 46. These extracts are characteristic. They reflect almost pathetic preoccupation with the need for recovery which looked so difficult to achieve in the German slough of despond.

** This view was presented in the March-April 1947 negotiations at the Moscow conference of the Council of Foreign Ministers; it was reiterated in the London meeting seven months later. Its first component was a demand for "an equitable sharing among the Occupying Powers of the costs of occupation of Germany, past, present and future." This was amplified by the specific demand that the repayment of the accrued deficit and external occupation costs in turn should have the "first charge on Germany's foreign exchange resources after her essential needs have been met." Until these needs were satisfied, "Germany shall not be called upon to make any reparation deliveries from current production." OMGUS, *A Summary*, 132, 135,

Finally, the deficit as the most tangible expression of German stagnation was converted into the measure of reparations potential. A deficit signified inability to pay reparations. Extraction of reparations from an economy with a deficit appeared illicit on its face since it would mortgage export proceeds which should be a "first charge" on imports and it would funnel out the foreign aid brought in to relieve the deficit. By implication this gauged reparations potential by potential ability to redress a foreign deficit.* In reality, the former turns upon forcing a margin between tax yields and allowable expenditure needs on the one hand and between total physical product and domestic consumption and investment on the other. The latter turns upon the willingness of the outside trading world to part with precious metals or needed imports in exchange for desired German products on a scale and on terms of exchange which can only partially be affected by German decision.[44] Practical expression of the distinction between these two aspects of reparation potential was given in the "transfer" arrangements for reparations payable under the Dawes Plan.** To wave this distinction aside was tacitly to apply "the

---

227; see also *Die Deutsche Frage auf der Moskauer Konferenz der Aussenminister, sonderheft, Europa-Archive,* II (1947), 706. For an analysis of the validity of this claim, see "Reparations Problems Again," *loc. cit.,* 32–33, nn. 22, 23.

* ". . . The annual surplus which German labor can produce . . . at home is no measure either theoretically or practically of the annual tribute which she can pay abroad." J. M. Keynes, *The Economic Consequences of the Peace* (New York, 1920), 208. See also the Dawes 1924 report.

** "There has been a tendency in the past to confuse two distinct though related questions, i.e., first the amount of revenue which Germany can raise available for reparation account, and second the amount which can be transferred to foreign countries. The funds raised and transferred to the Allies . . . cannot in the long run exceed the sums which the balance of payments makes it possible to transfer without currency and budget instability ensuing. But it is quite obvious that the amount of budget surplus which can be raised by taxation is not limited by the entirely distinct question of the conditions of external transfer." Budgetary balances can be precisely computed since it is "the sum of decisions taken by a single authority." By comparison "a country's economic balance defies exact calculation . . . and a potential economic balance is much more uncertain. It depends not on the decisions of a single authority but on the enterprise of individual merchants and manufacturers." See World Peace Foundation, *The Dawes Report,* 374. For an equally clear statement see the 1919 report of the banker's committee (Davis-Montagu-Loucheur) to the three chiefs of state on how the extent of reparations that could be realized ld or foreign currency "resolves [itself] entirely into how much can be saved many confining her exports to essentials and how much the consumptive he world can be increased" in P. M. Burnet, *Reparation at the Paris Peace*

theory of liquids to what is if not a solid at least a sticky mass with strong internal resistances."[45]

The difficulties anticipated and encountered during the Twenties in transforming internal reparations potential into a foreign trading surplus were given heightened force after 1945 by the nature of the real trading world in which Germany was to try its luck at overcoming its deficit. In this world the overwhelming bulk of gold and dollar reserves was owned or pledged to the United States which tended in the immediate postwar period to draw a constantly increasing share of them.[46] The fraction of reserves available for use by other countries was the object of desperate struggle and heightened possessory instincts. Without brutal utilization of her bargaining power as a source of coal exports, Germany could do little to acquire gold or dollars on a significant scale. Under these circumstances the German ability to maintain or redress her foreign balance was contingent essentially upon reversal of the trading currents which had drawn the world's monetary reserves to America and upon achievement of a more smoothly working multilateral trading system. This meant that Germans would not be permitted to devote a fraction of their working time and use of German productive facilities to repair damage wrought by Germans in Russia until the problem of "dollar scarcity" was solved or well on the way to solution. It was to this pitch of objective irrationality on the reparations question that Western thinking was carried due to its underestimation of reparations potential, its overestimation of the deficit and its identification of reparations potential with foreign trading ability.

Of course, this illusion-bound course of Western thought was not utterly beyond relief. It was permeated by dissonances which, though smothered over by the ideological atmosphere which came to accompany cold war in Germany, still gave it an uneasy balance and harbored certain possibilities for statesmanship. This potential for statesmanship could have been utilized by Soviet policy in pressing the issue of settlement. Indeed, very limited proposals for a reparations settlement were offered by the West.* But if a settlement was to result Soviet policy would need

---

Conference (New York, 1940, 2v.) I, 691. For a general survey, see any standard account of the reparations problem in the twenties, e.g., E. Dulles, "The Evolution of Reparation Ideas," A. H. Cole, ed., *Facts and Factors in Economic History* (Cambridge, 1932), 568 ff.

* Under Clay's direction, U.S.-Soviet discussions on the "technical" level were conducted in Berlin in the fall of 1946 to explore the feasibility of a settlement involving the lifting of dismantling levels, economic unification and current product

to have been astute, persuasive and subtle. It was crude, blundering and inept. Thus the Soviet method of demonstrating the existence of reparations potential was irritating in its casual self-assuredness.* The

reparations. The discussions were commented on extensively at the time in a hopeful way. Cf. "Reparations from Germany," *The Economist,* 23 and 30 November 1946, 833–4, 873–4; J. Alsop, *New York Herald Tribune,* 11 September 1946; *New York Times,* 11 December 1946. Don Humphrey who probably participated in or was close to the discussions characterized them as "informal" ones which "never reached the state of negotiations." The reasons alleged were that "the Soviet would not provide the requisite information and . . . were unwilling to treat Germany as a single political unit." D. D. Humphrey, German mss., Chapter XX, "The Soviets," 4. Nevertheless, Draper and Clay sponsored at least to a limited degree the program of a reparations settlement with the Soviets involving some kind of "deal" over upward revision of the dismantling plan. Clay alluded vaguely to his desire at Moscow to "develop the issue" which Dulles took the lead in inducing the American delegation to oppose. Clay, *Decision,* 149. The outcome of Clay's initiative was a curious proposal which offered the Soviets the dollar-for-dollar equivalent in current product of a fraction of the plant capacity entitled for dismantling under the March 1946 agreement but retained in Germany. And this limited compensation for a fraction of relinquished dismantlements was only to be paid when certain severely restrictive conditions were fulfilled. For the proposal, see U.S. Department of State, *Germany, 1947–1949,* 410. This proposal seems to have been guardedly discussed though the sources disagree in what detail and at what level. Mason cryptically asserts it was "never seriously discussed at Moscow"; while Clay states the proposal was "overlooked" by the Soviets though a favorable notice of it was explicitly taken by Vishinsky in a press conference and other sources allege the proposal was the main subject of a secret or closed session of the foreign ministers. *Die Deutsche Frage auf der Moskauer Konferenz,* 709; Middleton, *Struggle for Germany,* 101; *Tägliche Rundschau,* 4 April 1947; Mason "Reflections on the Moscow Conference" *loc. cit.* 381; Clay, *Decision,* 150. It is curious too that though Marshall alluded to this proposal in much detail in his report on the Moscow conference, the OMGUS compilation of conference agreements and the conference protocol contains no record of it. The ground for Soviet disinterest in the proposal as formulated is self-evident since the proposal would offer current product reparations of less value for a German settlement than the Soviet would extract with ease in six months from their zone of occupation.

* Molotov, *Speeches, Moscow Conference,* 53. A typical extract follows: "The Soviet delegation answers this question (of potential) without hesitation: there is nothing in these claims exceeding Germany's ability to meet them . . . If Germany uses even a fraction of her former war expenditures for partial compensation of the damage she caused to the Allied Powers, she will not only be able to ensure the ʰabilitation of her economy but also fulfillment of her obligations to the Allies." ʰre careful effort to prove the case was made in a letter from Eugene Varga, the Soviet economist, to *The Economist,* 3 January 1948, 13. He attempts to deʰroposition that Germany "could easily pay annually between $500 mil-

deficit which was overstressed by the West was treated with a benign unconcern. The accrued deficit which alarmed the West was attributed wholly to evil intention or Western mismanagement.* Finally, Soviet diplomats committed the egregious blunder of tossing away the one negotiational resource which could have been used to smooth the path toward settlement.

This recourse was the March 1946 level of industry agreement extorted by hard-driving Soviet negotiators who took full advantage of the fading Morgenthau orientations in American policy and General Clay's personal determination to reach agreement with the Soviets at German expense. This agreement actually conferred on the Soviets contingent title to a considerable segment of German industry, subject to dismantling. This title virtually amounted to an IOU on German industrial potential.

The trump card for Soviet diplomacy in quest of reparations settlement was the disaster to the German economy which collection of this IOU through dismantling would bring and the relief which would be offered by retaining some of the entitled plant in Germany and dividing its product for a series of years between German and reparations use. Relief offered in these terms would have commanded general German assent and would have mobilized the support of broad currents of opinion in the West which were in the process of revolting against the entire dismantling approach and the stringencies of the March 1946 agreement.

---

lion and $1000 million in reparations and at the same time could pay for food imports." It was unfortunate that this kind of thoughtful analysis was not presented as the Eastern position in earlier diplomatic exchanges.

* Characteristically the Soviets would reply to the issue of deficit that "of course" the "import-export plan" must not permit any deficit. "Furthermore, the Soviet delegation considers that the German economy should be established on the principle of a net balance, i.e., not showing any deficit." OMGUS, *A Summary,* 114. See also Molotov, *Speeches, Moscow conferences,* 53–55. Taking cognizance of the British deficit, Molotov merely noted that "if steps are taken for a proper development of German peacetime industry in the Ruhr and other parts of Germany then Taxpayers beyond the German frontiers will not have to bear the burden of expenditure on Germany's needs." This modest tone turned to harsh indictment of the Western zonal deficit at the London CFM session in November–December 1947. Importation of food was attributed to failure to carry out land reform; the necessity of importing certain miscellaneous military supplies was derided; the whole project of financial assistance of Western Germany was described as a means of establishing "control." cf. V. N. Molotov, *Über den Friedensvertrag mit Deutschland* (Leipzig, 1948), 30, 38 ff.

Such a suggestion—well timed and deftly worded, with the alternatives clearly put—would have strained sorely the Anglo-American reluctance to permit current product reparations.

Whether by design or inadvertance, the Soviets muffed the opportunity. In a careless move in July 1946 the Soviets swept aside as irrelevant or not controlling the Potsdam option on unification and the reparations and dismantling deal which was its outcome.* Rights over dismantled German industry won in sustained negotiations in Berlin were then thrown away by conceding the case for upward revision of the level of industry plan without *quid pro quo.*** Having played out all

* This sweeping aside of Potsdam was self-contradictory. In one paragraph General Clay was condemned for withholding fulfillment of dismantling under the Level of Industry Plan while in the next paragraph it was stated that "naturally" the reparations granted under the Potsdam agreement "must include not only equipment but also commodities out of current production." And then later in the speech it was insisted that "reparations from Germany to the amount of 10 billion dollars be exacted without fail." See Molotov's CFM Speech, 10 July 1946, reported *Tägliche Rundschau,* 11 July 1946. In the Moscow and London CFM negotiations the sweeping aside of the Potsdam agreement by verbal quibbles was unmistakeable. It was lamely explained that the Potsdam agreement "does not contain a single word against reparations from current production as envisaged by the decision of the Crimea Conference," as if very many words were needed for this purpose. Exegesis of the Potsdam text led to emphasis on the expression in the preamble which harmlessly alluded to the intent to carry out the Crimea decision. "This reference in the Potsdam Conference decisions made it unnecessary to mention the various specific aspects of the Crimea Agreement on reparations." Hence, the Soviet Union's claim to reparations from current production is "based upon the solid foundation of joint Allied decisions." Molotov, *Speeches, Moscow Conference,* 28, 34, 52.

** This critical action was taken toward the end of Molotov's second publicized speech on German questions before the Paris session of the Council on Foreign Ministers. Making specific reference to the March 1946 agreement Molotov stated that Germany's "peaceful industries must be given an opportunity to develop on a wider scale provided only that this industrial development is really used to satisfy the peaceful needs of the German people and the requirements of trade with other countries"; and this was amplified by the specific suggestion of raising the permitted level of steel production to near 10 million tons. See text of speech, given 10 July 1947 in newspapers or in U.S. Department of State, *Occupation of Germany: Policy and Progress,* 240. For text of the first speech, see *Tägliche Rundschau,* 11 July 1946. This relinquishment of the bargaining power inherent in the dismantling plan was ̄ntinued in the later negotiations. See Molotov, *Speeches, Moscow Conference,* 28–ʻ4 f. Molotov boasted of the generous Soviet attitude which "evidently closely ̣hes the British attitude" though other Powers "seem" to have "certain ap-̣ns regarding the development of Germany's peacetime industry." (54).

their trumps, the Soviets then asked for a showdown and asserted in Molotov's best sergeant-major tone their claim for ten billion dollars of reparations from all of Germany. To sweeten their claim, direct issue was taken with the American negotiator who had pushed through the Potsdam accord and the American right to attach conditions to dismantling was denied. By these moves the Soviet case for reparations was staked not on the realities of settlement or the achievements of the Control Council regime but on doctrinaire assertion of claims poorly supported and offensively argued. Understandably enough, this diplomacy helped to dissipate any potential for settlement on the Western side.**

Of course when it came down to programming, Soviet stipulations for upward revision usually included in vague form some mention of reparations removals but this seemed partly a defensive reaction. Cf. OMGUS, *A Summary*, 213.

** Offensiveness is indicated first by context which was an examination of Byrnes' pet project, the 25 year security treaty over Germany. Not accidentally did Byrnes lead off in reply: "When the United States is willing to make a drastic departure from its policies of the past and offers this treaty in order to help insure security for Europe, we resent having that offer met with irrelevant arguments on reparations and minor difficulties of the occupation." Molotov sharply condemned Clay's action in suspending dismantling and in this context presented his 10 billion dollar claim. The wide publicity obtained by Molotov's speeches inspired both Clay and Byrnes in the belief that they were primarily calculated to influence public opinion. Byrnes, *Speaking Frankly*, 174, 179; Clay, *Decision in Germany*, 129 ff. Byrnes commented that Molotov's speech "exhausted his patience." This was indicated by his grim words on reparations. "If the Chairman wants to discuss reparations I shall discuss reparations." He pointed out that the recorded Yalta text merely showed a promise to "study" a Soviet proposal, that this proposal was "considered" and "studied" and rejected by the West. At Potsdam, said Byrnes, "Marshall Stalin agreed to what the reparations program would be and it is set forth in the Potsdam Agreement and not in an *ex-parte* statement by Mr. Maisky back in the Crimea five or six months earlier." See text of speech in Ginsburg, *German Reparations*, 20 f. When you complain about General Clay's action, warned Byrnes, "you should remember his action is taken only to obtain justice for the United States under the Potsdam Agreement." Byrnes, *Speaking Frankly*, 174, 179. Thereafter the discussion on reparations was peppered with exchange on the priority of the Yalta or Potsdam texts. Citing the facts again at Moscow, Marshall concluded that "the position of the United States Government regarding reparations is that the agreements at Potsdam supercede the preliminary agreements previously reached at Yalta. We will not follow Mr. Molotov in a retreat from Potsdam to Yalta." U.S. Department of State, *Germany, 1947–1949*, 373. On the entire episode, see Clay, *Decision*, 129 ff.; J. Joesten, *Germany, What Now?*, 257 ff.; Drew Middleton, *The Struggle for Germany* (New York, 1949), 100 ff.

It was easier for the West to pull back and to respond in kind to Molotov's inept diplomacy and offensive legalism since new currents of thought and interest were rising to the surface in Western policy and were pulling against a course of settlement. The antagonism to the Germans was subsiding and that with the Soviets was steadily rising. Under the surface the Germans were still interested in the Western alliance which had been the hope and prayer of German wartime policy and thinking. Thus strong currents of thought and interest were working to forge an American-led French-German coalition of western Europeans having their main pivot in the Western controlled Rhine valley and the great industrial power of the Ruhr.[47] In how many ways and with what enticing persuasions was this program rationalized and defended. In a winged phrase: "we must begin with what we have in the West."[48] It was easy to feel that the Soviets were merely "stalling" for time or were deliberately procrastinating in order to obstruct Western European economic recovery. How easy to argue that the West had "bought" unity —or the eastern zone of Germany—at Potsdam and should not be "blackmailed" into buying the same horse "twice." The Soviet zone was disintegrating and thus was not worth "buying" in a "deal"; others urged that a strong Western Germany would "draw" eastern Germans like a magnet draws filings.[49] Such a Western Germany could, moreover, be shaped by Western hands to suit the needs for European integration into a larger federalized polity in which the cherished values of the liberal society would be protected against the democratic national state and the forms of creeping socialism which this state makes possible. German middle-class society was ready for the adventure and German political leaders were friendly, and pliable.

With these forces in the background pulling at the course of settlement, with the Western mind illusion-bound with regard to German reparations potential and with the tendency to drift into forms of vigorous action in and within the West, is it any wonder that the opportunity for settlement of the Control Council regime was muffed? Forgotten, erased from memory, or overlooked were the effects of partition in eastern satellite states. Forgotten or rubbed out of mind or overlooked was the ability of the communist world to reply in kind and to take like measures to consolidate a militant eastern regime in the borderland territories. Forgotten or rubbed out of mind or overlooked was the Soviet capacity to mobilize themselves and their friends and allies for militant action and to crush by police action and terror the hundreds of thousands of friends of western liberal thought living in the eastern borderlands. Or was it forgotten? Would not its mental anticipation merely serve to justify even more the course of rejection of settlement? The course of Western building was thus self-justifying and would tend to call into existence the grounds for its own action and thus manufacture its own rationale.

CHAPTER IX

DISINTEGRATION OF THE CONTROL COUNCIL REGIME

I. Sham Settlement

WITHOUT AGREEMENT which satisfied Soviet reparations demands on terms which would command American financial support and not exceed German capacity to pay, there was no chance for realizing the potential for settlement built up under the Control Council regime. This was the central conclusion which emerged from the extended canvass of the German situation by the foreign ministers of the occupying powers meeting at Moscow in the early spring of 1947.[1] But though the foreign ministers were unable to come to a real settlement, they shied away from a real showdown. Too much wartime ideology still carried over. Necessary allies had yet to be stiffened and mobilized. Public opinion at home and abroad needed to be prepared. On the German scene itself, Anglo-American efforts to consolidate their incipient form of West German government, by drawing into closer collaboration with it the West German and French leadership, would have been compromised if its opening and not its closing stages were accompanied by overt conflict.

Hence the policy of ambivalence was given another lease on life in the form of a sham settlement. The proceedings of the conference were adjourned to be resumed seven months later at another session in London. Preparatory to this meeting the deputies of the foreign ministers meeting in informal conference and the Berlin Generals acting as the Control Council were supposed, within a carefully prepared frame of reference, to canvass the controverted issues. This frame of reference distinguished between projects and subject matter according to level of preliminary disposition and according to scope of intended action.

Transmitted for "study" alone or for "information and study" were the vital economic and political questions which hinged upon overall settlement. The political issues—involving an election law, a bill of rights, merger of political parties and trade unions—were turned over to the Control Council for "information and study." The economic issues concerning reparations, import-exports, economic unity, financial reform and the like, were transmitted only "for information." At Bevin's instigation the West blocked referal "for study" of these materials by either the Control Council or the deputies of the foreign ministers. The distinction in terms of reference is significant though shadowy. There was a bare possibility for fruitful discussion of the specified political issues; there was no possible solution of the economic issues. Preclusion of further "study" of them was an indirect—and perhaps unintentional— way of indicating finality of divergence on these issues and of opening the possibility of interim unilateral action.

To this thin diet of informative and study materials, were added a limited number of action projects remitted to the Control Council to "negotiate and implement." These projects dealt with return of prisoners of war, occupation force limitation, demilitarization, denazification, DP camp administration, and the like. Though these projects were not central in a scheme of settlement, their collective import was large. They dealt in areas where the extent of apparent overlap in East-West policy was broad so that it was possible to define their scope, to set up targets for action and in some cases to indicate the nature of allowable standards and procedures. If we think of the Moscow 1947 agreement as a second version of the policy of ambivalence—Potsdam being the first—the contrast with Potsdam is self-evident. No large promises are extended, no broad vistas are envisaged. The zonal rulers are no longer resolutely commanded to gallop energetically in opposite directions. The instructions are comparatively business-like and drafted with economy and precision of language. In this more prosaic form, the policy of ambivalence contains fewer illusions and quicker prospects for withering away.[2]

II. Attempt at Implementation

That negotiation on reparations and allied issues had been effectively stopped at Moscow was borne out by the subsequent record. Within four months the work of listing and appraising plant capacity potentially subject to dismantling under the March 1946 level of industry plan was cut short. No additional allocation was made of plant capacity for general reparations; plant dismantling of equipment already allocated was slowed down. No effort was made jointly to revise the now outmoded level of industry plan. Contrariwise, the economic basis for partition appeared in the issuance of a revised level of industry plan for the western zones predicated on the separate existence of a western Germany and no payment of reparations eastward.[3] Further, no effort was made to break the quadripartite stalemate on financial reform; and the West began printing a separate currency for western monetary reform.[4]

Yet rupture in these areas was not formalized. The negotiations on monetary reform were not broken off; they merely lingered. And though the March 1946 reparations agreement plan was undermined in its fundamentals, certain of its provisions were considered binding and were applied in action. Thus general purpose equipment dismantled from war plants was allocated and appraised by quadripartite action under the Control Council. After much bickering, an agreement was reached with the Soviets on the makeup and value of their first westward shipment of "reciprocal deliveries" pursuant to the Potsdam agreement. In the same way, the existing structure of quadripartite agreement was serviced with amendments and a certain amount of new legislation filtered through. Chewing this daily cud, the hundreds of negotiators representing the four occupying powers whose collective meetings set in motion the processes of the Control Council regime managed to preserve their tempers and the fiction and some of the reality of a quadripartite government over Germany.[5]

This slow decay also characterized the controverted political items which were remanded for "study" to the Berlin Generals. The Soviets continued to advocate the nationwide merger of trade unions and political parties but now Britain and America joined France in opposition. The British vetoed the project for merger of political parties; an American interdict issued at a critical juncture of trade union unity negotiations flatly prohibited merger outside the bizonal area.[6] In connection with an election law the earlier division continued with the East favoring proportional representation as an umbrella for minority parties and the West favoring an electoral system which would weaken the role of the minority parties.

Similar stalemate characterized attempts to reach agreement on projects assigned to the Berlin Generals for concrete action. Only one was successfully completed, that which provided for withdrawal of restrictions on circulation of newspapers and publications originating in another zone. The foreign ministers' order to the Control Council to carry out land reform in all zones during 1947 was deemed fulfilled by reports which assured that this had been done. A similar placatory gesture occured in connection with refugee redistribution. At Moscow the British had pressed for revision of the original November 1945 agreement by which Eastern refugees were received into the densely populated British zone. Without a settlement producing unification of Germany, there was no possibility that the East would take back the surplus population which they had worked hard to get rid of. Hence the "investigation" of the subject ordered at Moscow produced only a record of acrimonious exchange.[7]

Not all the action projects designed at Moscow had so cursory an outcome. Most promising in this respect was probably the agreement on demilitarization. This directed the Berlin Generals acting collectively as the Control Council within 90 days to draw up an agreed list of armament plants and to complete the destruction of these plants within 12 months thereafter. A previously fixed deadline of 31 December 1948 was reaffirmed for the destruction of German fortifications, naval bases and other military installations. Finally, the institution of quadripartite inspection on these programs was ordered. Yet by the end of the year this relatively promising agreement remained unfulfilled. An agreed list of armament plants could not be drawn up. The British for their part appeared reluctant to destroy certain naval bases under their control.*

* The question of the naval bases rang through a succession of Control Council meetings and apparently was based on the fact that of German naval bases under British control only two were classified as military naval bases scheduled for destruction as such and that these two by 31 December 1946 were not demilitarized. *CFM Report*, Section I, Demilitarization, Appendix, British Progress Report on Clearance of Minefields, etc., 2. By some slip in November 1947 the British consented to an agreed CORC decision to subject the naval bases and ports to quadripartite inspection "in the shortest time possible." ACA, *Minutes of the Coordinating Committee*, Corc/M(47)46, para. 253. After the preparatory work for the departure of an inspection mission was completed, the British over indignant Soviet protest blocked the project on the obviously specious grounds that the actual agreement specified "investigation" and not "inspection." *Ibid.*, Corc/M(48)3, 4, paras. 24, 35. Even the American spokesman found it possible to state that "there was no doubt that an investigation could be carried out by means of an inspection but investigation did not necessarily imply inspection." According to the British report, only one naval base at Helgoland had been subject to demilitarization measures.

They tampered in some way with the listing of armament plant declarable under agreed standards.* The Soviets injected their note of controversy by showing an exaggerated concern over destruction of buildings convertible for civilian use and not specially designed or suited for armament plant.**

Running through this Anglo-Soviet dispute were the issues raised by inspection. At the time of the Moscow agreement inspection arrangements were in effect only for outright armament plants. One round of inspection in the four zones had been conducted.[8] With increasing difficulty after Moscow two other inspection commissions were sent out in 1947.[9] Efforts to widen the inspection program pursuant to the Moscow agreement stalemated.[10] The West believed that effective inspection involved unrestricted rights of entry into any facility or installation having possible military significance. The Soviets wanted inspection restricted to

---

See ACA, *Zone Commanders Semi-Annual Reports . . . on the Implementation of CC Directive No. 22*, Corc/P(48)14, 24 January 1948; and ACA, *Minutes of the Co-ordinating Committee*, Corc/M(48)3, para. 40.

* Soviet and French opposition was aroused by the British deletion of some 86 plants out of a previous listing (prior to March 1, 1947) of 284 armament plants; and by the end of the controversy the status of some 35 was in question. For a superficial summary of the history and major facts, see OMGUS, *A Summary*, 25–28; OMGUS, *Activities Directorate of Economics*, 96–99. It appears that of the 86 plants only 7 were deemed outright armament plants by the French and 35 by the Soviets, although there was an additional charge that "many war plants which were undoubtedly Category I plants were left off the lists while many small enterprises . . . were included." *Ibid.*, 98. Raised in May 1947, the issue was more or less dropped although in his famous statement on 21 November 1947 at the 75th meeting of the Control Council, Marshal Sokolovsky recurred to these matters. See *Sokolovsky November 1947 Statement*, 2–3. The issue is complicated by the fact that in the CFM Report submissions (*CFM Report*, Section IV, Part 2, Liquidation of German Economic, War and Industrial Potential), all four powers reported outright armament plants greatly in excess of the number reported after Moscow. Thus in the Soviet zone some 628 plants were listed, of which 311 were aviation plants; in the French zone, some 64 plants; in the British zone, 284 plants; and in the U.S. zone, some 117 plants. Yet quadripartite agreement was reached in May 1947 on 171 plants for destruction in the Soviet zone, 43 plants in the French zone, and 52 plants in the U.S. zone.

** For an excellent summary of the main issues, see OMGUS, *Activities Directorate of Economics*, 99 ff. Apparently only the question of buildings in 59 armament plants was in controversy although possibly the principles involved were capable of wider application. Short of case by case examination of the disputed plants and their facilities, it is difficult to determine where the sounder judgment lies.

designated categories and to listed items.[11] The Soviet objection that commissions empowered to "wander aimlessly" were unbusinesslike was obviously facetious.[12] Possibly the Soviets were protecting their uranium mining operations which got underway in 1948 on a large scale.* In any case, the issue was a vital one and no common ground was found.

The Moscow accord on denazification fared no better than demilitarization. The accord required that "appropriate measures" be taken to (a) "hasten the fulfillment" of previous Control Council denazification directives, (b) to complete the "removal" of Nazi activists from leading positions, (c) to "concentrate upon and hasten the bringing to trial of war criminals," (d) to ascertain the effectiveness of denazification among judges and prosecutors, and (e) to assure more "uniform treatment" in zonal directives. An American text noted laconically that "extensive negotiations at all levels of the Allied Control Authority have not yet (by the end of 1947) produced an agreed interpretation of the above five articles."[13] The West blocked Soviet proposals for quadripartite inspection of denazification tribunals. The Soviets alleged Western unwillingness to facilitate repatriation to eastern countries of suspected war criminals. But the major issue of difference concerned disposition of members of the SS, Gestapo and other Nazi cadre organizations which had been placed in a "war criminal" category by the judgment of the Nüremberg Tribunal in 1946. The issue at stake was simple and fundamental. Should membership in these organizations *per se* establish presumption of guilt? The West insisted that this presumption be contingent upon proof of "voluntary membership" and "knowledge of criminal purposes of the organization." In the Soviet view these conditions would "render very difficult the execution of justice and would allow major criminals to avoid responsibility for their acts." The West adhered to judicial safeguards evolved in a stable society and designed to minimize the risk of injustice to individuals. The Soviets were intent on expeditiously removing a social menace.[14]

The action-project on displaced persons was equally unsuccessful. By the time of the Moscow Conference the many-millioned mass of

* On these mining operations see the detailed report by a former Soviet officer, N. Grishin, "The Saxony Uranium Mining Operation," *Soviet Economic Policy in Postwar Germany* (NY 1953) 127–155. Mining operations were opened up in a belt of Saxony sites near the Czech frontier (see p. 37 for map). In 1950 some 10,000 Soviet personnel were involved, including military detachments, while German employees numbered approximately 92,000 (p. 143). The Soviet director was Maltsev, the organizer of the construction of the Moscow subway (p. 129).

displaced persons (DP's) found in the western zones at the end of the hostilities had been thinned out by repatriation to a so-called "hard core" of nonrepatriables. These chiefly comprised Balts, Poles and Polish Jews, accommodated for the most part in camps under military authority but administered by an international welfare agency (UNRRA). Soviet grievance arose primarily out of Western unwillingness to mingle camp administration with a dose of coercion strong enough to lead to repatriation. A fundamental principle of the Soviet social order—that the individual citizen has no right to emigrate—was impugned. But this sense of grievance was enhanced by the alleged inclusion within the DP population of German collaborators who were not screened out, by the tendency of camp administrations to discourage repatriation, and by the organization of DP males of military age into uniformed and disciplined groups under Western military control. Since the Soviets had early conceded the case on voluntary repatriation, the brunt of controversy resolved around these accessory conditions.

Perhaps the record on the first of these accessory conditions, concerning the screening out of German collaborators, is most clear. Most of the DP's were little people caught up in the vast migratory movements unleashed by a great war. However, included among the Baltic and Polish-Ukranian group were many who had served in German military units or as underlings in German supply or guard organizations.[15] The West had pledged that such Nazi collaborators were to be denied UN DP status and were to be handed over to the UN power concerned.[16] However, the western powers were undeniably lax in screening the camps though probably least so in the American zone; and efforts of UNRRA to improve matters were of little account.[17]

The Soviets had an equally strong case in their complaint that camp administration tended to foster non-repatriation. Partly this was a by-product of the standard of living and immunities of camp life which however rough by American standards afforded a sheltered and probably more comfortable existence than was likely to be obtained in the home country. Then too, it appears that little effort was made to segregate camp residents who were influential in opposing repatriation. Supporters of repatriation were not given official camp positions. The associations of the Polish DPs with London Polish welfare organizations which had come to Germany with the UNRRA and military detachments had not been cut. There were short spurts of vigorous effort, particularly in the American zone, to encourage though not to compel repatriation. But generally the attempt of the Western powers to encourage repatriation was minimal and cursory.*

The final count in the Soviet complaint grew out of the utilization in the western zones of DP males in uniformed and disciplined units under military control for the performance of guard, supply and police duties. The organization of uprooted and disloyal nationals in semi-military units under foreign allegiance and in the hostile soil of a neighboring country gave rise to a natural concern. Yet these organizations were constituted by the west for reasons primarily of a housekeeping nature.[18]

These three items of complaint were thrashed back and forth at Moscow and a five-pronged agreement was reached which apparently established common ground. It was agreed that war criminals among DP's were to be turned over upon "production of satisfactory evidence";

* "There is no doubt," states the second UNRRA report pursuant to Resolution 92, "that anti-repatriation propaganda is widely prevalent in DP camps and that liaison officers play a role in its dissemination." And their final report (CC(47)93, 30 July 1947, 14) concluded that "the repatriation policies of UNRRA have not been as completely carried out as UNRRA would have desired to. Adequate and appropriate information has been difficult to obtain in satisfactory form from home governments and in other instances there have been impediments to the dissemination of literature which was sent. The admittance of liaison officers to camps met with long delays due to lack of clearances by the occupation authorities either for entry into particular camps or for entry into the zones. As had been noted in previous reports . . . some liaison officers obtained necessary clearances only after months of negotiations. The work of those officers was thereby made substantially more difficult due to the long intervals of time during which the displaced persons have had no official contact with their governments of origin. Segregation both by nationality and attitude as well as screening have never been fully carried out by the occupation authorities. While the Administration is grateful to the military for the substantial action which they have taken it regrets that screening and segregation which are vital to repatriation have not been more fully carried out and that there has been a disturbing lag in the removal from UNRRA camps of displaced persons who have been declared ineligible for UNRRA assistance. Finally the activities of anti-repatriation groups within the camps have not been sufficiently curbed. This problem is complicated by the fact that unauthorized persons and organizations engaging in anti-repatriation activities have been able to enter the camps and carry on their activities in them." See also Hirschmann, *Embers*, 117–119, 178 ff. A large role also was played by the positive advantages to the DP's in staying. Moreover, for short periods vigorous efforts were made by the military authorities particularly in the American zone, and by the UNRRA camp administration, to induce repatriation. The most effective action in this regard was a 60-day ration made available to repatriates at their destination.

that distribution of literature and films emanating from the East and approved by the West was to be permitted within camps; accredited liaison officers were permitted the right of camp visitation under guard; all formal organization within and among camps and all propaganda of a "hostile" character to a UN member was to be banned; and voluntary repatriation was to be accelerated. Returned to Berlin, the agreement proved delusory in character. Outside the framework of a general settlement, the West showed little interest in appeasing Soviet complaints and negotiations were cut short by the brusque assertion that the Moscow agreement was outside the authority of the Control Council.

Reluctance to appease outside the frame of a general settlement also characterized Soviet attitudes to the Moscow agreement on return of some two million German prisoners of war in Allied custody.[19] After extended American prodding, agreement at Moscow was reached with the Soviets and French to return all German PW's under Allied custody by 31 December 1948. The Control Council was expressly ordered to formulate a "plan" for the detailed handling of the repatriations and the associated interzonal movements. For some months after Moscow, the Soviets cooperated in practical implementing action. But submission of detailed repatriation plans was turned down with the lame assertion that stipulating that prisoners of war would be returned in accordance with the Moscow decision satisfied the requirements of a "plan."[20]

A similar stalemate terminated the negotiations on limitation of occupation forces. This question had been broached by the Americans at the end of 1946 with the specific proposal to reduce occupation forces to 200,000 in the Soviet zone and 350,000 in the Western zones. At the Moscow Conference the Soviets accepted the American proposal amended to scale down the Western military quota by a hundred thousand. Under their proposal the French would have 50,000 and the Soviets and Anglo-American forces 200,000 each. This left the Western military forces greater than the Soviets—as initially proposed by the Americans—but with a lesser margin.[21] The divergence was not great and was compromisable. The project was accordingly passed on to the Control Council with an instruction to reach agreement. In Berlin, however, the will to agree had lapsed. Aside from an arid controversy over communication and service personnel, the chief dividing issue remained that of parity in strength between the combined Anglo-American and Soviet forces.[22]

III. Berlin as Focus for Tension

The inability to reach agreement on more than one of the Moscow limited-action projects indicated that the margins for tolerance and negotiation in the East-West peace settlement in Germany were running out. This took on particularly sharp significance in the administration of Berlin. There the occupying powers could not retreat to their respective sectors of the city as they could to their respective zones. They jostled one another in a crowded nervous city. Hence in Berlin the narrowing margins for compromise gave divergences a more explosive form.*

Thus a crisis arose as a consequence of city-wide elections held in October 1946. Campaigning on a clear position of resistance to Soviet power, the social democrats won a popular majority at the polls. Logically this brought them custody over the executive offices of city government including the mayor's office (Oberbürgermeister's office). The social democratic leader, Ernst Reuther, who was elected to this office, was unacceptable to the Soviets. The then incumbent mayor was unacceptable to the elected city assembly. The issue was carried to the highest Control Council levels. There both sides backed down and a compromise candidate was selected who was acceptable to the Soviets, to the West, and to the local SPD party leaders.[23]

A succession of disturbances followed the "Reuther affair." A flurry broke out over the character of quadripartite control to be exercised over communications between various parts of the Soviet zone which involved the East sector of Berlin or which transmitted Berlin East or West. The Western zone commanders reluctantly conceded exclusive Soviet management of such communications.[24] There were unilateral restrictions on political meetings and bans on demonstrations. Communist activities were hampered in one part of the city, bourgeois-liberal or Social-democratic activities in another.[25] Unified police and court administration broke down over a series of celebrated cases in which the Allies disagreed over treatment of German civilians.[26]

A prolonged controversy broke out over trade union election procedures, over the problem of wage policy, and over the issue of socialization. Even the question of social insurance contributions for German employees of the occupation forces became a controversial theme.[27]

Overshadowing these tensions were those arising out of the com-

* See for background earlier discussions of the "Berlin problem," pp. 21-4, 87-8.

mingled flow of economic interests in city supply and financing. One of the underlying supports for East-West condominium in the city was the pooling of coal imports and their unified distribution—together with coal-generated electricity and gas—throughout all sectors of the city on a non-discriminatory basis. In the fall of 1947 the supports for this system began to weaken. The Soviets diverted from the central coal pool for unilateral use within their sector some of their programmed coal imports. The occasion for this was the refusal of the Western powers to deem legitimate the coal consumption requirements of those Soviet sector plants working under Soviet contract for repatriations deliveries eastward. In Soviet eyes these plants were no more suspect than western sector plants producing for export to western Europe or to satisfy occupation force requirements.[28] As issues of this kind came forward, the possibility of condominium retreated.

This retreat turned to a rout under pressures arising out of the handling of Berlin trade with the western zones. Taking as occasion the installation of a new system for interzonal trade permits, the Soviets held that interzonal shipments originating from the Western sectors of the city would need Soviet endorsement for transit through the Soviet zone. The political motivation for the imposition of these controls is self evident. The underlying economic rationale is less obvious. It grew out of basic economic needs of the Soviet zone.

Strict frontier and customs control was required in the Soviet zone.[29] This was partly due to the severity of restrictions on the use of currency but more particularly to the impulse to capital flight. A like impulse was felt throughout Europe and in Britain but it was particularly intense in unstable countries caught in social revolution involving mass property displacements. In the case of the Soviet zone of Germany the urge to repatriate capital involved shipping assets westward to accompany or prepare for flight and emigration.* Already noticed by David

* This problem of capital flight is one of the basic politico-economic questions of the era and manifests itself in many forms. Though there is a running commentary on the effects of capital flight through the economic literature of the past three decades, there is to my knowledge no general monographic treatment of the problem from its incentive and technique aspects or even from the point of view of its lasting effects and modes of control. For an over-all appraisal chiefly in statistical terms of the importance of capital transactions of a "flight" character in the recent period and particularly in Britain, see United Nations, Department of Economic Affairs, *Economic Survey of Europe in 1949* (Geneva, 1950), 115 ff.; see also Lionel Robbins, "Inquest on the Crisis," *Lloyds Bank Review,* October 1947, 15–19. For an

Ricardo who assured his generation that "there are limits to the price which, in the form of perpetual taxation, individuals will submit to pay for the privilege merely of living in their native country," this outward movement of capital comprised the material basis for what latterday socialist thought has come to regard as "financial sabotage."*

Import and frontier controls are no stronger than their weakest link, which for the eastern zone economy obviously was Berlin. Illegal export and import movements involving capital repatriation could funnel through Berlin where frontier control was virtually non-existent and where transport facilities for interzonal transfer were readily available. In the Western sectors the German authorities regulated the flow of outgoing shipments. With superficial camouflage operations, which frequently were facilitated by the utilization of inter-branch exchange within a single firm, it was not difficult for firms to ship from Berlin assets originating within the Soviet zone. Frequently special assistance was provided for capital migration to facilitate re-establishment of enterprises in the Western zones. The fact that enterprises under property control in the Western zones had branch properties and that many residents of West Berlin had connections and access to Eastern Germany facilitated capital transfer.**

illuminating description of some of the devices for capital transfer, see Lovett's testimony, U.S. Congress, House of Representatives, *Third Supplemental Appropriation Bill for 1948*. Hearings before the subcommittee of the Appropriations Committee, 80th Congr., 1st sess., 241 ff. See also Thomas Balogh, *The Dollar Crisis* (Oxford, 1949), 116–120; R. G. Hawtrey, *Economic Destiny* (London, 1944), 126 ff.

* See David Ricardo, *The Principles of Political Economy and Taxation* (Everyman ed.) 164. See the basic works of Paul Sering, *Jenseits des Kapitalismus* (Nüremberg, 1946), 191 ff.; and E. F. M. Durbin, *The Politics of Democratic Socialism* (London, 1940), 286 ff.

** It is not easy to document cases of this traffic since it was inherently an "underground" phenomena. It was widely known among alert businessmen as one of the central currents of Berlin life but it was rarely written about and not very well understood by economic specialists, particularly those employed by military government. The author's personal contact with this sort of thing was chiefly confined to two interesting cases: a firm under property control with several warehouses of assets repatriated from the Soviet zone, and a large German construction company which managed to ship out via Berlin most of the key equipment from its Soviet zone branches. The author has seen a list of Eastern firms which had been "transplanted" successfully to the West, although frequently this involved only the shipment of "monetary" assets, good will and key staff personnel. On this, see *New York Times*, 30 March 1947. Moreover, since Berlin shipment involved violations of price and production control regulations, it became a principal focus of the Eastern

This capital transfer could be stopped by imposing effective restrictions on either the flow of commodity and personal traffic from the Soviet zone to Berlin or, alternatively, from the eastern sector of Berlin to the western sectors. But these restrictions either way would cut into a dense mass of local and suburban traffic and trade. Their effective application would cripple the use of the eastern sector of the city as a transport and communications business and commercial headquarters for the Soviet zone and would make a dead charge of their sector of the city with its expensive upkeep. Since the city frontiers were so extended, irregular and criss-crossed by rail, road and water networks, such restrictions would be difficult to apply effectively and would entail a dispro-

zone "black market" for disposal of key products in Berlin and procurement of "black market supplies" in Berlin. After the monetary reforms of 1948, the process of capital flight could easily take on a "monetary form" by sale of Eastern assets to obtain Western currency. The continuous depreciation during 1949 and 1950 of the Berlin rate of currency exchange considerably beneath the "purchasing power parity" of the Eastern and Western Currencies is an expression of the tremendous pressure for capital flight in the Eastern zone. See the interesting remarks of Walter Ullbricht, *Lehrbuch für den demokratischen Staats-und Wirtschaftsaufbau* (Berlin, 1949), 104–107, where specific cases were cited; and see also *Die Städtischen Körperschaften in der Berliner Krise*, 45 ff. The fact that the western sectors of Berlin have consistently partly lived on black market traffic with the Eastern zone is notorious. See Deutsches Institut für Wirtschaftsforschung, *Berlins Wirtschaft in der Blockade* (Berlin, 1949), 42 ff., 45. For remarks and information relevant to the entire problem, see particularly *ibid.*, "Die Wechselstuben," 135–138 and the following: E. Trost, "Die Berliner Währung," *Zeitschrift fur das gesamte Kreditwesen*, I (heft 10, 1948), 225 ff.; G. Abeken, "Das Geld-und Kreditsystem der Ostzone," *ibid.*, III (heft 8, 1950), 195 ff.; Berliner Zentralbank, *The Economy of West Berlin* (Berlin, 1949), II ff., 25 ff. (where cognizance is taken of the fact that transactions with the Soviet zone are "not noted by the authorities"); and a series of "Berlin Commentaries," included in the *German Economic Press Review* (prepared by German consultants for British Military Government, Office of Economic Advisor, Berlin, 1948–1949—mimeographed weekly), no. 14, 13 ff.; no. 30, 10 ff.; no. 24, 9 ff.; no. 20, 21, 17, 23, 41, 35. See also a number of "General Economic Comments" or "Surveys" attached to this Press Review, particularly no. 33, "The Black Market"; no. 6, "Reasons for the Different Valuation of West-Marks and East-Marks"; no. 32, "The German Clothing Industry," 14–17. Thus note the following almost naive comment from the study of the "Black Market": "In West Berlin the black market is a question of life and death. . . . It is no exaggeration if it is said that the success of the introduction of the West currency . . . depends on how the black market reacts. . . . Success will be dependent upon two factors. First, how will the Eastern zone react? Inflation exists there. Inflation favours export. For the Eastern Zone the West Sector is a foreign country. There will also be therefore a continued flow of goods from the East to West-Berlin. . . ." It goes without saying

portionate expenditure of funds, facilities and manpower. Hence, the Soviets did not seriously undertake to restrict traffic and movement between the eastern and western sectors of the city or between the eastern sector of the city and the eastern zone. Yet if these lines of traffic were open or were regulated only by crude measures, control over capital flight had to be attained by other means.

Like circumstances limited the efficacy of controls which could be successfuly administered directly within the Soviet zone.[30] A large scope for private enterprise remained within the zone; and many managers of nationalized enterprises were tied up with older ownership interests. Many of the regulatory bodies were unsympathetic or hostile. Diversion of property would be difficult to detect.[31] Under these circumstances, the most effective control involved direct Soviet regulation of shipments from Berlin by licensing individual transactions. Outgoing shipments had to be collected at central station points, so access would be relatively easy and means of enforcement would be simple to contrive.

---

that this black market movement has and had its reverse aspects: dependency of Berlin firms on the Eastern zone and sucking of key products to the Eastern economy through Berlin. Until the development of the Western trade embargo with the Eastern world or rather the gradual tightening of exchange and trade restrictions of the Western with the Eastern world, access through Berlin was not particularly important. Since the cumulative tightening of the embargo, Berlin has become a keyhole for the East as it remained a hole in the Eastern frontier control system. Moreover, even within Berlin exploitation of Eastern resources by a high exchange rate had its adverse aspects in penalizing trade prospects for many occupational groups in West Berlin. However, a detailed treatment of these problems involves monographic investigation which the author cannot pretend to have carried out to the detail required to obtain a clear picture. To a very considerable extent the negotiations to resolve the Berlin Crisis turned around methods to regulate this triangular picture of Berlin as center and diversionary point for East-West trade and black marketing. The "considerable flight of capital from East to West" was noted by J. P. Nettl, *The Eastern Zone and Soviet Policy in Germany, 1945–1950* (Oxford, 1951), 280. This capital flight from the Soviet zone was facilitated by the fact "that former entrepreneurs from the Soviet Zone, who had lost their factories and equipment to the Russians, now resided in West Berlin." HICOG, *Economic Assistance to West Berlin 1949–1951* (prepared by H. G. Schmidt, Historical Division, 1952) 2 f. "Piece by piece, by devious and illegal means, many trades and industries were transferred from the Eastern Zone to the comparatively freer Western Zones. . . . The important fur industry of Leipzig has been re-established in Frankfurt. Literally every piece of equipment and skilled craftsmen were smuggled over the 'Green border' " Arsen L. Yakoubain, *Western Allied Occupation Policies and Development of German Democracy, 1945–1951* (Dissertation, 1951, New York University, NY), 44, 46.

But though enforcement would be simple, control would be difficult. Repatriated capital knows many disguises. The mere fact that a firm desiring approval for shipments was of upright reputation and was not itself of Soviet zone lineage would count for nothing. A diligent intelligence investigation would be needed to prove that the firm was not being used as a "dummy" or "front" by friendly or concealed interests. Hence this mode of control would work considerable difficulties for Western sector commerce. Likewise, it was liable to gross administrative abuses. It easily shaded into political control. And it would evoke the intense opposition of the Western sector authorities who by this measure would be effectively deprived of economic power within the city. This basic issue of control over shipments going out was at the heart of the contentious spirit in Berlin during the winter and spring of 1947/48.[32]

IV. The London Conference

Heightened tension in Berlin, continued stalemate on the basic issues of settlement and narrowed margins for negotiation on limited action projects were brought to full expression in the London meeting in November–December 1947 of the Council of Foreign Ministers.[33] That the proceedings would be fruitless was indicated by an intemperate attack on the West, which marked Molotov's opening remarks.[34] When the German issue came on the agenda a two-day debate was required to agree on the discussion of a British paper on divergent issues.* On these issues there was persistent American effort to press the division on the reparations issue as controlling. "All these matters we have been discussing," noted Marshall out of turn, export-import programs, first charge on

---

* When the conference turned to economic questions, tempers were so strained that it seemed as if rupture would occur over procedure and not substance. There was a two-day debate on agenda. The Western spokesmen insisted, on Marshall's initiative, that the basis for discussion be constituted by a rambling British paper which had already been introduced into the Moscow conference as an outline of the British position. With bitterly worded and distractive commentaries, Molotov denied its adequacy as a text. On the 2nd day, the West consolidated in favor of the British document while Molotov presented a competing paper of his own containing three Soviet proposals. This provoked Marshall—certainly prematurely—to declare that the conference had turned into a blind alley. Every time Molotov rose, he denounced Western policy and finally acquiesced in use of the British document with the Soviet paper having supplementary status and with discussion free to cover other documents as well. This was quickly accepted on the third day and the session began to discuss the various paragraphs of the Bevin paper.

German exports, occupation costs, priorities on exports, "will revert to the question of reparations." It is impossible, he then asserted, "to have a clear picture of how all these matters can be put into effect unless we get a clear answer from the Soviet delegation on the question of reparations from current production." Marshall then emphasized the express determination of the United States not *"to agree to any program of reparations from current production as a price for the unification of Germany"* [italics added]. The divergence thus exposed, Marshall turned to the attack. Quickly sketching the background of the "critical state of Europe," he contraposed the deficits being shouldered by the British and American "taxpayers" for the support of western Germany to the substantial reparations being extracted out of current production from the Soviet zone. Thus, he added, "in effect much of the German economy operates for the Soviet account." This situation "needs to be corrected at once" and not "at some indefinite future time" when the German economy would probably be so wrecked "that its dead weight would drag down and submerge the economy of all Europe." Marshall then issued his ultimatum: he asked the Council of Foreign Ministers to prohibit after 1 January 1948 taking anything out of Germany "except for fair economic value in money or goods." If we cannot, he insisted, "take this economic decision which is of immediate vital significance, then we are wasting our time when there is no time to waste." As if this were not sufficiently explicit, Marshall added: "I feel we are entitled to a positive answer from Mr. Molotov now . . ."[35]

A few days later the challenge was made even more provocative. Marshall's point of departure was a British proposal calling for submission of regular reports on reparations removals from all zones. This was acceptable to the Soviets "in connection with a general agreement on the reparations question." Marshall then demanded that information on past reparations removals be tabled by each delegation by the coming Monday, December 15th. This brought an angry reply from Molotov. The Americans, he answered, desire a reparations report but for good reasons forego asking for reports on other questions. Would it be possible for the American and British delegations to supply data on purchases by foreign interests of German properties in their zones? On this his staff intelligence had misled him, but he came closer to the mark with a reference to "profits from the export of low-priced coal and timber." The Soviet Union, he closed, "would appreciate having this and certain other information on Monday, also relating to the French Zone."[36]

This was the setting when Molotov began later that afternoon to reply to Marshall's earlier challenge on the reparations question. "Three delegations," he pointed out, "have now united in a common front against reparations deliveries to the Soviet Union." He reminded his audience that their position was "in complete contradiction" with statements made during the war "when they resolved to support the Soviet Union and other Allies regarding reparations from Germany." Recalling the Yalta and Potsdam agreements he added: "The Soviet Union is not asking but demanding that the question of reparations at long last be decided." He pointed to the enormous damage and loss inflicted on the Soviet Union during the war. This was contrasted to the experience of America "which fortunately was not subjected to an enemy occupation and, what is more, enriched itself during the war." We are asked, he said, to cease taking reparations from our zone and to depend upon your dismantling programs. Up to 1 November 1947 you have dismantled and shipped some 33 million dollars worth of equipment for use by twenty countries. "Is this not a mockery?"

Molotov reflected bitterly that "as long as allies were needed in the war against the common enemy they mattered; not inconsiderable promises were made to them and obligations were entered into. . . . Little was left of these promises when came the time for peacemaking." He then reviewed the underlying economics of his reparations demands, pointed to the existence of reparations potential in the German economy, and offered to withhold reparations until industrial recovery was more advanced. He launched a sharp indictment which mixed exaggeration and barbs that hit home: you are holding back industrial recovery in your zones, you take out concealed reparations in the form of underpriced coal and timber exports, the subsidies you advance are extravagant and are connected with onerous conditions which will rob Germany of her political independence. "There is no longer," he said, "any point in talking about the independent development of Germany's economic and political life in the Western Zones." To no small extent this power over Germany will be "wielded by those who are not at all concerned with the German people but who would like to see Germany or at least her Western part for their expansionist aims and as a strategical base for aggressive plans." The Western partition, he charged, "gives a free hand to those who are anxious to lord it over the West." He classed as "groundless" Western claims for priority in reimbursement of their German subsidies. Lapsing into his sergeant-major tone, he stated that the Soviets "insist that the question of reparations be settled without delay in accordance with the Yalta and Potsdam Agreements."[37]

Thus the issue was drawn starkly in this bitter speech delivered in a setting of bitterness. Bevin and Marshall both rose to deny the groundless charges of commercial penetration into Germany. They avowed—and here the British were on shaky ground—that not "one penny" of profit from coal or timber exports "innured to the advantage of the Occupying Powers." Both men in different ways spit out their contempt for the Soviet position. Said the icy Marshall: "It is obvious that Mr. Molotov's remarks were not designed for serious discussion at this stage . . . and make it rather difficult to inspire respect for the dignity of the Soviet Government." Bevin countered in coarser strain: "I think Mr. Molotov could have wound up his speech by thanking us for so long listening to him." Bidault contented himself with the assertion that Molotov's references to France were "contrary to truth."[38]

With this exchange at its Friday session, the Council of Foreign Ministers established at Potsdam was clearly defunct. The Saturday meeting was postponed. On Monday Bevin read an intemperate and pointless reply to Molotov's peroration. Marshall with far more grace merely stated that the Soviet position on reparations, "put in its simplest terms was unacceptable." He then summed up the proceedings of the conference in a masterly indictment of Soviet policy on the German peace settlement. On all the "fundamental decisions" required for this settlement, "three delegations" have registered "their willingness to take them here and now . . . The Soviet Union alone refused to agree . . . Practical progress" was impossible "at this time." Hence he moved the "adjournment" of the session. Bevin assented and Bidault acquiesced. Molotov's reply, like Marshall's statement, was measured and restrained. On the adjournment proposal, he refused to give his assent or to object. It arose from "a desire to untie his (Marshall's) hands so that he can continue to act unilaterally as he has done in the past." We expect to be told, continued Molotov, "that on this point three delegations have already agreed and that there remains only for the Soviet delegate to agree." This, he said, "is always your response. . . . But it should not be forgotten that it is impossible to talk to the Soviet Government in the same manner as you talk to the present Greek government."[39]

The Conference then adjourned.

V. End of Control Council

Cessation of the Council of Foreign Ministers obviously undermined the Control Council regime. The zone commanders who in their collective capacity made up this regime dealt with each other and their issues on instructions from their governments. They thus dealt with each other as agents of the foreign ministers who had agreed to stop negotiations. These instructed agents could not long continue to meet together outside a semblance of a framework of settlement and without a higher level to which disputed questions could be referred. Hence as meetings continued, tension mounted.

One source of tension was the process of tripartite western agreement destined to bring the French zone into a consolidated and revitalized western Germany. The first day after the London conference disbanded a crucial member of the American delegation rejoined it in London after a round of discussions with French leaders and boasted of his "belief" that the "differences" between the three western powers "could be resolved and a trizonal agreement on western Germany could be reached." Bidault also so indicated at a closed western meeting. Within eight days after London, there was released the Ruhr coke agreement which was part of the assurance to France that her coal and coke needs would be taken care of. Thirty-two days later public announcement was made that tripartite conversations on Germany were to be held "at an early date." Six days thereafter, the first steps were taken in the cession to France of economic control over the Saar and within a month the arrangements for this cession were worked out.[40]

Within Germany daily evidence testified to the trend toward bifurcation. Before the London meetings adjourned the relatively independent Lemmer-Kaiser leadership of the liberal bourgeois party in the Soviet zone were driven from their neutralist position and out of zonal life. With them went a priceless asset for quadripartite settlement.* The

---

* Though the technical basis was the refusal of Kaiser to participate in a German unity congress sponsored by the SED en lieu of the torpedoed plans for an all-German *Repräsentation*, on other issues Kaiser had been growing more impatient of Soviet restrictions and policies; the possibilities for "bridge" and "mediating groups" were obviously becoming slim; Kaiser was personally irredentist on the Oder-Neisse issue and reacted against the sharpness of eastern zone attacks on American and British policy. See on this Otto Grotewohl, *Im Kampf um Deutschland, Reden und Aufsätzen* (2v., Berlin, 1948), II, 254 for date of 16 November 1947 as the time when Kaiser's willingness to break became apparent. In Kaiser's first open

day the London conference adjourned the German political leadership at Frankfurt commenced public meetings and studies on the problem of Western German government reorganization.[41] Only two days after London the loose arrangements for Anglo-American partnership over their fused zonal controls were worked over into provision for effective decision-making under American custody.[42] Eighteen days after London the moves for the organization of a formal government structure in Western Germany were mapped out; a few days later the Frankfurt German leadership asked for the immediate initiation of measures to crystallize such a west German government. Within two months the fundamental institutions of the new west German political structure were laid down in basic statutes.[43] In the dominant eastern zone party, the SED, the perspective of unification was relinquished as a realistic policy goal and hopes for economic revival were turned inward and Eastward. There was also a noticeable acceleration in the trend to centralized zonal power and economic control.[44]

These processes of rift without and tension within were given a curiously muted expression in the Control Council itself and its array of attendant committees and agencies. This apparatus was not brought to sudden halt in working order. The tendency rather was quietly to dismantle it by gradually disestablishing its rights and claims over successive layers of issues and problems. This was the treatment given after London to such major themes of Potsdam as denazification, demilitarization, industrial plant removal. In the same spirit projects of legislation

---

clash with the Soviet Military Administration on 22 December 1947, his public statement was moderate. Cf. account of this crisis in excerpts from OMGUS, *Daily Excerpts from German Publications* (Manpower Division—a set of excerpts devoted to the CDU crisis, mimeographed), 22 December 1947. In an illuminating statement, "Ein ordnendes Wort," *Tagesspiegel*, 18 February 1948, Kaiser noted that until the recent period "war bei allem Druck der auf der Bevölkerung, vor allem auf den Verantwortlichen der nichtkommunistischen Parteien lastete, noch eine gewisse Möglichkeit politisches Eigenleben zur Geltung zu bringen." His later programmatic speech of 6 March 1948 (*Tagesspiegel*, 7 March 1948) contains a fuller statement of the course of events which drove Kaiser, who belonged as he said, "zu den Männern die in der Verständigungsbereitschaft mit den Vertretern des Kommunismus bis an die Grenze die Möglichen gegangen sind." My friends and I, he says, followed this course out of compassion to bring security for the sixteen million eastern Germans and for the rest of Germany. But, he states, we could not tolerate the "popular front" drive with its sinister reminiscences of Hitler's street movements. See articles on the CDU crisis in *Civil Affairs in Occupied and Liberated Territory*, no. 196, 9, 10, 12, 44.

major and minor, which in some cases had been worked on within the Control Council hierarchy ever since its inception, were dropped on one ground or another. Of the more minor items it suffices to mention two innocent and meritorious agreements on highway transport and teacher training institutes.[45] The most significant of the major items concerned a social insurance law which had been decided in principle early in 1946 and which, after exhaustive negotiation and extended consultation with German interests, was finally given finished legal form and cleared through the lower organs of the Control Council machinery. The law was not plainly rejected but it was turned back into the negotiating machinery where it could be effectively killed.*

* The history of the project for nationwide reorganization of the social insurance system under Control Council auspices is an interesting type case of the potentialities and limitations of the kind of settlement attempted under the Control Council regime and of entanglement with both internal German and external pressures. The social insurance system obviously needed over-all readjustment in terms of rate structures, benefit provisions, and administration in accordance with changed post-war conditions. Continued structural uniformity of the social insurance system was obviously a requirement of German unification. A draft of principles for the revision of the social insurance system was worked out over the winter 1945/46 and approved by the Coordinating Committee in March 1946. See ACA, *Basic Principles of Social Insurance for Workers and Employees in Germany*, DMAN/P (46)11 rev., 7 March 1946. In working out the draft of the law, the comments and studies of the German trade union organizations and principal zonal bodies were solicited. "After two years of negotiation a compulsory social insurance law for Germany covering virtually the entire working population for sickness, maternity, funeral expenses, industrial accidents, invalidity and old age and death" was approved by the Manpower Directorate in December 1947. See OMGUS, *Report of the Military Governor*, Manpower, "Trade Unions and Working Conditions," no. 32 (cumulative review), February 1948, 27. As the law consolidated all types of social insurance including health groups and the position of employees and specially favored wage earner groups into a single system with benefit provisions favoring lower paid wage earners, the eastern zone union organizations heartily favored the law which had many complex provisions. On the whole, the more conservatively oriented west German organizations were critical. At the U.S. Zone Länderrat level the CDU and SPD opposed the measure but the Hessen Minister-President supported it with an interesting plea for the priority of measures which would promote unity. See "Parteien und Regierungen zur Reform der Sozialversicherung," *Zeitschrift für Versicherungswissenschaft und Versicherungspraxis*, I (October, 1947), 92–95; J. Kuczynski, "Die Hauptmotive der deutschen Sozialversicherung von Bismarck bis in die Gegenwart," *Arbeit und Sozialfürsorge* (official organ of the Soviet zone central labor administration in Berlin), I (1946), 298–300; "Einheitlicher Aufbau der Sozialversicherung in der sowjetischen Besatzung," *Ibid.*, II (1947), 61 ff.; "Materialien zur deutschen Sozialversicherung," *Europa-Archiv*, III (1948),

A similar outcome was accorded an agreement which had been submitted in its first form to the Berlin Generals late in 1945 and which had after extended negotiations finally been given what at the time seemed workable form. This agreement involved procedures and limitations with respect to occupation costs. It floundered on Soviet objections.* But perhaps the item which most fully indicated that all negotiating margins had run out was the project for an increase in the abnormally low price of Ruhr coal. This project was first launched by the British, who were responsible for the industry, in the fall of 1945. Approximately eighteen months of deficit financing occurred before the American and French delegations came to support a price increase. Another half year was consumed in negotiations before this project worked its way to the top levels of the Control Council machinery. As presented there, it involved

---

1287–1292, 1340–1344, 1671–1672. As it happened, the conservatively oriented German opposition got the ear of the visiting Case committee who raised the matter sharply with General Clay during a committee hearing and obtained an "off the record" review by the General of what he obviously deemed a delicate matter. U.S. Congress, House of Representatives, *First Deficiency Appropriation Bill for 1948*, Hearing before the subcommittee of the Committee on Appropriations, 80th Congress, 1st sess., 601–602; U.S. Congress, House of Representatives, Select Committee on Foreign Aid, *Final Report on Foreign Aid*, 80th Congr., 2nd sess., 131. The draft law was doomed regardless of Congressional interposition because of the almost united opposition of the political leadership of Western Germany and the senselessness of contracting at so late a date additional quadripartite agreements. But since the Soviets laid great store by the measure, which had been carefully nurtured through the Control Council machinery with its various coordinating actions and legal draftings, their reaction was extremely bitter. See ACA, *Minutes of the Control Council*, Conl/M(48)2, para. 11.

* The documentation on the occupation costs agreement would fill a small volume in tracing the course of its travels from the time a short document, "The Financing of Occupation Costs," DFin/P(64)4, 23 January 1946, was approved by the Coordinating Committee subject to certain rather cryptic revisions. See ACA, *Minutes of the Coordinating Committee*, Corc/M(46)6, para. 71. As finally elaborated, the agreement had most of its sting taken out but embodied certain significant understandings which would condition later agreements in this field. The Soviet disagreements hinged on relatively minor points which would affect very slightly the calculation of a bill that could never be repaid, i.e., external occupation costs. But to make the record consistent, the Soviets blocked agreement since they had so little interest in a measure designed primarily to serve as the basis for restrictions in the incurment of occupation costs. See the copious US brief, OMGUS, "Brief on Financing of Occupation Costs" for the Deputy Military Governor (Finance Division 1947—typewritten); ACA, *Financing of Occupation Costs*, Corc/P(47)41, 1st rev.; ACA, *Minutes of the Coordinating Committee*, Corc/M(48)2, 3, paras. 23, 24.

no practical Soviet interest since only Ruhr hard coal pricing was concerned and for the time being RM pricing had little meaning. The proposal was modest since it envisaged a price increase covering less than fifty percent of the losses being incurred. Nonetheless, the Soviets vetoed the measure and it was withdrawn from the agenda.[46]

Only one strange episode interrupted the trend of disintegration. This was a "last compromise proposal" on financial reform introduced by General Clay into the Control Council in January, 1948.[47] The details of the proposal, as well as of the course of the negotiations lasting approximately two months to which they led, are not clear. The American proposal involved reopening the stalemated financial reform project stripped of ancillary questions. The Soviets dropped their previous demand for parallel currency printing in Leipzig and Berlin and accepted exclusive printing in Berlin under quadripartite control. Arrangements for the initiation of currency printing in Berlin were undertaken.[48] Simultaneously the financial experts of the four powers resumed negotiations on unresolved aspects of financial reform. Agreement had previously been reached on the handling of old monetary accounts, problems of indebtedness, the issuance of new currency and credits. The negotiations for a capital levy showed agreement on fundamentals along with stubborn contention on lesser issues.[49] The delicate problem of allocation of currency to the occupying powers was handled successfully when Soviet requests were found substantially in line with Western ideas.[50] The principal difficulty appeared to hinge about the extent of political or economic union needed to support a common monetary reform. The Soviets urged the establishment of a joint central German bank and a joint central department of finance. The Western answer to this Soviet position was apparently negative.[51] In any case, the negotiations were broken off by the West when the Soviets brought an end to meetings which were becoming increasingly farcical in content.*

* Although Bennett asserts that the Soviets brought negotiations to an end with their stoppage of the Control Council machinery—"there remained no forum"—his memory does him injustice. Bennett, "The German Currency Reform," *loc. cit.,* 46. As Basil Davidson has noted, in their withdrawal from Control Council meetings the Soviets specifically exempted the monetary reform committees. Davidson, *Germany: What Now?* (London, 1951), 218. This is confirmed by the specific assertion in the Military Governor's report that the Soviets "indicated a desire to attend meetings of such bodies as the Currency Printing Committee and the Insurance Committee." OMGUS, *Monthly Report of the Military Governor,* March, 1948, 1–2. This discrimination between Control Council agencies was "unacceptable" to the

The Soviet action on March 20, 1948, took the form of walking out of a meeting of the Control Council. This occurred when the Western delegates refused to discuss in other than cursory terms a tripartite conference on Germany which had adjourned a few days before. Sokolovsky rose from his seat and after some bitter words declared the meeting adjourned. Clay later recorded his feeling then that "the Allied Control Council was dead." That it was killed by all its members is indicated by the simple fact that prior to later scheduled meeting dates the members whose turn at the chair was up circulated a note offering to hold a meeting upon request. No one requested.[52] Yet though killed by all its members, the Control Council was in a sense not killed by any. The members silently agreed to recognize that the Council had become devoid of function and a source of unnecessary complication, and that a fresh start would be required if a fruitful turn were to be taken in the course of the German East-West peace settlement.

Just as the disappearance of the Council of Foreign Ministers weakened the Control Council, the collapse of the Control Council as a functioning institution weakened the Berlin Kommandatura. Yet like the Control Council this did not disappear after what amounted to decapitation. It continued to function partly because the practical administration of the vast tissue of city ordinance and life had become adjusted to its existence. But it functioned with increasing difficulty. Kommandatura sessions had always been more stormy than Control Council meetings and ascerbity of expression increased toward the end. There

------

U.S. which in principle withdrew with British and French support its membership from Control Council agencies in view of the Sokolovsky action. There were certain interesting exceptions to this principle: the inter-allied Communications and Berlin Safety Secretariats, with important but more or less routine functions, continued to operate; the Berlin Kommandatura, illustrative as it was of the more important principle of Western rights in Berlin, was kept alive. *Ibid.*, April, 1948, 21; *ibid.*, May, 1948, 18. But the antidiscrimination principle was applied to the monetary reform negotiations. Thus the American position effectively completed a split which the Soviets began. That there was ambivalence on all sides is almost self evident. An informed French survey merely noted that after the bizonal government proclamation of 6 February 1948 the successful completion of financial reform negotiations "became more difficult." *La France en Allemagne*, I (October, 1948), 47. Likewise from the Soviet side—and, interestingly enough, from the SED—came a warning note about the pre-conditions to be fulfilled before a joint monetary reform —which was specified as of value only as facilitating the cause of German unification—would be desirable between eastern Germany and dollar-influenced western Germany. See Grotewohl, *Im Kampf um Deutschland*, I, 320 ff.

was no higher source to resolve difficult negotiations and the familiar process of rupture and withdrawal from the agenda ensued.[53] Finally, the Western sectors were placed under increasing pressure due to the trade control restrictions gradually put into effect by the Soviets after about the first of the year. As a result of these restrictions, which prohibited German civilian transport through the Soviet zone to a destination outside the zone without individual transaction approval, western Berlin trade shipments dwindled to a fraction of their former volume by April 1948.[54] Movement of military transport came into question and the first phase of the "air lift" was commenced when American military train service to and from Berlin was stopped due to American unwillingness to permit Soviet inspection.[55] Equally ominous was the "plane incident," involving destruction of a British plane over Berlin by contact with Soviet fighter planes ostentatiously buzzing about the Western air channels.[56]

The "bridge city" was becoming "bridge-head." Frequent indication was given of Soviet unwillingness to tolerate a Western enclave in the heart of their zone outside the framework of quadripartite settlement on Germany. This was countered by early expression of Western determination to hold on to the enclave. The makings of crisis in Berlin were thus ready to hand.[*] The Control Council regime at its origin was ballasted with and built around Berlin and a single currency. When ambivalence had run its full course, a crisis in Berlin induced by splitting of the currency would signify that the Control Council regime—and with it the possibilities for a unified peaceful Germany—had passed out of existence.

[*] Molotov in one of his London CFM speeches casually referred to the Western partition as separating the western part of Germany from "entire Germany and from Berlin, the capital city of Germany." Molotov, *London Speeches.* 28. Somewhat earlier, in October 1947, Clay had indicated that "only force" could cause American withdrawal from Berlin. On 19 December 1947 the *Tägliche Rundschau* ran an editorial prominently repudiating the suggestion that Western title to Berlin "real estate" was not contingent upon quadripartite government of Germany. This drew a flurry of press comment and denials by American officials. A few weeks later the *Tägliche Rundschau* ran a more strongly worded editorial which drew direct negatives from prominent Western authorities in Berlin and in the home countries. See *Tägliche Rundschau,* 19 December 1947, 11 January 1948; *New York Times,* 17 and 19 December 1947; *New York Herald Tribune,* 20 December 1947; *New York Times,* 11 and 12 January 1948; *Europa-Archiv,* III (1948), 1125.

CHAPTER X

THE STRUGGLE FOR BERLIN

I. Blockade and Airlift

THE BIPOLARIZATION of Germany had by mid-June 1948 undermined most of the grounds for unification built up into the Control Council regime. There survived chiefly those two underlying supports—a common capital and currency—around which the regime at the outset had been built.[1] These supports were now to be exploded away in a dramatic sequence of events.

The common currency was first to go. It disappeared with the institution of the now famous West-German monetary reform of June 1948. This reform action wiped out between 90 and 95% of old Reichsmark currency holdings or bank deposit claims and provided a new Westmark, issued and controlled solely by the Western powers. Devalued currency privately held would tend to seep across to East-Germany where this currency still exerted purchasing power and where it would add to the pressure of monetary demand, invigorate the black market and disrupt economic controls. Moreover, immense supplies of devalued currency at the discretion of the Western occupying authorities could be used in or around East Germany. Hence the Eastern authorities were compelled by the Western currency reform to carry out an offsetting reform in the East. Within six days of their official notification of Western action the Soviets were able to improvise currency stickers to be affixed on old currency notes; within the next four days the Eastern currency changeover was completed.[2] The new Eastern currency with its glued stickers was not a pretty sight; but Soviet intelligence was either weak in not detecting the secret preparations for currency changeover in Western Germany; or the Soviets preferred to be taken by surprise. But though inelegant the eastern currency was effective and the reality of two currencies—and all that would go with it by way of trading, pricing, and economic life—replaced the common currency which had been inherited by the occupation.

By itself the inauguration of separate currency systems in Eastern and Western Germany need not have endangered the last remaining piece of the Control Council regime, the common and jointly controlled capital city, Berlin. Berlin could have been outfitted with an independently issued currency under the control of the Berlin authorities. True, this course of action was not favored by Eastern and Western Berliners who, if out of despair or panic they did not ask that zonal reforms should be avoided, were in the main advocating integration with their respective areas.[3] American policy favored an independent Berlin currency and this was advocated in quadripartite negotiation.[4] The currency experts thought it feasible. A separate currency would have facilitated control by Eastern and Western monetary authorities of the depletion of Berlin resources through capital flight. Joint control over a separate Berlin currency would have brought its problems. But these problems were largely inherent in the task of economic management of a deficit urban area with extended trading relations. In other forms the same problems had already been encountered and to a degree grappled with.

Perhaps if time had been available for negotiation, this line of action would have been adopted as less undesirable than either of the two alternatives: retaining the old Reichsmark currency unchanged, i.e. converting Berlin into a currency cesspool for all of Germany, or splitting the city by introducing parallel currencies in the respective Eastern and Western sectors of the city. But time would have been required to negotiate a reform agreement and time was now short. The Western announcement of reform predated the actual reform by only two days. Quadripartite negotiating capabilities were depleted and the goodwill and comity required to bring such negotiations to successful conclusion was almost wholly lost.[5]

But even if more time had been available and even if a reform agreement could have been conjured up without difficulty by the Allied experts, would the Soviets have favored agreed action to further consolidate a unified capital city under quadripartite control? They would not have minded participating in control of such a city, with its corridors of access and its troublesome problems of frontier and customs control, located in the Western zones. But why compromise the integrity of their zonal control by allowing such an urban area to persist in that part of

Germany for which they had fought, which they had conquered and which they were allotted by joint Allied decision? They were willing in 1944 to detach the capital city from its zonal hinterland and to permit it to be garrisoned and controlled jointly by all the occupying powers in order to preserve the machinery of German national government, then located in Berlin, from predominant influence by the zonal power playing the host role. This machinery of German national government, under the original 1944 agreement, was to operate under the control of and subject to the direction of the Control Council. The various "Directorates" of the Control Council were to "exercise control over the corresponding German ministries and German central institutions."* But the Directorates and the Control Council had played out their role and were even formally no longer existing. The West-German monetary reform, and the London plan of West-German settlement which this reform spearheaded, accelerated the partition of Germany and put an irrevocable end to the Control Council for Germany as a whole. Maintenance of this regime over the city of Berlin which served as the headquarters for the evolving East-German state would not signify or facilitate German unity. The device of the Trojan horse has often been used to symbolize communist tactics of penetration in a hostile socio-political environment. But quadripartitely-controlled Berlin was the Trojan horse, operating under the camouflage of the search for German unity, which would enable the Western powers to consolidate a foothold in the very heart and center of the Soviet-controlled territory and to use this foothold to weaken or undermine Soviet control and to give predominance, in any future German peace settlement, to Western claims and drives. Under the auspices of quadripartite control West Berlin would serve as an extension or outpost of West Germany in the heart of East Germany, an alien lump which could become a source of trouble and diversion. Nor were the Soviets in this reading merely feeding their morbid suspicions. It was substantially in these terms that knowing Westerners, in their more candid and lucid moments, thought about Berlin. The So-

* See Article 3, b, iii and article 6, b, i of the agreement on "Control Machinery of Germany," signed November, 1944. See *Yalta Papers*, p. 126. Hence when Clay reached France in late 1944 he found that the staff that was to work under him, the U.S. Group Control Council, was "organized into divisions paralleling the German ministries which were to be seized on surrender and continued in operation under Allied Control." Clay, *Decision*, p. 8. Over the winter and spring of 1944/5 the Agreement on Control Machinery was modified to delete the cited passages and the implication running through them of a going machinery of national government.

viets would have had an excess of delicacy and soft nerves if they had not been guided in their Berlin policy in the spring and early summer months of 1948 by the fixed objective of weakening and undermining the Western enclave in Berlin and, if possible, driving the West by methods short of war out of the city.

To carry out this objective the Soviets had through the winter and spring months of 1947–8 hampered trading activities between West-Berlin and West-Germany and thus undermined the Western economic base in Berlin. Beginning in April at the lower levels and as of 16 June at the highest level they had brought the work of the Kommandatura—or the institutionalized practice of Allied control through negotiated agreements and regular consultation—to a halt. With the advent of Western monetary reform the Soviets attempted to strengthen their hold over the whole city of Berlin in two ways. First, they asserted in various ways formal authority over the whole of the city and particularly over the actions of the all-city Magistrat. No effort was made to enforce this authority within the Western-controlled sectors and little use was made of direct force with German authorities not directly functioning under Soviet sector control. Nevertheless, the assertion of a larger authority was reinforced by the Soviet invalidation of the Kommandatura and was correlated with the strongly expressed contention that the Western Powers no longer had a right to stay in Berlin.

To give meaning to this general position, the Soviets were adamant on excluding Western currency from circulation in Berlin—on this issue threats were voiced of effective retaliation—and conversely the whole of Berlin was to be included within the Eastern monetary reform. These purposes were spelled out in the last futile round of quadripartite negotiation conducted in Berlin on 22 June 1948 on the eve of the Eastern currency reform action. In this negotiation the Soviets evinced a sovereign disregard for any possible Western interest in Berlin monetary reform; they seemed to hold that this reform could not be modified under Kommandatura authority; and they insisted Soviet policy would control and regulate its details.[6] The Soviet financial reform law which was issued the day after reflected these contentions. The same law which applied in the Eastern zone was to apply to Berlin. In the letter of explanation to the mayor of the city it was only asserted coldly that Berlin "is located in the Soviet zone of occupation and economically forms a part of that zone."[7]

The value of monetary integration with the Soviet zone would have been considerable. The Soviets would have taken over certain priority positions of ultimate economic authority which would have afforded leverage for achievement of political goals or would have yielded, at the least, certain bargaining rights. They would have achieved control of terms of access by which additional supplies of currency, if needed, would be obtainable by the city of Berlin and particularly by its Western sectors. Politically, the monetary integration with Eastern Germany would have facilitated trading and dealing with the Eastern hinterland while a like degree of integration with the West would have required special arrangements. A considerable element of prestige too was involved. A government communicates and is exhibited before its citizens most extensively and frequently through its currency notes and coinage. A national currency distinguishes a people and its symbolism even passes into national folklore. The issuance of a national currency has become one of the decisive acts of national sovereignty; just so acquiescence in the use of another nation's currency constitutes an act of national denigration. Finally, currency integration in Berlin would have simplified the task of monetary management and economic control within the Soviet zonal area.

What then were the Western authorities to do with this usurpatory act of Soviet power which forced the issue of Berlin currency? The economic consequences of acceptance were not so ominous. There was a certain protection of Western interests in the fact that by express Soviet order the reform in Berlin was to be carried out under the authority of the Berlin Magistrat (in which the West exerted the largest influence) and through a network of city-owned banks most of which (though not the headquarters institution) were located within the Western sectors. Moreover, the Soviet zone law would have equipped the Berlin economy and banks with an ample supply of new currency; and since the payment relationships of Berlin with the Soviet zone were highly favorable to Berlin additional currency supplies would have in all likelihood gravitated to the city without formal application to Soviet zonal institutions.[8] Money is after all a mere token; and in a city with efficient economic management and use of rationing and allocation schemes even an inadequate token could be made to do.

Use of Soviet zone currency for the city would not hamper a vigorous program of exportation by the Western sectors in order to obtain Western deposit claims; these claims could be sold to Western importers to settle their claims for imports sold to Berlin; and a vigorous kind of traffic at the wholesale level could go on in which Western deposit claims served as money or as a means of payment without Western currency ever appearing in the city. If Soviet zone currency were to be inflated and access to new issuance were to be denied Berlin, or if the Soviets would discriminate against the Western sectors in the carrying out of the present reform, actual Western interests would be hurt. But with the injury realized proper redress could be sought; as yet the injuries were imaginary; and they might never become actual. There were some who pleaded along these lines in the headquarters of military government.[9]

The mood of conciliation on Berlin was unpopular among Western policymakers who were set against accommodation of Soviet claims to special financial prerogative in Berlin. Extravagant fears were voiced that the Soviets through control of the Eastmark would discriminate against or harm the West-Berlin economy. Irrespective of the merits of the Eastmark for the city, Western leaders felt it necessary to counteract the Soviet action to avoid making a precedent. It was important to show in action that the Western powers were to be masters in the Western sectors of Berlin. And forthright resistance to the Soviet action was prompted by interests even more fundamental. With the Soviets angry at a Western separate German settlement and determined to weaken the Western Berlin position, any scheme for joint East-West control over a unified city was unworkable. If the Western powers were seriously intending to stay in Berlin, they would need to pull together their sectors of the city, wrench them from the Soviet zone hinterland and East sector, tear apart the all-city government or convert it to a West-Berlin government and otherwise be able to govern and administer West-Berlin in close dependence upon Western Germany and with the least possible contact and association with the Soviets. Perhaps General Clay who made American policy in Berlin and directed it from day-to-day, and on the German side the aggressive leader of the Berlin social-democrats, Ernst Reuter, sensed this most clearly. These two determined men led the German and the Allied camp.[10] With these policy-makers in control, the Soviet program to undermine the Western powers in Berlin by assuming unilateral prerogative and by including the whole city within the Soviet currency area was going to be met head-on.

But why stay in Berlin? Physically battered by Allied air-war and the theater of bitter street fighting between German and conquering Soviet armies, with much of its choice plant dismantled by the Soviets in the first 50 days, the city was economically a deficit-area costing over

$250 millions a year to feed and supply. East-Germans could be reached by radio stations located on the extended zonal frontier line nearly as easily as from Berlin. East-Germans who were sufficiently desperate could always cross the extended zonal line. Why aggravate Soviet relations by fouling up their occupied territory just when we were trying to make a go of ours? Why try to feed and supply a city—even worse a segment of a city—located in hostile country and without secure and definite channels of access? Why not make a clean break and trade the Western interests in Berlin for satisfaction of some other desired Western objective such as the Austrian treaty and evacuation of Soviet troops from Austria? Why complicate an already disturbed peace settlement with troublemaking enclaves and corridors? It was in these terms that the author at the time analyzed the situation; and doubtless it was for these or comparable considerations that the French continually urged caution and withdrawal.[11] Many American policymakers still had an open mind on the question of withdrawal.

The desirability of staying in Berlin—of converting Berlin into a basic outpost of the Western alliance—in part reduces to the sheer reluctance to retreat from territory under pressure. Such a retreat would conjure up the images of defeat, of appeasement, of impaired prestige. It was in these terms that Clay urged on Washington skeptics that the U.S. must stay in Berlin.[12] Even more compelling were the obligations we had incurred to shelter our Berlin friends whom we had called into existence. But overlooking all this, if the West retreated from Berlin, would the West-Germans move into harness, play the role marked out for them in the London settlement and set up a separate West-German government and institutionally foster an economy of free markets, hard money and open association with the West? The London settlement was unattractive enough at best with its constitutional stipulations, its freezing of Ruhr control, its bias against social-democracy, its acceptance of overt partition, its barely restricted power of the Occupation.[13] If the West were merely going to assert authority in Western Germany and concede Eastern Germany to the Soviets, then the West-Germans would move on the London path more reluctantly. They would respond more enthusiastically to a Western alliance which tenaciously maintained a toe-hold in the Eastern zone and which was pledged to revision of the East-German-Polish frontier.

And not only the West-Germans would have been depressed by retreat from Berlin. The whole movement of Western Europe under

American leadership responded to the ideal of regaining the ancient European heritage in Eastern and in central Europe. In his rallying speech of 27 June 1948, Churchill urged vigorous support for a Western Berlin in order to stop the Soviets from turning the "Russian Zone into one of her satellite states."[14] The Belgian leader Spaak included Berlin in the list of European capitals where the presence of Soviet troops illustrated Soviet "aggression." If the Cold War is defined in Walter Lippmann's terms as a "diplomatic campaign to prevent Russia from expanding her sphere, to prevent her from consolidating it and to compel her to contract it," then the Cold War required maintenance of this "outpost of freedom," this "show-piece of democracy," this "symbol" of German unity lodged in Soviet-controlled territory.[15]

So with waverings and backslidings but with increasing firmness of policy as the main lines of cold war strategy under American leadership were developed, the West became determined to retain and to develop its Berlin outpost. Reflecting this determination the West decided to issue some 200 million marks of the new West-German currency for use in West-Berlin. New issuance for some months thereafter occurred at a monthly rate of nearly 50 million per month.[16] This currency was issued broadside to the whole population on a per capita basis and to business firms, financial organizations and public agencies. This currency or claims payable in it could be specified for payment in contracts and was to be legal tender to settle outstanding obligations.

But in two basic respects the Western counter-action showed an ingenious aptitude for moderation. In the first place though the currency was West-German money—this appealed to the predilections of the West-Berliners and satisfied their craving for tangible linkage with West-Germany—still the currency was stamped clearly to identify its origin. In this stamped form its circulation or use in West Germany could later be restricted or discouraged.

Secondly, the Western money was not issued to *supersede* the East-mark but only to *supplement it*. Counting on the head-quota alone the Soviet monetary reform would have allowed West-Berliners a free issue of 160 million new Eastmarks. Including the Eastmarks scheduled for issuance to business firms, savings banks and public institutions, it may be estimated that West-Berliners were in a position to receive not less than 500 million Eastmarks or between 10–15% of the total Eastern currency issuance, even if we allow for cancellation of the partial deposit claims built up by the Berlin city government and the Western occupy-in powers.[17] Western policymakers decided to encourage acceptance of Eastern currency and even to promote its use in the Western sectors. They made the currency legal tender; and for basic controlled payments—for rationed or allocated foods, house-rents, utility services, taxes—the payer was given the option of making payment either in Westmarks or Eastmarks at a 1–1 parity while the payee was obligated to accept payment. To further insure the use of Eastmarks, it was required that salaries or wages must be paid at least 75% in Eastmarks. Thus the use of Eastmarks was made virtually mandatory for basic transactions which dominated Berlin economic life or constituted its primary circuit flow. For other purchases or for capital transfers or wholesale transactions, it was permitted to contract for payment in either currency.

With this ingenious arrangement for two circulating currencies, the role of the Eastmark as the basic citywide currency was preserved. At the same time the use of the Westmark would prevent Soviet domination now or later of West Berlin finances; it would give all Berliners access to a currency which had outside value; it would facilitate direct trade with West-Germany; and it would provide for East-Germans or East-Berliners an instrument which would appeal to their hoarding instincts and to their desire for contact with the Western world. In a sense the two currencies were pitted against each other in the field of circulation to compete for public preference and as well to measure their relative purchasing power. If some accommodation to the exclusive use of the Eastmark should later be arranged, the withdrawal of the Westmark could be readily adjusted to. Perhaps the compromise aspects of the limited Western currency circulation in Berlin are best indicated by the intensity of opposition from West-Berliners which this scheme inspired. At first this opposition was clearly of a political character. The West-Berlin game-cocks could not understand why if the Soviets forbade the use of Westmarks in East-Berlin that the West should not reciprocate and forbid the use of Eastmarks in West-Berlin or at least not legally ensure their use. Perhaps the most objectionable feature of the dual-currency system was the inequalities of condition which the system permitted among wage-earners depending upon the percent of their earnings payable in Westmarks and among business enterprises required to sell services or products for Eastmarks at the option of the payee. Hence the West-Berlin business man and wage-earner added to the political clamor for an exclusive West-German currency in West-Berlin.[18]

In monetary history the experience with a dual currency in Berlin was a rare one which has not been studied with the care it warrants. But the Soviet response took little account of the subtleties of the Western currency program. The Soviets had been expressly defied in their *dictat* that the Westmark must not be introduced into Eastern Germany or Berlin. And their authority over the whole of Berlin was controverted. The Soviets knew that there was disunity in the Allied camp, that the French position was "soft," and that there were no visible preparations to defend the Berlin outpost. Hence the Soviets decided to treat the introduction of the Westmark as a *casus belli*, to deal out the sanctions which had been threatened, and thereby to test the firmness of the Western resolve.

The sanctions involved the blockade of West-Berlin. To this end the Soviets suspended on account of alleged "technical difficulties" all railroad passenger and freight traffic by rail or barge running through East-Germany and terminating in West-Berlin. The flow of electric power— coal reduced to energy—into West-Berlin from Eastern power stations was suspended, thereby cutting off two-thirds of West-Berlin's power supply.[19] The enforcement of the blockade of rail or barge access was comparatively easy. It was more difficult to stop the aroused West-Berliners from mobilizing needed goods from the surrounding Soviet-held territory which the Berliners knew, where they had many friends and from which they could draw support.[20] Apparently, truck routes of access through Eastern-Germany were open to "enterprising truckers" who managed to "evade Soviet controls and spirit produce from East Germany to West Berlin." In addition West Berlin trucks "drove out daily into the surrounding countryside and came back with vegetables," while individuals "returned by boat, train, subway or bicycle with wood, coal briquettes, potatoes and sundries."[21] Over the fall months the Soviets moved to scale down this traffic. By November some seventy-five control points were established on the intra-city West-Berlin frontier line to check the movement of goods. The zonal frontier was more carefully guarded and postal shipment through third countries was interdicted. The telephone circuit was rerouted. Parcels carried by West-Berliners across the sector line on the East-controlled elevated railways were subject to confiscation. The campaign to seal off the intra-Berlin Western frontier from personal traffic and petty trading greatly irritated West Berliners.[22]

This was the Eastern "blockade" of West-Berlin. The West replied

in kind by suspending all trading from Western to East-Germany including the vital shipments of Ruhr hard coal and steel upon which
East-German metal-working industry was partly dependent. To supply
West-Berlin the Western Powers stepped-up the small-scale or "baby-
airlift" which had been supplying the needs of the Western occupation
forces since late spring. The airlift was now to bring in enough food,
coal and essential industrial materials to enable a population of nearly
two millions to survive.

The duel between the airlift and the blockade brought us close to
the edge of war. Coercion on a mass scale was involved; the conflict of
purpose was fundamental and pervasive; and compromise and recon-
ciliation were forgotten. Nor was trade alone interdicted. Property and
bank deposits of persons or organizations domiciled across the East-
West zone line were blocked or liable for seizure.[23] But the struggle was
waged with limited methods. However vigorous their assertion of
authority over the whole of Berlin, the Soviets respected the practical
control of the Western powers within the Western sectors. They even
granted a kind of immunity to West-Berlin leaders who, however, were
frequently harassed and nagged. As Clay reported the Soviets avoided
"with care" measures "which would have been resisted with force."[24]
But the Western governments did not choose to believe that the Soviet
government would have shirked the fight if we were, as Clay proposed,
to push an "armed convoy" up the access routes to Berlin.[25] Similarly,
the Soviets probably felt the West would not shirk the fight if they
challenged the Western airways to Berlin.

The duel between the airlift and the blockade lasted for nearly
eleven months. In the process all semblance of a unified city government together with the institutions of shared East-West condominium
were destroyed. The nucleus for partition in Berlin existed from the start
in the control by the occupying powers over their so-called Bezirk (or
borough) administrations and the separate sector control over imported
commodities, over political behavior, police administration and radio
and newspapers. The sheer disappearance of the Kommandatura, i.e. of
an institutionalized system of negotiated Allied agreements regarding
all-Berlin action, greatly strengthened tendencies toward disintegration
of the all-Berlin city government. Since the city government offices were
largely located in the Soviet-controlled sector, the Soviets had the advantage of local access and immediate physical control. But the all-city
legislative assembly was predominantly and vigorously Western; and

most of the important officials and the civil service staff were also Western in sympathy. Many preferred a neutral course but they were forced to choose sides. All Western-controlled city bureaus and the facilities of city government were eventually driven from the Soviet sector. An Eastern-controlled city government manned by SED members and a limited number of liberal allies or neutralists was set up and became a functioning organization by the end of the year. The process of setting up dual governments in the city took some time since both sides catered to local and world public opinion and sought to disguise the nature of the splitting actions which were best motivated in defensive terms or as merely practical adjustments to certain troublesome situations. Though weakened by transplantation and stripped of the key requisites for a bureaucratic existence—desks, offices and typewriters—a Western all-city government was reorganized and consolidated. With the move of the Berlin supreme court to West-Berlin in February 1949, "the last remaining city-wide governmental function had been divided."[26]

To this administrative partition there corresponded a polarization social and cultural. The unified trade union movement, which had been developed since the occupation under communist or SED leadership was split; in the course of the blockade an anti-communist trade-union center was formed which won a strong following among organized Berlin workers and became legally established in the Western sectors. The bulk of the communists or SED members or supporters either lived in, or moved to, the Eastern sector of the city. Since the SED did not participate in the late 1948 Western city elections, this party nearly disappeared from West-Berlin public life. Similarly, the Western parties were driven out of East-Berlin or were reconstituted under acceptable leadership. The mass dismissals and counter-dismissals of city officials and leaders, numbering some 2000 on the Western side, amounted "almost to an exchange of population."[27] Newspapers and magazines were confined in their mass circulation according to their vintage to the Eastern or Western part of Berlin or Germany. Educational institutions shifted their domicile according to their political sympathies.[28] Socialization was accelerated in East-Berlin; while controlled properties were released for private use in open markets in West-Berlin. In the one area the profit motive was checked by controls and public enterprise; in the other area controls were relaxed and profits were reconstituted as the guiding agency of the economy. This transformation had revolutionary effects in the East-sector since under the Control Council regime the public administration of the Sector and many of its key institutions had been led by West-Germans.[29] For West-Berlin the changeover also had revolutionary implications. The power of the communist movement over organized labor was broken; its influence within the city administration and in public life generally was greatly reduced. In the process of supporting the blockade the West-Berlin population had become mobilized either in public service, on the job or in street rallies and demonstrations. The spirit of the anti-fascist front was burned out and highly militant anti-Russian—perhaps even more an anti-communist—mood was inspired. The latent antagonism was released between the communists supported now by the resident Soviet power and the whole string of bourgeois-democratic parties now sheltered and identified with the West. The East-Berliners developed sharper methods of struggle, and considerable restraint needed to be exerted to prevent strong popular feelings from exploding in local street fights or mob-action in which isolated communists in the Western sectors or West-German officials or demagogues in the Eastern sector were man-handled.

The conflict between the Allies was thus amplified as it was worked out in the German community. It widened the German perspective, opened the German sense of power, and made impossible the restoration of the Control Council regime. This presupposed the unity of the occupying powers set against a rather apathetic and submissive German world which at its bottom layer was preoccupied chiefly with private ends and was still in the spell of recoil from the total defeat of the Hitler Reich. We could put it, perhaps, this way: the Western German parties were no longer willing to collaborate with a German communist-influenced SED, the West-German leadership had lost the confidence of the Soviet occupying authorities, and the Western powers would no longer tolerate a Soviet veto on the form and terms of their associated dealings.[30]

II. The Diplomatic Negotiations and Settlement

We thus see that in addition to carrying on the struggle by the physical means of blockade, airlift and counterblockade, both East and West sought to become consolidated in the sectors of the city which they controlled. We shall now see that the struggle opened up by the Berlin crisis was not confined to the use of physical force or of political strategy in Berlin. Both sides endeavored to further their cause through diplomatic negotiations. These commenced in a sense with the quadripartite meeting of financial experts on 22 June 1948. They were then resumed during early July in correspondence and in personal meetings of the zone commanders in Berlin. In August there were formal meetings between diplomatic emissaries of the Western powers and top Soviet government leaders. Then there was a week of intense negotiations at the zone commander level in Berlin. This was followed with diplomatic correspondence which at a certain point came to a head. Thereafter, the negotiations were transferred to the Security Council of the UN. In this forum a more formal kind of diplomacy was in place and allies, friends and some neutral onlookers were drawn into the discussions. It is interesting to reflect that the negotiations petered out at about the time when a settlement was in the making. These tortuous negotiations cannot be traced in detail here.[31] But we shall endeavor to decode the negotiations and to show how they became another means to carry on the struggle for Berlin.[32]

One purpose of the negotiations was to intimidate the other side indirectly by threatening war or a more aggressive use of force. Thus the tone of the diplomatic exchanges was austere and threatening. They spoke of firm intentions, absolute positions and of threats to the peace. The Western Powers "categorically" asserted that they would not "be induced by threats, pressure or other action" to abandon their "rights" in Berlin. The Soviets in reply asserted an intention not to "enter into discussion of this statement" both because the Soviets "have no need for a policy of pressure" and because "by violation of the agreed decisions concerning the administration of Berlin" the Western powers "themselves are reducing to naught their right to participation in the occupation of Berlin."[33] This note of mutual intimidation, slightly toned down in the French messages, was kept up to the very end. But neither side was really intimidated. Perhaps if the West had had serious military power in being on the Continent, its veiled threats might have earned more respect. But this power was nominal; and only the first steps were in process to develop an integrated Western command. Only two available American divisions could have been moved to the Continent. A fleet of 200 long-range strategic B-29 bombers equipped with atomic bombs was shifted to an English airbase on 15 July. But no other military moves were made to back up the intimidating language. Of course the Soviets could never quite tell what turn Western policy might take. The Anglo-American leaders were determined men who would not shrink from what Bevin in his September UN speech called "the black fury, the incalculable disaster of atomic war." But even this implicit threat did not deter the Soviets. They did not think that the policy of long-distance atomic strategic bombing of Soviet cities would be decisive; they had once faced without flinching a more formidable opponent; and they knew that their ground forces could sweep across Western Europe with little organized opposition.[34] Sheltered by the atomic bomb the West did not flinch either although there were anxious moments. "When tension (at Berlin) was at its height, Bevin confessed that he now realized what agony Neville Chamberlain must have endured in September 1938."[34a]

With negotiation by intimidation was interwoven the reciprocal negotiation of options of peace-by-concession. The options were usually given a veiled expression to disguise their true nature and to make them more palatable to onlookers and neutral public opinion. But in them the "other side" was asked to concede the particular advantages which had been sought through struggle. Thus the Soviets continually offered to withdraw the blockade and fully to recognize the quadripartite status of Berlin if the program of the Western London settlement to erect a West German state would be suspended. This possibly appealed to the French. But they had already given their assent to the settlement. The British and Americans would obviously never undo what all the resources of their diplomacy and power had barely contrived. The West expressed this in diplomatic language by refusing to discuss their Western German settlement while under duress; and they also reassured the Soviets that the action taken under the London plan would not conflict with the larger needs of the German settlement. What this in fact meant was that the Soviet Zone territories could leave Soviet control and join the Western Germany being constructed under Western leadership. The Soviets were obviously disinterested.[35]

Besides offering peace by concession on the basic issue of Eastern or Western Germany, both the Soviets and the Western Powers developed programs for limited surrender in Berlin, i.e. for achieving predominance over the split city unified only by exclusive use of Eastern currency. Both programs coupled with this withdrawal of Western currency from Berlin and the lifting of the blockade and counter-blockade and of associated restrictions on trade and movement. But in other respects the programs differed markedly. The Soviet program contemplated agreed control positions which would have permitted the Soviets to curtail or, if they were so inclined, to disrupt the economic trade of West-Berlin with Western Germany.[36] The Soviets would also tie up or control the use by Western Powers of the "counterpart funds" growing out of the sale in West Berlin of the Western foodstuffs and supplies provided by Western subsidies. These counterpart funds provide much of the leverage for economic assistance and rehabilitation growing out of external subsidy. Control over these funds to the extent achieved greatly enhanced American power in shaping political and economic reconstruction under the Marshall Plan.[37] Unhampered use of these funds was in the American view a legitimate concomitant of the role of occupying power.[38]

On the currency front, the Soviets were willing to exchange East-marks for circulating Westmarks on a 1–1 basis and to set up a four-power financial commission with general authority over the arrangements for currency changeover and for the continued provision and use in Berlin of the Eastmark. But action by this commission would be subject to Soviet veto; and the Soviets were willing to concede only the empty verbiage of the principle of "equal treatment" throughout the city and the right of the West sectors to apply for loans to meet budgetary deficits or occupation costs. The Soviets in advance indicated that they would provide little or no funds for West-Berlin budgetary deficits or occupation expenses. And they would not concede to the Western Powers any access to claim upon the East-zone central bank which they insisted should, under Soviet control, regulate currency and credit policy for the Soviet zone and for Berlin.[39]

Finally, the Soviet program would have put Western air traffic under some kind of quadripartite customs control; and no distinct recognition was to be given or implied as to the general legitimacy of the quadripartite status of Berlin and of the Western position in the city. Quite clearly the Soviets were still seeking in their limited settlement program to achieve the ends for which the blockade was launched. If accepted by the Western Powers they would concede a paramount position in Berlin economics to the Soviets. Contact and communication with West-Germany would be greatly hampered; and the Western position in the city would be weakened. Understandably this Soviet offer could be attractive to the West if the airlift were doing very poorly or if the Berliners or French were weakening under the strain. Both the French and the Berliners held firm and the airlift developed surprising power. Hence the West was not interested.

In turn the West developed a compensatory scheme of aggression just to show that its diplomatic capacities were respectable and to give the Soviets a convenient line of partial retreat if they or their allies or satellites should weaken under the strain. This program contemplated the Soviet surrender of the blockade and counter-blockade in exchange for withdrawal of Westmarks and the acceptance of Eastmarks in all Berlin. But the price for this acceptance was heavily in Western favor. First, the West would have a free hand in organizing and carrying out the trade of West-Berlin with West-Germany, thus cutting across the trade restrictions applied by the Soviets over the winter and spring of 1947-8. To safeguard the Soviet zone from economic disruption or economic-drainage through this trade the West conceded the Soviets a free hand in isolating their controlled territories around West-Berlin so as to permit only sanctioned and self-balancing transactions.[40] Second, the Soviets were to subsidize the costs of operating the economically derelict and bankrupted West-Berlin enclaves by furnishing sufficient currency to meet the heavy West-Berlin budgetary deficits and charges for so-called occupation expenses, i.e. expenses for maintaining in Berlin the Western occupation troops, governing establishments, public media and the whole retinue of supporting organizations and personnel.[41] The Western formula for budgetary support was unrestricted though at the time the budget deficit was running around 50 million marks monthly. Somewhat later the new West-German government, when asked to take over a similar blanket responsibility, baulked.[42] Third and most important, the Soviets were to provide far-reaching safeguards to ensure that use of Eastern currency in Western Berlin could not possibly hamper its access to new currency or transfer ultimate monetary authority to the Soviets.[43] The West asked for no less than Western participation in the management of the central bank of the Soviet Zone. True this participation was to be confined to issues arising in regard to the currency changeover and to the "continued provision and use of the Eastmark in Berlin." But virtually all the operations of the East Zone Central Bank would affect the "provision and use" of that currency in Berlin. To ensure that this Bank would have sufficient lending power to take care of Berlin needs, the Western Powers would be negligent if they did not limit use of bank credit for the support of other areas or projects. The Western Powers could be dissatisfied with the quality of reports furnished by the managers of the bank and could ask for quadripartite inspection of its records and facilities. The Western Powers could reject loans requested by East Zone German governments on the grounds that these governments were illegitimate.[44] Central banks generally are pivotal agencies of political power. Over no German agency was a stricter Western control exercised under the London settlement than over the West-German central bank.[45] The Western insiders knew that under cover of loosely-drawn terms of reference the Western Powers were staking a claim in their limited surrender program for what could be turned into a veiled copartnership regime over the entire Soviet zone.[46] The Soviets could see that the Western program "practically meant completely subordinating financial policy and currency both in Berlin and the Soviet zone to their control and influence."[47] Clearly the Soviet Union would not be interested in withdrawal of Western currency from Berlin and release of the counter-blockade if paid for with such a price.

While the peace-with-concession programs of East and West were possibly given an excessively stringent character, these programs essentially reflected both the balance of power achieved and the relative disinclination of either side to attempt to return to the quadripartite administration over a formally unified city or even a city unified in any essential respect. This disinclination arose partly out of the antagonism engendered by the head-on collision at currency reform. But even more this disinclination was grounded in mutual awareness that the presuppositions had disappeared for an East-West operating partnership in Berlin however restricted in scope. There was no way the Soviets could give guarantees that Zonal monetary policy would not hamper credit access to Berlin without making it possible for the Western Powers to hamper and disrupt their zonal management. Likewise there was no way the Western Powers could give guarantees that West-Berlin trade would not have disorganizing influence on the East-German economy unless that economy was at Soviet expense insulated from West-Berlin. Arrangements that would rigidly operate regardless of changing conditions would be unsuitable for application to a city destined to experience a wide diversity of economic and political conditions. But arrangements that would depend upon judgment or negotiated agreement would place one side or the other in a subordinate position. A neutral committee of experts canvassed the controversy in the conscientious search for grounds for conciliation to resolve disagreements which appeared to the distant observer "so small and technical."[48] They came up with an ingenious framework for a negotiated settlement which probably was equally dissatisfactory to both parties and which would, in practice, have operated fairly well granted good will and the desire to make a partnership function.[49] But it was just this desire which had eroded, not only on the part of the Allies but also in the now schismed German community. Hence without ill-will the plan was rejected by both East and West. Both sides preferred to continue the duel of blockade and airlift rather than to take on the torment of a quadripartite solution.

If the contending parties were to settle the conflict it seemed clear that they would need frankly to accept the fact of a split city, juridically recognize the line of partition, insulate the West-Berlin enclave as much as possible from the East-German hinterland, permit the enclave to go its own way in trade, currency and politics and thus to draw close and become integrated with its West-German homeland. With this settlement the blockade and counter-blockade could be lifted and the acute threat to the peace overcome. This was the line of settlement which would have generated the fewest elements of strain; and it was a line of settlement which the Western delegations in their informal suggestions at the UN discussions recommended.[50] Because this line of settlement now appeared so inevitable, the Western powers on 20 March withdrew the legal tender privilege of the Eastmark from West-Berlin and arranged for additional currency grants to enable the Westmark to become the established money in West-Berlin.[51] It was substantially the line of settlement that was in fact negotiated in the agreement reached on 4 May 1949. In that agreement both sides undertook to lift restrictions imposed by East or West since 1 March 1948 and within eleven days thereafter to initiate diplomatic discussions at the foreign-minister level on the German and Berlin problem as a whole. So tense was the note of struggle that run through these negotiations that it was not found feasible to release from "blocked" status the property and deposits located on one side of the East-West line in Germany but owned on the other side. Nor were the sequence of events and the bounds of discretion that were involved in the "blockade" and in the "counter-blockade" respectively properly defined. The original May agreement only specified that "all restrictions imposed since 1 March 1948" by the four Occupying powers on transportation, communication or trade between the respective zones and sectors of Germany were to be "lifted." In the June agreement at the Foreign Minister level each Occupying power undertook the additional obligation, "to ensure the normal functioning and utilization of rail, water and road transport," by taking "the necessary measures" within their zones. This tended to tie down Soviet access through pre-existing routes. But with regard to resumption of East-West interzonal trade, for which the mere lifting of the "restrictions" imposed by the Occupying Powers would signify little, the West rejected Soviet proposals that would specify the nature and procedure for such trade and promised only to "recommend" to the "leading German bodies" in their zone "to facilitate the establishment of closer economic ties . . . and more effective implementation of trade and other economic agreements."[52] This left the matter of resumption of East-West trade in a haze of ambiguity; the West was not tied down; and in fact during German negotiations to reach a new trading agreement, the U.S. representatives maneuvered behind the scenes to restrict the volume of trade that would be carried on.[53] But though the Soviets were obligated to open up "access" on previously used routes to Berlin, they retained the right to "screen" Berlin exports according to procedures in force on 1 March 1948; and by manipulation of screening "rights" and "access procedure" they could exert a corresponding pressure on the West-Germans. And though the West-German economy was less dependent upon this trade than East-Germany, the trade was highly beneficial to West-Berlin which received on Western account nearly a third of East-German exports.[53a] Both sides thus had an interest in carrying out the agreement to "lift" restrictions; both sides could police the agreement; and both sides could inflict enough injury to compel a rough equivalence in mutual advantage. In February of 1950 an American spokesman characterized the situation as "off again and on again" with Eastern restrictions "mainly against trucks" answered in part by a "counter steel embargo." It was not a "healthy situation" but it is "a much better situation . . . than it was with the airlift."[54] The terse characterization by the responsible American commander of the original 1944 Kommandatura agreement—"as a legal document it stinks but as a rough note on what you've been talking about it's all right"—applies in full to the 1949 agreement which ended the blockade and airlift and permitted the struggle for Berlin to be carried on with less disruptive means.[55]

But why did the Soviets accept the defeat of their purposes and relinquish what they had sought to achieve by the blockade? Why did they let the West have, hold and use its Berlin outpost on such cheap terms? The plausible answer is that continuation of the struggle by means of the blockade was shown to be imprudent. If the airlift carried the city—and if the city would support the airlift—over the winter months of need, then the maintenance of the Western position in Berlin could not be undermined or disintegrated through continuation of the blockade. The use of large aircraft and more efficient organization was steadily increasing the tonnage carried to Berlin. By spring the airlift brought in 8000 tons daily which was as much as the West "had been able to bring into Berlin by rail and water prior to the blockade."[56] The financial cost of the airlift to America and England was insignificant, only one-half million dollars daily.[57] The most repressive measures feasible could only scale down but not completely dry up the support from the Soviet zone and from East-Berlin organized by a small army of enterprising black marketeers possessed of abundant supplies of East-marks and of the valuable Westmark currency.[58]

If the blockade could not weaken the Western economic position in Berlin, it in turn became a stimulus for political revival in the whole Atlantic community which was responding to and accepting vigorous American leadership. Thus within Germany itself the visible struggle over Berlin probably helped to turn the balance of German sentiment and public opinion in favor of the London plan of Western settlement and thus promoted the rise of that Western Germany which it was the purpose of the blockade to help deter. Partly this outcome owed to the fact that the Social Democratic Party, which was most sensitive to the satellite status marked out for the forthcoming Western German state and the highly restricted range of German decision, had in its Berlin establishment taken the lead in fighting for a Western Berlin. Then too the Western Berlin leaders urged the course of West-German collaboration with the Western program. The position of the West-German communist party was greatly weakened by its opposition to the struggle to preserve West-Berlin. The airlift too convinced many German leaders of the tenacity of Allied purpose in the Cold War. It gave promise of a growing Anglo-American-German alliance which would seek ultimately to achieve German unity, i.e. to push back the Soviet armies and release the East-Germans from Soviet control.[59]

The Berlin crisis had a tonic effect not only in Germany. It was consolidating the whole of Western Europe under American leadership and inducing closer forms of association and common defense arrangements. It was a stinging thought that when the Western forces in Berlin were first challenged the Atlantic coalition could make so slight a showing of military force. The beginnings of the NATO Pact antedate the Berlin crisis; but the formation of the NATO alliance and the program of rearmament was immensely stimulated by that crisis and the sustained duel which followed it.[60] Moreover, the duel between the airlift and blockade caught the imagination of the Western public; it symbolized and tended to justify the Cold War; it helped to erase from Western minds the memories of German aggression now replaced by the image of the "stout-hearted democrats of Berlin."

Finally, the blockade-airlift duel with insignificant economic costs to the West, aside from the impoverishment of West Berlin, served substantially to retard economic revival in East-Germany. East-Germany was deprived by the counter-blockade of the equipment and industrial supplies badly needed to sustain industrial operations or permit the desired rate of economic progress. Though the absolute quantity of East-West interzonal trade was barely a fifth of the prewar level, many of the goods moving were not readily replaceable within the Eastern world. Current index reports on industrial performance in East-Germany are not available, but there is scattered evidence to support the surmise that the pressure of the counter-blockade played an important role in bringing about a settlement.[61]

These are reasons enough. Soviet foreign policy has realist traditions; and Soviet policymakers are trained in a political philosophy which calls for continuous appraisal of a strategic line and willingness to modify or even to reverse it if this seems called for in the light of realized results and a changed situation.

But while partition in Berlin and encapsulation of West-Berlin and its assimilation into West-Germany resolved the 1948-9 Berlin crisis, it only created the groundwork for a much more enduring problem. Eastern and western Germany were now crystallizing in divergent social and political moulds and becoming imbued with the deepest hatreds of the 20th century. These Germanies were drawn into trade partly in order to provide more adequately for West-Berlin. Yet West-Berlin also constituted a potential source of tensions arising out of frontier administration, transport access and political disturbance. For the time being these tensions were muted as the Germans of all faiths and location concentrated their energies on renewal of their economic life. Ordinary people wanted a respite. Time was needed to heal wounds, repair factories, reunite families, find new markets, and build up again a stock of goods and a standard of more comfortable living. Along with this economic renewal would come institutional invigorizing and new attitudes and forms of social and personal life. But this would make ever more anomalous the role of West-Berlin. The enclave would be cast in ever-sharper opposition to its hinterland and in closer connection with its homeland. Would the West-Berliners behave themselves? Would the East-Germans refrain from petty persecution of unwelcome neighbors cast in their midst? Would peaceful trade exert a healing influence? Would "incidents" be avoided? Or was Berlin a permanent incitement to Cold War, a block to the peace, an inspiration to a continuous state of tension?

III. Postscript

The crisis in Berlin together with the West German monetary reform which touched it off had profound repercussions. In the Berlin crisis the tension between the United States and the Soviet Union rose to the brink of war. Under the spell of crisis, the remnants of wartime ideology of East-West alliance were dissipated, the moral unity of the Western world under American leadership was enhanced, and the formation of a viable West German republic was accelerated.

The explosiveness of these developments attests to the emergence of a historic watershed. On one side of this watershed was the old Control Council regime with its possibilities for quadripartite settlement in a united and neutralized Germany. Realization of these possibilities, as we have tried to show in this book, was not guaranteed. But neither was it foredoomed. Such realization could draw support on a wide variety of resources. Intermediary social forms appropriate for a country which was to serve as a buffer between East and West were being created. And neither zonalization nor internal social differentiation had blighted German capacity to work out a mutual accord.

After June 1949 this entire line of possibilities which had been gradually narrowing became closed. A quadripartite settlement involving a united Germany was no longer possible. There could be no return to the kind of East-West condominium which had grown up after 1945, thrived for a while, decayed and then died. By the end of the period even reparations no longer commanded the leverage in settlement which it once had. Nor could eastern and western Germany develop a livable accord with one another. The resources of policy and agreement, the drift of historic momentum, the very personalities which would have made it possible—had been used up. The social moulds of divergent regimes had hardened.

FOOTNOTE ANNEX

Unless otherwise indicated all manuscripts and mimeographed materials cited, including all Control Council, Bipartite and other Allied documentation on Germany, will be found in the collection of German materials deposited in the library of the Littauer School, Harvard University.

NOTES FOR CHAPTER I

1. Cordell Hull, *The Memoirs of Cordell Hull* (2v., New York, 1948), II, 1451–58.

2. Cf. my conclusions in this chapter, section III.

3. This aspect is well brought out in Hull's detailed account. Hull, *Memoirs*, II, 1570–1582.

4. See the detailed story told in P. E. Mosely, "The occupation of Germany: New Light on How the Zones were Drawn," *Foreign Affairs*, XXVIII (1950), 580–604; H. Feis, *Churchill Roosevelt Stalin* (Princeton, N.J., 1957) 362 ff.

5. "Statement on Control Machinery in Germany," one of the agreements reached in the winter and early spring of 1944/5 by the European Advisory Commission, signed and promulgated on 5 June 1945. Office of Military Government for Germany (U.S.), *Enactments and Approved Papers of the Control Council and Coordinating Committee* (7 v., Legal Division, Berlin, 1946–48), I, 14. The same principle was embodied in other documents signed at the same time.

6. For this agreement see the "Declaration regarding the Defeat of Germany," issued 5 June 1945 and its supplement, an intergovernmental agreement on "Certain Additional Requirements to be Imposed on Germany," issued as Control Council Proclamation no. 2, 20 September 1945. *Ibid.*, 10–15, 81–96. These two documents embody the bulk of the original "terms of surrender" instrument which, through the curious course of events recited by Mosely, was replaced by an *ad hoc* instrument considerably reduced in scope. See P. E. Mosely, "Dismemberment of Germany: The Allied Negotiations from Yalta to Potsdam," *Foreign Affairs*, XXVIII (1950), 496 ff.

7. Cf. H. R. Trevor-Roper, *The Last Days of Hitler* (New York, 1947), 102 f., 121 ff., 134 f.; Office of Strategic Services, Mission for Germany, USFET, Field

Intelligence Studies no. 31, *Political Implications of the 20th of July* (15 October 1945), 28 f., 42 ff.; F. Reuter, *Der 20 Juli und seine Vorgeschichte* (Berlin, 1946), 28 f.; H. B. Gisevius, *To the Bitter End* (Cambridge, 1947), 461, 472, 480, 521, 526 f., 532 f. The OSS Study cited as probable an estimate of 4,980 executions connected directly or indirectly with the plot. *Political Implications*, 55. See also Trevor-Roper, *The Last Days of Hitler*, 34 ff. For a recent survey of literature see A. Grosser, *The Colossus Again* (trans. N.Y. 1955) 64 ff., p. 83, n 6.

8. Kraus and Almond, "The Social Composition of the German Resistance," *Struggle for Democracy in Germany*, 64.

9. A . D. Kahn, *Betrayal, Our Occupation of Germany* (Warsaw, 1950) 20–41.

10. These local movements, generally called ANTIFA, were encountered "almost without exception as Allied troops captured the larger cities" according to the reliable account of Kraus and Almond, "Social Composition of the German Resistance," *loc. cit.*, 65 ff. See the detailed account provided of the ANTIFA movement in Hamburg which "in the latter years of the war" involved the activities of one or two thousand persons. Spurning doctrinal programs, ANTIFAS "occupied Nazi party and labor front local offices; they erased Nazi slogans and changed streets names; took over houses, clothing and food from Nazis; and made space available to returning concentration camp victims." The Kraus-Almond summary is confirmed by many sources of varying reliability. Describing the ANTIFA activities in Leipzig, a student of the Soviet zone observed that "in varying form that story could be repeated for most of the towns taken over by the Russians." G. Schaffer, *Russian Zone of Germany* (SRT Publications. U.S.A., 1947), 16. The Schaffer account of Leipzig is confirmed by an OSS study of that period. See Office of Strategic Services, Mission for Germany, USFET, *Field Intelligence Studies*, "The Political Situation in the Ruhr and in the Adjacent Industrial Region to the South," no. 7, July 1945, 5–7, 12 ff, 17 ff, 20 ff; *Ibid.*, "Trade Union Developments in Essen and Adjacent Cities." no. 22, September 1945, 17 ff. The claim to near-universality of these ANTIFA movements is also testified to by other observers. Tibor Mende, *Europe's Suicide in Germany* (London, 1946), 89. L. Krieger, "The Interregnum in Germany: March-August 1946," *Political Science Quarterly*, LXIV (1949), 513; Paul Sweezy, "Germany from the Ruins," *New Republic*, 22 April 1946, 585 ff; J. P. Nettl, *The Eastern Zone and Soviet Policy in Germany* (Oxford, 1951), 76–9; H. O. Lewis, *New Constitutions in Occupied Germany* (Foundation for Foreign Affairs, Pamphlet no. 6, Washington, 1948), 2.

11. On land reform and Junker liquidation, see the now definitive works of A. Gerschenkron, *Bread and Democracy in Germany* (University of California Press, 1943); Philip M. Raup, *Land Reform in Post-war Germany: The Soviet Zone Experiment* (doctoral dissertation, University of Wisconsin, Madison, Wisconsin, 1949), chaps. I–V.

12. The depth of the need for corporate reorganization is indicated by the striking fact that even an apostle of neo-liberalism such as Röpke included in his postwar German plan a far-reaching corporate reorganization of heavy industry. See W. Röpke, *The Solution of the German Problem* (translated from the German, New York, 1946/7) 172 ff, 174 ff, 203 ff.

13. On the role of centralized economic planning in circumstances of this type, see the important work of W. A. Lewis, *The Principles of Economic Planning* (2nd

ed., London, 1951). The American experience of partial planning for limited mobilization in 1951–3 is an instructive episode in this regard. Decentralized enterprise functions best by making relatively small adjustments in a universe with well-defined outlines. Where the future is obscure or the displacements massive in proportions, the characteristic responses of the market economy become disorganized, random and wasteful. See J. M. Keynes, *The General Theory of Employment, Interest and Money* (N.Y. 1936), chap. XII; J. Schumpeter, *The Theory of Economic Development* (translated, Cambridge, Mass. 1934), chap. II.

14. On the pattern of Nazi war finance, with its deficits ranging between 35–50 per cent, see R. W. Lindholm, "German Finance in World War II," *American Economic Review*, XXXVII (1947), 122 ff.; Eduard Wolf, "Geld- und Finanzprobleme der deutschen Nachkriegswirtschaft," Deutsches Institut fur Wirtschaftsforschung, *Zwei Jahre Nach Dem Zusammenbruch* (Berlin 1947), 196 ff. While the net amount of the monetary overhang increased after the war due to repatriation of currency from outlying areas, credit expansion to cover budget deficits and military mark issuance, Wolf pointed out that these were approximately offset by measures of monetary sterilization. *Ibid.*, 206–222. Whereas 1946 national income calculated at prevailing legal price and wage levels had sunk from a prewar 60–80 billion RM to around 34–40 billion and national wealth had fallen a third, the total of fixed income claims payable in legal tender currency and of liquid assets had risen four to fivefold. *Ibid.*, 196–206. OMGUS, *A Plan for the Liquidation of War Finance and the Financial Rehabilitation of Germany* (a report submitted by the Colm-Dodge-Goldsmith mission to Germany which includes the text of the report and a collection of supporting studies collected in a separate volume of appendices, preface dated 20 May 1946, Berlin) [hereafter cited CDG Report], Appendices A, E and J. The recognized and registered public debt had risen some tenfold, ran to four times the prospective national income at prevailing price-wage levels, and debt service for 1944 was budgeted as 12 billion RM although many obligations were unfunded or floating at low interest rates. *Ibid.*, Appendix J; Wolf, "Geld-", *loc cit.*, 201 ff.

15. "It was a bad sign that in 1944 more and more establishments and even official ones had to promise material premiums for higher efficiency mostly in the form of cigarettes." Schwerin von Krosigk, "Die Kriegsfinanzierung seit 1939" (a statement about wartime financial policy written in confinement under American custody in 1945 by the one-time minister of finance in the Nazi Reich), 14.

16. On financial reform thinking in the eastern zone, see an unpublished resolution of the central committee of the Social Democratic Party in the Soviet Zone, "Wirtschaftsaufbau und Finanzen" (6 November 1945—unpublished); J. Kuczinski, "Geld und Geldwert in der Ostzone," *Die Wirtschaft*, I (1946), 114–115; *Neuaufbau der Deutschen Wirtschaft, Referat und Diskussion über die Richtlinien der KPD zur Wirtschaftspolitik* (Berlin, 1946), 31–39; 103–105; Bruno Gleitze, "Deutschland's finanzpolitische Lage Ende 1947," *Deutsche Finanzwirtschaft*, I (1947), 1–9. Antagonism to a policy of relaxation of price and wage controls and support for monetary reform was about as decided in the western zones. Cf. reports of a German conference on monetary reform, held on December 1945, Frankfurt, Germany. Paul Binder, "Die Sanierung von Deutschlands Währung und Finanzen" (Tübingen 1945–mimeographed), 29 ff.; G. Keiser, "Die Verfahren zur Beseitigung des Kaufkraftüberhanges" (Hamburg, 19 Dec. 1945–typed report), 4;

OMGUS, *Report of the Military Governor,* Finance and Property Control, December 1945, No. 6, 9. See also the survey of German opinion as presented in Wolf, "Geld–", *loc. cit.,* 234–55; *CDG Report,* Appendix Q. For examples of contemporary German thought, see the report published by a committee of Munich trade union and SPD leaders, *Plan G. Ein Gesamtplan für Regelung der schwebenden Währungs- und Finanz-Probleme* (Munich 1945), 21 ff.

17. For this flat judgment, see the *C-D-G Report,* 25–26; Walter Heller, "Tax and Monetary Reform in Occupied Germany," *loc. cit.,* 218 ff.: *Deutsche Finanzwirtschaft,* I (November, 1947), 1 f.; *Ibid.,* II (January–February, 1948), 1 f. Taxation approaches "tolerance limits" only as a variety of indexes indicate the accumulation of strain. See on this the interesting analysis in W. Gerloff, *Die Öffentliche Finanzwirtschaft* (Band 1, Allg. Teil, Frankfurt, 2d ed., 1948), 222–236.

18. For supporting analysis, see my papers on the capital levy, "The Capital levy and Deadweight Debt in England," *Journal of Finance,* VIII (1953); "The Capital levy after WWI," *Public Finance,* VII (1952).

19. Winston Churchill, *Closing the Ring* (v.V. of the series, "The Second World War," Boston 1951) 406. Allies in context meant Churchill, Stalin and Roosevelt.

20. Hull, *Memoirs,* II, 1620–1621, from memoranda of the President to Secretary Hull on 29 September and 20 October 1944. The President concluded the first memo with this note: "we cannot afford to get into a position of merely recording protests on our part unless there is some chance of some of the protests being heard."

21. Churchill, *Closing the Ring,* 290. In his survey of Teheran Churchill wrote that "The political aspects were at once more remote and speculative. Obviously they depended upon the results of the great battles yet to be fought and after that upon the mood of each of the Allies when victory was gained." *Ibid.,* 405.

22. On the position of the American Army chiefs, see P. E. Mosely, *Face to Face with Russia* (Foreign Policy Association, "Headline Series," No. 70 1948), 8–9; Mosely, Occupation of Germany," *loc. cit.,* 583, 585, 588, 595. On the partitionist position of Roosevelt and Churchill, see the evidence collected in Mosely, "Dismemberment of Germany," *loc. cit.,* 887–898. Supplementary evidence indicates that the American position remained basically partitionist through to the preparations for the Potsdam conference. R. E. Sherwood, *Roosevelt and Hopkins, An Intimate History* (New York 1948) 904; W. D. Leahy, *I Was There, The Personal Story* (New York 1950) 390; Hull, *Memoirs,* II, 1620 ff. On the American division, see *Ibid.,* 1602–1622; James F. Byrnes, *Speaking Frankly* (New York, 1947) 181–187; H. L. Stimson, G. McBundy, *On Active Service in Peace and War* (New York 1947) 568–583. For a useful general survey, see Mosely, "Dismemberment," *loc. cit.,* 489–495. While there is no record of division on the subject within the Soviet government, it may be noted that Stalin's attitude was ambivalent and combined support of partition with a strain of opposition. See the evidence in *Ibid.,* 488 ff, 493 ff. See also Sherwood, *Roosevelt and Hopkins,* 798 ff.; Churchill, *Closing the Ring,* 400.

23. These agreements on terms of surrender, zonal boundaries, the Control Council system and various other documents signed on 5 June 1945 may be found in many official collections. OMGUS, *Enactments and Approved Papers,* I, 1–18.

24. See the text of JCS 1067, reproduced in U.S. Department of State, *Germany, 1947–1949, The Story in Documents*, Department of State Publication no. 3556, European and Commonwealth Series 9 (Washington, 1950), 22–23. Cf. Mosely, "Occupation of Germany," *loc. cit.*, 592 f.

25. *Ibid.*, particularly paragraphs 2, 3e, 11, 14b-c, 17, 18a, 21, 22, 25, 28, 39, 40, 45c, 46, 48c-d-e, 49.

26. *Ibid.*, paragraphs 3g (Austria), 62 (denazification proclamation), 7b (demilitarization proclamation), 47 (Reich public debt service).

27. These services included transport, communications, power, finance, foreign affairs, and production and distribution of essential commodities. *Ibid.*, paragraphs 3c, 39b, 6a, 7b.

28. *Ibid.*, paragraphs 3b-c-f, 4, 18b, 38, 39b, 40, 43, 45c, 46, 48, 49c. In some of these paragraphs the "pending" formula was replaced with words to similar effect, such as an injunction to carry out a specific policy "subject to any agreed policies of the Control Council."

29. For examples, see G. Boss, *Berlin von Heute, Stadtverwaltung und Wirtschaft* (Berlin, 1929), 27 ff. "Berlin und die Provinz Brandenburg sind volkisch und wirtschaftliche auf engste miteinander verbunden." Approximately one-fourth of the non-Berlin-born segment of the prewar Berlin population came from Brandenburg. *Ibid.*, 28. "Berlins Güterverkehrswirtschaftliche Verflechtung 1938 mit den jetzigen Besatzungszonen," *Berliner Statistik*, I (1947), 202. Paul Goeths, *Berlin als Binnenschiffahrtsplatz* (G. Schmoller u. P. Sering, ed., "Staats. u. Sozialwissen. Forsch.," VII, Leipzig, 1910). 20–40; Boss, *Berlin von Heute*, 14 ff. With a show of reason an east German spokesman boastfully could assert that "every economist knew that Berlin and east Germany comprised the basis for Hamburg trade." W. Ulbricht, *Der Fünfjahrplan und die Perspektiven der Volkswirtschaft* (Berlin, 1950), 12.

30. "Berlins güterverkehr. Verflechtung," *loc. cit.*, 202.

31. For the broad product groups of electrical equipment and clothing the percentage share of Berlin in 1936 is 49.0 percent and 38.4 percent respectively. A finer product breakdown which would exclude handicrafts and concentrate on main product lines would give Berlin a yet stronger position in both these fields of economic activity. OMGUS, Special Report of the Military Governor, *Economic Data on Potsdam Germany* (1947), 20; E. Rossel, "Die Berliner Elektroindustrie," *Die Wirtschaft*, I (1946), 213–214. The main offices of Germany's increasingly more centralized financial and banking organizations were located in Berlin which housed one-fourth of all financial employees working in Germany. One-fourth of Germany's corporations likewise had Berlin headquarters. Berlin served as one of the major cultural centers of Germany and almost two million visitors added tourist revenues to the income streams feeding the city's economic life. Boss, *Berlin von Heute*, 13–15.

32. Deutsches Institut fur Wirtschaftsforschung, *Berlins Wirtschaft im Übergang* (Berlin, 1947), 18.

33. See Mosely, "Occupation of Germany," *loc. cit.*, 587–591. There was no ambiguity about the European Advisory Commission agreement which specified that "the area of Greater Berlin will be occupied by forces of each of the four Powers" while its "administration" will be "jointly directed" by the four Commandants sitting as the Kammandatura. OMGUS, *Enactments and Approved Papers*, I, 16.

34. The premise of U.S.-British staff planning in London, that an integrated national organism would be taken over with its central administrative services intact, is variously indicated. See Lucius D. Clay, *Decision in Germany* (New York, 1950), 8 ff.; H. Zink, *American Military Government in Germany* (New York, 1947), 88 ff.; W. Friedmann, *The Allied Military Government of Germany*, London Institute of World Affairs, "The Library of World Affairs," eds. G. Keeton and G. Schwartzenberger (London, 1947), 14 ff.

35. This restates Mosely's judgment that the ready Soviet acceptance of the British proposal for a zone of about a third of Germany as well as a Berlin enclave "appeared a sign of a moderate and conciliatory approach to the problem of how to deal with postwar Germany," particularly if it is borne in mind that the Western powers had not yet landed in France. Mosely, "Occupation of Germany," *loc. cit.*, 591.

36. Alfred Weber and A. Mitscherlich, *Freier Sozialismus* (Heidelberg, 1946), 49; Frank Howley, *Berlin Command* (New York, 1950), 44 ff; A. Z. Carr, *Truman, Stalin and Peace* (New York, 1950), 63 ff.

37. Eisenhower, *Crusade*, 396–403. For critical appraisal see Feis, *op. cit.*, 602 ff.

38. Leahy, *I Was There*, 349, 379, 382; Clay, *Decision*, 10, 24–30; U.S. Department of State, *Germany, 1947–1949*, 205. See Feis, *op. cit.*, 633 ff.

39. General Hilldring, *Occupation Currency Transactions*, 115. As soon as it became plain that the Soviets were in earnest the State Department urged that duplicate plates be furnished the Soviet government since "it would be a pity to lose the great advantage of having one currency used by the three armies," a symptom of "a degree of solidarity which was much to be sought." The Treasury proved obstructive. It alleged that accountability would be difficult, that detection of counterfeiting would be hampered, that the private printing contractor under bond would be displeased, and that certain delays would be brought about. Morgenthau in direct conversations with the Soviet Ambassador turned down the project, alleging as the principal obstacle the strong legal position of the private currency printing company which was unwilling to jeopardize security practices by providing a duplicate set of plates to the Soviet government. As might have been expected, the Soviets "expressed their opinion to Harriman that they could not accept the explanation of a private printing company interfering with the program under consideration." *Ibid.*, 152–153, 175–182, 182–184.

40. In May of 1944 the precious cargo of printing supplies and inks was got off in five planes. *Ibid.*, 186, 207. There was an implied understanding to employ militarily issued marks for procurement or payment within the German economy if regular Reichsmark currency were not used. Perhaps even nothing so strong as an "understanding" may be construed from the Soviet letter which stated that "the wish of the British and American governments to collaborate in the issuance of military currency in Germany . . . is shared by the Soviet Government," but this at any rate is an intimation of an understanding. *Ibid.*, 148. But there was no agreement on the rate of exchange for purposes of troop pay or official military purposes; there was no specific agreement which would prevent the overlapping of serial numbers; there was no understanding about reporting of issuance.

41. The Soviets expressed interest in receiving American proposals with

respect to the rate of exchange of the mark, but no common action was taken; and the U.S.-British 10 cent mark decision was communicated to the Soviet government *ex post facto*. To the American request that formal agreement be reached to treat military marks and Reichsmark currency on a one for one basis, that a general purpose rate of exchange should not be fixed for some time, that the desirability of uniform cross conversion rates should be noted—to all this, no reply is indicated. Laxity about serial numbering was even more amazing. At the time the plates were transmitted, the serial numbers then reached in the Washington printing were itemized. Assuming that the American printing had been completed, the Soviets picked up at the nearest rounded figure above the highest recorded American number. The starting numbers of the Soviet serials were communicated in June 1944. Yet it appears that the U.S. continued printing even though our numbering overlapped considerably with that of the Soviet notes. *Ibid.*, 148, 158–160, 196, 214–215.

NOTES FOR CHAPTER II

1. See the authoritative survey by the Foundation of Foreign Affairs, "The Polish-German Frontier; Polish Claims and Diplomatic History," *American Perspective*, I (1947), 211–235.

2. Note the coupling of the Rhine and the Oder and the general defense of emphasis on river channels as a criteria for frontier making in Louis F. Aubert, *Securité de l'Occident Ruhr-Rhin* (Paris, 1946), 7.

3. See Churchill, *Closing the Ring*, 283, 362 ff., 396 ff., 403, 406; Byrnes, *Speaking Frankly*, 30 ff.; Hull, *Memoirs*, II, 1438 ff.

4. For the basic American policy, whose crux was rejection of the Soviet territorial acquisitions which grew out of the Nazi pact period, see *Ibid.*, 1165–1173. Hull weakened to the extent of not objecting—which implied tacit approval of a kind—to a British-Polish-Soviet agreement on revisions. *Ibid.*, 1439 ff. At Teheran and at Yalta, however, the Americans solidarized themselves with the British. Byrnes, *Speaking Frankly*, 29 ff.; Stettinius, *Roosevelt and the Russians* 38 ff.; 86 ff., 184 ff., 210 ff.; Leahy, *I Was There*, 210 ff., 316, 322.

5. See N. A. Voznesensky, *Soviet Economy During the Second World War* (Trans. Int. Pub., 1949), p. 129 f.

6. See later, p. 155 ff.

7. 15 billion RM for the value of industrial equipment and machinery, see J. H. Furth, *American Economic Review*, XX XXXVIII (1948) 929; R. Stucken, "Die Grosse Vermögensabgabe und das heutige Finanzproblem," *Finanz Archiv*, II (1948), 242 f.; we can build up this valuation from replacement costs of the known inventory of German machine tools, extended by a factor relating machine tool stocks to other types of equipment and an aging factor. A cross-check is afforded by the fact that Control Council valuation of dismantled equipment averaged about 1–1.2 million RM per plant dismantled. See OMGUS, *Special Report of the Military Governor*, Three Years of Reparations (November 1948) 4; The United States Strategic Bombing Survey, *The Effects of Strategic Bombing on the German War Economy* (Overall Economic Effects Divisions, 1945), 43–48, 218.

8. Henry Morgenthau, *Germany is our Problem* (New York, 1945) 64 ff., 76 ff.

9. Roosevelt believed, according to Hull, that the "real nub of the situation is to keep Britain from going into complete bankruptcy at the end of the war" and that elimination of German industrial potential was a means for achieving this end. Hull, *Memoirs*, II, 1620 ff. That this was no freak is indicated by Roosevelt's stress on it in his presentation at the Yalta conference.

10. Though Stettinius was charged specifically by Roosevelt with seeing to it that the Yalta "conclusions" were "carried forward," these "conclusions" were apparently overlooked by the interdepartmental cabinet discussions which had been in course ever since September 1944. U.S. Department of State, *Postwar Foreign Policy Preparation, 1939–1945,* Department of State Publication 3580, General Foreign Policy Series, 15, (Washington, 1949), 396. These terminated with a draft policy statement, approved by the President on 23 March 1945, which included among other things a clear statement of the Morgenthauist position on reparations. About all that appeared to carry over from the Yalta discussion was a penumbra of approbation around the 50% share formula. See the detailed excerpts from and summarization of the policy in Edwin Pauley, "The Potsdam Program Means Security," *Prevent World War III*, III (1947), 39–41; Isadore Lubin, Reparations Problems," *Proceedings of the American Academy of Political Science,* XXI (1946), 64 ff.; D. D. Humphrey, German mss., Chap. II, "The Background of Potsdam-Yalta," 9–15. The document of 23 March was a parent to the basis U.S. directive in the early days of the occupation JCS 1067. It was also the document used by the American delegation at the Potsdam conference and it was the basis for the rigid instructions to the American delegation to the Moscow Reparation Commission which were so out of tune with the spirit of the American negotiations at Yalta. U.S. Department of State, *Postwar Foreign Policy Preparation,* 370–1; Byrnes, *Speaking Frankly,* 185–7; H. S. Truman, *Memoirs* (2v. N.Y., 1955) I, p. 16 f. This policy outcome would perhaps have met with more opposition if the three persons most familiar with the Yalta reparations negotiations—Roosevelt, Hopkins and Stettinius—had not been removed or incapacited shortly after the conference. Stettinius it appears dropped out of central policy responsibilities shortly after Yalta. Hopkins was removed immediately by illness. Roosevelt of course approved the March 23 policy statement which ran contrary to the line indicated in the Yalta discussions. This may have been not uninfluenced by his physical condition, though it also may indicate that the Yalta understanding, or its implications for economic policy, he accepted only tentatively to smooth out the course of the meeting. D. D. Humphrey, in his German mss., Chap. II, "The Background of Potsdam-Yalta" also noted the strange fact that the March 23 reparations document embodied a point of view irreconcilable with the Yalta understanding. (p. 10.)

11. Maisky is reported as having said that "in order to make Germany pay there had to be strict tripartite control over Germany." E. R. Stettinius, *Roosevelt and the Russians,* 130. See another expression of this view in a statement made between August and October 1944 by a key British foreign office spokesman, Sir W. Strang, in F. H. Smith, "The Rise and Fall of the Morgenthau Plan," *United Nations World,* I (1947), 36.

12. This provision of Potsdam textually reads as follows: "Payment of reparations should leave enough resources to enable the German people to subsist without external assistance. In working out the economic balance of Germany the necessary

means must be provided to pay for imports approved by the Control Council in Germany. The proceeds of exports from current production and stocks shall be available in the first place for payment for such imports." *Ibid.*, Potsdam Protocol, II, paragraph 19, p. 50. Modified by the insertion of one phrase, this provision is textually identical with the so-called "Principle 8" of a series of American sponsored principles on reparations urged during the 1945 Moscow session of the reparation commission and accepted but for this "Principle 8." For the text of the eight principles, see an article by Jacques Rueff, the French representative on the reparations commission, "Les Nouvelles Réparations Allemandes," in L. F. Aubert and others, *Nouveaux Aspects du Problème Allemand* (P. Hartmann, ed. Centre d'Études de Politique Etrangère, Paris, 1947), 196–197. Ambiguity is present, however, because Rueff states that the eight principles were worked out by the commission and transmitted to the Potsdam conference, whereas, according to the accounts of Isadore Lubin and Edwin Pauley, the eighth principle was not accepted by the Soviets and was handed over unresolved to the Potsdam conference. Lubin, "Reparations Problems," *loc. cit.*, 65–66; Pauley, "The Potsdam Program Means Security," *loc. cit.*, 39 ff. One vital clause which very much restricted the application of the principle was inserted at the time it was adopted at Potsdam— the phrase "in working out the economic balance of Germany." This curiously worded clause makes sense as an eliptical expression referring to the elaboration of a balance sheet of the German economy which would show surplus plant capacities available for dismantling as reparations. Read in this context the principle appears as an instruction to the Control Council that in computing required economic capacity in Germany "the necessary means must be provided to pay for imports approved by the Control Council." The final sentence with reference to confinement of export proceeds refers to imports which are both approved by the Control Council and are involved in the "working out of the economic balance of Germany." Cf. David Ginsburg, *The Future of German Reparations* (National Planning Association Pamphlets 57–58, Washington, 1947), 7–9, 21–28.

13. The two paragraphs which are meaningful when linked together in this manner may be found in the preface to the section of the Potsdam Protocol dealing with Germany and in paragraph 2 of the agreement on "Political and Economic Principles," *Ibid.*, 48. The preface to the protocol is not included in this collection, but it is available in others. It reads: "Agreement has been reached at this Conference on the political and economic principles of a coordinated Allied policy toward defeated Germany during the period of Allied control."

NOTES FOR CHAPTER III

1. See for the social-democratic underground the report of the central committee, which was recognized by the Soviets, written by one of the members of the underground central committee, Max Fechner, in 40. *Parteitag der sozialdemokratisches Partei Deutschlands, 12–20 April 1946* (Berlin, 1946), 38–45; J. Joesten, *Germany—what now?* (Chicago, 1948), 64–67. On the CDU side Joesten reports—and he is an unusually accurate source on early events—that "as soon as the ban on political activity had been lifted . . . a number of prominent Catholic and Protestant politicians got together to form a new party," merging together the

old Centrum party, the old Democratic party, members of the Christian trade unions and personalities from the right resistance of 20th July. *Ibid.,* 87–92. On the Liberal Democratic party leadership, see *Ibid.,* 105–109. Enough has been said to indicate that the newly formed German leaderships, while selected from among those willing to collaborate with a Soviet occupation, in no significant sense embodied mere "puppet" appointees. J. P. Nettl in his *The Eastern Zone and Soviet Policy in Germany, 1945–1950* (Oxford 1951) commits the egregious error of asserting that the two leftist parties were installed in the eastern zones "first" but that in the autumn two "large middle-class parties had been organized in the British and American zones and applied for Russian permission to organize in the Soviet zone." The author who thus cooly invents occurrences, embroiders them with plausible motivation by asserting that "since it was not yet the fashion to denounce as Fascist political parties which had the open approval of the Western Allies, the Russian permission was given." *Ibid.,* 75, 80. Although the book is untrustworthy in other matters also, it is a useful account and one which may be drawn upon.

2. OMGUS, *Government and its Administration in the Soviet Zone of Germany* (prepared by Civil Administration Division, November, 1947), paras. 191, 193.

3. This must be conceded if a democratic character is not to be denied liberal Western states such as England or America where control over the press and facilities of meeting and propaganda is quite lopsided. The extent of imbalance in the Soviet zone can be over-stated. The two bourgeois parties each published five newspapers in the Soviet zone in contrast to the SED's eleven—a distribution not too out of proportion with party memberships. See ACA, *Report to the Council of Foreign Ministers from the Allied Control Authority in Germany* Conl/P (47) 7–15, February 1947 (hereafter cited CFM Report), Section III, Democratization, Part 2, 12. During the election campaign in the Soviet zone in 1946 American correspondents could see only SED posters and placards, but it is an issue of judgment how vital a role visual aids play in changing voter preferences.

4. Fritz Löwenthal, *News from Soviet Germany* (trans., by E. Fitzgerald, London 1950) 286 f.

5. OMGUS, *Government and Administration, Soviet Zone,* paragraphs 43–44.

6. For instances see later in this chapter p. 61 f. (p. 297 f. in the cited work of Raup).

7. Nettl, *Eastern Zone,* 95–96.

8. Statement of Hugo Buschmann, *Tagesspiegel,* 6 December 1946.

9. See F. Dahlem, "Die antifaschistische Einheit in den Konzentrationslagern," *Einheitsfront der Antifaschistisch-Demokratischen Parteien* (Berlin, 1945), 38–41.

10. For text of this agreement signed 14 July 1945, see *Einheitsfront,* 44–45; and for an accurate translated summary, Schaffer, *Russian Zone,* 71.

11. Altogether some 5.02 million expellees were received in the Soviet zone, according to an official quadripartite report. *CFM Report,* Section VII, Population Transfers, App. L. On the importance of the work of settlement, see Tschesnow, "Einige Betrachtungen zum Umsiedler-Problem," *Die Wirtschaft,* I (1946), 14–17; Schaffer, *Russian Zone,* 164–167. Available West German estimates range between 4–4.4 million expellees. See P. H. Seraphin, *Die Heimatvertriebenen in der Sowjetzone* (Berlin, 1954) ch. 2, p. 44 ff.

12. During 1946/7 it was reliably estimated that the proceeds of current

withdrawals from German product for occupation use were distributed 50–50 between utilization within Germany by the occupation forces and export as reparations. See Eduard Wolf, "Aufwandungen für die Besatzungemächte, öffentlich Haushalte und Sozialprodukt in den einzelnen Zonen," Deutsches Institut für Wirtschaftsforschung, *Wirtschaftsprobleme der Besatzungszonen* (Berlin, 1948), 120 ff. Source reports on Soviet reparations withdrawals uniformly contain undistributed total withdrawals without reference to allocation between occupation requirements and shipment abroad. For review of evidence on Soviet occupation spending, see later.

13. During 1946 the Soviets drained about two-thirds of zonal tax proceeds for their use. In regard to the amount of current product reparations extracted from the Soviet zone, withdrawals diverted to shipment eastward as reparations probably ran to 500 million dollars annually during 1946–1948 and in combination with occupation maintenance the total utilization of German resources probably was near a billion dollars anually in current values, with a mark value of between 2 and 3 billion RM. A billion dollar total is that found in the more careful estimates; it is consistent with the findings of Eduard Wolf, the most well-informed investigator; it is consistent with Soviet admissions regarding reparations withdrawals and reparations receipts by Poland; and it is consistent with known data on the allocation of Soviet zone industrial production for reparations and occupation costs (running at 17 and 8 percent respectively during 1948 and 1949). See A. Gerschenkron, "Russia's Trade in the Postwar Years," *Annals of the American Academy of Political and Social Science*, v. 263 (1949), 89 f.; F. L. Neumann, "Soviet Policy in Germany," *Ibid.*, 175 ff.; F. H. Furth, review in *American Economic Review*, XXXVIII (1948), 931; "Die Reparationsleistungen der Sowjetischen Besatzungszone Deutschlands," *Europs-Archiv*, IV (1949), 2029–2034; Wolf, "Aufwendungen," *loc. cit.*, 120–125; F. H. Sanderson, "Germany's Economic Situation and Prospects," *The Struggle for Democracy in Germany* 162 ff.; *Die Wirtschaft*, sonderheft "Der wirtschafts-plan 1949/50," July, 1948, 23. The Soviet admission was that by Dec. 31, 1950 3.66 billion dollars had been withdrawn as reparations of which 768 millions were elsewhere identified as capital withdrawals. See *Die Sowjetische Reparationspolitik seit 1945* (Vorstand der SPD, Sopade Denkschrift no. 29, Hannover, 1950), 35 ff.; N. A. Voznesensky, *Soviet Economy during the Second World War* (translated under auspices of International Publishers, New York, 1949), 132–134; B. R. von Oppen, *Documents on Germany Under Occupation 1945–1954* (Oxford, 1955) 489.

13a Under communist and left socialist inspiration, local government in the eastern zone was based upon reconstitution of elective rather than appointive patterns which at village, county and city levels were put in the hands of relatively autonomous legislative assemblies, elected by proportional representation, to whom executive agencies were subordinated. See OMGUS, *Government and Administration, Soviet Zone*, paragraphs 68–73, 84, 85, 87, 89. The broad philosophy of liberating local self administration—under which this legislation was designed—is indicated in the statement of local government policy formally adopted in 1946 by the SED with an introductory statement by Max Fechner who, although a member of the central secretariat of the SED, was a former leader of the "Kommunalepolitischen Zentrale" of the SPD in the pre-1933 period. See *Die Kommunalpolitischen Richtlinien der*

SED (Berlin, 1946), 6–7. "Ein Staat, der von dem Willen des Volkes bestimmt und getragen wird, muss als die Grundlage als die freie, sich selbst verwaltende Gemeinde haben." The self-governing gemeinde, said this SED secretary who would have been an excellent spokesman for the local government department of Civil Administration Division of OMGUS, "ist die politische Hochschule in einem demokratischen Staate für die Weckung und Förderung des politischen Gemeinsinne seiner Bürger. Eine Gemeinde aber die von dem staatliche gelenkten Büroapparat geschulmeistert wird, kann keine kraftvolle und vom Eigenleben erfüllte Zelle des Staates sein." And Fechner even emphasized that the Weimar democracy was paralyzed partly because "in der untersten Gemeinschaft in der Gemeinde die Einwohner nicht zur tätigen Mitarbeit herangezogen hatte." For a similar point of view, which was born of repugnance to traditional German bureaucratic patterns constraining local government, see the work of another SED notable in local government affairs, the mayor of Dresden, W. Weidauer, who emphasized that under the old regime "die allmächtige Burökratie drosselte und erstickte fast alles fortschrittliche kommunale Leben." Hence, "der aufbau einer wirklich demokratischen Selbstverwaltung in den Gemeinden und Kreisen war nicht möglich ohne einem völlig neuen Weg in der Regelung der Beziehungen der Gemeinden zu den sogennanten übergeordneten Behörden einzuschlagen." This was achieved. The county directors were elected and not appointed and the range of delegated functions was decreased. Marx's Proudhonist sympathies for "self-governing communalism" in his *Civil War in France* provided some of the ammunition for Weidauer, but his program could have been taken over by American military government without a qualm. SED responsibility under the occupation appeared to evoke a real interest in breaking up bureaucratic patterns of governmental organization inherited from the past. "Wir bekämpfen nur die Burökratie als staatliche Einrichtung weil sie ein unheilvolles Erbe ist, dass wie ein Alpdruck nicht nur auf dem Volke sondern auch auf den Beamten selbst lastet." Grotewohl, *Deutsche Verfassungspläne*, 30, 36. Furthermore, the files of *Demokratischer Aufbau*, the eastern zone journal of local government, are saturated with the philosophy of self-government. W. Weidauer, *Neue Wege der Kommunalpolitik* (Voco Verlag, 1948), 50, 58, 40–63. The main restriction on local government appeared to operate through budgetary controls which were made effective chiefly through interlocking grants and subventions whose operation has been imperfectly studied. A competent Western student of eastern zone practise concluded that there was evidence that financially "die Idee der Selbstverantwortung im Osten sehr lebendig ist." Dreissig's conclusion was that "während im Westen die öffentlichen Gebietskörperschaften in viel zu starkem Masse von Länderüberweisungen abhängig sind, auch wenn sie die Ausgaben weitgehend selbst bestimmen können, leben sie im Osten im wesentlichen aus eigenen Mitteln die sie aber nicht selbständig verausgaben können." W. Dreissig, "Der Finanzausgleich seit der Besatzung," *Deutsche Finanzwirtschaft*, I (December 1947, no. 9), 16, 18. See also A. Riewald, "Die finanzielle Selbstverantwortung der Gemeinden," *Ibid.*, I (June 1947, no. 3), 21–25.

14. For a characteristic statement of the left SPD position, see the programmatic address of Grotewohl, *Wo Stehen Wir, Wohin Gehen Wir* (Berlin, 1945) delivered in September 1945.

15. That it in fact was the programmatic basis for fusion seems clear and this

was frequently emphasized by Grotewohl in his addresses at the time and later. "Die Kommunistische Partei von heute ist ebensowenig von 1932 wie die SPD dieselbe ist." After 1918 the SPD was lost in revisionism and "hatte sich in den Gebundenheiten der Weimarrer Demokratie verstrickt, die politische Bewegungsfreiheit und die Kampfkraft verloren. Die KPD orientierte sich damals an den grossen Vorgängen der Russischen Revolution und den Auffassungen der dritten Internationale. Während dem die einen in der sozialistischen Reform mit dem Spatzen in der Hand zufrieden waren, strebten die andern nach de Taube auf dem Dach. Das Ends von Lied aber war dass die Arbeiterklasse weder dem Spatzen noch die Taube hatte." Out of all this there was much to learn. For the SPD there was the need to go back to Marx and Engels and for the KPD the need to recognize democracy "als ein Kampfmittel. Weder der eine noch der andere Partner der Vereinigung ist berechtigt dem anderen diese Umstellung als ein Maneover vorzuwerfen. Sie ist kein Maneuver sondern das Ergebnis einer ernsten Lehre aus dem Jahren von 1914 bis 1945." Grotewohl, *Im Kampf um Deutschland*, I, 44, 111–112. Citing the passage in the KPD declaration of 10 June 1945 which announced the communist goal of a parliamentary democratic republic, Grotewohl declared: ". . . mit diesem Grundsatz schuf die KPD zwei politische Tatsschen, die sich für den Wiederaufbau Deutschlands segensreich auswirken werden. Sie begrub damit das Kriegsbeil zwischen der kommunistischen und sozialdemokratischen Arbeiterschaft und schuf damit die ideologische Voraussetzung zur Beseitigung des Bruderkampfes." Speech of August, 1945 in *Die Berliner Konferenz* (Berlin, 1945), 25. The later program of the SED, the party of communist-socialist fusion, gave full evidence of this programmatic shift. See also, Carola Stern, *Porträt einer bolschewitischen Partei* (Köln 1957) ch. I, II, p. 22 f., 46 ff.

16. That the desire for unification was widely shared during the early days of the occupation is attested to by many reliable sources. See Eliaeberg, "Political Party Developments," *Struggle for Democracy In Germany*, 255; Hill, *Struggle for Germany*, 187 ff.; *Jahrbuch der Sozial-demokratischen Partei Deutschlands, 1946* (Göttingen, 1947), 114; Tibor Mende, *Europe's Suicide in Germany*, 87 ff.

17. See Marx's comments in the *Neuen Rheinischen Zeitung* on the need for a unified German republic, given in Marx-Engels, *Die Revolution von 1848* (Berlin, 1949), 40 ff.; F. Engels, *Germany: Revolution and Counter-Revolution* (translated for International Publishers, New York, 1933), 132, 142 ff., 144 ff.; Grotewohl, *Deutsche Verfassungspläne*, 53–57; Alfred Meusel, *Kamp um die Nationale Einheit in Deutschland* (Berlin 1947), 10–32.

18. The comrades who wish us to introduce total planning and socialism, said Ulbricht once, should realize "dass gegenwärtig eine Besatzung da ist, und zwar von vier Mächten, unter denen drei kapitalistische Mächte sind . . . In den letzten Monaten haben wir uns—und das ist natürlich—vor allem mit den Fragen der Wirtschaftspolitik in der sowjetisch besetzten Zone beschäftigt. Aber unser Blick war stetz gerichtet auf die Notwendigkeiten in allen deutschen Gebieten." Cited from Ulbricht's concluding remarks in *Neuaufbau der Deutschen Wirtschaft Referät und Diskussion über die Richtlinien der KPD zur Wirtschaftspolitik* (protocol of KPD conference held 29 December 1945 to 7 January 1946, Berlin 1946), 106, 114. "Würden wir . . . einen Schritt weitergehen, so bestände die Gefahr der Zerreissung Deutschlands. Wir wollen den reaktionären Kräften in anderen Zonen keinen

Vorwand geben zur Weiterführung ihrer föderalistischen Politik." From this came the rule that "alle Massnahmen, die wir gegenwärtig im demokratischen Aufbau und in der Demokratisierung der Wirtschaft durchführen, müssen so erfolgen, dass sie in allen Teilen Deutschland verwirklicht werden können." Ulbricht, *Demokratischer Wirtschaftsaufbau* (Berlin, 1946), 36 f. Sooner or later the real course of zonal development would be recognized but this was classified by Ulbricht in another important address as an example of the "Dialektik der Entwicklung." ". . . Es geht nicht so," he noted, "wie wir uns das frührer so schön vorgestellt haben, dass man in allen Teilen Deutschlands alles gleichmässig organisiert. . . . Nun, wir, geben uns die grösste Mühe euch möglichst gute Beispiele zu geben." Ulbricht, *Der Plan des demokratischen Neuaufbau* (Berlin, 1946), 45.

19. Raup, *Land Reform Soviet Zone*, 258–263.

20. See the detailed account in Raup, *op. cit.*, chap. V; Hoernle, *Bodenreform*, 27 ff.

21. As Raup points out in his authoritative account violence was chiefly invoked in forcing old owners to leave their estates and the local communities concerned. Most of these were forced out, he notes, "roughly and with hardly more than their immediate personal possessions" 287. But no instance has been reported of the deaths, cruelties and murders indicated in the account of Howard Becker, "Changes in Social Stratification in Germany," *American Sociological Review*, XV (1950), 333–357.

22. See Raup, *op. cit.*, 373–384.

23. This was ascribed a major role by Ulbricht. "Es ist eine falsche Auffassung, dass die Sicherung der Versorgung eine rein wirtschaftliche Frage ist. Solange noch Faschisten im Dorfe herrschen, kann es keine geordnete Versorgung geben, denn sie sabotieren. Also die Demokratisierung des Dorfes ist der erste Schritt zur Sicherung der Volksernährung." W. Ulbricht, *Demokratischer Aufbau*, 26 f.

24. Although considerable reliance was placed upon the incentive aspects of the differentiated market and two-price system, it does not appear to have worked out very successfully. See Ulbricht, *Demokratischer Wirtschaftsaufbau*, 30 ff.; Liebe, "Die Organisations der Landwirtschaft . . . ," *loc. cit.*, 199 ff.

25. See Raup, *op. cit.*, 355–358.

26. *Ibid.*, 337–372.

27. "Die Betriebe die wieder produzieren haben in der Regel wenig oder kein Geld." That the need for money in the eastern zone led some producers to produce articles for direct sale in the black market was indicated. *Neuaufbau der deutschen Wirtschaft*, 65 f. See also later, 171 ff.

28. See earlier, p. 8 f. and later, p. 97 f.; Schaffer, *Russian Zone*, 146–154; B. Gleitze, "Deutschlands finanzpolitische Lage Ende 1947," *Deutsche Finanzwirtschaft*, I (no. 8, 1947), 8 f.

29. On Soviet financial reform and its effects on economic life, see G. Stolper, *German Realities* (New York, 1948), 110 f.; Schaffer, *Russian Zone*, 45 ff.; *Neuaufbau der Deutschen Wirtschaft*, 31–33; and see later, 181–183.

30. E. Heinzelmann, "Ein neuer Kredit-apparat," *Die Wirtschaft*, I (1946), 74–77.

31. G. Sobottka, "Kohle and Kohlenhandel," *Die Wirtschaft*, I, (1946), 79–81. During 1947 these properties were taken over by the Länder through a nationaliza-

226   THE GERMAN PEACE SETTLEMENT AND THE BERLIN CRISIS

tion act which covered all mining properties. See "Die Kohle: Eigentum des Volkes," *Ibid.*, II, (1947), 211 ff. Considerable overlapping exists in the coal industry because about a third of the coal mining properties were in Soviet SAG form; while actual ownership of the remaining properties is in Länder hands although they are centrally administered. See Deutsches Institut, *Wirtschaftsprobleme*, 230–233. It appears that the Land nationalization action of 1947 had chiefly formal significance since most of the enterprises were already expropriated. See "Die Wirtschaftliche Entwicklung in der sowjetischen Zone Deutschlands seit Potsdam," *Europa-Archiv*, II (1947), 1029.

32. See *Ibid.*, 1030–1032; F. Seume, "Organisationsformen der industrie in der sowjetischen Besatzungszone"; Deutches Institut, *Wirtschaftsprobleme*, 218–232.

33. Announced Soviet motivation for sequestration was twofold: to take reparations through production rather than by dismantling the plants and to safeguard German employment. "Zweihundert Grossbetriebe, die ursprünglich für die Demontage vorgeschen waren, wurden in Sowjetaktiengesellschaften umgewandelt, um den Arbeitern und Angestellten die Arbeitsmöglichkait zu erhalten," Sokolowski's statement, cited in *Die Wirtschaft*, II (1947), 33. See Schaffer, *Russian Zone*, 172–174 for an interesting description of the early reaction of the plant forces and works councils to the sequestration at the Buna and Leuna works. See also his description of the way the sequestration was rationalized. *Ibid.*, 50 ff. For indication of possible return of the properties, see later 228, n. 1.

34. On this, see Nettle, "Inside the Russian Zone," *loc. cit.*, 203–210; Schaffer, *Russian Zone*, 54, 177 ff.; Buschmann, "Plan for Organization," 14; Löwenthal, *News from Soviet Germany*, 130 ff., 225–234.

35. *Befehle des Obersten Chefs*, I, 29, 51.

36. This in general was the significance of the Soviet order no. 234. On this, see the official documents, *Steigerung der Arbeitsproduktivität und Verbesserung der materiellen Lage der Arbeiter und Angestellten* (Berlin, 1947.)

37. Seume, "Organisationsformen der Industrie," *loc. cit.*, 245 ff. The drive for "profitability" ("Rentabilität") became a major theme of eastern zone economic literature and moved its conceptions of industrial organization and business incentives close to Western norms. See particularly the interesting remarks of Bruno Gleitze, "Deutschlands finanzpolitische Lage Ende 1947," *loc. cit.*, 7–9.

38. Nettle, "Inside the Russian Zone," *loc. cit.*, 208–215; OMGUS, *Government and Administration, Soviet Zone*, paragraphs 19–39; Nettl, *Eastern Zone*, 114–125.

39. See G. G. Kromrey, "Entwicklung der Planungsarbeit," *Methoden der Wirtschaftsplanung* (a special collection edited and published by *Die Wirtschaft*, December 1947), 3 f. Indeed, the orientation of SED and KPD policy through the first 18 months or more of the occupation was to urge local initiative, mass pressure and development of new leadership. Ulbricht's analysis is sufficiently clearly focussed to be worth citing: "We stellen wir uns unter diesen Bedingungen die Organisation des Neuaufbaus der Wirtschaft vor? Wir schlagen vor, dass die Wirtschaft von den Landesverwaltungen geleitet wird; dass bei den Landes ... ein Planungsamt geschaffen wird, dem die Planung und Lenkung der Produktion die Rohstoffzuteilung, die Kontrolle der Reparationslieferungen und die Planung der Verteilung obleigt; dass beiden Landes-verwaltungen die Abteilung für Industrie und Brennstoff ausgebaut wird, die Aufgabe hat, dafür zu sorgen dass die Produktions-

aufträge verteilt und richtig durchgeführt werden." The total emphasis was on a method of economic planning and reconstruction which would make possible "die ganze Volksinitiative zu entfalten, damit die Produktion gesteigert, die Bevölkerung besser versorgt und die Städte schneller aufgebaut werden." Ulbricht, *Plan des demokratischen neuaufbau,* 29–30. It was characteristic of the early period that a statement of "demokratische Wirtschaftsplanung muss auf den drei Planungs-ebenen: Betrieb, Kreis und Land entwickelt, durchgeführt und Kontrolliert werden." Ernest Schloz, "Planung in den Kreisen," *Methoden der Wirtschaftsplanung,* 11.

40. Thus even in the distribution of foodstuffs there was complaint that "die tatsachlich Versorgung war trotz einheitlicher Rationen in den Ländern ungleich weil ein gewisser wirtschaftlicher Particularismus dazu führte dei eingegangenen Lieferverpflichtungen, auf denen der Versorgungsplan aufgebaut war, nicht immer in vereinbarten Umfange einzuhalten." It was noted that "besonders in Sachsen entstanden dadurch in der Lebensmittelversorgung zeitweise ernste Schwierig-keiten." "Deutsche Wirtschaftskommission an der Arbeit," *Die Wirtschaft,* III (1948), 134. Hence also Fritz Selbmann, the able economic minister in Saxony, could complain that "wir heben . . . noch eine ungenügende Koordinierung unserer Pläne untereinander." Fritz Selbmann, *Reden und Tagebuchblätter,* 1933–1947 (Voco Verlag, 1947), 115. Thus also Lola Zahn in a notable discussion remarked that "aus der Besorgnis um eine laufende Rohstoffversorgung heraus haben Betriebe vielfach ihre noch vorhandenen Bestände verschwiegen. Dieser Betriebsegoismus vieler Einzelbetriebe floss zusammen in den Wirtschaftspartikularismus des ganzen Landes. Nicht nur die dem Lande unbekannten sondern auch die ihm bekannten Bestände erschienen in den Plänen nich . . . Wenn die Planung eines Landes ein Doppelgesicht zeigt, eihen Januskopf mit einem der Zone und der Wirtschafts-kommission zugekehrten Gesicht und einem anderen dem Lande und seinen ange-blich besonderen Interessen zugewandten verschmitzt lächelnden Gesicht, so wird damit eine wirkliche Planung sehr erschwert." Lola Zahn also mentioned the case of Saxony: "Das Land Sachsen versorgt seine Bevölkerung mit brauchbaren Textilien und behandelt Mecklenburg als fünftes Rad am Wagon der Textilversorgung." What would Saxony say if "Mecklenburg ihm statt Roggenmehl Kleie liefern würde." Lola Zahn, "Einige kritische Bemerkungen zur Wirtschaftplanung." *Einheit,* III (1949), 509–510. In the course of the reconstruction, noted Ulbricht, "unserer demokratischen Ordnung von unten nach oben ohne Vorhandensein eines zentralen Organs ein gewisser Partikularismus entwickelt hat. Dieser Partikularismus hat uns bei der Wirtschaftplanung recht grosse schwierigkeiten bereitet und würde dem einheitlichen wirtschaftlichen Aufbau und der Mobilisierung aller Reserven hindernd im Wege stehen." W. Ulbricht, *Lehrbuch für den Demokratischen Statts—und Wirtschaftsaufbau* (a compilation from speeches and addresses, Berlin, 1949), 32 f. In the early period of local administration, "setzte ein Warenpartikularismus ein, dessen Domäne manchmal nicht über den Sichtbereich des Kirchturms hinausging." Kromrey, "Entwicklung der Planungsarbeit," *loc. cit.,* 3. In an illuminating treat-ment of the problem of coordination in planning, it was startlingly announced that— though the "kernel" of planning involved "coordination" of segmental and regional plans, and that ample provision for this was made on the local, business, county and state level—"im Gegensatz zu den Ländern gab es bis vor kurzem in der Zonenebene noch keine Organisations-form für die Plankoordinierung." This zonal coordination

was handled "case to case" by improvised committees made up of the "interested" central and land agencies. P. Strassenberger, "Koordinierung der Pläne." *Methoden der wirtschaftsplanung,* 12–25. An early report noted that the local and Land planning and management agencies have not "keineswegs voll gewachsen. Sie treiben noch oft einen schadlichen Wirtschaftspartikularismus." "Sechs Monate Industrie-Planung," *Die Wirtschaft,* I (1946), 99.

41. See the trenchant critique of the eastern zone planned economy in the well-informed article, "Kritisches sur Wirtschaftsplanung" *Die Wirtschaft* II (1947) 218–220. "Eine Rationalisierung," noted Ulbricht in one of his characteristically caustic comments, "in Berichterstattung und Statistik ist daher eine dringende Notwendigkeit. Damit der Verwaltungsapparat ernsthaft verkleinert wird." W. Ulbricht, *Unsere Wirtschaftspolitik, 1949* (Berlin, 1949), 68. "Es gibt noch," said Selbmann, "einen gewissen Bürokratismus, eine allzu starke Belastung der Produktionsunternehmen mit Fragebogen, Meldebogen und einem ganzen Apparat von Kontrolleinrichtungen. . . ." Selbmann, *Reden,* 11 f.

42. Thus even in 1949 it was necessary for Ulbricht to use assuring language such as that "niemand denkt daran die Landesparlament beiseite zu schieben oder auszuschalten." He then suggested that the states would retain the functions of implementation, adaptation, "Konkretisierung." But he could not have been wholly blind to the fact that this would displace the focus but not eliminate the basis of central-local conflict. Ulbricht, *Lehrbuch,* 33. With his tendency to dramatize Nettl reports that with the formation of a central Economic Commission in 1947 "what had been a mere shadow of centralization at the time of the Central Administrations became now a powerful reality." *The Eastern Zone,* 133. But by the nature of the structure of administration and operational control, the attempt at centralization could only be imperfect, as was clearly brought out in the judicious OMGUS survey, *Government and Administration, Soviet Zone,* paragraph 38, which brought out the tendency of the "state SMA's" to continue to "give orders to the state governments which conflicted with those sent out by the Commission" and noted that the "Practical accomplishments" of the centralization move "remained exactly nil."

NOTES FOR CHAPTER IV

1. See D. Sternberger, "Parties and Party Systems in Postwar Germany," *Annals of the American Academy of Political and Social Science,* V. 260 (1948) 20. ". . . at first these parties had different names in different German regions but in a relatively short time they separately merged and consolidated . . ." See also V. F. Eliasberg, "Political Party Developments," *The Struggle for Democracy in Germany* (G. A. Almond, ed., Chapel Hill, 1949), 233 ff., 239 ff.; M. Meyerhoff, "Parties and Classes in Postwar Germany," *South Atlantic Quarterly* XLVI (1947).

2. The principal laggards were the British who had to be pushed in this direction by the Americans. See W. Friedmann, *The Allied Military Government of Germany* (London Institute of World Affairs, London, 1947), 85 ff., 88 ff., 108 ff.

3. In the American zone the budgeted expenditures for DP camps and UNRAA during 1946/7 was 176 million RM. See Office of Military Government for Germany (U.S.), *Report of the Military Governor,* Finance, no. 24. cumulative review, 15.

4. See Sanderson, "Germany's Economic Situation and Prospects," *loc. cit.,* 150.

5. Civilian air transport was unrestricted for licensed Western air lines. A "co-ordinated German organization" on a tripartite basis was "formed under tripartite supervision" for the Rhine waterways early in 1946. G. R. Clemens and J. H. Verhey "The Rhine," *Engineering News Record,* 16 October 1947, 6. OMGUS, *Report of the Military Governor,* Transportation, no. 26 (cumulative review), 12–23. L. D. Clay, *Decision in Germany* (New York, 1950), 283.

6. See earlier, Chap. III, p. 59 f.

7. On the tendency to use clerical advice, see Harold Zink, *American Military Government in Germany* (New York, 1947), 92, 134. For the celebrated case of the early Aachen regime, see Paul Padover, *Experiment in Germany* (New York, 1946); Kahn, *Betrayal,* 17–24. Kahn's analysis of the early regime of Mainz (37–41), Blum's regime in Frankfurt (59–71) and the Schaffer regime in Bavaria (80–94) appears reliable.

8. Eliasberg, "Political Party Developments," *loc. cit.,* 95 ff., *passim;* Fried-mann, *Allied Military Government,* 27 ff. For a more sympathetic picture, see the articles in French zonal publications and "Colony on the Rhine." *loc. cit.,* 69–70.

9. L. D. Clay, *Decision,* 67 ff., 69 ff., 258–262; J. H. Herz, "Fiasco of Denazi-fication," *Political Science Quarterly,* LXIII (1948), 569–594; Zink, *American Mili-tary Government,* 130–147. The withdrawal of occupation surveillance is dramati-cally described in Arsen L. Yankoubian, *Western Allied Occupation Policies and Development of German Democracy* (Ph.D. Dissertation, N. Y. University Library, 1951) Chap. III, pp. 95–109.

9a. See J. D. Montgomery, *Forced To Be Free* (Chicago, 1957).

10. For this characterization, see the outstanding analysis of Leonard Krieger, "The Inter-regnum in Germany: March–August 1945," *Political Science Quarterly,* LXIV (1949), 515 ff., 522 ff., 544. See also Kraus and Almond, "Social Composition of the German Resistance," *loc. cit.,* 88.

11. OMGUS, *Report of the Military Governor,* Finance, cumulative review, no. 24, 10–12; OMGUS, *Governmental Organization in the Occupied Zones of Germany* (Civil Administration Division, Berlin, 1947), 7–9; Friedmann, *Allied Military Government,* 85 ff.; W. Menzel, "Verwaltung der Britischen Zone," *Des Sozialistische Jahrhundert,* I (1947), 82 ff.

12. On this "stagnant inflation," see Horst Menderhausen's illuminating paper, "Prices, Money and the Distribution of Goods in Postwar Germany," *American Economic Review,* XXXIX (1949), 652 ff.; OMGUS, *Report of the Military Gov-ernor,* Trade and Commerce, no. 21, 19 ff. See also Stolper, *German Realities,* Chapter V, "Country without Currency," 95–108.

13. For an incisive picture see W. Eucken, F. W. Meyer, "The Economic Situa-tion in Germany," *Annals,* V. 260, 58–60.

14. The question of management incentives and status was explored most thoroughly in U.S. Coal Control Group, *Review of Hard Coal Production,* Bib/P(48) 92; see also partial text of report by Robert Moses, *New York Herald Tribune,* 30 July 1947.

15. This was the key conclusion of a study of the Ruhr by a competent econ-omist, F. Sanderson, "Report on Trip."

16. For the judgments rendered and data cited, see D. D. Humphrey, mss. on

Germany, "Black Gold," 12, 14; D. Ginsburg, *The Future of German Reparations* (National Planning Association Pamphlets no. 57–58, Washington, 1947), 40.

17. Cf. HICOG, *Food and Agricultural Programs in West Germany* (prepared by H. G. Schmidt, Historical Division, 1952) 8–12.

18. For record of this, see E. L. Hutton, D. W. Dobbins, *Postwar German Foreign Trade* (JEIA, Höchst, Germany, December, 1947), 5–20. Clay notes that "our first joint step toward facilitating foreign trade was to reduce existing restrictions so that German firms could contract directly with their foreign customers subject to final approval of contracts by Joint Export-Import Agency." Clay, *Decision,* 199.

19. Humphrey, German mss., Chapter XVII, "Clay Establishes Dollar Trade in the Heart of Europe," 1–13. The remarks in the text largely are borrowed from Humphrey's brilliant analysis.

20. *Ibid.,* 13. On the costs of the policy see also JEIA, *Suggested Change in Foreign Trade Policy,* JEXIM/P(48)12, 9 February 1948; JEIA, *Policy in Regard to Trade with Neighboring European Countries,* JEXIM/P(48)49, 11 June 1948. During 1948 a few concessions were made by way of programmed trade agreements.

NOTES FOR CHAPTER V

1. OMGUS, *Enactments and Approved Papers of the Control Council and Coordinating Committee* (7v., Legal Division, Berlin, 1946–1948), I, 95, 97; IV, 47.

2. *Ibid.,* I, 131, 176, 225, 308.

3. Among the fields of systematic application of this assumption were finance, money, prices, wages, taxation, budgets.

4. R. W. Van Wagener, "Cooperation and Controversy among the Occupying Powers in Berlin," *Journal of Politics,* X (1948), 86 ff.; on the Soviet side, see G. Klimov, *The Terror Machine* (trans. N.Y. 1953) ch. 7.

5. *Final Report to the Secretary of the Army on the Nuernberg War Crimes Trials under Control Council Law no. 10* (prepared by T. Taylor, Washington, 1949), 26.

6. General Clay once expressly alluded to this. See his testimony in U.S. Congress, Senate, *Military Government in Germany.* Hearings before the Committee on Investigation of the National Defense Program, 80th Congress, 1st session, Part 42 (Washington, 1946), 25880; L. D. Clay, *Decision in Germany* (New York, 1950), 135 ff.

7. Tendencies to conviviality, as R. W. Van Wagener implied, ran in peculiar "affinities." See his "Cooperation and Controversy," *loc. cit.,* 97.

8. F. Utley, *The High Cost of Vengeance* (Hinsdale, Ill., 1950), 25 f.

9. Clay, *Decision,* 28; F. Howley, *Berlin Command* (New York, 1950), 57–59.

10. Hence during the three year period preceding monetary reform, monetary transfers were unrestricted between the Soviet zone and the city but were permitted only on current transactions between the city and the western zones. Howley, *Berlin Command,* 97–99; OMGUS, *A Four Year Report* (Office of Military Government, U.S. Sector, Berlin, 1 September 1949), 14, 67, 112; G. Stolper, *German Realities* (New York, 148), 109; Allied Control Authority, Allied Kommandatura, Berlin,

Accumulated Bank Clearings at the Berliner Stadt Kontor, BK/R(46)152, 13 April 1946.

11. Although there is abundant evidence that pooled treatment was confined to foodstuffs, coal and public utilities there is also indication that the Magistrat effort to coordinate in other economic fields was effective particularly in the early period and with regard to construction activity, trade and handicrafts, transport and communications. Also a deposit is on record of ACA activity for such items as clothing for Berlin police, linen requirements for hospitals, pharmaceutical supplies and trucks. *Die Wirtschaft,* I (1946), 133–134, 195; II (1947), 425–426; Bipartite Control Office, *Supplies for Berlin,* Bico/P(48)94, 31 March 1948; Robert Nieschlag, "Probleme der Berliner Wirtschaft," Deutsches Institut für Wirtschaftsforschung, *Wirtschaftsprobleme der Besatzungszonen* (Berlin, 1948), 287 ff.; *Berlin im Neu-aufbau, das erste Jahr, Rechenschaftsbericht des Magistrats der Stadt Berlin* (Berlin, 1946), 59–70, 88–109, 120–133; OMGUS, *Activities of the Economic Directorate* (Special Report of the Office of the Economics Advisor, August, 1946), 129, 223, 322.

12. This included, for example, appointments to high city office, decrees, ordinances and appropriations. See the provisional constitution, OMGUS, *ACA Enactments,* IV, 47.

13. Controversies arose over such questions as Radio Berlin, Berlin University, the provisional constitution, the Berlin police and recognition of political parties. *Ibid.,* III, 170, 153–154; IV, 77–83; Howley, *Berlin Command,* 111 ff., 12 ff., 142, 152 ff. On the intimate character of Berlin administration see also HICOG, *Berlin: Development of its Government and Administration* (prepared by E. Plischke, Historical Division, 1952), 34 ff.

14. OMGUS, *ACA Enactments,* I, 139, 173, 136; II, 64, 129; III, 6, 51, 79; IV, 65; V, 12, 49, 10. The wide range of agreements and decisions not formally codified at the Control Council level may be found briefly summarized in ACA, *Report to the Council of Foreign Ministers from the Allied Control Authority in Germany,* CONL/P(47)7–15 (hereafter cited *CFM Report*), Section III, "Democratization," Part 3, Religious Affairs; Part 4, Education; Part 5, Reorganization of the German Judicial System and Reform of the German Procedural and Substantive Law; Part 8, Public Welfare; Part 7, Formation of Free Trade Unions, Social Insurance.

15. See *Ibid.,* Section III, *passim.*

16. *Ibid.,* Section IV, "Economic Problems," Part VIII, Economic Unity, 6–8 Part IX, Transportation, 4–5; Part X, Currency and Finance, (b) Budgets, (c) taxation, (e) banking, (g) prices; (h) wages; OMGUS *ACA Enactments,* I, 136, 140, 301, 321; II, 68, 88, 90, 111, 116, 118, 161; III, 26, 122, 126, 129, 175. On the tax legislation see particularly OMGUS, *Germany: Postwar Tax Program* (prepared by E. Gomberg, assistant to the American member on the ACA tax committee Berlin 1946—mimeographed).

17. *CFM Report,* Section II, "Denazification." For the significance of these measures, see C. J. Friedrich, "The Peace Settlement—Political and Military," *Annals of the American Academy of Political and Social Science,* 257 (1948), 124 ff.

18. *CFM Report,* Section I, "Demilitarization." For the significance of these measures, see Friedrich, "The Peace Settlement," *loc. cit.,* 123–124.

232   THE GERMAN PEACE SETTLEMENT AND THE BERLIN CRISIS

19. ACA Directive no. 39, "Liquidation of German War and Industrial Potential," adopted in October 1946 was the high point of this program. Subsequent to its adoption an important agreement with respect to carrying out quadripartite inspection of armament plants was reached; the machinery for implementing both agreements was instituted; and the first quadripartite inspection team actually was sent out in January 1947. Another directive, no. 22, was equally stringent and covered the destruction of fortifications and military facilities. Time limits for this work were prescribed. On these, see *CFM Report*, Section I, "Demilitarization," parts 3, 5; OMGUS, *Activities of the Economic Directorate*, 105 ff.; OMGUS, *ACA Enactments*, V, 6.

20. *Ibid.*, I, 199 ff. For some details of the programmed movement of 5 million persons, see *CFM Report*, Section VII, "Population Transfers," Part 5, Transfer of German Population (Expellees) and Appendix L. The Western zones agreed to accept 3 of the 5 million persons. General Clay slips in presuming that the Control Council agreement on Polish expellees did not include German inhabitants of the Oder-Neisse area, Clay, *Decision*, 313. For evidence to the contrary, see ACA, *Progress Report to the Coordinating Committee with Regard to Section XIII of the Resolutions of the Potsdam Conference*, DPOL/P (45)12, 19 September 1946. For a somewhat unsifted collection of materials bearing on the movement of persons, see V. Gollancz, *Threatened Values* (U.S. ed., Hinsdale, Ill., 1948), 129–147. For an authoritative and fair review see E. Wiskemann, *Germany's Eastern Neighbors* (Oxford, 1956) ch. 13, 14, 16.

21. *Ibid.*, 169 ff., 188 ff.; *CFM Report*, Section IV, "Economic Problems," Part 8, Level of Industry and Industrial Production. Expert Soviet economists who worked on the plan knew it "was unrealistic and unrealizable." Klimov, *op. cit.*, 201.

22. *Ibid.*, Section II, Pertinent Decisions of the Allied Control Authority, 2–7, Part 9, Transportation, 3–5.

23. For detailed information, see *Ibid.*, Section V, "Reparations," 2–4. For a sample of an inspection report by an Inter-Allied Commission, see ACA, *Report of the Inter-Allied Commission of Textiles*, SCGG/SEC(47)2, 15 February 1947.

24. This pattern of listing capacities—retained and surplus for valuation, allocation, notification and dismantling—is derived from compiled summaries in *CFM Report*, Section IV, Part 1, Section V, Part 4, "Progress Report on Final Reparations Plan based on Data Submitted to the Control Council."

25. *Ibid.*, Section V, "Reparations," Part 5, Valuations and Physical Removals.

26. See W. Röpke, *The Solution of the German Problem* (E. W. Dickes, translator, New York, 1946), 242; F. Joesten, *Germany; What Now?* (Chicago, 1948), 228 ff.; *CFM Report*, Section IV, Part 7, Appendix "C," 12. H. Wegner, "Die Zonen und der Aussenhandel," Deutches Institut, *Wirtschaftsprobleme*, 104, 109; K. Moldenhauer, "Ein Jahr Interzonal Handel," *Die Wirtschaft*, II (1947), 66 ff.; R. Appelt, "Der Interzonen-und Aussenhandel der Ostzone," *Ibid.*, III (1948), 346 ff.

27. That is, within two to six months. See Clay, *Decision*, 110; *CFM Report*, Section VI, "Central Administrations," The proposed central bank is classified as one of the agencies.

28. For analysis, see OMGUS, Special Report of the Military Governor, *Central German Agencies* (1946), 2–5.

29. *CFM Report,* Section III, "Democratization," Part 2, Reconstruction of democratic political life, freedom of speech, right of assembly, and public discussion . . . , 1–2; *Ibid.,* Part 7, Formation of free trade unions . . . , 4–5. Proposals for nationwide merging of political parties and trade unions were debated at high Control Council levels in October 1945 and March 1946 before the first flush of East-West cooperation had faded. Clay, *Decision,* 110, 119.

30. On the trade union aspect of the case, see World Federation of Trade Unions, *Report of Activity of the World Federation of Trade Unions, 15 October 1945–30 April 1949* (Milan, 1949), 425–446; Paul Phillips, "The German Trade Union Movement under American Occupation, 1945–1949," *Science and Society* XV (1951), 294 ff.; F. Apelt, *Der Weltgewerkschaftsbund und die Deutschen Gewerkschaften* (Berlin, 1947); Fritz Tarnow, "Labor and Trade Unionism in Germany," *Annals,* 260 (1948), 93 ff.; *Die Arbeit,* I (1947), 137 ff., 233 ff., 329 ff.; II, 65 ff.; OMGUS, *Report of the Military Governor,* Manpower, "Trade Unions and Working Conditions," no. 24, 3; *Ibid.,* no. 26, 2–3; *Ibid.,* no. 32, cumulative review, 11. On the political party aspect, see "Ansätze einer deutschen Repräsentation," *Europa-Archiv,* III (1948), 1144–1145; Dolf Sternberger, "Parties and Party Systems in Postwar Germany," *Annals,* 260 (1948), 20, 24–25; Joesten, *Germany: What Now?,* 95 ff., 106–114.

31. Clay, *Decision,* 39.

32. See later, p. 182 f.

33. J. F. Byrnes, *Speaking Frankly* (New York, 1947), 169–170; testimony of General Echols in April 1946, U.S. Congress, Senate, *Military Government in Germany,* Part 42, 25803. Clay seems always to have felt a pang of regret about the French veto. Clay, *Decision,* 77, 43, 131.

34. E. Wolf, "Geld-und Finanzproblem der deutschen Nachkriegswirtschaft," Deutches Institut, *Die Deutsche Wirtschaft Zwei Jahre Nach dem Zusammenbruch* (Berlin, 1947), 207 f., 219–222.

35. This was the pattern in Austria and its repetition in Germany could be anticipated. Cf. F. H. Klopstock, "Monetary and Fiscal Policy in Postliberation Austria," *Political Science Quarterly,* LXIII (1948), 108–109. See also typewritten account by the author, "Highlight Report of Vienna Trip, November 25–27, 1946," (OMGUS, Finance Division, 28 December 1946); OMGUS, *Financial Exploitation of German Resources by the USSR* (Finance Division, November, 1947), 6.

36. That substantial sums could have been involved is indicated by the hiatus in the known disposition of the 12 billion of currency reserves carried by the Berlin Reichsbank as unissued currency of which only some 6 billions has been accounted for. Cf. "Der Deutsche Geldumlauf," *Statistiche Praxis,* I (1946), Karteiblatt; OMGUS, *Report of the Military Governor,* Finance and Property Control (October 1945, no. 4). In any case some 3 to 4 billion RM were available to trickle into Potsdam Germany by illicit means.

37. See *CFM Report,* Section VI, Central Administration, 5, for a brief discussion of projects for central German agencies covering fields of statistical control, narcotic control, a patent office, a hydrographic office, and the like.

38. The pathways by which central German agencies were within two months converted into a projected provisional German government were well shown in

OMGUS, Special Report of the Military Governor, *Central German Government* (1946).

NOTES FOR CHAPTER VI

1. A condensed version of this chapter with fuller documentation has been published in *Finanzarchiv* n.f. Bd XVII (1957) 398–417 under the title: "Failure of Quadripartite Monetary Reform" [hereafter referred to as "Finanzarchiv Version"].

2. See authorities collected in "Finanzarchiv Version," p. 398 n. 2.

3. Allied Control Authority, *Elimination of Excessive Concentration of Economic Power in Banking*, Dfin/BC/Memo(46)15, 21 June 1946. Hans Adler, "The Postwar Reorganization of the German Banking System," *Quarterly Journal of Economics*, LXIII (1949), 322–325; ACA, *Report to the Council of Foreign Ministers from the Allied Control Authority in Germany*, CONL/P(47)7–15 [hereafter cited *CFM Report*], Section IV, Part 10, (e) Banking, 2–4.

4. Edgar Morin, *Allemagne Notre Souci* (Paris, 1947), 28–51.

5. Before the arrival of M. Leroy-Beaulieu, the latter French representative referred to in the text, the French position was sufficiently ambiguous and conservatively hued that the principal British representative could confidentially assert a belief that the French "appear in general to favor the British views." S. P. Chambers, "Anti-Inflationary Measures in Germany" (29 December 1945—mimeographed), 6. M. Leroy-Beaulieu's predecessor was connected with conservative French banking and commercial circles. Morin, *Allemagne Notre Souci*, 43. Nevertheless the protocol of financial reform debates in the Finance Directorate of the Control Council shows that the French clearly rejected the anti-reform British position, although on the positive side they merely asserted willingness "to study objectively" other proposals. ACA, "Stenographic Notes, Finance Directorate, 12th Meeting," 28 November 1945 (typewritten), 11; *ibid.*, 14th Meeting, 14 December 1945, 7–9. An officially inspired article indicated that the French favored a policy midway between the Soviet and the British positions. "Le Passé et L'Avenir du Reichsmark," *La Revue de la Zone Française*, II (1946), 52.

6. See "Finanzarchiv Version," p. 399, n. 2.

7. "So far as the French are concerned they find it exceedingly difficult to take part in the discussion of problems which are inevitably of a central character and in which their main policy of opposing any central German Government is involved." Chambers, "Anti-Inflationary Measures in Germany," 7.

8. ACA, *Proposal for a Non-recurring Property Levy*, Dfin/P(46)5, January, 1946.

9. See "Finanzarchiv Version," p. 400, n. 2.

10. See *ibid.*, p. 400, n. 4.

11. Cf. *Ibid.* p. 401, n. 2.

12. Cf. *Ibid.*, p. 401, n. 3.

13. *Idem.*

14. See later, Chapter X.

15. See "Finanzarchiv Version," p. 402, n. 1.

16. B. Bernstein, "Memo for the Files" (12 June 1945—typewritten). "Mr.

Chambers made clear in the discussion that the only reason for wanting to set up a central ministry of finance for the three Western zones is that it is his feeling it is absolutely essential to balance the budget in Germany, that it could be balanced only by a Central Ministry for Western Germany. . . . During the course of the discussion Mr. Chambers made clear that he believed that a balanced budget is the very essence of government."

17. S. P. Chambers, "The Major Problems of German Finance and Proposals for their Solution" (9 June 1945—typewritten). This memo also states that "the most urgent action required to enable the banks to make available their normal loan facilities is to restore the postal services and other means of communications. . . . It will not be enough to reconstitute the existing tax machinery and to enforce the existing tax laws. . . . The problem of making revenue meet expenditure must of course be tackled on the expenditure side as well as on the revenue side."

18. See ACA papers cited in "Finanzarchiv Version," p. 402, n. 2.

19. Chambers, "Anti-Inflationary Measures," 4; ACA, "Stenographic Notes, Finance Directorate, 12th Meeting," 12; and papers on prices and taxation cited in the preceding note.

20. *Proposals for Amendments in the German Tax System* (no file number, n.d.), 1.

21. Chambers, "Anti-Inflationary Measures," 3; ACA, "Stenographic Notes, Finance Directorate, 14th Meeting," 7–8.

22. For source and additional citations, cf. "Finanzarchiv Version," p. 403, n. 2.

23. See *Occupation Currency Transactions*, 232–236 for the text of this directive. See also a memorandum by two famous economists then serving as consultants to the Federal Reserve Board, H. S. Ellis and G. Haberler, "Recommendations concerning certain Financial Questions confronting the Allied Military Government of Germany" (Washington, n.d. but approximately May, 1944—mimeographed). This memo outlined the necessity for an over-all inflation control policy dealing with excessive monetary assets and public debt and recommended that some variant of a scheme of blocking of bank deposits and debt moratorium be employed.

24. See *Occupation Currency Transactions*, 246–250 for the text of the memorandum and revised directive issued by the director of the Civil Affairs Division of the War Department recommending that the revised directive which apparently had been prepared by the Treasury Department be approved for issuance.

25. Cf. the financial section of JCS-1067, as cited in U.S. Department of State, *Germany 1947–1949, The Story in Documents* (Department of State Publication 3556, European and Commonwealth Series 9, Washington, 1950), 31–33.

26. L. D. Clay, *Decision in Germany* (New York, 1950), 18–19.

27. This Treasury representative was Colonel B. B. Bernstein. For details see "Finanzarchiv Version" p. 404, n. 2.

28. For details see "Finanzarchiv Version" p. 404, n. 3.

29. Clay, *Decision*, 209–210. It appears that Washington objections sprang chiefly from the War Department and that strong proponents of the monetary reform plan in the State Department helped to carry the day.

30. OMGUS, *A Plan for the Liquidation of War Finance and the Financial Rehabilitation of Germany* (a report submitted by the Colm-Dodge-Goldsmith mis-

sion to Germany which includes the text of the report with a preface dated 20 May 1946 and a collection of supporting studies and appendices, published separately as volume II and dated 10 June 1946). The main text of the report has been republished, with a valuable introduction by Dr. H. Sauermann, in *Zeitschrift für die Gesamte Staatswissenschaft* III (1955) heft 2. [The Report will hereafter be cited *CDG Report*].

31. See earlier chapter I, pp. 8–9.

32. See earlier chapter, p. 10; also "Finanzarchiv Version," pp. 405–6.

33. See for extended discussion of the question of "private indebtedness," "Finanzarchiv Version," p. 407–8, n. 1.

34. See "Finanzarchiv Version," p. 409 n. 1, for an account of criticism of the C-D-G plan. In correspondence with the author Dr. Colm has argued that fund managers were to be endowed with authority to pay out claims according to priorities and that preference was to be given small holdings. The whole plan was to be framed in the interests of *rehabilitation*. But according to the plan property losses were to constitute the main criteria for awarding benefits.

35. For details and documentation, cf. "Finanzarchiv Version," p. 409, n. 2, 3.

36. See for a full statement of evidence "Finanzarchiv Version," p. 410, n. 1.

37. See for a full statement of evidence, "Finanzarchiv Version," p. 410 n. 2, 3, 411 n. 1, 2.

38. *Idem.*

39. Clay, *Decision*, p. 208.

40. F. A. Southard, *The Finances of European Liberation with Special Reference to Italy* (New York, 1946), 22. Assistant Secretary of War Petersen informed a Senate Committee that some 75 different foreign currencies were involved. *Occupation Currency Transactions*, 3, 53.

41. This project was advocated in a high level financial conference of U.S. Army and Department of State financial personnel held on 30 May 1945 after the menace of excess currency conversion had been realized. But the suggestion was rejected for lack of Congressional approval and because it would be contrary "to the ingrained rule that a soldier's pay is inviolate and that he can spend it as he considers best." *Ibid.*, 344.

42. It threatened to impair the public credit or supplant indigenous currencies; and constituted a potential dollar drainage on the U.S. at such time as the currency in question would become a means of purchase against U.S. exports. Cf. Southard, *The Finances of European Liberation*, 5.

43. This facility of ready and instant conversion to dollars at a protected rate contributed immensely, it was felt in high Army quarters, to the "peace of mind and effectiveness" of the "combat soldier." *Occupation Currency Transactions*, 2–6; cf. Southard, *The Finances of European Liberation*, 4, 5, 122 ff.

44. *Occupation Currency Transactions*, 6.

45. For citations see "Finanzarchiv Version," p. 413 n. 2.

46. *Occupation Currency Transactions*, p. 51.

47. *Ibid.*, 52, 448 ff., 466 f., 475, 513, 480.

48. *Ibid.*, 596.

49. The Staff Studies on this move by the Frankfurt Theater Staff and by the

War Department General Staff are reprinted in *ibid.*, 513–516, 536, 551–555, 555–563, 593–601.

50. Cf. *ibid.*, 327 ff., 346, 347, 348, 357.

51. Thus for the months of August, September, and October 1945, total pay disbursement was 9.2 million dollars and conversions were 15.5 million dollars, a sizeable gap but a minor contribution to the Army mark deficit. After October the institution of the Control Book system apparently cut down the specific Berlin deficit. *Ibid.*, 439 ff.

52. *Ibid.*, 3, 9, 97, 551.

53. *Ibid.*, 121.

54. *Ibid.*, 3, 551, 555, 597; Clay, *Decision*, 63; Bennett, "German Currency Reform," *loc. cit.*, 44.

55. For documentation cf. "Finanzarchiv Version," p. 414 n. 2.

56. *Occupation Currency Transactions*, 2, 23, 60, 290. Note particularly para. 3, a, b, of Finance Circular Letter by the Office of the Fiscal Director, 22 March 1945. In the basic Washington currency directive issued 8 September 1944 disbursing officers were permitted to convert authorized local currencies without making a cumulative individual record and subject only to the loosest of restraints. *Ibid.*, 254–269, particularly 258; cf. also 316–318, 320 ff.

57. See the copious reference to the inspired newspaper accounts and statements by alarmed Congressmen in "Finanzarchiv Version," p. 414 n. 3, 415 n. 1, 2.

58. For documentation see "Finanzarchiv Version," p. 415, 3.

59. For documentation and analysis of other motives to the printing stalemate, see "Finanzarchiv Version," 416, 1.

NOTES FOR CHAPTER VII

1. ACA, *Report to the Council of Foreign Ministers from the Allied Control Authority in Germany*, CONL/P(47) 7–15 hereafter cited *CFM Report*, Section IV, Part 3, 11–12; Office of Military Government for Germany (US), *Activities of the Economic Directorate, 1945–1948* (Special Report of the Office of the Economics Advisor, Berlin August, 1949), 131.

2. Hans Liebe, "Agrarstruktur und Ernährungspotential der Zonen," Deutches Institut, *Wirtschaftsprobleme der Besatzungszonen* (Berlin, 1948), 3 f. 84. The Soviet zone share of prewar population was 22 percent; the Soviet zone prewar per capita calorie food output approximately equalled prewar consumption, 2900–3000 calories. OMGUS, *Economic Data on Potsdam Germany*, 2, 13. But total Soviet zone population had increased 13.7 percent by the October 1946 census count. Inclusive of feeding responsibilities for Berlin (a little over a million non-self suppliers) and the concentration of population increase in the non-self supplier category, the total non-self supplier population would increase by some 20 percent. Thus prewar food output with a 1946 non-self supplier population would yield food consumption crudely calculated at about 2500 calories. OMGUS, *The Population of Germany* (2v., Civil Administration Division, Berlin, November, 1947), 4; *CFM Report, Section IV*, Part 3, Food and Rationing, Table III. On a *Stärkewert* basis the Soviet zone food output in 1946 is estimated at 60 percent of prewar. Liebe, "Agrarstruktur und Ernährungspotential," *loc. cit.*, 31. Official Soviet reports indicated in

238 THE GERMAN PEACE SETTLEMENT AND THE BERLIN CRISIS

the 1945/6 crop year an availability through the rationing system of 1388 calories per non-self supplier. *CFM Report,* Section IV, Part 3, 27. For the 1946/7 crop year Soviet plans projected a per capita calorie yield of 1957 calories, although Liebe reported a sharp drop in crop availabilities. From all this it is clear that no food surplus in fact or in potential existed in the eastern zone.

3. Ruhr coal was sent to the eastern zone only on an explicit exchange of equivalent basis. See ACA, *Minutes of the Directorate of Economics,* DECO/M/ (45) 14, 20 November 1945, paragraph 157; *Ibid.,* DECO/M(45) 15, 26 November 1945, paragraph 169. The same was true of interzonal food exchange. OMGUS, *Activities of the Economics Directorate,* 187.

4. Clay, *Decision,* 94 ff.

5. *Ibid.,* 169, 171.

6. *Ibid.,* 172.

7. For general surveys of this early form of bizonal fusion, see OMGUS, *The Evolution of Bizonal Organization* (Civil Administration Division, Berlin, 1948), 1–4; Council on Foreign Relations, *The United States in World Affairs, 1947/8* (prepared by J. C. Campbell and staff. New York, 1948), 79–87; "The Battle of Minden," *Economist,* 26 April 1947, 609–611.

8. For the text of this agreement, see U.S. Department of State, *Germany, 1947–1949,* 450–453. Key provisions set up the goal of immediate achievement of a self-sustaining economy, which had deadly implications for coal export policies; pledged a food ration level of 1800 calories for the normal consumer; and provided in the financial terms of partnership for a capital endowment, specified sustaining revenues, methods of recovery and agencies for expenditure.

9. See earlier, p. 89 f.   –

10. Incompatibility of social and economic regimes was believed by many to have cut away the basis for settlement which had crystallized in other respects. See Friedrich, "The Peace Settlement," *loc. cit.,* 120–129 for review of the extent to which the work of the Control Council regime favored settlement and for a clear expression of the thesis of social and political incompatibility.

11. The Soviets attacked the West bitterly for its Ruhr regime but did not hesitate to demand the exemption of property "acquisition . . . in connection with reparation receipts." OMGUS, *A Summary,* 115. The West attacked the Soviets and demanded the dissolution of their SAG empire, although it asserted that during the "period of military occupation, no special regime [of quadripartite character] for the Ruhr is necessary." *Die Deutsche Frage auf der Moskauer Konferenz der Aussenminister,* prepared as a special issue of *Europa-Archiv,* II (1947), 724.

12. This latter point would have been of particular concern to the Americans. See Clay, *Decision,* 200, 293 for emphasis on the principle of "political neutrality" on the issue of socialization which was also imprinted in the basic U.S. occupation directive of July 1947. U.S. Department of State, *Germany, 1947–1949,* 40.

13. See the excellent paper by Martin J. Hillenbrand, *The Ruhr in the Postwar World,* U.S. Department of State, Foreign Service Institute Monograph Series (May, 1950—mimeographed), 8 ff., 33 ff., 43 ff. Like Hillenbrand, I find the report of the German Steel Trusteeship Administration, *The Decartelization and Reorganization of the Iron-Producing Industry* (translated in OMGUS, 6 July 1948—mimeographed) highly illuminating, particularly Chapter III with its anal-

ysis of the history of the formation of combines used in the Ruhr industry. Cf. also Fritz W. Hardach, "Betriebswirtschaftliche Fragen bei Neuordnung der Kohlen- und Eisenwirtschaft nach dem Gesetz Nr. 75," *Zeitschrift für Handelswissenshaftliche Forschung*, Neue Folge, I (heft 6, 1949), 242–288.

14. See David Ginsburg, *The Future of German Reparations* (National Planning Association Pamphlets no. 57–58, Washington, 1947), 28 ff., 33 ff.; Stolper, *German Realities*, 135–171; CFM Report, Section V, Reparations, Parts 4 and 5.

15. For documentation on the French position, see Ministere des Affaires Étrangères, Services français d'Information, *Notes, Documentaires et Études* [hereafter cited France, *Notes*], "Les Quatre Grands et l'Allemagne," no. 685, 7 August 1947, 5–12. For general expositions of the French viewpoint, see L. F. Aubert, *Securité de l'Occident Ruhr-Rhin* (Paris, 1946); L. F. Aubert and others, *Nouveaux Aspects du Probléme Allémand* (Paul Hartmann, ed., Centre d'Études de Politique Étrangère, Pub. no. 17, Paris, 1947); Georges Bidault, "Agreement on Germany: Key to World Peace," *Foreign Affairs*, XXIV (1946), 571–578; and the illuminating essays in E. M. Earle, ed., *Modern France, Problems of the Third and Fourth Republics* (Princeton, 1951). It was no accident that the first presentation of the French delegation at the Moscow conference was "Le Probléme Démographique de l'Allémagne," France, *Notes*, no. 593, 5 April 1947. French interest in German manpower was manifested soon after the war in connection with her systematic use of prisoners of war on a scale comparable, population considered, to that of the Soviets. At the Moscow conference the French holdings of PWs were reported at 631,483 against 890,532 for the Soviets and a surprisingly large total of 435,295 for the British. *Die Deutsche Frage auf der Moskauer Konferenz der Aussenminister*, prepared as a special issue of *Europa-Archiv*, II (1947), 679. Only with strong American pressure did the French launch a program to scale down her PW holdings. J. F. Byrnes, *Speaking Frankly* (New York, 1947), 670. At the Paris reparations conference the American delegate strove unsuccessfully to obtain an accounting for PW labor services as an item in the reparations bill. At that conference both the British and the French favored use of PW labor for an extended forward period. At that time the French were employing some 800,000 prisoners. "In addition the U.S. had undertaken to transfer another 520,000 prisoners to France and still another 450,000 if U.S. military authorities in Germany judged that they were available. It was known moreover that the French desired to use these prisoners for a considerable period."

16. See Joesten, *Germany: What Now?*, 40; P. E. Mosely, "The Occupation of Germany: New Light on How the Zones were Drawn," *Foreign Affairs*, XXVIII (1950), 600; Economic Cooperation Administration, *The European Recovery Program*, Country Studies, Chapter XVII, "Western Germany" (Washington, 1948 —mimeographed), 53–63; U.S. Congress, Senate, *Extension of European Recovery*. Hearings before the Committee on Foreign Affairs, 81st Congress, 1st session (Washington, 1949), 276 f. In the hearing the flat statement was made that "as a separate economic and political entity the French zone would face an almost impossible task in achieving viability during any reasonable period of time."

17. See U.S. Congress, House of Representatives, Select Committee on Foreign Aid, *Final Report on Foreign Aid*, 80th Congress, 2d. session, May, 1948, 154–168.

Thus on 26 August 1947 dollar purchases except of cereals, coal, fats and oils were suspended; on September the bread ration was reduced to 200 grams daily; and precious French gold and dollar reserves were expended in buying American coal; inflation was continuous and gold reserves could not last much longer. See U.S. Congress, House of Representatives, *Third Supplemental Appropriation Bill for 1948*, 80th Congress, 1st session (Washington, 1947), 223–252, 291–299. On the journalistic level see "Uneasy Balance in France" and "The French Economic Crisis," *Economist*, 26 July 1947, 37–39, 156–157; "The French Economic Crisis, II," *Ibid.*, 2 August 1947, "France's Struggle for Bread," *Ibid.*, 16 October 1947.

18. This was essentially the means by which French adhesion to Bizonia ultimately was obtained. Clay, *Decision*, 193, 321 ff.

NOTES FOR CHAPTER VIII

1. Access to additional information and closer calculation has made it worth-while to settle on estimates somewhat higher than those worked out in my "Reparations Problem Again," *loc cit.*, 28 ff.

2. For current product withdrawals, see authorities collected above ch. III, The minimal dismantling estimate comes from N. A. Voznesensky, *Soviet Economy during the Second World War* (International Publishers, 1949), 132–4. It was there unambiguously asserted that the value of the industrial equipment transferred from Germany as reparations amounted only to .6% of total property damage estimated at 128 billion dollars. See also G. H. Harmssen, *Reparations, Sozialprodukt Lebenstandard; Versuche einer Wirtschaftsbilanz* (summary report with 12 Anlage, Bremen, 1947), Anlage X, "Demontage und Bewertung der Entnahmen," 5–17. According to Harmssen the Soviet valuation may be doubled to obtain true value. This alleged true value would be out of accord with the estimated prewar value of 3.75 billion RM for all industrial equipment in the Soviet Zone. However, dismantling was also extensive in public utility equipment, office equipment and rail-road cars and track. Of course valuations of used equipment is essentially arbitrary; and much of the dismantled equipment did not render very useful service when reinstalled by the Soviets. The used equipment will not often meet user needs in optimal fashion; there is not the same range of choice as when buying new. See detailed accounts by Soviet experts in *Soviet Economic Policy in Postwar Germany* (ed. R. Slusser, N.Y., 1953), 14–56.

3. Richard Castillon, *Les Reparations Allémandes, 1919–1952*, Paris, (1955) 156 (citing value of 20 million dollars). This is plausible since the two-thirds of the German merchant marine allocated to the Western Powers are valued at 173 million RM (1938). See Dept. of State, *Germany 1947–1949* (1950) 428.

4. We have on record a reliable estimate of 45 million dollars for Hungary, 128 millions for Finland and 600 millions for Austria. Considering these figures an allowance of one billion dollars for total realizable foreign assets seized by the Soviet Union is not greatly out-of-line. Book values might have been greater but realizable and transferrable values are another story. See Castillon, *op cit.*, 152; *Harmssen Report*, Anlage XII, p. 21 f.; P. E. Mosely, "The Treaty with Austria". *International Organization* IV (1950) 229 ff. Realized foreign German assets treated as reparations by Western countries were valued only at 293 million dollars (Castillon, *op.*

cit., 156 f.). In comparison with this the one billion dollar estimate seems generous.

5. The original dismantling program evolved out of the March 1956 Control Council agreement indicated about 2000 plants for dismantling from the Western Zones. As originally stepped down in late 1947 the Western dismantling program comprehended about 868 plants; under American pressure tied in with Marshall-Plan aid the dismantling was scaled down by about a third in 1949 and in 1950. Final dismantling involved 668 plants with an equipment value (1938) of 713 million RM. Of this final total the actual Soviet share was around 20 million dollars. Allowing for reciprocal deliveries they could not have received much more even with a liberalized dismantling program. See Castillon, *op. cit.*, 153 ff.; *Germany 1947–1949*, 415 ff., 423 f.

6. The possible magnitude of previous fulfillment range from an official (though unsupported) British estimate of 7 billion dollars (Cornides and Volle, *Um den Frieden*, 35) to an official but unpublished U.S. (Berlin) estimate which ran to over ten billion dollars. (OMGUS, *Progress of German Reparations*, Economics Division, November 1947, p. 2). See also for other efforts at valuations, J. H. Furth, *American Economic Review*, XXXVIII (1948) 924–932; American Association for a Democratic Germany "Reparations-Claimed and Collected", *Facts About Occupied Germany*, VI (1947) 2 ff.; *Harmssen Report*, Anlage XII, 22; J. P. Nettl, *The Eastern Zone and Soviet Policy in Germany 1945–1950* (Oxford 1951) 207–225.

7. On the Western-German Debt Settlement of 1952, see the summary treatment in H. Wallich, *Mainsprings of the German Revival* (New Haven, 1955) 258–261. German reluctance was indicated in the complex negotiations; but acceptance of the Allied claims which go back in principle to the war debts of the Twenties, was a condition for relaxation of Occupation-control. See the account of the negotiations in Elmer Plischke, *Allied High Commission Relations with the West German Government* 1949–1951 (Bonn, 1952) 47–64. The assumption of prewar debts had, to my knowledge, never been voiced in presentation of Western claims on Germany during negotiations with the Soviets. These debt-claims would have been laughed out of court. But the component of claims honored at London for Western "economic assistance" rendered after 1945 was always specified as an American claim with high priority for reimbursement. How odd that barely after denying the ability of Germany to pay the Soviets for damage sustained by German aggression, the Allies insisted on foisting on a Western Germany their depreciated claims of a faraway past. Of course the guiding authorities in the Occupation were drawn from the circle of international bankers which had negotiated the first round of German Settlements in the Twenties, had worked out the standstill arrangements in the Thirties and now were sitting in judgment over a vanquished Germany. Understandably, the Western bankers included interest arrears—going back in some cases to 1932—but then generously scaled down the accumulated value. See E. Achterberg, "Der Londoner Schuldenplan." *Zeitschrift für das Gesamte Kreditwesen* (Heft 17, 1952), 437–442.

8. German social product in 1950 was assessed at values 77% over 1936 levels for Western Germany and some 71% (for industrial product only moving at controlled prices) for Eastern Germany. See W. F. Stolper, "The Labor Force and Industrial Development in Soviet Germany," *Quarterly Journal of Economics, LXXI*

(1957) p. 542, Table Xnl; *Statistisches Jahrbuch für die Bundesrepublik Deutschland 1954* (Wiesbaden 1954) 519–523. Commodity price indexes for the industrial sector were by 1950 85% over 1938 levels and in 1949 they were near 90% over. (See *ibid.*, 1957 ed., p. 458). However, other price-structures were less inflated.

9. Stolper, *loc. cit.*, 527 f.

10. B. U. Ratchford and W. D. Ross, *Berlin Reparations Assignment* (Chapel Hill, 1947) 79 f. The Soviet economist Varga in an interesting letter to the London *Economist* 3 January 1948, p. 13 illustrated this higher German living standard by citing figures for meat and milk consumption per capita.

11. Varga, *idem.*

12. *Jahrbuch, 1954*, p. 408.

13. Though Berlin was badly damaged by Allied air-raids, these were generally night-area-raids which accordingly did little unrepairable damage to industrial facilities. See United States Strategic Bombing Survey, *Area Studies Division Report* (Sept. 1945). Berlin ranked low as an air-raid target (see App. A. iv. f.) and its distance from London handicapped the air-war on it. Hence it was attacked heavily only after November 1943 and it received only 35,000 tons of bombs as against around 30,000 for Essen and Cologne and 25,000 for Hamburg. (See listing of cities with tonnage and other data in *ibid.*, p. 18, Table N. Study of the production curtailment arising out of area raiding indicated that for every 15,000 tons of bombs "dropped in area raids a loss of one percent of annual production was imposed on Germany" (p. 18). Of the production loss half was induced by absenteeism and disorganization and half by damage to facilities. So much of this damage was repaired that it was estimated that "not more than an estimated 6.5% of all machines tools in Germany were damaged or destroyed by air attack," p. 22). For the German economy was a whole the great bulk of the bomb tonnage was aimed at industrial or military targets (nearly twice as great as general "area-raids"). It appears that during 1944 (during which year % of all bomb tonnage was dropped in Germany) only some 6.5% of existing machine tools were damaged or destroyed by air raids of all kinds. See U.S. Strategic Bombing Survey, *The Effects of Strategic Bombing on the Germany Economy* (1945) p. 45. From all this it may be inferred that damage through air raids to the industrial capacity of Berlin was of a minor order. Dismantling was more significant; yet the author has not seen any well-authenticated evaluation of dismantling in Berlin. The 55 days in May and June before Western troops entered the city were hardly sufficient to permit as massive a dismantling as is often suggested. Thus the charge that Berlin's industrial capacity was reduced down to a third or less of prewar by bombing and dismantling is not well-supported. For this charge see Deutsches Institute, *Berlin's Wirtschaft in der Blockade* (Berlin 1949) 35 f.; "Was Kann Berlin's Industrie Leisten," *Wirtschafts Zeitung* II (10 September 1947). The charge specified that capacity in the electro-technical industry was removed down to 17% of prewar. R. Nieschlag, "Probleme der Berliner Wirtschaft," Deutsches Institute, *Wirtschaftsprobleme der Besatzungszonen* (Berlin 1948), 285. A published account of this industry affirmed that (in 1946) "as yet only 35%" of its capacity was "put back into operation" while actual capacity was "still higher." E. Rössel, "Die Berliner Elektro-Teindustrie," *Die Wirtschaft*, I (1946) 214. Moreover between

1936 and 1944 industrial capacity in German industries was significantly enlarged to make possible war production. Hence considerable capacity could have been destroyed or removed by dismantling and still left capacity exceeding that of 1936. We are inclined to accept as more reliable the more common attribution of Berlin's retarded economic revival to shortage of materials and parts, disorganization of supply and markets, inability to make long-range plans and hindrances of access due to transport and commercial restrictions. See Deutsches Institut, *Berlins Wirtschaft in Übergang* (Berlin 1947) 22–26; "Berlin zwischen den Zonen," *Wirtschaftszeitung*, II, November 14, 1947; E. Dusiske, "Planung in einer Dreimillionenstadt," *Die Wirtschaft*, I (1946) 133 ff.; "Berlin—lebenswichtiges Zentrum im deutschen Wirtschaftsaufbau," *ibid.*, 194–20," I (No. 1, 1948) 7 ff.; *Berlin im Neuaufbau das erste Jahr* (Berlin 1947) 70–87; "Wirtschaftslage Berlin 1947," *Wirtschftslatt für Berlin*.

14. I once ventured to describe a report to Military Government in those sharp terms the effects of Allied Property Control. See the essay "Stingy Finance and Laissez-Faire" cited p. 70, n. 7, 8 of my paper, "The German Economic Potential".

15. In my "German Economic Potential," p. 68 ff. these statements are documented.

16. See my "Stingy Finance and Laissez-Faire" for an effort to appraise in economic terms what I ventured to call "mass smuggling in open black markets" paras. 57–59. See also Hans Gurski "Devisenüberwachung und Kapitalflucht" *Aussenhandel*, I (1948, no. 14) 3 ff. The existing memoir accounts by occupation personnel paint distressing pictures of blackmarketeering by Allied personnel, both East and West in search for personal enrichment. On the Soviet side see the interesting account of personal looting in G. Klimov, *The Terror Machine*, 103 ff., 118 ff., 163, 178 f. For the American side see H. Zink, *The United States in Germany 1944–1955* (N.J. 1957) 136 ff. "It would not be fair to conclude", writes Zink, "that looting was all-prevailing among American forces in Germany, but there was a good deal of it" (p. 136). But as for black-marketeering "it almost seemed like the classical story of Diogenes going about with a lantern to seek out an honest man", 138. See interesting personal accounts in Ratchford and Ross, *op. cit.*, 14–18; A. D. Kahn, *Betrayal, Our Occupation of Germany* (Warsaw 1950) 95–111.

17. Though a complex internal budgeting machinery was installed with varying degrees of effectiveness by the different Army commands, and though a wide variety of policies were instituted to abridge the procurement authority of local commanders who at the outset were delegated with unrestricted requisitioning power without regard to monetary costs, the results were still far short of those obtaining with normal governmental expenditures control patterns. See the detailed survey of controls and budgeting devices on the American side in OMGUS, *Report of the Military Governor*, Finance, no. 24, cumulative review, 24–26. See also comments in OMGUS, *A Plan for the Liquidation of War Finance and the Financial Rehabilitation of Germany* (a report submitted by the Colm-Dodge-Goldsmith mission to Germany which includes the text of the report with a preface dated 20 May 1946 and a collection of supporting studies as appendices, paged non-continuously and dated 10 June 1946), Appendix D, "Government Budgets and Taxation," 6.

18. Byrnes, *Speaking Frankly*, 167 ff.; U.S. Department of State, *Germany 1947–1949*, 445. The CDG Report stipulated that reductions of occupation costs to 3 to 4 billion RM annually was an indispensable condition of success for monetary reform. *C-D-G Report*, 25.

19. Article XI of the Dawes Plan settlement resolved into a single financial claim "all amounts for which Germany may be liable . . . including reparations, restitutions, all costs of all armies of occupation, clearing house operations, . . . commissions of control and supervision." World Peace Foundation, *The Dawes Plan* (Boston, 1923), 385.

20. *Report of the First Committee of Experts*, Part I, VIII, a (German ed., Berlin, 1924) p. 10.

21. See copious references in my "German Economic Potential," p. 74, n. 15, 16.

22. See *idem*, n. 17. The tax reforms carried out in both Eastern and Western Germany in late 1948 and during 1949 both gave a good deal of tax relief while at the same time in both areas total tax revenues increased due to economic revival. See for detailed study, G. C. Weigand, "Business and Finance in Communist Germany," *Illinois Law Review* vol. 46 (Jan-Feb 1952) 868–878.

23. See my "German Economic Potential," *loc. cit.*, p. 77 f. for documented support of these and like assertions of fact.

24. For detailed analysis, see "German Economic Potential," *idem*.

25. The authors of the report of the "Overall Economic Effects Division" included J. K. Galbraith (later Professor of Economics at Harvard University), Paul Baran, B. H. Klein, N. Kaldor.

26. See chart of GNP in billions of 1939 RM USSBS, *The Effects of Strategic Bombing on the German War Economy* (Oct. 1945) p. 22.

27. *Ibid.*, p. 44.

28. *Ibid.*, p. 230, Table 37.

29. *Ibid.*, p. 46 f.

30. *Ibid.*, p. 43 and entire chapter, "The Supply and Use of Capital Equipment" p. 43–53.

31. *Ibid.*, p. 106.

32. *Ibid.*, p. 108.

33. See "German Economic Potential" for detailed appraisal, p. 77.

34. For this pattern of integration into the world economy, see "German Economic Potential," 85–87.

35. See A. Gerschenkron, *Bread and Democracy in Germany* (Berkeley, 1943), 59 ff., 200 ff.; B. Harms, ed. *Strukturwandlungen der deutschen Volkswirtschaft* (2v., Berlin, 1929), I, 394, 422 ff. For a contemporary statement which brings this point of view up to date, see H. Schacht, *Abrechnung mit Hitler* (Hamburg, 1948), Chapter XII, "Das deutsche Problem."

36. Angell, *The Recovery of Germany* (New Haven, 1929), Chapters I and II.

37. Making allowance for debt service and travel and currency remission items, the net deficit for 1927-9 ranged near 2.5 billion DM. See the careful study in S. P. Gilbert, *Bericht des Generalagenten für Reparationszahlungen* (Berlin, 1930), 311 ff. Deficits naturally were a function of the breadth of domestic income flow,

but the late Twenties experienced no inflation and there was continuous market pressure and accumulating unemployment.

38. The role of price relationships is indicated by the fact that though the German import-export balance showed an annual average surplus during 1935–1937 of 370 million RM this would have yielded a deficit of 630 million RM at 1928 prices. Statistisches Reichsamt, *Statistisches Jahrbuch* (Berlin, 1936), 256. It may be noted peripherally that to some extent the use of an aggressive trade agreement program and trading controls merely offset retention by Germany of the "old" parity for the Mark which was not devalued in the British and American pattern. See H. S. Ellis, *Exchange Control in Central Europe* (Cambridge, 1938).

39. See analysis and sources in "German Economic Potential," *loc. cit.*, 85, 87, as well as the Mendershausen article cited above.

40. See "German Economic Potential," 83 ff. and notes 33, 34 and 35, for adjustment of the prewar balance of trade for wartime losses and notice of the principle schemes that have been worked out showing the various conditions of economic balance achievable under the new conditions.

41. The following discussion is a condensed and recast version of an analysis initially presented in "Reparations Problems Again," *loc. cit.*, 38–41.

42. See "Reparations Problem Again," *loc. cit.*, 39 n. 38.

43. U.S. Department of State, *United States Economic Policy toward Germany*, Department of State Publication 2630, European Series 15 (Washington, 1946), 106. The assumption is made here that the American share would lapse in favor of Germany.

44. See "Reparations Problem Again," *loc. cit.*, 34–8 nn. 24, 25 for a more detailed version of this analysis and for sources.

45. J. M. Keynes, "A Rejoinder," *Economic Journal* (1929), cited here as republished in *Readings in the Theory of International Trade* (Blakiston Series, 1949) 167.

46. For the clearest expositions of this, see T. Balogh, *The Dollar Crisis*, 1–18, 77 ff., 175 ff.; Seymore Harris, "Dollar Scarcity," *Economic Journal*, LVII (1947), 165–178. Also see sympathetic comments by J. H. Williams, *Postwar Monetary Plans and Other Essays* (3rd ed., New York, 1947), cxx ff.; J. K. Galbraith, *Beyond the Marshall Plan* (National Planning Association Pamphlet no. 68, Washington, 1949), 24 ff.

47. These currents of thought and interest were perhaps most clearly elucidated and were given strongest leadership by John Foster Dulles who shortly before the Moscow March-April 1947 conference had been appointed advisor to the Secretary of State. He came to Moscow with a program which rejected outright any reparations agreement and which aimed flatly at creating an American-led, anti-Soviet West European coalition pivoting on Germany. This was the implicit content of the Dulles speech of 19 January 1947 and the explicit content of a policy memorandum which served as the basis for the discussion of the German problem in Berlin. This memorandum emphasized the danger of a Germany "subject to 'political penetration' by the Soviet Union or a Germany 'independent of both East and West' which would have an 'enormous bargaining power.' " It concluded on the note that " 'the European settlement should seek primarily to solidify and

strengthen Western Europe.'" The conflict with Clay's viewpoint was a sharp one and Clay later announced that he could "not be responsible for the execution" of the Dulles line which Clay reported involved opposition to any reparations settlement. See J. F. Dulles, *War or Peace* (N.Y. 1950) 102 ff.; and the Dulles speech of 10 February 1947 as excerpted and commented on in J. P. Warburg, *Put Yourself in Marshall's Place* (N.Y. 1948) 11. See Clay, *Decision,* 149. By the fall of 1948 the antagonism was still strong enough so that Howley could report that on Dulles' visit to Berlin, "ice" divided the two men and that "the only subject on which Clay and Dulles appeared to agree was Rhine wine." F. Howley, *Berlin Command* (N.Y. 1950) 223.

48. U.S. *European Recovery and American Aid,* Report by the President's Committee on Foreign Aid (D.C. 1947) 34. In the section on Germany this statement was set off by the remark that "two years ago" East-West unification in Germany would have been "highly desirable." This being "almost impossible" to achieve, and delay being "too costly," we must "start" in the West with "what we have."

49. The concept of Western Germany as "magnet," with its naive hopefulness or its cold cynicism, was espoused openly in Germany during 1947. "Passivität bedeutet heute für Deutschland Vernichtung des Lebens," exhorted Kurt Schumacher at the June 1947 convention of the western Social Democracy. "Wenn man Deutschland gesund machen will," he added, "so ist es nach den realen Möglichkeiten heute nur auf dem Wege zun erreichen, dass mann die Bizone ökonomisch so lebendig macht, dass von ihr ein unwiderstehlicher Magnetismus auf andere Zonen ausgeht . . . denn eine Zonenvereinigung ist wirtschaftlich nur denkbar und möglich, wenn der Westen stark genug ist, das ökonomischeVakuum der Ostzone bei einer Vereiningung auch auzufüllen." So also the influential editor of the Berlin *Tagesspiegel,* Erik Reger, in a programmatic series of articles which were republished as a pamphlet: " . . . in diesem Sommer, da jede mit 'Schritten' ausgefüllte Minute ein unwiederbringlicher Verlust ist, genügt das Mikrokosmische nicht mehr." He outlined a program of twelve-pronged action which anticipated later Western policy. See Kurt Schumacher, *Deutschland und Europa* (Frankfurt, 1947); Erik Reger, *Zwei Jahre Nach Hitler* (Hamburg, 1947), 52 ff. Victor Gollancz and Wilhelm Röpke warned against fusion with eastern Germany to avoid "opportunities for the Russian policy of infiltration." W. Röpke, *The Solution of the German Problem* (trans. E. W. Dickes, New York, 1946), 217; V. Gollancz, *Our Threatened Values* (U.S. ed., Hinsdale, Ill., 1948), 120. Ginsburg warned of "the progressive economic deterioration in the Soviet zone . . . [which] threatened breakdown for lack of raw materials and essential supplies and equipment." Ginsburg, *The Future of German Reparations,* 48. Even Walter Lippmann advised that "the economic unification of Germany, a central German government, a demilitarization treaty are not things to be bought eagerly from Mr. Molotov. They are things to be sold him reluctantly on carefully considered terms." Cited in *Ibid.,* 54. In this period, Lippmann devoted his persuasive pen to the campaign for the creation of a western Germany. See his column, for example, *New York Herald Tribune,* 12 September 1946; *Ibid.,* 5 October 1946. Only later in 1947 did Lippmann urge against a policy of Western partition. E. S. Mason attributed the failure of the Moscow Conference to bargaining tactics "by now all too familiar." Mason, "Reflections on the Moscow Conference," *loc. cit.,* 475. Elsewhere he stated that an alternative explanation "is

in terms of a possible Soviet estimate of its own bargaining position. The USSR may not have sought agreement because it considered that the probable course of events favored delay." E. S. Mason and J. K. Pollock, "American Policy toward Germany," *Foreign Policy Reports*, XXIII (November 1, 1947), 210. Clay's and Byrnes' thinking was, at least, retrospectively, simple. "Soviet representatives not only did not intend to reach an agreement but were deliberately delaying discussion in the belief that the resulting conditions in Germany would be favorable to their expansion program." Clay, *Decision*, 130, 154. Clay also believed that "it was in Soviet interest to permit relationships to deteriorate, to wage a war of nerves recreating the fear in Europe which alone could make possible the further advance of Communism." *Ibid.*, 160. General Marshall also said that the divergence of purpose between the U.S. and the USSR about promoting the recovery of a "solvent and vigorous Europe" was the "cause of many of the present differences between the U.S. and Russia" and that "with the removal of this cause the East-West tension would lessen." U.S. Department of State, *Germany, 1947–1949*, 10. Cf. also "New Deal for Germany," *The Economist*, 1 November 1947, 707. Either in more serious or more sloganized terms the program of building in the West with what we have was widely espoused. Thus see Tibor Mende, *Europe's Suicide in Germany* (London 1946) 6 ff.; Lewis Brown, *A Report on Germany* (N.Y. 1947); Stolper, *German Realities*, 107 ff.; Friedrich, "The Peace Settlement with Germany," *loc. cit.*, 128; G. D. H. Cole, *The World in Transition* (N.Y. 1949) 191 ff. The example of Cole shows how even the most enlightened and uninvolved leaders of the Western Left shared the premises and suppositions which induced the leaders of the Western Right to drive for a separate Western Germany and to give up, for the time being, the policy of settlement.

NOTES FOR CHAPTER IX

1. The best general survey of the Moscow Conference is found in Council on Foreign Relations, *The United States in World Affairs 1947/8* (prepared by John C. Campbell and staff, New York 1948), chapter III, "Germany: The Moscow Conference and After."

2. For the texts of the Moscow Agreements and their relevant contexts in discussion, see *Die Deutsche Frage auf der Moskauer Konferenz der Aussenministern*, prepared as a special issue of *Europa-Archiv, II* (July, 1947) and hereafter referred to as *Die Deutsche Frage, Moskau*, 736–7. These texts are also available in ACA papers and in scattered form in Office of Military Government for Germany (U.S.), *A Summary of Agreements and Disagreements on Germany* hereafter referred to as *A Summary* (1st ed., Civil Affairs Division, 1948), 20, 50–51, *passim*. For the relevant discussion of the terms of reference of the economics question, see *Die Deutsche Frage*, 735 f.; V. N. Molotov, *Speeches and Statements at the Moscow Session of the Council of Foreign Ministers, 1947* (published by Soviet News, London, 1947), 106.

3. For brief discussion, cf. *The United States in World Affairs 1947/8*, 83 ff.

4. J. Bennett, "The German Currency Reform," *Annals of the American Academy of Political and Social Science*, v. 267 (1950) 43–7; L. D. Clay *Decision in Germany* (New York, 1950), 211.

5. The peculiar nature of the rupturing is indicated by the monetary reform negotiations which were resumed in August 1947 with a modified version of the American currency printing plan. See Allied Control Authority, *Minutes of the Coordinating Committee* Corc/M(47)19; para. 91, para. 436; ACA, *Minutes of the Control Council* Conl/M(57)19, para. 91. On allocations of general purpose equipment through latter 1947, see OMGUS, *Enactments and Approved Papers of the Control Council and Coordinating Committee* (7v., Legal Division, 1946–1948) VIII, 26 ff, 59–62, 63–73, 90–97. On the reciprocal delivery agreement, see *Ibid.,* 86–90. For the entire record of quadripartite agreement see this volume, *passim,* and the review given by Clay, *Decision,* 152–162.

6. See Clay, *Decision,* 290 ff.; OMGUS, *Report of the Military Governor,* Manpower no. 32 (cumulative review) 11–12; OMGUS, *A Summary,* 53–54, 61; *Sokolovsky November 1947 Statement,* 7 f., (this statement was presented by Sokolovsky to the 75th meeting of the Control Council on 21 November 1947 and was separately translated and reproduced).

7. For land reform, refugee-redistribution and zonal publications, see OMGUS, *Activities of the Directorate of Economics, 1945–1948.* Special Report of the Office of the Economics Advisor, August 1949) 32–37; ACA, *Minutes of the Control Council,* Conl/M(48)1, para. 3; ACA, *Distribution Between the Zones of German Refugees Since the Cessation of Hostilities,* Conl/P(47)464, 28 December 1947; OMGUS, *A Summary,* 67.

8. The achievement in October 1946 of the principle of inspection on armament plant as embodied in CORC Directive 39, the actual organization and dispatch of an inspection commission during January 1947, the submission and consideration of a report of visitation, and promulgation of an agreed code for the organization and handling of interzonal inspections—all this embodied a very important forward step in the East-West peace settlement in this field. See OMGUS, *Activities Directorate Economics,* 105 ff.; and OMGUS, *Enactments and Approved Papers,* V, 6. The report of the commission in the U.S. zone was an illuminating document showing a lax state of affairs on the plant level. See ACA, *Report of the First Disarmament Inspection Commission Visiting the U.S. Zone,* CLMP/P(47)7.

9. There was an illuminating CORC debate on the reports of the second inspection commission. See ACA, *Minutes of the Coordinating Committee,* Corc/M (47)48, para. 556 and ACA, *General Report of the Second Inter-Allied Inspection Commission for Checking the Liquidation of German Industrial War Potential,* Corc/P(47)234, 20 November 1947. The 3rd commission did not submit an agreed report.

10. The Moscow agreement textually reads that the Control Council "shall verify with the aid of quadripartite commissions the operations for the liquidation of war potential provided for in the preceding paragraphs" which included operations covered in CORC directives 22 and 28. If inspection were to cover operations under those directives it would become significantly widened to cover handling of underground and ground installations and facilities and military materials of all kinds. See OMGUS, *A Summary,* 20.

11. This conflict over the scope of inspection had been going on since the spring of 1946 and more or less took the form of British-American coupling of inspection of military facilities, installations, personnel, and supplies with inspection

of economic facilities. See L. D. Clay, *Decision in Germany* (New York, 1950), 126–128. If this had political or ulterior overtones, the Soviet insistence that inspection be confined only to pre-arranged visitations at scheduled facilities obviously would have greatly hampered the effectiveness of inspection which requires in some form right of unprepared visitation.

12. ACA, *Minutes of the Control Council*, Conl/M (48) 1, para. 5.

13. OMGUS, *A Summary*, 92.

14. *Sokolovsky November 1947 Statement*, 7; OMGUS, *ACA Enactments*, I, 310; ACA, *Minutes of the Coordinating Committee*, Corc/M (47) 48, para. 558; Corc/M (47) 37, para. 411.

15. See Ira B. Hirschmann, *The Embers Still Burn* (New York 1949) 122 f.; E. M. Kulischer, *Europe on the Move* (New York 1948) 269 ff.; Institut für Besatzungsfragen, *Das DP Problem* (Tübingen 1950) 16–19. See comments on the Ukrainian group in the last cited publication, 17 f. A reliable military government report cited the following composition of a large Baltic DP Camp: members of the Wehrmacht, 2.45%; members of police organizations (Gestapo, etc.), 3.74%; wearing German uniform (16%); coming to Germany voluntarily, 57.5%; persecuted by the Nazis, 7.9%; persecuted by the Russians, 54.2%.

16. See U.S. Department of State, *The United States and the United Nations*, State Department Publication no. 2735, Report Series 7 (Washington, 1947) 118–122; UNRRA, *Reports of the Administration on Displaced Persons Operations (per) Resolution 92* (mimeographed compilation of documents relating to and reports growing out of the adoption of UNRRA Resolution 92 of March 1946, requiring bimonthly reports on expediting repatriation), 1st report.

17. For evidence, see the innumerable testimonies to this effect collected in the UNRRA, *Reports . . . Resolution 92*. Thus in the first report (1 June 1946) of the UNRRA Central Headquarters in Germany, the facilities for screening were so inadequate that it was reported "absolutely impossible . . . to conduct a screening program which may be considered effective by even the most minimum standards." *Ibid.*, 18. In the British Zone, screening activity had been virtually nonexistent and in the American zone sporadic, spasmodic and (in UNRRA's judgement) inadequate. Though screening activity was most prominent in the American zone, in UNRRA's judgment it was "ineffective and inaccurate" because of inexperience and in efficiency of personnel and, as in the British and French zone, it boiled down to determination of eligibility for UNRRA assistance rather than disclosure of collaborationist elements. See *Ibid.*, third report, CC (47) 11, 28 January 1947, 9 ff.

18. See OMGUS, *A Summary*, 184–185; UNRRA, *Reports . . . Resolution 92*, special report CC (47) 81, 12 June 1947, 6 (UNRRA disapproved of these organizations).

19. Byrnes had given this issue great emphasis. See James F. Byrnes, *Speaking Frankly* (New York 1947) 167–169. Throughout 1945 and most of 1946 the French desire to utilize labor services of almost a million PW's working in France was a major obstacle to repatriation. See also OMGUS, *A Summary*, 199.

20. *Ibid.*, 199–203; ACA, *Minutes of the Control Council*, Conl/M (48) 1, para. 4.

21. See for references, earlier Chapter VIII; Byrnes, *Speaking Frankly*, 166; OMGUS, *A Summary*, 269.

22. *Ibid.;* Clay, *Decision,* 155.

23. On the "Reuther affair," as it was called, see OMGUS, *ACA Enactments,* VII 78 ff.; Clay, *Decision,* 143 ff.; OMGUS, *Monthly Report of the Military Governor* June 1947, 42; Frank Howley, *Berlin Command* (New York, 1950), 142–145; *La France en Allemagne,* no. 6 (September, 1947), 79 ff.; *Ibid.,* no. 7 (November, 1947), 84 ff.

24. ACA, *Minutes of the Coordinating Committee,* Corc/M (47) 39, para. 435; *Minutes of the Control Council,* Conl/M (47) 19, para. 90.

25. ACA, *Minutes of the Coordinating Committee,* Corc/M (48) 3, para. 42; Sozialdemokratische Partei Deutschland, *Jahrbuch, 1947* (Hannover 1948), 30 ff.; Howley, *Berlin Command,* 152 ff.

26. The most prominent was the "Fried" case; the case of a Western sector official, Bliemister, arrested in the Soviet sector; and the Soviet-appointed Berlin police chief, Markgraf. ACA, Allied Kommandatura Berlin (hereafter cited AKB) *Minutes of the Commandants,* BKC/M (48) 7, para. 49; *La France en Allemagne,* No. 9 (November 1947) 89; Control Commission for Germany (British Element), *Monthly Report,* III (March 1948), 47 ff.

27. Howley, *Berlin Command,* 152 ff., 168 ff.; SPD *Jahrbuch,* 1947, 39–41; *Minutes of the Berlin Kommandatura* through March and April 1948; *La France en Allemagne,* no. 9 (November 1947), 89 ff., 94 ff.

28. See Bipartite Board, *Agreements with Soviet Authorities Concerning Supply of Coal and Power to Berlin,* BIB/P(47)131, 18 December 1947; ACA, AKB, *Report of Kommandatura Coal Receipts,* BK/R(48)44, 24 January 1948; ACA, AKB, *Implementation of Agreement on Supply of Fuel and Electricity,* BK/R(48)93, 13 March 1948.

29. For the history of action and discussion on this question from August 1947 through to February 1948, see ACA, AKB *Interzonal Trade Permits,* BK/R(48)80, 3 March 1948. The crucial action of requiring Soviet sector countersignature on Western sector interzonal trade permits was taken on 12 January 1948. See also *Die Städtischen Körperschaften in der Berliner Krise, Tatsachen und Dokumente* (a collection issued by the Berlin West Magistrat, 1949), 7 ff.

30. This would take the form of increased socialization, development of trading Kontors, stimulation of "mass" and union controls, increased police action and terrorization and other similar measures. Already at the second SED Congress in his basic report, *Brennende Fragen des Neuaufbaus Deutschlands* (Berlin, September, 1947), Ulbricht described the "Kampf dem Schiebertum"—"gegen des Schwarzen Markt, gegen die Kompensationsseuche und Korruption führen"—as one of the most urgent tasks in the Eastern zone. *Ibid.,* 18 ff. He called for a policy involving mobilization of unions, work councils and party members behind a campaign to obtain strict accounting for materials and product shipments. *Ibid.,* 29–31. Of course this campaign would probably have been called for even in a closed economy under such adverse conditions; but inner tensions and black marketing acquire another significance when the economic frontiers are open.

31. For some materials on this point, see W. Kling, "Der Kampf um das Volkseigentum," *Die Wirtschaft,* III (1948), 513–515; "Wirtschaftssabotage sächsischer Textil-Grosshändler," *Ibid.,* 549–550; "Die Warenbewegung muss vereinfact werden," *Ibid.,* IV (1949), 554 ff.

32. This was the kernel of Reuter's insistence at the time on "die Verbindung mit dem Westen"; without this "wäre die Stadt nicht nur politisch sondern auch wirtschaftlish verloren." Ernst Reuter, "Kommunele Aktion," *Das Sozialistische Jahrhundert*, II (May, 1948), 191–193.

33. Several available sources on the conference have been consulted in the preparation of this account. The best condensed day by day summary of the proceedings is that compiled by W. Cornides and H. Volle, "Die Londoner Aussenministerkonferenz der vier Grossmächte," *Europa-Archiv*, III (January, 1948), 1067–1086. This is cited hereafter as *Londoner Konferenz*. The full texts of Molotov's principle speeches can be found in V. M. Molotov, *Über den Friedensvertrag mit Deutschland* (a pamphlet compilation, Leipzig, 1948) (hereafter cited as Molotov *London Speeches*). Shorter Soviet comments or verbal exchanges may be found in the unusually full Tass and ADN accounts as reproduced in *Tägliche Rundschau*, 25 November–15 December 1947. A reliable textual account of the formal decisions of the conference may be found in OMGUS, *A Summary, passim*. American accounts on this, as on other events dealing with Germany in a public setting, have been exhaustively set forth in the weekly digest of press opinion, *Civil Affairs in Occupied and Liberated Territories* (prepared by Analysis Branch, Public Information Division, Department of the Army), nos. 193, 194, 195 (4, 11, 18 December 1947). *New York Times* reports especially those by Middleton and Mathews, are sometimes informative. Clay's account (*Decision*, 344–349) is impressionistic. On the French side there is available a documentary history of the conference which contains the texts of the main papers and speeches, including several of Bidault's which are available only in summarized form elsewhere. Ministére des Affaires Étrangères, *Notes, Documentaries et Études*, "La Conference de Londres," no. 868, 1 April 1948. The best secondary source summary is that of the Council on Foreign Relations, *The United States in World Affairs, 1947/48* (prepared by John C. Campbell and staff, New York, 1948), 459–467.

34. See Molotov, *London Speeches*, 5–11.

35. For text of Marshall's statement made on 10 December 1947, see *NY Times*, 11 December. Emphasis is given the statement by the fact that it was made outside the proper order of discussion as indicated by the fact that Molotov did not reply and by the fact that the specific subject under discussion was para. XX–XXII of the British paper dealing with occupation deficits and their mode of repayment. See *Londoner Konferenz*, 1080. American preoccupation with the reparations issue was also indicated by the fact that Marshall had raised it—prematurely—during the two-day debate on agenda. Picking up a reference to the reparations problem from one of Molotov's diatribes, he asked if the payment of the ten billion dollars in reparations was a Soviet condition for a settlement. If the interpretation were correct, Marshall asked his Soviet colleague to "state specifically how he would propose for the German people to meet such an obligation. Perhaps the answer to these two questions will enable us to leave generalities and engage in discussion which may enable us to make some progress." See text of statement, *NY Times*, 6 December 1947.

36. *Tägliche Rundschau*, 13 December 1947. See OMGUS, *A Summary*, 232, for texts of proposals constituting the basis for discussion.

37. For the text of the speech, see *New York Times*, 13 December 1947; Molotov, *London Speeches*, 32–40.

38. See *Londoner Konferenz*, 1083. The occasion of Marshall's comment, stated Clay, "was the only time I ever saw Molotov wince perceptibly." Clay, *Decision*, 348.

39. *Londoner Konferenz*, 1083–1085; *New York Times*, 16 December 1947; and for the long British speech, see France, *Notes*, "La Conference de Londres," 33–35.

40. See interview with Dulles on 15 December reported in N.Y. *Herald Tribune*, European edition, 17 December 1947; *N.Y. Times*, 14, 16 December 1947; Clay, *Decision*, 211; France, *Notes*, "Accords Franco-Anglo-Americains sur le charbon," 5–6. Coke exports in 1936 totalled 6.8 million tons or 22% of total coal exports and coke export tonnage during 1946 and 1947 was 3.3 million tons. The agreement stipulated that upon recovery of daily output in Germany to 300,000 daily tons, some 7.6 million tons of coke would be exported and with a further rise of coal output 8.4 million tons of coke would be exported. See analysis in Deutsche Kohlenbergbauteitung, *The Coal Economy in the Year 1947 and Towards the End of the Winter 1947/8* (Essen, March 1948—mimeographed), 58. On the agreement and the August-September 1947 conference which it grew out of, see also *The Uinted States in World Affairs 1947/8*, 93 ff.; Clay, *Decision*, 321 f. On the whole development, see *The United States in World Affairs 1947/8*, 461 ff., 467 ff. For action on Saar, see France, *Notes*, "Accords . . . sur le charbon," 7–8; Bipartite Board, *Minutes*, Bib/M(48)3, para. 288; Bipartite Control Office, *Trade Negotiations with the Saar—Coal Deliveries*, BICO/Sec(48)359, 11 June 1948.

41. See the following articles: "Germans in West Draft Plan Giving Them Added Powers," *New York Times*, 16 December 1948; "Germans Drafting Federation Plans," *Ibid.*, 14 December 1947; "Politicians Plan Zone Government," *Ibid.*, 17 December 1947.

42. For brief notice see *The United States in World Affairs 1947/8*, 464 ff.; Clay, *Decision*, 178 ff.; and the detailed commentaries on this agreement given in contemporary Congressional hearings.

43. See OMGUS, *Evolution of Bizonal Organization* (Civil Administration Division, 1948) 7–12; Clay, *Decision*, 177–184; Bipartite Control Office, *Memorandum Presented to Military Governors by the President of the Bizonal Economic Council on January 8, 1948*, Bico/Sec(48)16. The document commences by declaring: "The London Conference has failed to bring about the reunion of the Zones of Occupation longed for by all Germans and indispensable to both Germany's and Europe's political and economic recovery." This disappointment brings preparations "made for the recovery" in Bizonia. "If the danger is to be met measures must immediately be initiated which will give the population . . . assurance that hope for improvement . . . has not vanished." Among these were listed labor enactments, removal of transport restrictions, certain aspects of coal export policy too delicate to mention publicly, tax reform, and above all monetary reform.

44. ". . . Ist es an der Zeit klar zu erkennen und ebenso klar auszusprechen dass die angliederung der Sowjetbesatzungszone an die Bizone, das heisst an das System monopolkapitalischer . . . kolonialpolitik, das deutsche Elend nur vergrössern wurde . . . Die Hoffnung auf eine gesamtdeutsche Regelung durch einen gerechten Friedensvertrag für Deutschland ist durch das Verhalten der West-

mächte geringer geworden." We must accordingly change our line, our policy perspectives; we must speed up denazification, cut occupation costs, convert our zonal agencies into a central government, etc. See Grotewohl, *Im Kampf um Deutschland*, II, 328, 329, 335. This speech, "Was Müssen Wir Tun?" was also published in the *Tägliche Rundschau*, 11 February 1948. Although this statement was not highly publicized, it marked, along with the formation of the Volkskongress and the sharpening of the propaganda attack—much of it raucous and crude—a decisive turn in the life of the eastern zone.

45. ACA, *Minutes of the Coordinating Committee*, Corc/M(48)2, 3, paras. 29(c), 38.

46. The history of the coal price action in the ACA would make an interesting monograph, for it was the result of a meandering round of negotiations, papers, conferences on a unilateral British level, an internal US level (chiefly price control and finance), a U.S.-British level, a tripartite level, and then on the ACA level in two directorates and their respective committees. For the history of the problem through July, 1947, see OMGUS, "Brief to Director of Finance Division accompanying Price Policy Committee Report on Ruhr-Coal Pricing," (Finance Division July 1947—typewritten). For the final paper, see ACA, *British Memorandum on the Increase in the Price of Hard Coal*, Corc/P(48)12; ACA, *Minutes of the Coordinating Committee*, Corc/M(48)2, 3, paras. 27, 36.

47. C. J. Friedrich, in his "Rebuilding of the German Constitution," *American Political Science Review*, XLIII (1949), 468 states that this was pushed by the British. Evidence on the record does not point in this direction. Clay (*Decision*, 211) merely states that Bevin and Marshall jointly instructed Robertson and Clay to "make a last effort . . . to obtain quadripartite agreement." Clay's initiative in designing the specific reform proposal and in sponsoring its presentation in the Control Council and the Clay-Robertson exchange at the Bipartite Board meeting concerned suggest that Clay more than Robertson was the initiator. See Bipartite Board, *Minutes*, "Currency Reform," BIB/M(48)3, para. 291.

48. See reports in the *New York Times* and *New York Herald Tribune* as collected in *Civil Affairs in Occupied and Liberated Territory*, no. 204, 19 February 1948, 9, 11, 17; *Ibid.*, no. 205, 15.

49. See earlier references and discussion, Chapter VI, p. 112 f.

50. In fact it may be said that virtually complete agreement was reached on terms for conversion, allocation of currency to occupying powers, handling of banking and insurance, and some components of a *Lastenausgleich*. Clay's memory perhaps does him wrong when he asserts that "our new proposal in the A.C.A. did not meet with direct Soviet refusal but with their usual delaying tactics." Clay, *Decision*, 211.

51. According to Jack Bennett, agreement was complete except for a Soviet demand for the creation of a "German central department of finance." J. Bennett, "The German Currency Reform," *Annals of the American Academy of Political and Social Science*, Vol. 267, 45. A long and manifestly inspired editorial outlining the Soviet position, appearing in the *Tägliche Rundschau* at the time, stipulated the creation of a central bank and of a central finance ministry as forerunners for the other central administrative agencies. The Soviets obviously were trying to use the necessary German organization to handle monetary reform as a wedge to lead

to German unification and evinced no concern with the possibilities for a limited monetary union.

52. See Clay's version of the entire incident, *Decision,* 355–357; OMGUS, *Monthly Report of the Military Governor,* March 1948, 1–2.

53. Accomplishments were so few and the sparring so intense that the Soviets were able to call off meetings of the lower organs of the Kommandatura on 2 April 1948. See *La France en Allemagne,* no. 10 (October 1948), 49. See also HICOG, *Berlin: Development of its Government and Administration* (prepared by E. Plischke, Historical Division, 1952) 38 ff.

54. See earlier in this chapter, p. 174 and see the documentary collection, *Die Städtischen Körperschaften in der Berliner Krise,* 7 ff.; Deutsches Institut, *Berlins Wirtschaft in der Blockade,* 69 ff.

55. See Clay, *Decision,* 359 ff. Somewhat reluctantly, the French and British followed suit. See Great Britain, *Germany: An Account of the Events Leading up to a Reference of the Berlin Question to the UN* (White Paper, CMD 7534, 11 October 1948), 15 ff.

56. Control Commission for Germany (BE), *Monthly Report,* "Berlin Air Disaster," III (April, 1948), 16–19.

NOTES FOR CHAPTER X

1. See earlier Chap. I, p. 21 ff.

2. Soviet currency was derogatorily labelled "Klebemark" or "Tapetenmark" (wall-paper currency).

3. The dominant group in the Magistrat and particularly Dr. F. Friedensburg belatedly in May 1948 saw catastrophe approaching and made every effort to hold it off. See his work, *Berlin-Schicksal und Aufgabe* (Berlin 1953) 25 f., 29 f. For a summary account see W. P. Davison, *The Berlin Blockade* (Rand Corp., 1958) 78 ff. For documentary citations see Magistrat von Gross-Berlin, *Die Städtischen Körperschaften in der Berliner Krise, Tatsachen und Dokumente* (Berlin, 1949), 12–19. Friedensburg asserted in the debate immediately following that he and his associates had "bewusst und planmässig darauf verzichtet, rechtzeitig eine besondere Berliner Währungsreform vorzubereiten" (p. 18). A tendency to recommend a separate Berlin currency may be found in a very thoughtful and well-informed article by a Berlin Social-Democrat, H. Zank, "Berliner Gulden," *Das Sozialistische Jahrhundert,* May 1948, p. 211–212. A well-informed Berlin economist writing in an official report in West-Germany stated that Berlin circles strongly leaned to a currency-partition and the West-Berlin inclusion in the West-German reform. This program was "stark propagiert." The currency specialist for the Berlin Tagesspiegel asserted (see issue of 23 June, "Währungsgespräche") "for months" he advocated this solution to facilitate trade with the West, to be consistent with the desired economic structure of Berlin and for political-psychological reasons. This solution was also desired on the West-German side. The Frankfurt Economic Council on being informed that Western reform action was imminent officially resolved that "rapid preparations must be made to include the city of Berlin in currency reform." Folder 29, *Economic Council,* 17th Plenary Meeting, 15 June, p. 3. On the Eastern side H. Acker, an SED Berlin finance leader, rejected as unsound an independent

Berlin currency and argued strongly that Berlin should use Eastern currency. See *Berliner Zeitung* 6 May 1848.

4. Clay, *Decision In Germany*, p. 364. According to J. Bennett, the American financial representative at the quadripartite conference of 22 June 1948 (on it see n6 below), suggested a separate Berlin currency issued under the Kommandatura. J. Bennett, "The German Currency Reform," *Annals of the American Academy of Political and Social Science*, v. 267 (1950) 51 f.

5. Failure to give the Soviets more advance notice, however well motivated by the need to achieve surprise, greatly offended Soviet sensibilities and violated the code of comity which plays a role in facilitating joint work and successful negotiation. Even Colonel Howley thought that failure to inform the Russians "gave them a very good excuse for a walkout." F. Howley, *Berlin Command* (N.Y. 1950) 180. Marshal Sokolovsky informed General Clay that the lack of prior notice put "the Soviet occupation authorities in a difficult position" and compelled immediacy of response. Ministry of Foreign Affairs of the USSR, *The Soviet Union and the Berlin Question* (Moscow, 1948) [hereafter cited as SU, *Berlin Crisis*] p. 26. The Western action was the more disagreeable since the main principles for an all-German solution had been quadripartitely worked out since quadripartite negotiations had at American initiative been carried on through to 20 March 1948. See Chap. VI above, p. 113 f. for details. All this while the West was printing a separate currency and planning for a separate Western reform. Sokolovsky in his quite personal letter to Clay indirectly reproached the American General by stating that the Soviet authorities "favored the currency reform for the whole of Germany that was being prepared within the framework of the Control Council, but for political and moral considerations it did not think it possible to make preparations for a separate currency reform in its own zone" (*ibid.*, p. 28). The Western authorities did think it possible—"their morals and ours"—and thereby committed what, if the positions were reversed, Americans would call a treacherous act or even a kind of Pearl Harbor. Americans after all still feel indignant about the unannounced Japanese attack on their naval base even though the general order of the attack was suspected by an alert intelligence. Actually Clay arranged for printing of the separate Western currency during October 1947 (Clay, *Decision*, p. 211).

6. This last "futile round" of quadripartite negotiation was held between financial representatives of the Military Governors on 22 June to endeavor to take agreed action on Berlin currency reform. Apparently, at the conference the West, at French instigation and insistent urging, offered to accept the Eastern mark (a) if it would be introduced under quadripartite auspices (i.e. as a Kommandatura order), (b) if it would be equally applied throughout the city, (c) if the Western rights to the mark proceeds of the imported food and fuel sold in West-Berlin would be appropriately handled. These three conditions to acceptance of the Eastmark are indicated. They are mentioned in Clay's account (*op. cit.*, p. 364), in authorized French accounts (*N.Y. Times*, H. Callender, 24 June, 1948) and in the Soviet news release (DNA) on the meeting (see *Tägliche Rundschau*, 24 June 1948). Clay also asserts that in the meeting the West asked for "a trade agreement which would not place the industry of Berlin under Soviet domination." (p. 364). But this explosive issue would have been out of context and in Bennett's account (see "The German Currency Reform," *loc. cit.*, 51 f.) neither this issue is mentioned or that of the import

proceeds. But Bennett adds that the "Kommandatura or some other four power body" might determine the amount of new money from the East to be issued in the city "as well as the terms of conversion and city banking policy in the conversion." According to this account the West offered only to accept the Soviet zone currency and not the law under which the currency was issued and which controlled the terms and quantity of its issuance. In the published news release (published in NYC papers 24 June) the West claimed that "The SMA insisted that it alone would write the currency law for the city of Berlin." Furthermore the SMA refused to recognize the prerogatives of the Kommandatura "as the supreme law-making body of Berlin." But if the West wanted to quadripartitely fix the amount of currency that could be drawn out of the Soviet zone treasury it was seeking, in a way, to trespass on Soviet rights. In the Soviet-inspired news release, the Soviet financial delegate, Maletin, at the meeting is quoted as asserting: "'Wir warnen sowohl Sie also such die deutsche Bevölkerung von Berlin dass wir wirtschaftliche und administrative Sanktionen anwenden werden, die den Übergang zu einer einzigen Währung in Berlin—der Währung der sowjetischen Besatzungszone—erzwingen werden.'" Thus was the West threatened. Apparently the representatives engaged in a "sharp discussion" of the principle of a Kommandatura, i.e. of the four-power regime for the city, and Maletin is quoted as having argued that the Kommandatura regime disappeared with Western partition. However, Maletin was willing to concede that the Western powers should remain in Berlin. Thus he thought that the problem of handling Western subsidized food and fuel imports could be handled under some clearing scheme. "Die Verrechnungen für diese Vier-Mächte-Lieferungen nach Berlin erfolgen durch Buchungen auf die Konten der Militärverwaltungen." Finally, the original American report of the conference stated that the Soviet position allowed for Kommandatura "recommendations" on the financial-reform law; this position only claimed that "the final arbiter would remain the Soviet Command." From all this it seems that the Soviets had developed an aggressive position, but that the Western delegates or at least the Americans developed certain issues provocatively.

7. Letter of Ltnt. Gen. Lukjantschenkos to Major Schroeder, *Tägliche Rundschau,* 23 June 1948.

8. The basic fact that payment relations of Berlin with the East Zone were favorable and increased the deposit balances maintained in Berlin, was demonstrated by the author in a memo 24 June, "The Currency Reform Crisis in Berlin" addressed to General Clay and Mr. L. Wilkinson, his Economic Advisor. I quote para. 8: "Once the reform is carried through a quite different order of question emerges, namely, the subsequent administration of monetary and credit policy in the city. This question in turn subdivides into three: (a) the possible need for additional currency, (b) rules for banking policy, and (c) administration of banking policy. While the initial currency and bank deposit "quota" of Berlin as given by the reform may be adequate in the first instance, suppose Berlin needs additional currency in the future. On what terms and conditions may it receive credits from the Sovzone Central Bank? Fortunately this dangerous situation is not likely to arise and it is accordingly not necessary at the present time to achieve guarantees that it would be properly handled. Additional currency needs may arise in three ways: (1) export of currency to the West, (2) export to Sovzone, or (3) greater internal needs. Item

(1) can be eliminated as the Berlin deficit with the Western trade must be financed by Western subsidy and not by currency shipments. Item (3) can probably be met by credit and deposit expansion, or other-wise by officially restricting price and wage increases. This leaves item (2), a payment deficit with the Sovzone. The experience of 1946 and 1947 indicate that just the opposite is likely to occur: not a payment deficit but a payment surplus. During 1946 the bank clearing account between Berlin and Sovzone were approximately balanced; during 1947 there was a payment surplus of about 2 billion RM. This surplus resulted partly from large export of "services" of Berlin to Sovzone, meeting large payrolls here but also due to net inflow of remittances, capital transfers, deposits of government reserves and the like. As all the causes which produced this favorable balance are not likely to disappear, the monetary and banking situation in Berlin would be correspondingly eased. It is accordingly suggested that worry over meeting future currency deficits need not block agreement now." In a basic canvass of the problem of Berlin currency reform an able West-German economic expert, writing on 12 June 1948 gave a full analysis of the Berlin-East-Germany payment balance.

9. See my memo cited n. 8 above.

10. On this see Clay, *Decision*, Ch. 19, 20; and Davison, *Berlin Blockade*, 83 ff., 103 ff., 149 ff., 231 f.

11. This was in fact the central contention of a little booklet, *Berlin Crisis and an Honourable German Peace Settlement* (October, 1948, privately mimeographed and privately circulated). The author served as the US member of a Tripartite working party set up to investigate and report on the trade deficit of West Berlin and the means for its financing. See Report 30 July 1948. "It is possible to imagine the evacuation of Berlin within the framework of a negotiation and against a counterpart," wrote M. Schuman, president of PRP in *Aube*, newspaper organ of PRP. *N.Y. Times*, H. Callender, 28 June, 1948. Ambassador B. Smith felt that however great the need to remain in Berlin as a "temporary measure" that "it was a liability to be disposed of at the first auspicious moment." Clay, *Decision*, 376. Even in U.S. Hqs. in Berlin for several weeks after the blockade had started, there were still "discussions about the advisability of withdrawing from Berlin," (Davison, *Blockade*, 150).

12. The messages are quoted or summarized in Clay, *Decision* 361 ff.; and Davison, *Blockade*, 71–75, 149 ff.

13. An initial West-German reluctance Davison summarizes as follows: "If the London Recommendations had been the only major issue in June and July of 1948, the Western powers would have faced a group of sullen parliaments and a recalcitrant Economic Council in West Germany," *Blockade*, 283. The German opposition to the London Settlement was complexly motivated and was partly demagogic. It was rather easily dissipated. See Clay, *Decision*, 409 ff.

14. *N.Y. Times*, 27 June, 1948. J. Kaiser in a barnstorming speech in Munich proclaimed "The Russians need Berlin to completely control the eastern zone." *Munich American*, 15 August 1948.

15. Walter Lippmann, *The Cold War* (London, 1947), p. 28.

16. *Germany 1947–1949*, 271; for summary details of *Report of the Bank Deutscher Länder* [BDL] *1948 and 1949* (Frankfurt A/M, 1950) p. 37–40.

17. The Magistrat legally approved carrying out both the Eastern and Western reform plans in the city and the unrestricted use of both currencies. The West virtually requested the use of Eastmarks. Eastmarks comprised the bulk of the circulating currency of West-Berlin. See Deutsches Institut für Wirtschaftsforschung, *Berlins Wirtschaft in der Blockade* (Sonderhefte N.f. Heft 3, Berlin, 1949) 80 f.; *Die Städtischen Körperschaften,* 19–23; *Report BDL 1948–9,* 37. Eastmark deposits made up 65% of total deposits in West-Berlin banks in Dec. 1948. *Berlin 1948 Jahresbericht des Magistrats* (Berlin 1950) p. 75. Contemporary newspaper accounts indicate that the Berliners were thriving in the first week of the new money on the double conversion. Davison reports Berliners "were instructed also to exchange a part of their old currency for Eastmarks." p. 132. *Die Berliner Zeitung* of 25 June reports that West Berliners were privileged to convert currency in East-Berlin and "on the first day this privilege has been widely used." "Everybody was trading money, trying to get rid of old marks and looking for hard currency or real property." "The news of the total blockade at first was lost in the confusion which the currency reform brought with it. We were all so occupied with questions as to where and how we would change our money, should we also change money in East Berlin, will we have enough money to get along, and so on . . ." (Davison, *Blockade,* 133–4). The East-German monetary authorities were apparently scrupulous in converting according to their published law the 1.2 billion RM of Magistrat balances into 300 million Eastmarks. *Berlin 1948,* p. 148. Of the total reported Eastmark issuance of 4.1 billion DM, West-Berlin probably received its near per-capita share, 16%. Gunther Kohlmey, *Das Geldsystem der Deutschen Demokratischen Republik* (Berlin 1956) p. 31. This indicates by the way that Berlin economics could exert a potent monetary influence in East-German economic life.

18. See editorials in *Tagesspiegel* July 4 ("Berliner Währungskrieg"), July 7 ("Der Weg der D-Mark"), July 6 ("Die Lage"), July 14 ("Westberlin fordert"). The political opposition was here clearly dominant. But the Berliners also objected to a certain tendency toward *stinginess* in Western currency policy, i.e. a concern lest excessive amounts of currency be issued in Berlin. The West-Berliners did not merely want a Valuta-currency which would be used chiefly for black market purchases. "The 25% rule is neither politically nor economically bearable." The symbolic and political aspects of the case were uppermost in a petition of German business organizations to American Military Government (See Davison, *Blockade,* p. 233 f.). Of course the people wanted to be paid in Westmarks and to spend chiefly Eastmarks. As early as November 3 the Magistrat by resolution requested that the Westmark be installed in West-Berlin (see *ibid.,* 262 ff.). See also E. Trost, "Die Berliner Währung," *Zeitschrift für das gesamte Kreditwesen* (1948, heft 10, 225–6).

19. *Berlins Wirtschaft Blockade,* p. 111.

20. It must not be forgotten that in July 1948 private business men controlled many factories, most of the small shops and most wholesale and retail trade; these business men were generally sympathetic with the West, had connections with Berlin and doubtless did much to feed supplies into West Berlin while, in the process, obtaining black market prices or the precious West-German currency. The wholesale traders particularly, though set up with 51% public funds, in many cases

diverted products, so charged Ulbricht, to the black market and to West-Berlin. Ulbricht cited alarming reports of field investigations concerning disappearances of shoes, leather, textiles and other commodities. W. Ulbricht, *Lehrbuch für den Demokratischen Staats—und Wirtschaftsaufbau* (Berlin 1949) 104–107. In East-German plans a large role was still left for private business and SED worked only through a bloc policy (cf. p. 236 f.).

21. Davison, *Blockade,* p. 196.

22. *Ibid.,* 196 ff., 325.

23. Blocking of deposits accounts continued long after the restrictions on trade were removed. This subject deserves careful research. Cf. R. C. Loehr, *The West German Banking System* (Historical Division, HICOG, 1952) p. 110.

24. Clay, *Decision,* 374.

25. For Clay's proposal see *idem.* Truman in his *Memoirs,* v. II (1956) describes the deliberations of the American War Council meeting on 22 July 1948 to decide whether to reinforce the airlift or to attempt to push through to Berlin with "armed convoys" (p. 124–7). The fateful decision—the world hovered on the brink of catastrophe—was for the airlift as involving "less risk" (p. 126).

26. Elmer Plischke, *Berlin: Development of its Government and Administration* (Historical Division, HICOG, 1952), p. 148. The process of governmental split is faithfully described in Davison, *Blockade,* 201–219, 229–235.

27. Davison, *Blockade,* 206.

28. *Ibid.,* 208.

29. *Ibid.,* 200–209.

30. *Ibid.,* 202.

31. The negotiations can best be followed through document collections, memoirs and monographs. Of basic importance are the three "White papers": SU, *Berlin Crisis;* the British paper, *Germany, An Account of the Events Leading Up To a Reference of the Berlin Question to the United Nations,* Cmd 7534, 11 Oct., 1948 [cited as Br, *Berlin Crisis*]; U.S. Dept. of State. *The Berlin Crisis* (pub. no. 3298 Sept. 1948 [cited as US, *Berlin Crisis*]. The important memoir accounts are: Clay, *Decision,* 369–376, 379; T. Lie, *In the Cause of Peace* (N.Y., 1954) Ch. XII, "Mediation in Berlin," J. F. Dulles' *War or Peace* (N.Y. 1950) Ch. XI; See also *Germany 1947–1949,* 207–272. Reliable secondary accounts can be found in Boris Meissner, *Russland, Die Westmächte und Deutschland* (Hamburg, 1953) 170–189; Council on Foreign Relations, *The United States in World Affairs 1948–49* (N.Y. 1949) pp. 133–149, 452–464; 1949 (N.Y. 1950) 33–45; and Davison, *Blockade,* 158 ff., 183 f., 237 ff., 225 f., 264–275. Soviet views at the publicist level are fully reported in *New Times.*

32. This paraphrases a Soviet paraphrase of the famous thesis of Clausewitz: "If war is a continuation of politics, only by other means, so also peace is a continuation of struggle, only by other means." Cited in H. A. Kissinger, *Nuclear Weapons and Foreign Policy* (Anchor ed., 1958), p. 65.

33. G.B., *Berlin Crisis,* p. 48, 52.

34. At least this was the Washington estimate of the situation. See Truman, *Memoirs,* II, 243 ff.; Davison, *Blockade,* 156 f., 241 f.; the *U.S. World Affairs 1948–9,* 512 ff. See for a non-quantitative but first-hand appraisal of Western defense capabilities on 6 Oct. 1949 when NATO became activated with American

military assistance the 4th semi-annual report to congress on the *Mutual Defense Assistance Program,* 14 Feb., 1952, 82C, 25, HD 352, p. 17 ff. Kissinger probably overstates the degree to which the Soviet minimization of the significance of the atomic bomb was wholly a matter of "iron discipline" and "cold-blooded effrontery" as was involved in Stalin's claim that "atomic bombs are intended to frighten people with weak nerves but they cannot decide the outcome of a war." (Kissinger, *op. cit.,* p. 81 ff.). After all our high-ranking naval officers in 1949 pleaded before a Congressional Committee that strategic area bombing could not under existing conditions render decisive service in a war against the USSR, that anti-aircraft defenses would greatly hamper unescorted bomber sorties, that bombing precision at high altitudes was crude, that radar defenses were well-developed, and that the size of the area devastated by atomic bomb was vastly overrated. See Committee on Armed Services, House of Representatives, 81C, 1st S., Hearings, *The National Defense Program—Unification and Strategy,* Oct. 6–21, 1949; and Committee Report, *Unification and Strategy* 81C, 2nd S, House Doc. 600, Mar. 1, 1950.

34a. Lord Strang, *Home and Abroad* (London 1956) 298.

35. In a slightly veiled form Acheson made this clear in his 29 April 1949 pledge that "this Government will agree to no general solution for Germany into which the basic safeguards and benefits of the existing Western German arrangements would not be absorbed." *Germany 1947–1949,* p. 20. It was not until the May-June CFM meeting that the West actually proposed to unify Germany by asking for the East-German states to "join" the Bonn Government. *N.Y. Times* text, 29 May, 1949.

36. The Soviets attempted to justify this publicly by arguing that unregulated trade would "practically mean opening broad channels for every sort of speculative trade transaction in the Western sectors of Berlin, which might do irreparable damage both to the economy and to the currency of the Soviet zone and Berlin." The "uncontrolled import and export of commodities . . . would have the effect of turning Berlin into a centre of currency and commodity speculation . . . which would be bound to result in the complete disorganization of economic life in the Soviet zone." SU, *Berlin Crisis,* 77, 82. This tendency to disorganization would exist in a unified city with open channels of trade and access to Eastern Germany. But if the Western Berlin enclaves were partitioned off by frontier controls and a *cordon sanitaire,* then a free Western hand in West Berlin would not be critical for the fate of East-Germany though it would probably entail some diversion of resources via black marketing and capital flight.

37. The first chief of the Marshall Plan once asserted that "counterpart funds as you know constitute the only recovery fund" and "we trade dollars for counterparts." Cf. U.S. Congress, House of Representatives, *Foreign Aid Appropriation Bill for 1950.* Hearings before the subcommittee of the Committee on Appropriations, 81 Cong., 1st sess. (Washington, 1949) 54 ff. Control over counterpart funds was an unprecedented penetration of foreign power with distinct control and guidance overtones and it was recognized and treated as such. The American Congress was first "tempted," as Kindelberger has put it, to assert complete control over these funds and their use in the participating countries. See C. P. Kindelberger, *International Economics* (1953) 484. But only in Germany did America assert predominant control over the detailed use of the counterpart funds. In England

they were, aside from a 5% quota, quietly sterilized. The degree of influence and of utilization of the funds in other countries varied from case to case. See for muffled accounts H. P. Ellis, *The Economics of Freedom* (1950) 12–14, 273 ff., 319 f., 213 ff. In West Berlin the American-controlled German agencies played a crucial role in guiding investment programs in Berlin and in underwriting American influence in the city. See Hubert G. Schmidt, *Economic Assistance to West Berlin 1949–1951* (Historical Division, HICOG, 1952) chapters 2–4. This predominance in using counterpart funds owed to the master role of occupying power. A like predominance was achieved in the Soviet zone of Germany through analogous relationships involving varying degrees of direct penetration into the economic and social life of the occupied community. The 1949 Amendment to the ECA Act declared that "there should be no doubt" that uses of counterpart funds "are related also to the 'declaration of policy' which opens up American influence to the full range of policymaking comprehended by the program." See U.S. Congress, Senate, *Extension of European Recovery Program*, Report of the Committee on Foreign Relations, Report No. 100, March 8, 1949, p. 14. The quarterly reports of the ECA Administration give a valuable account of the use of counterpart funds which, as the 8th Report asserted, "played an important role in the progress toward the economic recovery of Western Europe." See ECA *Eighth Report to Congress* (Quarter ending March 31, 1950, D.C. 1950) p. 78 f.

38. Use of the counterpart funds was posed as a distinct issue only in the Berlin September negotiations between the Berlin Zone Commanders though the issue was not discussed. See BR, *Berlin Crisis*, p. 57. But in their 14 September communication the Western Powers asserted for the first time the "right of each of the occupying powers to control the proceeds from food and fuel imported for the use of the Berlin population and industry," (*ibid.*, 59). In a later statement of "clarification" of their position the Soviets obliquely proposed to make the cost of imported food and fuel a "liability" of the Berlin city government which consistently therewith, under quadripartite direction, would have had the disposal of the funds. An interesting compromise was suggested by the UN Committee of Neutral Experts who proposed that the counterpart funds could be used to finance occupation expenses not financed on Berlin budgets and deficit budgetary expenditures but must otherwise be used only with four-power agreement. See *Germany 1947–1949*, p. 240, 255.

39. This summary reduces the formal language of diplomacy to its lowest common denominator power-equivalent. There perhaps was a tendency for Stalin— who showed up in the negotiations as unusually astute, efficient and open—to concede a larger measure of control over Berlin currency and Soviet zone central bank operations than the final Soviet agreement permitted. Was he overruled by his Politburo colleagues, as has been suggested? And was this Politburo controversy on this subject a cause of Zhdanov's sudden death on 29 August, just as the Moscow negotiations concluded? Did the protest of the German Soviet field command stiffen up Soviet policy?

40. For this safeguard which would involve "appropriate controls . . . over economic intercourse between [Eastern] areas and Western Berlin," latterly conceded, see *Germany 1947–1949*, p. 267, 269.

41. The original Western proposals would ensure access to Soviet Zone currency to provide "adequate funds for budgetary purposes and occupation costs."

The Soviets countered by asking that Berlin budgets be balanced and that occupation costs be borne by zonal budgets. The British report of the 2nd round of discussions with Stalin asserted that the Western delegates "showed a similar desire to be helpful over the Soviet desire to reduce occupation costs and to balance the Berlin city budget." The American report makes no such allegation. Exercising skill in reconciling divergent policies, Stalin produced a draft which ultimately was reduced to the following near-nonsense: Financial arrangements in Berlin shall ensure "the provision of sufficient currency for budgetary purposes and for occupation costs reduced to the greatest extent possible and also the balancing of the Berlin budget." BR, *Berlin Crisis,* 36, 56. Occupation expenses in '46–7 in Berlin were estimated at 363 million RM for recognized expenses only and 460 million RM for the total, or some 20% of tax revenues; in the summer of 1948 they were running at 300 million marks. See E. Wolf, "Aufwendungen f.d. Besatz . . .," DIW, *Wirtschaftsprobleme der Besatzungszonen* (1948) 120, 126, 128; see "Report on the Trade Deficit of West-Berlin," cf. 11 above. The occupation expenses for the American element alone in 1950, including all occupation-induced expenses, ran to 58 million DM; and this bill was incurred when the city was under our management and we had a full incentive, so to speak, for economy. See Schmidt, *Economic Assistance to West Berlin 1949–1951,* p. 95. Manifestly, to request the Soviets to finance our lavish living in the city and our large facilities was to add insult to injury.

42. The episode is worth citing in full. "Because of the urgency of West-Berlin requirements and the need of definitely settling the matter of Berlin participation in the investment program, ECA negotiators asked that there be included in the agreement a statement of the responsibility for the West German Federal Republic to provide West Berlin with such amounts of Deutsche Mark as may . . . be required for the economic maintenance and development of that area." The West German negotiators were understandably reluctant to make a promise which might be hard to keep if literally interpreted. "Their persistent objections led in the end to a considerable modification of the draft agreement wording." The modified draft clause promised such aid as it might be found expedient to give in negotiated agreements. Schmidt, *Economic Assistance to West Berlin,* 6–7.

43. For explanation of the "access" problem in terms of "keeping-in-step" with Soviet zone credit expansion, see *Germany 1947–9,* p. 267.

44. There is some indication that the British and French position on this subject was less aggressive than the American. Thus a French-British proposal tabled on 7 Sept. 1948 would have confined the "control" of the Berlin Kommandatura to "approval" of an agreement to be negotiated between the all-Berlin Stadtkontor and the zonal central bank. But the Berlin Stadtkontor was a Magistrat institution. Thus the proposal would have shifted the problem of negotiation and of safeguards partly to the German level. But still "in the exercise" of its functions the Soviet Zone Central bank "shall act under the control of the Finance Commission and will furnish the Commission with such relevant statistics as it may need for its purposes." *Germany 1947–9* 237 f. The cloven hoof of hostile intention stands out even in this "mild" document.

45. Interestingly, the central bank system and the whole banking regime of West Germany was shaped by direct military edict and law. The central bank

(BDL) constituted by allied authority, was controlled in its policy-making decisions by direct allied order. Long after an ostensible self-governing West-German government was established, its central bank operated under the direct control of an Allied Commission. For the persistence of this control see the valuable and revealing monograph by R. C. Loehr, *The West German Banking System* (Hist. Div., HICOG, 1952). Loehr notes that "In the background" of the operation of the BDL "was the Allied Bank Commission, constantly reviewing the activities of the bank, and encouraging, supporting or admonishing the bank officials according to the exigencies of the situation," p. 24.

46. With his keen eye for power positions Clay felt that "the most significant comment he [Stalin] made was that, without reservation, he did not object to four-power control of the German Bank of Emission . . . Stalin's comment was not incorporated in the written directive despite utmost effort by the representatives of the Western Powers." Clay then makes the revealing comment that "Our insistence in Berlin that the final agreement reflect this comment led in large part to the breakdown of negotiations." Clay, *Decision*, p. 369–370. However, this is not sinister in intent. Clay knew the Soviet Foreign Office "had no intention of really permitting quadripartite control of this bank for any purpose." Clay was not striving to obtain control over the East Zone. But he wanted to maintain an effective Western position in Berlin; and if this were to be done in a unified city linked with Eastern currency then Clay would not shirk this most audacious demand out of delicacy of feeling. But Clay was quite content to accept control of West-Berlin on a let-alone, leave alone basis.

47. SU, *Berlin Crisis*, p. 69. The Soviet foreign office added that this was done "with the ultimate intention of forcing the USSR to withdraw" from its zone. (*Ibid.*, p. 55–6.)

48. Lie, *In the Cause of Peace*, 206. A UN Secretariat member thought "there had rarely been so small a difficulty in so major an international dispute." (p. 204.) But what seem like banking technicalities from a distance or in the ordinary functioning of a liberal-bourgeois society make up a vital agency in the power-structure of the society. Perhaps this reflects an ancient canon of political science that political power in a state is indivisible and must have a single locus of ultimate authority.

49. The main documents involved in the work of the Committee of Experts may be found in *Germany 1947–1949*, 230–271; see also Lie, *ibid.*, 214 ff.; Davison, *op. cit.*, 243–249. All honor is due to G. Myrdal and his associates for *trying*.

50. See Memo dated 4 Feb. 1949 by the three Western Currency Experts, *Germany 1947–1949*, p. 270.

51. See the revealing justification in *Germany 1947–1949*, p. 272, and in Davison, *Blockade*, p. 263.

52. For the texts of the May and June 1949 agreements see *Germany 1947–1949*, p. 274, 69–70. On Soviet trading proposals and their fate see Meissner, *op. cit.*, 202; and *NY Times* dateline 19 June, 21 May, 14 June.

53. See the detailed and documented account of the behind the scenes dealings in which apparently the German Government "did not entirely carry out its assurances" regarding curtailing of East-West interzonal trade. Elmer Plischke, *Allied High Commission Relations with the German Government* (Historical Division,

HICOG, 1952) 65–69. Adenauer felt that the West Germans were free to negotiate with East-Germans without Allied controls and though he promised "prior notice" of "important measures" the German representatives violated Allied "instructions" and signed a trade agreement of which the Allies disapproved (p. 67). This was embarrassing since "at the request of the federal authorities the High Commission had agreed not to send observers to the negotiations in order that the federal negotiators would have greater freedom of action." If Bonn refused to ratify the agreement "the Eastern negotiators would regard the Allies as responsible, and this would destroy the common front of the High Commission and the Federal Republic." Ultimately the agreement was ratified "despite the solemn assurances of the Federal Government." The High Commission capitulated "not wishing to afford the East an opportunity of holding the Allies responsible for disrupting the economic unity of Germany." (p. 69.) We owe this candid reporting in the best tradition of American scholarship to the high standards maintained by Professor Roger H. Wells under whose general supervision the HICOG Historical Series of monographs was prepared and edited. The adverse American attitude toward expanding interzonal trade was fully indicated in the HICOG *5th Quarterly Report Oct. 1– Dec. 31, 1950,* pp. 72–78 which closed with the admonition that "no trade can be fostered which contributes to the economic division of Germany" or which lends support "to an uneconomic armament-producing development in Eastern Germany," p. 78. As originally developed in the 1947–8 version of the Marshall Plan American policy favored resumption of East-West trade; and even the Congress supported this goal. See the Senate Report, 80 C., 2nd S, No. 935, Feb. 26, 1948, *European Recovery Program,* p. 41. "The Committee accepts and approves the assumption concerning the desirability of East-West trading." But increasingly during 1948 and particularly after outbreak of conflict over Berlin American export to Soviet-controlled or affiliated territory was cut back by mid-'49 to a near fifth of its 1947 average. By that time American influence in Europe was used to restrict East-West trade. After the Korean conflict broke out American trade with the East Bloc was brought to a virtual halt and Congress made "cooperation" with the American program a condition for receiving assistance. See the survey in the so-called Battle Report, 82C, HR, No. 703, July 16, 1951. The report noted "the reluctance of the West Germans to accept the Russian zone of Germany as a foreign country and to impose satisfactory border controls." (p. 9.) Actually the zonal frontier line was loosely supervised; illegal trade was flourishing, control over traded items was weak. See the Staff "Report on Export of Strategic Materials From Western Germany to Communist Countries" in Senate Report No. 944, *Export Controls and Policies in East-West Trade,* Oct. 12, 1951 pp. 19–50. This staff report recognized that the May 1949 agreement to lift trade restrictions imposed since 1 March 1948 "seriously restricts the possibility of effecting trade relationships with the Eastern zone on the same basis as trade with a satellite country." (p. 50.) For a survey see *U.S. In World Affairs 1952,* pp. 40–7, 88 f.

53a. The "triangular" nature of East-West interzonal trade and supply of Berlin was already worked out in the coal-power Anglo-Soviet agreements of 1945–7. Thus see Bipartite paper, *Agreements with Soviet Authorities Concerning Supply of Coal and Power to Berlin,* BIB/P (47) 131. The November 1949 Frankfurt agreement on interzonal trade stipulated that one-third of the East zone exports were to go to Western Berlin. HICOG, *5th Quarterly Report on Germany* (1951) p. 76. This pattern prevailed through to 1956. Berlin commodity receipts of East zone deliveries averaged 125 million DM between 1953–6; her deliveries were a third as much. Berlin received about a fourth of East zone shipments. See BRD, *Statistisches Jahrbuch 1957* (Statistiches Bundesamt, 1957) p. 275.

54. Hearings, House Appropriations Committee, *Foreign Aid,* testimony of J. J. McCloy 29 Feb. 1950, p. 467 f. General Clay in testifying before the same Committee on May 18, 1949 stressed the balance of interests that made it possible for the local authorities to work the problem out. (p. 897 f.) Actually, the resumption of interzonal trade was in Berlin negotiations in June 1949 made contingent upon "assurances" for transport access. See *NY Times* dateline 3 June 1949.

55. Howley, *Berlin Command,* p. 56.

56. See Clay's report in *Decision,* 382–386. With the bigger planes under way this tonnage "could be doubled" if necessary (p. 386); *Berlins Wirtschaft in der Blockade,* p. 18.

57. See *Berlins Wirtschaft in der Blockade,* 70 ff., 135 ff.

58. In the early months of Blockade Sokolovsky asserted that the commodity drainage out of the Soviet zone to support Berlin amounted to 900 tons of necessities daily. SU *Berlin Crisis,* p. 63. The head of the economic control administration of East-Germany also complained bitterly of the drainage into West-Berlin by the dealing of "thieves and black marketeers" to procure products sold for Westmarks in West Berlin. *Die städtischen Körperschaften,* p. 45. See above no. 20 and citations from Ulbricht. Ample evidence supports these contentions. A business "underworld" of smugglers or black marketeering had grown up under the Occupation; and persisted in fact in Western Berlin. E. Butler in his later report *City Divided: Berlin 1955* (N.Y. 1955) wrote respectfully of the organized "smugglers" who now violate the regular customs service (p. 88 f.). The expert economist of the Deutsches Institut für Wirtschaftsforschung explained that "Inoffeziel kamen aber immer noch beträchtliche Lebensmittelmengen auf allen möglichen Wegen nach Berlin und zwar besonders auch in die Westsektoren." All unrationed food procurements were estimated at near 10% of total Berlin food consumption. (200 calories per capita daily.) *Berlins Wirtschaft in der Blockade,* pp. 16, 22–3. Another contribution to the volume spoke of the "considerable" import surplus of West-Berlin with the East zone, p. 70. A British MG economic survey estimated black market commodity drainage from the East zone at 150 million DM. "General Economic Comment" in *German Economic Press Review* no. 33, the Black Market. According to a Gallup poll 52% of the families purchased in the free market; price history was detailed. An alert American journalist exaggerated the case by reporting that "The black market, not the airlift, was responsible for the unexpected splurging" and he provides interesting detail. D. Bess, "What did the Airlift Really Prove," *Saturday Evening Post,* 25 June 1949. This amazing trade was heavily financed by Westmarks, it seems. With their local circulation provided by Eastmarks the Westmarks were used for procurement. Thus 40% of the Westmarks issued by 31 December 1948, or 240 million DM, were returned to West Germany partly through direct trade but partly indirect trade via the Soviet zone. See *BDL Report 1948–49,* p. 42 ff.; also private BDL reports of the period. Partly the bourgeois circles of East Germany rallied to the support of West Berlin and supplied goods; but partly the

trading agencies of the Soviets, anxious to obtain Westmarks (for propaganda, intelligence or for trading purposes) are alleged to have sold Eastmarks at high discount or goods for Westmark currency. Private BDL reports so alleged; see also the "German Economic Press Review," series on "Berlin-Commentaries," No. 14; "Berlin's Currency War," *Economist* (London) July 3, 1948, p. 2. Procurement in East-Germany was also often paid for at premium Eastmark prices; the Eastmark funds for this purpose were obtained from the thriving currency-exchange traffic with a monthly volume of 10–12 million DM monthly through registered agencies. The Eastmark traded at heavy discount—3 and 4 to 1—partly because of Soviet currency sales to buy Westmarks, partly for psychological reasons, partly because outside rationed goods in free market prices in East Germany were very high, but also because the East German bourgeosie was wherever possible converting assets to goods or money and selling this in Berlin for Westmarks. As Klingelhöfer noted: "The better Westmark became a means of hoarding and of capital-and-tax-flight." *Berlin 1948,* p. 97.

59. In two valuable chapters, Ch. VII, "The Soviet Defeat in West Germany" and Ch. VIII, "Why Berliners Resisted" Davison has traced this process of political invigoration within West Germany and in West Berlin.

60. Both the NATO pact and the final carrying out of the London plan of West German settlement including acceptance of the Bonn Constitution were carried to completion during the Blockade. See the triumphant accounts in B. Meissner, *op. cit.,* p. 183 f. *U.S. in World Affairs 1948–49,* Ch. V "Progress of European Recovery," Ch. XII, "The West Agrees on Germany," and Ch. XIII, "Defense of the West."

61. See Davison, *Blockade,* p. 275; J. P. Nettl, *The Eastern Zone and Soviet Policy in Germany, 1945–1950,* 276 f.

INDEX

Ambivalence: defined, xiv–xv; draw-backs, 15–16; at Potsdam, 38–39; in unification policy, 97; in monetary reform policy, 101–102; and overlap, 128; demise of, 128–129, 135, 188; at Moscow, 164–165

American attitudes to Allies: availability of materials, xi–xii; author's identification, xii; ambivalence, 17, 19, 97; Berlin, 23–24, 188, 191, 194–196, 199, 201; eastern frontier, 27, 36; reparations, 32–36, 123, 154–155, 157, 178–179; at Potsdam, 36, 39; level of industry plan, 93, 135; French veto, 97; British financial policies, 109–110; currency question, 116–117; economic unification, 123–125, 129; bizonal fusion, 129, 162–164, 166; Soviet sequestration, 132; deficit, 154–157, 179, 204; at London, 178–181; French in western Germany, 182; access to Berlin, 188. *See also* Cold war; Clay, Lucius D.; Morgenthau plan; Roosevelt, Franklin D.; Western attitudes to Allies

American attitudes to German problems: response to German situation, 4, 6, 10–13, 71–74; ambivalence, 17; reparations, 32; denazification, 73; planning, 74; export-import arrangements, 79, 82–84; responsibilities to Berlin, 87; financial institutions, 102–103, 111; monetary re-

form, 111–17; bizonal fusion, 162–164, 166

Anti-Fascists: of the right, 4–5; of the left, 5–6; eastern zone, 43–47; western zones, 71–72

Balance of power: wartime equilibrium, 1–2; Berlin crisis, 206

Banks: eastern zone nationalization, 58, 65; American and French zone, 70, 76, 111; Berlin, 88; monetary reform, 102–103, 104, 105, 108, 205–206; Western Germany, 206. *See also* Financial institutions

Berlin: importance, 21, 130, 174–178, 190–192, 194–196, 201, 209–211; pre-war pattern, 21–22, 143; planning for post-war, 23, 191; Soviet attitudes, 23–24, 190–192, 208–210; Western attitudes, 23–24, 188, 191, 194–196; Western access, 24, 87, 188, 195, 198, 204; drainage on western zones, 70, 142, 195; coal, 87, 88, 174, 198; military government, 87–88, 199; German government, 88, 173, 192, 194; political parties, 173, 199–201; communications through, 173, 198; capital flight through, 174; interzonal trade, 174–178, 188, 192, 203–204, 205, 208; airlift, 188, 199, 204, 208–210; money for, 190, 192–194, 196–198, 204, 205–206, 209; as cold war catalyst, 195–196, 209, 210–211; blockade, 198, 207–210; partition, 199–201, 206–208, 210–211. *See also* Magistrat; Kommandatura; Settlement in Berlin; and other Berlin headings

Berlin and eastern zone: communications, 173; Soviet view of trade, 174–178; black market, 175–177n, 209; Berlin's money, 190, 192–194, 196–198, 204, 205–206, 207; blockade, 198, 208, 210; Berlin's partition, 199–201; significance of Berlin crisis, 209–211

Berlin and western zones: western German support, 70, 142, 195; capital flight from east, 174–175, 175–177n; trade, 188, 192, 208; Western attitudes, 188, 191, 194–196; German attitude, 195; blockade, 198, 208; Berlin's partition, 199–201; significance of Berlin crisis, 209–211

Berlin's city government: Bezirke and sectoral military government, 87, 199; Magistrat, 88; mayorality, 173; Bezirke and trade, 175; Soviet attitude, 192; partition, 199–201. *See also* Magistrat; Kommandatura

Bizonal fusion: economic planning, 75; food, 80; foreign trade, 82–83, 151–152; rationale, 129–130, 162; elaboration, 182–183

Black market: eastern zone, 58; western zones, 76–77; and currency reform, 99; and U.S. currency conversion, 117; and economic recovery, 144; and Berlin, 175–177n, 209

British attitudes to Allies: ambivalence, 17; eastern frontier, 27; Morgenthau plan, 33; reparations at Yalta, 34; level of industry plan, 93, 135; financial policies, 107–110; bizonal fusion, 129; political and economic unification, 131, 133, 166; reparations, 155; at Moscow, 165, 167; demilitarization, 167–168; at London, 178–181; Berlin crisis, 203. *See also* Churchill, Winston; Western attitudes to Soviets

British attitudes to German problems: German situation, 6, 10–12, 71–74; coal, iron and steel, 70, 77–79, 133;

denazification, 72; economic planning, 74–75; responsibilities to Berlin, 87; financial institutions and policies, 102–103, 107–110, 112

Capacity to pay reparations: principles: 140; recovery in 1950's, 140–142; 1947 evidence, 142; drags on, 142–145; financial capacity, 145–146; strategic bombing survey, 147–149; need for imagination, 154–155; and deficit issue, 155–157; Soviet attitude, 158. *See also* Industrial capacity

Capital levy: purpose and need, 8–10, 100; socialization potential, 10; eastern zone, 63; Soviet attitude, 105, 113, 115; British attitude, 109, 113, 115; C-D-G plan, 113–115; aid in unification, 132; and World War I reparations, 146; final status, 186

C-D-G plan: origins, 111–112; characteristics, 113–115; negotiations, 115–116

Central agencies: importance, 14, 128–129; and JCS 1067, 21; at Potsdam, 39, 96; in Control Council, 96, 97; and monetary reform, 100; and economic unity, 125

Central German government: planning, 14; in JCS 1067, 20; and reparations policy, 35; at Potsdam, 39; and eastern zone, 66; and monetary reform, 100; and settlement, 130–132; after Moscow, 166

Churchill, Winston: on post-war planning, 16; on territorial advance, 23–24; on Morgenthau plan, 33; on Berlin, 196

Clay, Lucius D.: on level of industry plan, 93, 159; on monetary reform, 112, 186; on currency, 116; on currency conversion, 120; on end of Control Council, 187; on program for Berlin, 194, 195; on Berlin blockade, 199

Coal: eastern zone nationalization, 58–59, 63; for eastern zone, 65; western export, 68, 79, 83, 179, 181; western sequestration, 70, 77–78, 143; for German economy, 75;

price, 77–78, 108, 185; management, 78–79; zonal outputs compared, 80; and foreign trade, 83–
84, 151, 157; for Berlin, 87, 88, 174,
198, 199; French attitudes, 97, 136,
139, 182; and economic unification,
124; and bizonal fusion, 129; occupation use, 144; and Berlin blockade, 198–199
Cold war: forebodings, 162–163; pre-
liminaries at London, 178–181; Berlin as catalyst, 195–196, 209–210;
furthered in Berlin, 211
Comparisons between zones: agricultural production, 56; property control, 60; general, 67–71; coal output, 80; 1947 economic status, 80
Control Council: plans, 18; in JCS 1067,
21; significance of Berlin, 24, 173,
188; significance of common currency, 25, 188; description, 85–87,
166; Kommandatura, 86, 89; accomplishments, 89–95; French veto,
97; British finance policies, 108–
109; monetary reform, 112, 116,
121–122, 186; reparations, 123,
125; failures, 128–129; and settlement possibilities, 130–135, 137,
164, 172, 173; and economic recovery, 142–144; and Moscow conference, 164–165, 167, 169, 171–
172; and London conference, 182;
gradual demise, 183–186; dissolution, 187
Current product reparations: principle,
28; advantages, 31; Morgenthau
plan, 33, 35; and unification, 35;
Soviet zone, 48, 138; and western
deficit, 124; Soviet demand for, 135;
effect on German economy, 140;
and foreign deficit, 152–157, 179;
and American and Soviet views at
London, 178–181. See also Capacity to pay reparations; Industrial
capacity
Currency: importance, 25, 104, 188–
189; eastern zone, 58; western
zones, 76–78; in interzonal trade,
89, 95–96; monetary reform, 99–
101, 105, 116–117; Allied access,
104, 107, 115, 186; British view,

108–109; new printing, 116, 121,
186; separate for western zones,
166, 189, 190, 196; separate for
eastern zones, 189, 198; for Berlin,
190, 192–194, 196–198, 204, 205–
206, 207. See also Military currency

Decartelization: eastern zone, 51, 62;
and Soviet sequestration, 59; in
Control Council, 89; and settlement
possibilities, 132–133
Deficits: western zone, 80, 82–84, 124,
127; and reparations claims, 139,
152; in foreign trading position,
149–154; and reparations policy,
154–157; Soviet attitude, 159; at
London conference, 179; in Berlin,
195, 204, 205
Demilitarization: eastern zone, 51; Control Council, 91, 130; at Moscow,
165; and inspection, 167–169
Denazification: eastern zone, 48, 52, 55,
60, 62–63, 65; western zone, 67,
70, 72–73; Control Council, 91,
130; at Moscow, 165, 169; issues,
169; and displaced persons, 170.
See also Property control
Dismantling: principle, 28; difficulties,
29–31, 135; Morgenthau plan, 33;
and zonalization, 35; "withdrawals"
at Potsdam, 38; for Soviets from
western zones at Potsdam, 40–41,
92, 138, 160–161, 166; Soviet zone,
47–48, 138; level of industry plan,
92–95, 126, 159–160, 166, 180;
stopped by Americans, 125
Displaced persons: western zones, 67;
and black market, 144; and occupation costs, 144; at Moscow, 165,
171–172; Soviet views and western
actions, 170–172
Drift: discussed, xiv, xvii–xviii; and ambivalence, xiv–xv, 17; and western
attitudes, 162

Eastern frontier: rationale, 12, 26–27;
western accession, 37, 137; east
German acceptance, 44, 47; and
reparations, 135; and formation of
Western Germany, 195. See also
Expellees

Price and wage controls: eastern zone, 58, 64; western zones, 75, 76–78; Control Council, 89, 90n; British views, 108

Prisoners of War: and reparations labor, 29; at Moscow, 165, 172

Property control: western zones, 60, 70, 73; eastern zone, 60–63, 65; and economic recovery, 77–79, 143; Control Council, 85; and settlement potential, 132–134; and capital flight, 175; and Berlin blockade, 199, 207

Property equalization: *See* Capital levy

Quadripartite agreements: during war, 2, 18, 27, 33–34, 135; on Berlin enclave, 23; access to Berlin, 24, 87; and ideological overlap, 89; and punitive action against Germans, 90–95. *See also* Control Council; Kommandatura; London conference of foreign ministers; Potsdam agreement

Reparations: Soviet rationale, 26, 27–28, 180; basic principles, 28–29; basic difficulties, 29–31; Morgenthau plan, 32–33, 34; World War I experience, 33, 140, 145–146, 156–157; Potsdam arrangements, 38, 92, 135; and partition, 38–39; and unification, 40–42; extent of Soviet withdrawals, 47–48, 138, 166; level of industry plan, 92–95, 123, 135, 159–160; Soviet proposals, 135, 138, 160–161; magnitude of claims, 138–139; limited western desire for, 138, 153–154; German capacity to pay, 140–149; at Moscow, 165; American position at London, 178–179, 181; Soviet position at London, 179–181. *See also* Capacity to pay reparations; Current product reparations

Reparations from Soviet zone: dismantling, 47–48; current production, 48; 1947 status, 138; in 1950's, 142

Repatriation: displaced persons, 170–172; prisoners of war, 172

Reuther, Ernst: mayorality, 173; program for Berlin, 194

Roosevelt, Franklin D.: on Soviets, 16; on American occupation planning, 19; on Morgenthau plan, 33; at Yalta on reparations, 33–34

Ruhr: and eastern zone, 65, 199, 210; sequestration, 70, 77–79, 133; French attitude, 136, 139, 182; and economic recovery, 143, 149; war damage, 148–149; and bizonal fusion, 162. *See also* Coal

Separation of Power: in conduct of war, 1–2; in wartime agreements, 1, 3; in zonal authority, 19–20. *See also* Partition, Zonalization, Zone Commanders

Sequestration: *See* Economic Controls; Expropriation; Property Controls; Socialization

Settlement: defined, xv; and leadership, xvi–xvii; possibilities, xviii; difficulties, 129; bases for, 130; possibilities of, 130–137, 164, 172–173

Settlement in Berlin: settings for negotiations, 202; intimidation and concession in negotiations, 202–203; Soviet program for Western surrender, 203–204; Western program for Soviet surrender, 205–206; disinclination to unification, 206–207; and committee of neutrals, 206–207; lines of partition, 207–208; reasons for Soviet submission, 208–210; danger in Berlin, 210–211; end of unification in fact of partition, 211

Social bases of German problems: eastern zone, 49, 51, 57–58, 63–64; comparison between zones, 67–68, 71–72; western zones, 73–74, 76–77; fissure between zones, 96, 132, 162–163. *See also* Economic bases of German problems; Political bases of German problems

Social Democratic party: eastern zone, 45, 51–52; western zones, 96, 209; Berlin, 173, 194, 200, 201, 209

Socialization: advantages, xii–xiii; postwar situation, 10–11; potential of

capital levy, 10, 114–115, 132; eastern zone, 50; potential of sequestration, 132–134. *See also* Banks; Capital levy; Coal; Denazification; Economic controls; Expropriation;
Land and local government; Land
reform; Property control
Soviet attitudes to Allies: difficulty of
knowing, xi; existence of Berlin enclave, 23–24, 188, 190–192, 202,
204; military currency, 24–25; reparations, 26, 27–28, 29, 31, 40–41,
135, 138–139, 140, 157–161, 179–
181; eastern frontier, 26–27; Yalta
on reparations, 33–34, 135; at
Potsdam, 36–37, 135; political and
economic unification, 42–43, 49, 96,
126, 127–128, 131, 133, 135, 166;
level of industry plan, 93, 126, 135;
French veto, 97; currency question,
121; Ruhr, 132–133; deficit, 155;
issues raised at Moscow, 168–172;
Berlin's trade, 174, 188, 192; bizonal fusion and Western Germany,
180–181, 187, 203; Berlin's money,
190, 192–193, 198, 206; Berlin
blockade, 198–199, 207–208; settling Berlin crisis, 206–208; reasons
for Soviet submission, 208–210
Soviet attitudes to German problems:
German situation, 4, 6, 10–12, 71;
Anti-Fascists, 43–47, 52; occupation requirements, 47–48, 64; occupation objectives, 48–49, 53; sequestration, 59; economic controls,
64–65; monetary reform, 105–107,
112; reparations capacities, 140;
formation of Western Germany,
180, 201
Strategic bombing survey: and German
industrial capacity, 147–149

Taxation: in Control Council, 89, 90n;
and drainage in eastern zone, 106;
British attitude, 108; and occupation costs, 143–144; and capacity to
pay reparations, 146
Trade unions: eastern zone, 46; western
zones, 68, 73; Control Council, 89,
96, 97; at Moscow, 165; after Moscow, 166; and partition in Berlin,
200, 201

Unification: merits and demerits of policy, 14–15, 17; in JCS 1067, 21;
and Berlin, 24, 130, 173, 189, 191;
and common currency, 25, 189; and
reparations policy, 35, 178–179; at
Potsdam, 39–41, 160; after Potsdam, 42, 127–129, 166, 172; eastern German interest, 52–54; Control
Council premise, 95; French veto,
97, 104; and monetary reform, 100,
112, 121–122; and economic unity,
125–126, 142; and settlement possibilities, 130–135, 164; unaccep-
able in Berlin, 206–207; its end in
fact of partition, 211

West German attitudes: formation of
Western Germany, 182–183, 195;
among Berliners, 190, 194, 196,
197, 198, 201; importance of Berlin,
191, 195, 201; German communist
party, 201; Berlin's deficit, 205; significance of Berlin crisis, 209–211
Western attitudes to Soviets: importance
of Berlin, 23–24, 188, 191, 194–
196, 202; eastern frontier, 27, 37;
political and economic unification,
40–42, 96, 123–125, 166, 203; reparations, 123, 127, 154–157, 178–
179; export-import arrangements,
124; issues raised at Moscow, 168,
169, 170–172; at London, 178–181;
trade permits in Berlin, 178; access
to Berlin, 188; Berlin's money, 190,
193–194, 196–197, 205–206, 207;
Berlin blockade, 199; Berlin's partition, 201, 206–207; settling Berlin
crisis, 206–208. *See also* American
attitudes to Allies; British attitudes
to Allies; Cold war; French attitudes to Allies
Western attitudes to German problems:
Anti-Fascists, 6, 71–72; political
and economic reorganization, 10–
12, 72–74; political parties and
trade unions, 96; reparations, 157;
bizonal fusion, 162–164; formation
of Western Germany, 183, 203; in
Berlin, 195; significance of Berlin
crisis, 209–211. *See also* American
attitudes to German problems; Brit-